Get the eBook FREE!
(PDF, ePub, Kindle, and liveBook all included)

We believe that once you buy a book from us, you should be able to read it in any format we have available. To get electronic versions of this book at no additional cost to you, purchase and then register this book at the Manning website.

Go to https://www.manning.com/freebook and follow the instructions to complete your pBook registration.

That's it!
Thanks from Manning!

Azure Storage, Streaming, and Batch Analytic

A GUIDE FOR DATA ENGINEERS

RICHARD NUCKOLLS

MANNING

SHELTER ISLAND

For online information and ordering of this and other Manning books, please visit
www.manning.com. The publisher offers discounts on this book when ordered in quantity.
For more information, please contact

> Special Sales Department
> Manning Publications Co.
> 20 Baldwin Road
> PO Box 761
> Shelter Island, NY 11964
> Email: orders@manning.com

Manning Publications Co.
20 Baldwin Road
PO Box 761
Shelter Island, NY 11964

Development editor:	Toni Arritola
Technical development editor:	Robin Dewson
Review editor:	Ivan Martinović
Production editor:	Deirdre S. Hiam
Copy editor:	Ben Berg
Proofreader:	Jason Everett
Technical proofreader:	Karsten Strøbæk
Typesetter:	Dennis Dalinnik
Cover designer:	Marija Tudor

ISBN: 9781617296307
Printed in the United States of America

This book is dedicated to my loving wife, Joy.

brief contents

contents

preface

This book started, like any journey, with a single step. The services in Azure were running fine, but I still had a lot of code to write for the data processing. I was months into the implementation when I saw Mike Stephens's email. I wondered, "Is this legit?" Why would a book publisher contact me?

I'd been raising my profile as an Azure developer. Writing code, designing new systems, and migrating platforms are part of a team lead's work. I was going to conferences on Azure technology too, and writing up what I learned for my company. Put it on social media; if you don't tell someone, how will they know? Writing a book seemed like the next step up. So I jumped at it.

I've always enjoyed teaching. Maybe I should say lecturing because when I open my mouth, I end up explaining a lot of things. I got my MCSD certification after a few months of studying for the last test. I told others they should get it too. That's what I wanted to write: a study guide for my next certification, based on this new analysis system I was building. Studying reveals how many options you have and I love to have options. Like any long journey, writing a book presents many options too. This journey ended up rather far from where I imagined that first step would lead.

This book was written for the Microsoft technologist. I chose from the multitude of options available specific services that tightly integrated with each other. Each one does its job, and does it well. When I started, the exam "Perform Big Data Engineering on Microsoft Cloud Services" included Stream Analytics, Data Lake stores, Data Lake Analytics, and Data Factory. I've used these services and know them well. I thought I could write an exam preparation book about them. The replacement exam

"Implementing an Azure Data Solution" shifted focus to larger services that do almost everything, like Azure Databricks, Synapse Analytics, and Cosmos DB. Each of these services could be a book unto itself.

The services chosen for this book, including Azure Storage, Data Lake stores, Event Hubs, Stream Analytics, Data Lake Analytics, Data Factory, and SQL Database, present a low barrier to entry for developers and engineers familiar with other Microsoft technologies. Some of them are broadly useful in cloud applications generally. So I've written a book that's part exam guide, part general introduction to Azure. I hope you find these services useful in your cloud computing efforts, and that this book gives you the tools you need to use them.

acknowledgements

I would like to first thank my wife, Joy, for always supporting me and being my biggest cheerleader.

Thank you so much Luke Fischer, James Dzidek, and Defines Fineout for reading the book and encouraging me during the process. Thanks also to Filippo Barsotti, Alexander Belov, Pablo Fdez, and Martin Smith for their feedback. I also need to mention the reviewers who gave generously of their time and whose comments greatly improved this book, including Alberto Acerbis, Dave Lobban, Eros Pedrini, Evan Wallace, Gandhi Rajan, Greg Wright, Ian Stirk, Jason Rendel, Jose Luis Perez, Karthikeyarajan Rajendran, Mike Fowler, Milorad Imbra, Pablo Acuña, Pierfrancesco D'Orsogna, Raushan Jha, Ravi Sajnani, Richard Young, Sayak Paul, Simone Sguazza, Srihari Sridharan, Taylor Dolezal, and Thilo Käsemann.

I would like to thank the people at Manning for supporting me through the learning process that is writing a technical book: Deirdre Hiam, my project editor; Ben Berg, my copyeditor; Jason Everett, my proofreader; and Ivan Martinović, my review editor. I'm grateful to Toni Arritola for patience and advocating for explaining everything. Thanks to Robin Dewson for an expert review and easy to swallow criticism. And thanks to Mike Stephens for giving me the chance to write this book.

about this book

Azure Storage, Streaming, and Batch Analytics was written to provide a practical guide to creating and running a data analysis system using Lambda architecture in Azure. It begins by explaining the Lambda architecture for data analysis, and then introduces the Azure services which combine into a working system. Successive chapters create new Azure services and connect each service together to form a tightly integrated collection. Best practices and cost considerations help prevent costly mistakes.

Who should read this book

This book is for developers and system engineers who support data collection and processing in Azure. The reader will be familiar with Microsoft technologies, but needs only a basic knowledge of cloud technologies. A developer will be familiar with C# and SQL languages; an engineer with PowerShell commands and Windows desktop applications. Readers should understand CSV and JSON file formats and be able to perform basic SQL queries against relational databases.

How this book is organized: a roadmap

This book is divided into 13 chapters. The first two chapters introduce data processing using Lambda architecture and how the Azure services discussed in the book form the system. Each service has one or more chapters devoted to the creation and use of the technology. The final chapter covers a few topics of interest to further improve your data engineering skills.

- Chapter 1 gives an overview of data engineering, including what a data engineer does.
- Chapter 2 describes fundamental Azure concepts and how six Azure services are used to build a data processing system using Lambda architecture.
- Chapter 3 shows how to set up and secure Storage accounts, including Blob Storage and Queues.
- Chapter 4 details creating and securing a Data Lake store and introduces the Zones framework, a method for controlling use of a data lake.
- Chapter 5 builds a resilient and high-throughput ingestion endpoint with Event Hubs.
- Chapter 6 shows how to create a streaming data pipeline with Stream Analytics, and explores the unique capabilities of stream data processing.
- Chapter 7 creates a Data Lake Analytics service, and introduces batch processing with U-SQL jobs.
- Chapter 8 dives into more complex U-SQL jobs with reusable tables, functions, and views.
- Chapter 9 extends U-SQL jobs with custom assemblies, including machine learning algorithms for unstructured data processing.
- Chapter 10 shows how to build data processing automation using Data Factory and Key Vault.
- Chapter 11 dives into database administration when using SQL Databases.
- Chapter 12 demonstrates multiple ways to move data into SQL Databases.
- Chapter 13 discusses version control for your Azure services and building a data catalog to support your end users.

Because each service integrates with other services, this book presents the eight Azure services in a specific order. Some services, like Stream Analytics and Data Factory, rely on connecting to preexisting services. Many chapters include references to data files to load into your system. Therefore, it's best to read earlier chapters before later chapters. The appendix includes code snippets in Azure PowerShell language for creating instances of the required services. Using these PowerShell snippets, you can create any required services if you want to jump straight into a chapter for a particular service.

About the code

Chapters 3–12 include Azure PowerShell commands to create instances of the services discussed and to configure various aspects of the services. Some chapters, like chapter 5, include demo code written in PowerShell to show usage of the service. Other chapters, especially chapter 10, show JSON configuration files that support the configuration of the service. The code is available in the GitHub repository for this book at https://github.com/rnuckolls/azure_storage.

The appendix includes guidance for installing the Azure PowerShell module on your Windows computer. You can also run the scripts using Azure Cloud Shell at https://shell.azure.com. The scripts were created using version 3 of Azure PowerShell, and newer versions also support the commands. The appendix collects the service creation scripts too.

This book contains many examples of source code, both in numbered listings and inline with normal text. In both cases, source code is formatted in a `fixed-width font like this` to separate it from ordinary text. Sometimes boldface is used to highlight code that has changed from previous steps in the chapter, such as when a new feature adds to an existing line of code.

In many cases, the original source code has been reformatted; we've added line breaks and reworked indentation to accommodate the available page space in the book. In rare cases, even this was not enough, and listings include line-continuation markers (➡). Additionally, comments in the source code have often been removed from the listings when the code is described in the text. Code annotations accompany many of the listings, highlighting important concepts.

Author online

Purchase of *Azure Storage, Streaming, and Batch Analytics* includes free access to a private web forum run by Manning Publications where you can make comments about the book, ask technical questions, and receive help from the author and from other users. To access the forum, go to https://livebook.manning.com/#!/book/azure-storage-streaming-and-batch-analytics/discussion. You can also learn more about Manning's forums and the rules of conduct at https://livebook.manning.com/#!/discussion.

Manning's commitment to our readers is to provide a venue where a meaningful dialogue between individual readers and between readers and the author can take place. It is not a commitment to any specific amount of participation on the part of the author, whose contribution to the forum remains voluntary (and unpaid). We suggest you try asking the author some challenging questions lest his interest stray! The forum and the archives of previous discussions will be accessible from the publisher's website as long as the book is in print.

about the author

RICHARD NUCKOLLS has a passion for designing software and building things.

He wrote his first computer program in high school and turned it into a career.

He began teaching others about technology any time he could, culminating in his first book about Azure.

He recently started Blue Green Builds, a data integration company, so he could do more in the cloud.

You can follow his personal projects and see what he builds next at rnuckolls.com.

about the cover illustration

The figure on the cover of *Azure Storage, Streaming, and Batch Analytics* is captioned "Dame génoise," or Genoese lady. The illustration is taken from a collection of dress costumes from various countries by Jacques Grasset de Saint-Sauveur (1757–1810), titled *Costumes de Différents Pays*, published in France in 1788. Each illustration is finely drawn and colored by hand. The rich variety of Grasset de Saint-Sauveur's collection reminds us vividly of how culturally apart the world's towns and regions were just 200 years ago. Isolated from each other, people spoke different dialects and languages. In the streets or in the countryside, it was easy to identify where they lived and what their trade or station in life was just by their dress. The way we dress has changed since then and the diversity by region, so rich at the time, has faded away. It is now hard to tell apart the inhabitants of different continents, let alone different towns, regions, or countries. Perhaps we have traded cultural diversity for a more varied personal life—certainly for a more varied and fast-paced technological life. At a time when it is hard to tell one computer book from another, Manning celebrates the inventiveness and initiative of the computer business with book covers based on the rich diversity of regional life of two centuries ago, brought back to life by Grasset de Saint-Sauveur's pictures.

What is data engineering? 1

This chapter covers

- What is data engineering?
- What do data engineers do?
- How does Microsoft define data engineering?
- What tools does Azure provide for data engineering?

Data collection is on the rise. More and more systems are generating more and more data every day.[1]

> *More than 30,000 gigabytes of data are generated every second, and the rate of data creation is only accelerating.*
>
> —Nathan Marz

Increased connectivity has led to increased sophistication and user interaction in software systems. New deployments of connected "smart" electronics also rely on increased connectivity. In response, businesses now collect and store data from all

---

[1] Nathan Marz and James Warren. *Big Data: Principles and Best Practices of Scalable Real-Time Data Systems.* Shelter Island, NY: Manning Publications, 2015.

aspects of their products. This has led to an enormous increase in compute and storage infrastructure. Writing for Gartner, Mark Beyer defines "Big Data."[2]

> *Big Data is high volume, high velocity, and/or high variety information assets that require new forms of processing to enable enhanced decision making, insight discovery, and process optimization.*

> —Mark A. Beyer

The scale of data collection and processing requires a change in strategy.

Businesses are challenged to find experienced engineers and programmers to develop the systems and processes to handle this data. The new role of data engineer has evolved to fill this need. The data engineer manages this data collection. Collecting, preparing, and querying of this mountain of data using Azure services is the subject of this book. The reader will be able to build working data analytics systems in Azure after completing the book.

1.1   *What is data engineering?*

Data engineering is the practice of building data storage and processing systems. Robert Chang, in his "A Beginner's Guide to Data Engineering," describes the work as designing, building, and maintaining data warehouses.[3] Data engineering creates scalable systems which allow analysts and data scientists to extract meaningful information from the data.

Collecting data seems like a simple activity. Take reporting website traffic. A single user, during a site in a web browser, requests a page. A simple site might respond with an HTML file, a CSS file, and an image. This example could represent one, three, or four events.

- What if there is a page redirect? That is another event.
- What if we want to log the time taken to query a database?
- What if we retrieve some items from cache but find they are missing?

All of these are commonly logged data points today.

Now add more user interaction, like a comparison page with multiple sliders. Each move of the slider logs a value. Tracking user mouse movement returns hundreds of coordinates. Consider a connected sensor with a 100 Hz sample rate. It can easily record over eight million measurements a day. When you start to scale to thousands and tens of thousands of simultaneous events, every point in the pipeline must be optimized for speed until the data comes to rest.

---

[2]   Mark A. Beyer and Douglas Laney. "The Importance of 'Big Data': A Definition." Gartner, 2012. http://www.gartner.com/id=2057415.

[3]   Robert Chang. "A Beginner's Guide to Data Engineering—Part I." Medium, June 24, 2018. http://mng.bz/JyKz.

1.2   *What do data engineers do?*

Data engineers build storage and processing systems that can grow to handle these high volume, high velocity data flows. They plan for variation and volume. They manage systems that provide business value by answering questions with data.

Most businesses have multiple sources generating data. Manufacturing companies track the output of the machines, employees, and their shipping departments. Software companies track their user actions, software bugs per release, and developer output per day. Service companies check number of sales calls, time to complete tasks, usage of parts stores, and cost per lead. Some of this is small scale; some of it is large scale.

Analysts and managers might operate on narrow data sets, but large enterprises increasingly want to find efficiencies across divisions, or find root causes behind multi-faceted systems failures. In order to extract value from these disparate sources of data, engineers build large-scale storage systems as a single data repository. A software company may implement centralized error logging. The service company may integrate their CRM, billing, and finance systems. Engineers need to support the ingestion pipeline, storage backbone, and reporting services across multiple groups of stakeholders.

The first step in data consolidation is often a large relational database. Analysts review reports, CSV files, and even Excel spreadsheets in an attempt to get clean and consistent data. Often developers or database administrators prepare scripts to import the data into databases. In the best case, experienced database administrators define common schema, and plan partitioning and indexing. The database enters production. Data collection commences in earnest.

Typical systems based on storing data in relational databases have problems with scale. A single database instance, the simplest implementation, always becomes a bottleneck given increased usage. There are a finite amount of CPU cores and drive space available on a single database instance. Scaling up can only go so far before I/O bottlenecks prevent meeting response time targets. Distributing the database tables across multiple servers, or *sharding*, can enable greater throughput and storage, at the cost of greater complexity. Even with multiple shards, database queries under load display more and more latency. Eventually query latency grows too large to satisfy the requirements of the application.

The open source community answered the challenge of building web-scale data systems. Hadoop makes it easy to access vast disk storage. Spark provides a fast and highly available logging endpoint. NoSQL databases give users access to large stores of data quickly. Languages like Python and R make deep dives into huge flat files possible. Analysts and data scientists write algorithms and complex queries to draw conclusions from the data. But this new environment still requires system administrators to build and maintain servers in their data center.

1.3   *How does Microsoft define data engineering?*

Using these new open source tools looks quite different from the traditional database-centric model. In his landmark book, Nathan Marz coined a new term: *Lambda architecture*. He defined this as a "general-purpose approach to implementing an arbitrary function on an arbitrary data set and having the function return its results with low latency" (Marz, p.7)[4]. The goals of Lambda architecture address many of the inherent weaknesses of the database-centric model.

Figure 1.1 shows a general view of the new approach to saving and querying data. Data flows into both the *Speed layer* and the *Batch layer*. The Speed layer prepares data views of the most recent period in real time. The *Serving layer* delivers data views over the entire period, updated at regular intervals. Queries get data from the Speed layer, Serving layer, or both, depending on the time period queried.

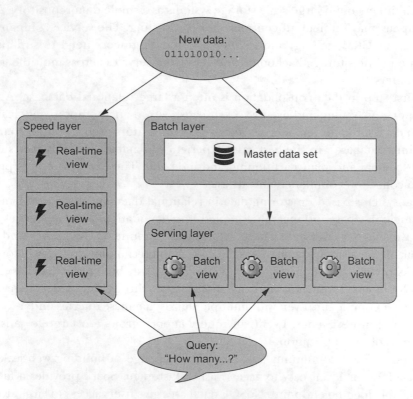

Figure 1.1   Lambda analytics system, showing logical layers of processing based on query latency

---

[4]   Marz and Warren. *Big Data*.

Figure 1.2 describes an analytics system using a Lambda architecture. Data flows through the system from acquisition to retrieval via two paths: batch and stream. All data lands in long term storage, with scheduled and ad hoc queries generating refined data sets from the raw data. This is the batch process. Data with short time windows for retrieval run through an immediate query process, generating refined data in near-real time. This is the stream process.

1 Data is generated by applications, devices, or servers.
2 Each new piece of data is saved to long-term file storage.
3 New data is also sent to a stream processor.
4 A scheduled batch process reads the raw data.
5 Both stream and batch processes save query output to a retrieval endpoint.
6 Users query the retrieval endpoint.

Figure 1.2 shows the core principle of Lambda architecture: data flows one way. Only new data is added to the data store; raw data is never updated. Batch processes yield

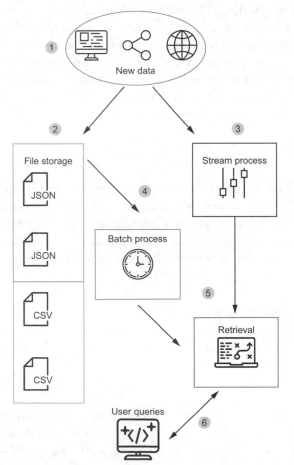

Figure 1.2 Lambda architecture with Azure PaaS services

data sets by reading the raw data and deposit the data sets in a retrieval layer. A retrieval layer handles queries.

Human error accounts for the largest problem in operating an analytics system. Lambda architecture mitigates these errors by storing the original data immutably. An *immutable* data set—where data is written once, read repeatedly, and never modified—does not suffer from corruption due to incorrect update logic. Bad data can be excluded. Bad queries can be corrected and run again.

The output information remains one step removed from the source. In order to facilitate fast writes, new bits of data are only appended. Updates to existing data doesn't happen. To facilitate fast reads, two separate mechanisms converge their outputs. The regularly scheduled batch process generates information as output from queries over the large data set. Between batch executions, incoming data undergoes a similar query to extract information. These two information sets together form the entire result set.

An interface allows retrieving the combined result set. Because writes, reads, queries, and request handling execute as distributed services across multiple servers, the Lambda architecture scales both horizontally and vertically. Engineers can add both more and more powerful servers. Because all of the services operate as distributed nodes, hardware faults are simple to correct, and routine maintenance work has little impact on the overall system. Implementing a Lambda architecture achieves the goals of fault tolerance, low latency reads and writes, scalability, and easy maintenance.

Mike Wilson describes the architecture pattern for Microsoft in the "Big data architecture style" guide (http://mng.bz/2XOo). Six functions make up the core of this design pattern.

1.3.1   Data acquisition

Large scale data ingestion happens one of two ways: a continuous stream of discrete records, or a batch of records encapsulated in a package. Lambda architecture handles both methods with aplomb. Incoming data in packages is stored directly for later batch processing. Incoming data streams are processed immediately and packaged for later batch processing. Eventually all data becomes input for query functions.

1.3.2   Data storage

Distributed file systems decouple saving data from querying data. Data files are collected and served by multiple nodes. More storage is always available by adding more nodes. The Hadoop Distributed File System (HDFS) lies at the heart of most modern storage systems designed for analytics.

1.3.3   Data processing

A distributed query system partitions queries into multiple executable units and executes them over multiple files. In Hadoop analytics systems, the MapReduce algorithm handles distributing a query over multiple nodes as a two step process. Each

Hadoop cluster node *maps* requested data to a single file, and the query returns results from that file. The results from all the files are combined and the resulting set of data is *reduced* to a set fulfilling the query. Multiple cluster nodes divide the Map and Reduce tasks between them. This enables efficient querying of large scale collections. New queries can be set for scheduled updates or submitted for a single result. Multiple query jobs can run simultaneously, each using multiple nodes.

1.3.4 Data queries

A real time analysis engine monitors the incoming data stream and maintains a snapshot of the most recent data. This snapshot contains the new data since the last scheduled query execution. Queries update result sets in the data retrieval layer. Usually these queries duplicate the syntax or output of the batch queries over the same period.

1.3.5 Orchestration

A scheduling system runs queries using the distributed query system against the distributed file system. The output of these scheduled queries becomes the result set for analysis. More advanced systems include data transfers between disparate systems. The orchestration function typically moves result sets into the data retrieval layer.

1.3.6 Data retrieval

Lastly, an interface for collating and retrieving results from the data gives the end user a low latency endpoint for information. This layer often relies on the ubiquitous Structured Query Language (SQL) to return results to analysis tools. Together these functions fulfill the requirements of the data analysis system.

1.4 What tools does Azure provide for data engineering?

Cloud systems promise to solve challenges with processing large scale data sets.

- Processing power limitations of single-instance services
- Storage limitations and management of on-premises storage systems
- Technical management overhead of on-premises systems

Using Azure eliminates many difficulties in building large scale data analytics systems. Automating the setup and support of servers and applications frees up your system administrators to use their expertise elsewhere. Ongoing expense of hardware can be minimized. Redundant systems can be provisioned as easily as single instances. The packaged analytics system is easy to deploy.

Several cloud providers have abstracted the complexity of the Hadoop cluster and its associated services. Microsoft's cloud-based Hadoop system is called *HDInsight*.

According to Jason Howell, HDInsight is "a fully managed, full spectrum, open source analytics service for enterprises."[5] The data engineer can build a complete data

---

[5] Jason Howell. "What is Apache Hadoop in Azure HDInsight." Microsoft Docs, February 27, 2020. http://mng.bz/1zeQ.

analytics system using HDInsight and common tools associated with Hadoop. Many data engineers, especially those familiar with Linux and Apache software, choose HDInsight when building a new data warehouse in Azure. Configuration approaches, familiar tools, and Linux-specific features and training materials are some of the reasons why Linux engineers choose HDInsight.

Microsoft also built a set of abstracted services in Azure which perform the functions required for a data analysis system, but without Linux and Apache. Along with the services, Microsoft provides a reference architecture for building a big data system. The model guides engineers through some high-level technology choices when using the Microsoft tools.[6]

> *A big data architecture is designed to handle the ingestion, processing, and analysis of data that is too large or complex for traditional database systems.*

> —Mike Wilson

This model covers common elements of the Lambda architecture, including data storage, batch and stream processing, and variations on an analysis retrieval endpoint. The model describes additional elements that are necessary but not defined in the Lambda model. For robust and high performance ingestion, a message queue can pass data to both the stream process and the data store. A query tool for data scientists gives access to aggregate or processed information. An orchestration tool schedules data transfers and batch processing.

Microsoft lays out these skills and technologies as part of its certification for Azure Data Engineer Associate (http://mng.bz/emPz). Azure Data Engineers are described as those who "design and implement the management, monitoring, security, and privacy of data using the full stack of Azure data services to satisfy business needs." This book focuses on the Microsoft Azure technologies described in this certification. This includes Event Hubs, Stream Analytics, Data Lake store and storage accounts, SQL Database, and Data Factory. Engineers can use these services to build big data analytics solutions.

1.5   Azure Data Engineers

Platform as a service (PaaS) tools in Azure allow engineers to build new systems without requiring any on-premise hardware or software support. While HDInsight provides an open source architecture for handling data analysis tasks, Microsoft Azure also provides another set of services for analytics. For engineers familiar with Microsoft languages like C# and T-SQL, Azure hosts several services which can be linked to build data processing and analysis systems in the cloud.

Using the tool set in Azure for building a large scale data analysis system requires some basic and intermediate technical skills. First, SQL is used extensively for processing streams of data, batch processing, orchestrating data migrations, and managing SQL

---

6   Mike Wilson. "Big data architecture style." Microsoft Docs, November 20, 2019. http://mng.bz/PAV8.

databases. Second, CSV and JSON files facilitate transferring data between systems. Data engineers must understand the strengths and weaknesses of these file formats. Reading and writing these files are core activities of the batch processing workflows. Third, the Microsoft data engineer should be able to write basic C# and JavaScript functions. Several cloud tools, including Stream Analytics and Data Lake Analytics, are extensible using these languages. Processing functions and helpers can run in Azure and be triggered by cloud service events. Last, experience with the Azure portal and familiarity with the Azure CLI or PowerShell allows the engineer to create new resources efficiently.

1.6 *Example application*

In this book, you will build an example data analytics system using Azure cloud technologies. Marz defines the function of the data analytics system this way: "A data system answers questions based on information that was acquired in the past up to the present." (Marz, p.6)[7] You will learn how to create Azure services by working through an overarching scenario.

The Jonestown Sluggers, a minor league baseball team, want to use data to improve their players' performance and company efficiency. They field a new sensor suite in their players' uniforms to collect data during training and games. They identify current data assets to analyze. IT systems for the company already run on Microsoft technology. You move to the new position of data engineer to build the new analytics system.

You will base your design on the principles of the Lambda architecture. The system will provide a scalable endpoint for inbound messages and a data store for loading data files. The system will collect data and store it securely. It will allow batch processing of queries over the entire data set, scheduling the batch executions and moving data into the retrieval endpoint. Concurrently, incoming data will stream into the retrieval endpoint.

Figure 1.3 shows a diagram of your application using Azure technologies. Six primary Azure services work together to form the system.

1 Event Hubs logs messages from data sources like Azure Functions, Azure Event Hubs SDK code, or API calls.
2 Stream Analytics subscribes to the Event Hubs stream and continually reads the incoming messages.
3 A Data Lake store saves new JSON files each hour containing the Stream Analytics data.
4 Data Lake Analytics reads the new JSON file from the Data Lake store each hour and outputs an aggregate report to the Data Lake store.

---

[7] Marz and Warren. *Big Data.*

5 SQL Database saves new aggregate query result records any time the Stream
   Analytics calculations meet a filter criteria.
6 Data Factory reads the new aggregate report from the store, deletes the previous day's data from the database, and writes aggregate query results to the database for the entire batch.

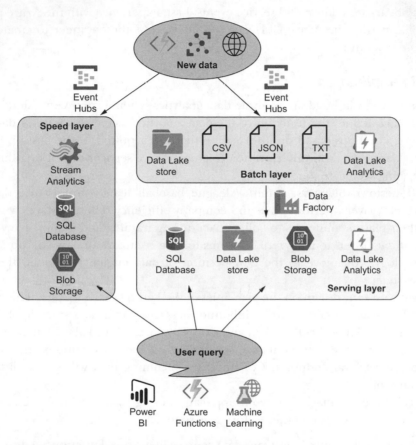

Figure 1.3   Azure PaaS Services analytics application

Multiple services provide methods for processing user queries. The SQL Database
provides a familiar endpoint for querying aggregate data. Engineers and data scientists can submit new queries to Stream Analytics and Data Lake Analytics to generate
new data sets. They can run SQL queries against existing data sets in the SQL Database with low latency. This proposal fulfills the requirements of a Lambda architecture
big data system.

   In order to build this analytics system, you'll need an Azure subscription. Signing
up for a personal account and subscription takes an email address and a credit card.
Most of the examples in this book use Azure PowerShell to create and interact with

Azure services. You can run these PowerShell scripts using Azure Shell, a web-based terminal located at https://shell.azure.com/. Nearly all of the examples in this book are also shown using the Azure Portal. PowerShell scripts, with the Azure PowerShell module, allow a more repeatable process for creating and managing Azure services. A recent version of an integrated development environment (IDE) like Visual Studio 2019 is optional, if you want to build the C# code examples or create your own projects using the various Azure software development kits.

Summary

- Many challenges come with the growing data collection and analysis efforts at most companies, including older systems struggling under increased load and shortages of space and time. These take up valuable developer resources.
- Increased usage leads to increased disruption of unplanned outages, and the risk of data loss is always present.
- The database-centric model for data analysis systems no longer meets the needs of many businesses.
- The Lambda architecture reduces system complexity by minimizing the effort required for low latency queries.
- Building a Lambda architecture analytics system with cloud technologies reduces workload for engineers even further.
- Azure provides PaaS technologies for building a web-scale data analytics system.

Building an analytics
system in Azure

2

This chapter covers

- Introducing the six Azure services discussed in this book
- Joining the services into a working analytics system
- Calculating fixed and variable costs of these services
- Applying Microsoft big data architecture best practices

Cloud providers offer a wide selection of services to build a data warehouse and analytics system. Some services are familiar incarnations of on-premises applications: virtual machines, firewalls, file storage, and databases. Increasing in abstraction are services like web hosting, search, queues, and application containerization services. At the highest levels of abstraction are products and services that have no analogue in a typical data center. For example, Azure Functions executes user code without needing to set up servers, runtimes, or program containers. Moving workloads to more abstract services reduces or eliminates setup and maintenance work and brings higher levels of guaranteed service. Conversely, more abstract services remove access to many configuration settings and constrain usage scenarios. This chapter introduces the Azure services we'll use to build our analytics system. These services range from abstract to very abstract, which allows you to focus on functionality immediately without needing to spend time on the underlying support systems.

2.1 Fundamentals of Azure architecture

Before you dive into creating and using Azure services, it's important to understand some of the basic building blocks. These are required for creating services and configuring them for optimum efficiency. These properties include:

- Azure subscriptions—service billing
- Azure Regions—underlying service location
- Resource groups—security and management boundaries
- Naming conventions—service identification

As you create new Azure services, you will choose each of these properties for the new service. Managing services is easier with thoughtful and consistent application of your options.

2.1.1 Azure subscriptions

Every resource is assigned a subscription. The subscription provides a security boundary: administrators and resources managers get initial authorization at the subscription level. Resources and resource groups inherit permissions from their subscription. The subscription also configures the licensing and payment agreement for the cloud services used. This can be as simple as a monthly bill charged to a credit card, or an enterprise agreement with third-party financing and invoicing.

All Azure services will have a subscription, a resource group, a name, and a location.

- A *subscription* groups services together for access control and billing.
- A *resource group* groups related services together for management.
- A *location* groups services into a regional data center.
- *Names* are globally unique identifiers within the specific service.

Every Azure service, also called a *resource*, must have a name. Consistently applying a naming convention helps users find services and identify ownership and usage of services. You will be browsing and searching for the specific resource you need to work with, from a resource group to a SQL Database to Azure Storage accounts.

> **TIP** Because caching exists in many levels of Azure infrastructure, and syncing changes can occur between regions, recreating a service with the same name can be problematic in a short time frame (on the order of minutes).

2.1.2   Azure regions

Microsoft Azure provides network services, data storage, and generalized and specialized compute nodes that are accessible remotely. Azure doesn't allow access to their servers or data centers, and users don't own the physical hardware. These restrictions makes Azure a cloud provider.

Cloud providers own and maintain network and server hardware in data centers. The data center provides all the power, Internet connectivity, and security required to support the hardware operations that run the cloud services. Azure runs data centers across the world.

Azure data centers are clustered into regions. A region consists of two or more data centers located within a small geographic area. There are many regions for hosting Azure resources across the globe, including the Americas, Europe, Asia Pacific, and the Middle East and Africa.

Data centers within a region share a high-speed network for low latency. Service and data replication between data centers in a region provide critical disaster recovery safeguards. All Azure services exist in more than one region and some are available in every region. Keeping related services within the same region maximizes system performance. Choosing a region near to your users minimizes latency between the user and the services.

This book uses the East US 2 region for any Azure PowerShell scripts which require a specific region, because all resources in the book are available in that region.

> **TIP**   You can learn more about the global nature of Azure regions at http://mng.bz/pz28. You can see the current list of Microsoft Azure services by region at http://mng.bz/OvGR.

2.1.3   Azure naming conventions

You should create a resource group before creating any services. Use this first step to plan your naming conventions and region preferences at the start of your project. A resource naming convention should be applicable across all resources types and follow these guidelines:

- It should align with security or management boundaries.
- It should decrease the cognitive load for the user in identifying a resource.
- It should produce a name which is globally unique within the service.
- Ideally, a naming convention will allow meaningful sorting by name.

An approach moving from broadest to narrowest classifications can fulfill these requirements.

1   The broadest element is the Azure region or location. Most services will have a definite location. Keeping related services in the same region limits charges for network egress. Define a set of acronyms to use.
2   Define a platform name. What project, product, or client does the collection of services support? When you have dozens or hundreds of the same service, several levels of discrimination helps to target the correct service.

3 Separate services by release promotion. Continuous deployment, to a development or production environment, is one of several release strategies that rely on deployment to more than one environment for testing and validation. Dev, Stag, Test, Load, and Prod all work for defining release environments.

4 Adding a service type descriptor helps group similar services.

5 A use case descriptor is better than a number for expressing a particular service instance's function. For example, a system may use multiple Azure databases such as Content, Users, and Logs, each with distinct usage periods and patterns. Adding usage descriptors to the database names makes their purpose clear.

6 All other options being equal, a fixed-width numeric ID is a final differentiator. A random string of alphanumeric characters also serves as a valid ID for automatically provisioned services.

Figure 2.1 lays out these six elements.

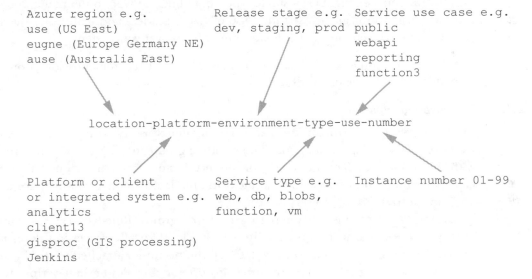

Figure 2.1 Resource naming in Azure

As an example, picture a design for an analytics system hosted in the Australia Southeast region.

- A resource group name of `ause-analytics-dev-grp`
- An app service hosting a Web API site named `ause-analytics-dev-web-api-01`
- Two databases named `ause-analytics-dev-db-raw-01` and `ause-analytics-dev-db-curated-01`
- An Azure Storage account named `auseanalyticsdevblob`

Some services, like Azure Storage, have a length limit for the name. You'll see the specific requirements for setting up Azure Storage in the next chapter, including the naming restrictions. Other resource creation throughout the book will present similar details. Use the components of the naming convention that make sense for your situation.

> **NOTE** An Azure *Storage account* is an umbrella resource that hosts services, including Blobs, Queues, Files, and Tables. The Storage account Blob Storage stores files of all sizes. You can learn more about Azure Storage accounts in chapter 3.

Your services may all be in a single location and not need the location in the name. Your release process may involve creating new services with the latest configuration and changing an endpoint setting to the new services. In this case, your environment variable must be more flexible than "dev" and "prod", instead specifying a release ID. Perhaps your projects can be separated by subscription, so you don't need a project. Or all your services might be a single type, so adding the type to the name would be redundant. If you plan for expanded use of Azure services and features at the start, your naming convention will be flexible enough to cover your system.

> **NOTE** For another take on service names, Microsoft recommends some formats at http://mng.bz/wB8B.

2.1.4 *Resource groups*

Resource groups in Azure are organizing containers. Every Azure service has one. Every resource group has a region. The resource group anchors a service to a region, with the primary configuration data for the service stored in that region. This is especially true for some services, like Cosmos DB and Traffic Manager, which are global and have infrastructure in every region.

Every Azure resource belongs to a resource group. Role-based access control (RBAC) can be managed at the resource group level for all services in the resource group. Deleting a resource group deletes all the resources attached to it. This book uses `ade-dev-eastus2` as the resource group for any PowerShell scripts which require it.

Every resource needs a resource group, so let's create one now. The `New-AzResourceGroup` command creates a new resource group. Provide the resource group name using the `Name` parameter and the Azure region using `Location`. Execute this script in PowerShell with the Azure Modules loaded.

Listing 2.1 New resource group

```
New-AzResourceGroup -Name "ade-dev-eastus2" -Location "East US 2"
```

This PowerShell script will return an error if a group by that name exists. Otherwise it will create a new resource group.

TIP You can find the current list of Azure regions at http://mng.bz/YxgB.

2.1.5 Finding resources

In the Azure portal, common filters include name, subscription, resource group, service type, location, and tags. *Tags* are key-value pairs you can add to any service for filtering. Azure provides multiple methods for filtering by type.

NOTE Remember, in the Azure portal, the content layout containers are called *blades*.

Using the Azure portal, you can search in the All Services blade, use the type filter in the All Resources blade, or use Favorites to navigate directly to a specific service type blade. Filtering by name, location, and tags is available from the All Resources blade, or from a specific service type's blade.

You can even use Azure PowerShell to get services by type. Access Azure PowerShell by visiting Azure Cloud Shell at https://shell.azure.com/, or clicking the >_ header menu in the Azure portal. See appendix A for more details about setting up PowerShell and using it to create and configure services in Azure. Listing 2.2 shows the module command for getting a list of Azure Storage accounts.

Listing 2.2 Azure PowerShell list Storage accounts

```
Get-AzResource -ResourceType Microsoft.Storage/storageAccounts | ft
```

Listing 2.2 includes the `Format-Table` alias `ft`, which formats the command output as a table instead of a column of property values. Listing 2.3 shows the output of the `Get-AzResource` command. The subscription contains a single Azure Storage account.

Listing 2.3 Azure PowerShell list Storage accounts output

```
Name          ResourceGroupName ResourceType                        Location
----          ----------------- ------------                        --------
adedeveastus  ade-dev-eastus    Microsoft.Storage/storageAccounts   eastus
```

From listing 2.3, you can discern the naming convention in use is platform-environment-location. Now that you can locate services in Azure, let's take a look at how we'll design the analytics system.

2.2 Lambda architecture

Lambda architecture seeks to combine the best of real-time processing and fast querying, with the ability to query over huge amounts of collected data. All of the data that enters the system gets a time stamp. The time stamp puts the data in order, which is split into multiple time windows based on the time stamp. Data follows two paths through the system. The real-time "hot" path prepares data for querying with low latency, on the order of seconds or minutes. The hot path has access to the most recent data; therefore its calculations are accurate over a short window of time, but may not be accurate over all time. The batch "cold" path prepares data over the entire data window. The cold path has access to all the data before the batch execution, so the calculations are accurate up to the time of the last batch. Typical latency for the cold path is on the order of hours or days. Together the hot and cold paths contain data from all the time windows.

In an analytics system designed with a Lambda architecture, user queries are submitted to two processors, depending on the targeted time window. For real-time or low latency data sets, a *speed layer* returns query results from the hot path. For longer windows of time, a *serving layer* returns results from various batch processes which cover the time window. Figure 2.2 shows queries submitted to two layers.

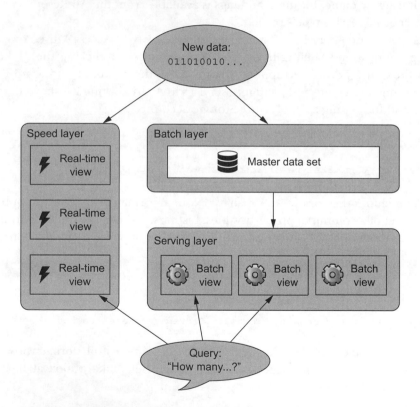

Figure 2.2   Lambda analytics system, showing logical layers of processing based on query latency

To build a Lambda analytics system in Azure, you need to select technologies and services that provide the functions of these layers. Let's look at some of the services offered by Azure that can be used.

2.3   *Azure cloud services*

Microsoft Azure is a cloud services provider. This means Azure provides data center services and software that an enterprise traditionally hosted in their own offices or data center, or in a hosting provider's data center. These were "on-premise" resources, to be distinguished from resources hosted "in the cloud." IT engineers usually have physical access to on-premise resources, but not to cloud resources.

Cloud services providers, like Microsoft Azure and Amazon Web Services, provide three main types of services, classified by the end-user management of the underlying operating system and software.

1 The lowest level of abstraction provides *Infrastructure as a Service* (IaaS). IaaS provides resources like virtual machines, routers, and firewalls. The provider manages the hardware in their data center, and the end user manages the software and operating system. IaaS resources require technical and developer support to manage operating system and software installation, and create code to run on the servers.

2 The next level of abstraction provides a *Platform as a Service* (PaaS). PaaS provides server application hosting such as web servers, databases, and storage. The provider manages the hardware and operating system running in their data center and manages server applications running on the operating system. The end user configures and uses the applications. PaaS resources require developer support to create code to run on the server applications.

3 The third level of abstraction provides *Software as a Service* (SaaS). SaaS provides user applications delivered over the internet. Typical SaaS applications include web-based email services or web-based file sharing services that charge a subscription. The SaaS provider manages all aspects of the hardware, operating system, and software. The end user configures and uses the application. Microsoft has transitioned many of their operating systems, desktop, and server applications to IaaS, PaaS, or SaaS resources available in Azure.

Microsoft Azure offers both open-source and Microsoft technologies in its cloud services. HDInsight is available for Hadoop engineers and data scientists. HDInsight manages containerized Hadoop processing nodes, with plenty of configuration access and overhead. Azure also provides Databricks, a SaaS abstraction of the Apache Spark analytics engine. Both provide viable options for operating large analytics systems in the cloud. A third option exists: By using the tight integration provided by Azure products, Microsoft data engineers can build their own sophisticated and flexible analytics system using familiar technologies like C#, SQL, and Git. This book will discuss these services and how to use them to build a complete analytics system in the cloud.

Leveraging interconnected services allows you to focus on the business logic of the application. Contrast this with writing and hosting the software yourself, and you can see the value of creating your application in the cloud first. The comparison also demonstrates the source of expenses in cloud service usage. Engineers and developers at Microsoft must design and maintain software that operates at an impressive scale, is resilient to failure, tolerates updates and new features, and supports end user's changing usage.[1]

> *Cloud-native software is highly distributed, must operate in a constantly changing environment, and is itself constantly changing.*

> —Cornelia Davis

Azure services were developed as *cloud-native software*. You pay for the benefits that accrue from this software design, like on-demand scaling and high availability. You can take advantage of the resilient and agile nature of cloud-native software by creating your own analytics application with these interconnected services. In this book we'll build a robust analytics processing system that can scale with demand.

2.3.1 *Azure analytics system architecture*

Imagine your company wants to analyze user behavior in their main website to provide relevant suggestions for further reading, to promote user retention and higher page views. A solution would allow generating suggestions based on historical data, recent personalized actions, and machine learning algorithms. Further, the same system could also analyze error events in real-time and provide alerts. You can build a system in Azure to do the analysis work. The rest of this book walks through use cases, technical trade-offs, and design considerations when creating and operating each piece of our proposed analytics system. Before we dive deeply into each of the services, let's take a look at the system as a whole.

This architectural design uses the six Azure services discussed in this chapter.

- Events Hubs for real-time ingestion
- Stream Analytics for real-time query processing
- Data Lake Storage for data retention and batch query processing support
- Data Lake Analytics for batch query processing
- Data Factory for batch scheduling and aggregate data movement
- SQL Database for interactive queries

Let's look at each of these services.

2.3.2 *Event Hubs*

Azure Event Hubs provides a PaaS scalable message ingestion endpoint, including built-in integrations with Blob Storage and Stream Analytics. Our analytics system will use Event Hubs as the entry point to our data processing pipeline. This provides our system with a scalable and reliable buffer to handle spikes in the volume of incoming events. Event Hubs accepts HTTPS, Advanced Message Queuing Protocol

---

[1] Cornelia Davis and Gene Kim. *Cloud Native Patterns: Designing Change-Tolerant Software.* Shelter Island, NY: Manning Publications, 2019.

(AMQP), and Apache Kafka packets for event messages. Clients are available for these protocols in your language of choice. Messages in Event Hubs can be read by one or more subscribers.

Events Hubs scales in two ways. First, the endpoint processes incoming messages with a *throughput unit*, a measure of maximum throughput at a fixed cost. Adding more throughput units allows a higher message rate, at a higher cost. Second, Event Hubs partitions the messages. Adding more partitions allows the Event Hub to buffer more messages and service parallel reads by subscribers. We'll cover setup and design considerations with Event Hubs deeply in chapter 5.

2.3.3 Stream Analytics

Azure Stream Analytics processes streaming data. Streaming data is ordered by a time element, which is why it's often referred to as *events* or *event data*. Stream Analytics accepts streams from Event Hubs, IoT Hubs, and Blob Storage, and outputs processed information to one or more Azure endpoints. It uses Structured Query Language to query the data stream. The data process can be thought of as fishing a river with a net made of particular shapes. The data flows by the net, which captures the bits that match the shapes. The fisherman hauls in the net regularly to review his catch. In the same way, the queries pull result sets out of the stream as it flows by.

Stream Analytics scales in two ways. First, each Stream Analytics job can utilize one or more *streaming units*, a synthetic metric describing CPU and memory allocation. Each step in the job uses between one and six streaming units. Second, planning parallelism in your stream queries allows you to take advantage of the available parallel processes. For example, writing data to a file in Blob Storage or Data Lake Storage can use multiple connections in parallel. Writing data to a SQL Server table uses a single connection, for now. A single query operation can use up to six streaming units. Each job can have more than one query operation. Planning the streaming unit allocation along with the query structure will allow for maximum throughput.

2.3.4 Data Lake Storage

Azure Data Lake Storage stores files. It provides a folder interface over an Apache Hadoop file system, which supports petabytes of data. Multiple open-source and native Azure cloud services integrate with Data Lake Storage. Fine grained access via integration with Azure Active Directory makes securing files a familiar exercise.

2.3.5 Data Lake Analytics

Azure Data Lake Analytics (ADLA) brings scalable batch processing to Data Lake Storage and Blob Storage. ADLA jobs use familiar SQL syntax to read files, query the data, and output results files over data sets of any size. Because ADLA uses a distributed query processor over a distributed file system, batch jobs can be executed over multiple nodes at once. To run a job with parallel processing, just move the slider past one.

Azure Data Lake Analytics uses a new coding language called *U-SQL*. U-SQL is not ANSI SQL. For starters, WHERE clauses use C# syntax. Declarative statements can be extended with C# functions. Query data comes from tables or files. We'll discuss this new language more in chapter 8.

2.3.6   *SQL Database*

Azure SQL Database (SQLDB) supports most functions you're familiar with from the on-premises SQL Server. Most functionality matches: CRUD actions, views, stored procedures, table creation, indexing, and partitioning. Many database applications can be ported to directly. In addition, you get backup management, on-demand scaling of processing power, nearly unlimited databases and storage space, and multi-zone failover.

2.3.7   *Data Factory*

Azure Data Factory automates the data movement between layers. With it, you can schedule an ADLA batch job for creating aggregate data files. You can import those files into SQLDB and execute stored procedures too. Data Factory connects to many different endpoints for input and output and can build structured workflows for moving data between them. Data Factory schedules, executes, and monitors these repeated activities.

2.3.8   *Azure PowerShell*

Azure offers Cloud Shell as an option for managing resources via the command line, as PowerShell or Bash commands. You can access Cloud Shell from the Azure portal, or by connecting to https://shell.azure.com. This book uses Azure PowerShell scripts throughout for provisioning Azure resources.

2.4   *Walk-through of processing a series of event data records*

In this system, incoming event data follows both a hot and cold path into the user query engine. To illustrate how the event data flows through both paths, let's trace the flow of a typical user action event through both paths. This system monitors error rates and provides "users also viewed" suggestions. We can see how each path fulfills part of our imagined business requirements for this system.

2.4.1   *Hot path*

1 New data events are submitted to the Event Hub endpoint. The data events contain both error data and page view data.
2 The Event Hubs endpoint stores the events for retrieval.
3 A Stream Analytics job reads events from Event Hubs as they are submitted. The job runs two steps.
   a The first step prepares updates for a Power BI dashboard. This could be a simple error rate query from the last hour, or a machine learning API call. The query limits the updates to one per second.

     b The second step saves data directly to SQL Database. To match the project requirements, the query reads the last 24 hours of streaming data and finds the top three most visited pages by same-session users. It then writes this data.

  4 The website reads the most recent list of recommendations for a particular page view from the SQL Database.

2.4.2 Cold path

  1 New data events are submitted to the Event Hub endpoint. The data events contain both error data and page view data.

  2 The Event Hub endpoint stores the events for retrieval.

  3 A Stream Analytics job reads events from Event Hubs as they are submitted.

  4 The Stream Analytics job runs one step—writing the raw data events to Data Lake Storage files.

  5 Each day, Data Factory runs a scheduled pipeline. This pipeline has multiple steps.

     a Data Factory submits a Data Lake Analytics job to calculate next page visit probabilities based on previous page visits.

     b To match the project requirements, the job query reads the last 30 days of stored page visit data and finds pages visited by same-session users.

     c It then writes this data to an aggregate file.

  6 Data Factory imports the aggregate file into the SQL Database.

     a It also moves 24 hour "hot" data to an archive table.

  7 The website reads the most recent list of recommendations for a particular page view from the SQL Database.

Figure 2.3 shows how all six services can be assembled into an analytics processing system providing real-time and batch-time outputs.

2.4.3 Choosing abstract Azure services

There are multiple functions that a modern analytics platform must support. Some platforms put all the functions in one monolithic system; others require building the system with many discrete services. You can design a platform in Azure using the second approach, using the advantages of PaaS software.

First, the system must collect event data. This can be user input, server actions, or error logging. If you can build new logging functionality into your systems, using Event Hubs as a logging endpoint makes sense because:

- Event Hubs can handle high traffic loads.
- Event Hubs can easily save all event data to disk.
- Event Hubs comes with a good service level agreement.
- Event Hubs is a convenient gateway to Stream Analytics for real-time processing of the event data.

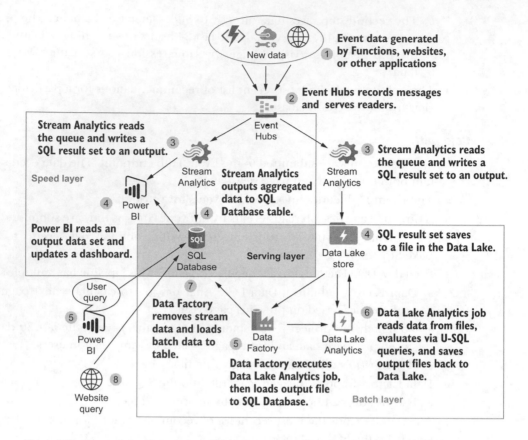

Figure 2.3   Azure abstract service analytics system, showing Lambda architecture layers over hot path and cold path data processing steps

For applications built on the .NET framework, the NuGet package from Microsoft provides a client for integration into application code for logging events. The .NET client includes built-in retry logic.

Second, the system must process events in real-time. Stream Analytics queries a streaming data set from Event Hubs in real-time.

- Stream Analytics includes built-in support for reading from Event Hub endpoints as a streaming source.
- Stream Analytics supports outputting results to SQL and Cosmos databases, Blob Storage, Power BI, and Azure Functions.
- Stream Analytics has multiple methods for enhancing data with machine learning algorithms.
- Stream Analytics lets us leverage our existing SQL skills.

The result set will be emitted in small batches when a calculation is completed. Figure 2.4 shows Stream Analytics reading from Event Hubs and writing to Data Lake

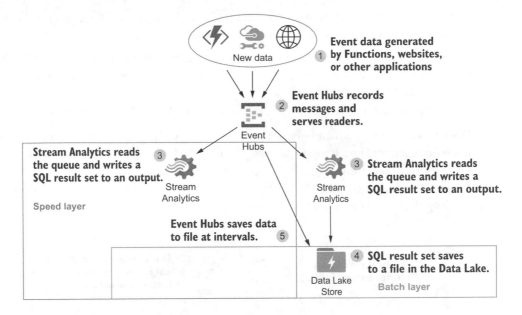

Figure 2.4　Event Hubs reads discrete messages and serves the set to readers.

store. Power BI integration makes adding results to dashboards quick work. Writing the emitted result set to a SQL Database keeps queries up to date, continuously adding new data as it enters the system. For projects where real-time logging is not an option, log files can be loaded into Blob Storage for near-real-time processing by Stream Analytics. Figure 2.5 shows Stream Analytics evaluating SQL statements and writing results to SQLDB and Data Lake store.

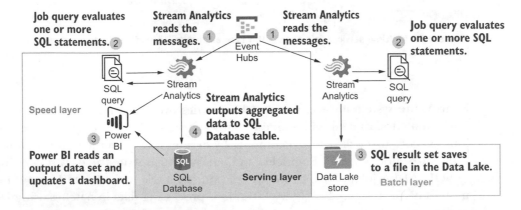

Figure 2.5　Stream analytics reads streams of data, evaluates SQL queries, and emits data sets.

Third, the system must store all the data securely while allowing easy access. Both Blob Storage and Data Lake Storage can fulfill this role.

- Data Lake Storage has no practical limit to the volume of data that can be stored.
- Data Lake Storage uses a familiar read/write/execute security model over a hierarchical folder structure.
- Authentication is controlled through Azure Active Directory accounts.

Data Lake Storage, which is based on the Hadoop file system, allows access by many analytics services, including Data Lake Analytics, HDInsight, and Databricks. For projects where real-time logging is not an option, log files can be loaded into Data Lake Storage for batch processing by Data Lake Analytics. Figure 2.6 shows multiple tools loading data to Data Lake store for batch processing.

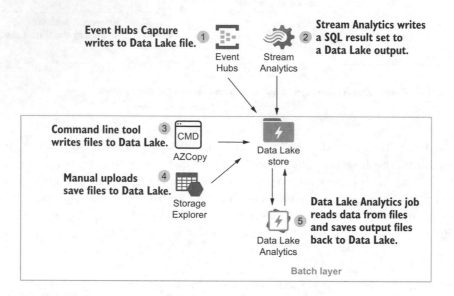

Figure 2.6   Multiple services can access Data Lake Storage for read and write operations.

Fourth, the system must enable batch analytics over any and all of the data. Data Lake Analytics, as the name suggests, runs analytics jobs over data lake files. ADLA jobs execute using distributed compute by design, with a simple slider defining the number of nodes to use. Engineers and data scientists write the data processing job in SQL. ADLA job processing nodes read one or more data files and output one or more data files. Figure 2.7 shows ADLA jobs processing data in batches using U-SQL queries.

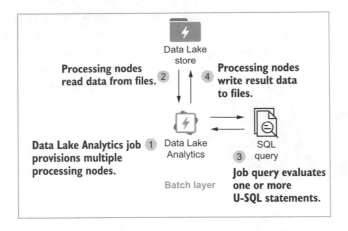

Figure 2.7   Data Lake Analytics reads data files, evaluates SQL queries, and save result sets as files.

Fifth, the system must be capable of updating user query result sets. Data Factory is a great fit for automating these other services.

- Data Factory connects to Azure endpoints like Blob Storage, Data Lake Storage, and SQL Database.
- Data Factory provides multiple methods for moving and transforming data between endpoints.
- Data Factory can access on-premises files and databases, through an on-premises Integration Runtime.
- Data Factory pipelines can copy file data to and from databases, execute ADLA jobs, and run stored procedures.

Data Factory orchestration manages the end-to-end data movement requirements of this analytics system. Figure 2.8 shows Data Factory scheduling batch processing and moving data into the serving layer.

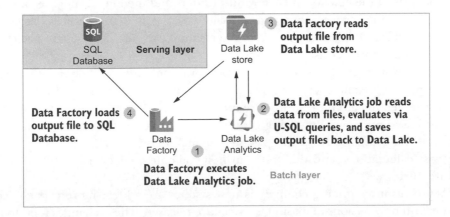

Figure 2.8   Data Factory schedules jobs and moves data between files and databases.

Sixth, the system must be capable of returning results to user queries in near real-time. SQL Database uses a familiar RDBMS query engine with a scalable storage system that supports TBs of data. Because SQL Database uses SQL for querying data, many tools exist which can connect and submit queries. Power BI is one such tool. Figure 2.9 shows end user queries run against SQL Database in the serving layer.

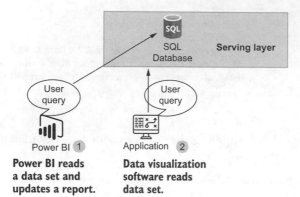

Power BI reads
a data set and
updates a report.

Data visualization
software reads
data set.

Figure 2.9   SQL Database provides data query endpoint.

This example focuses on connecting abstract services together into a working system. Each service offers an optimized tool designed for easy setup, high throughput, and minimal maintenance. The services take full advantage of the consumption model of cloud computing. Let's look more closely at the main cost considerations for building a system with these services.

2.5 Calculating cloud hosting costs

When building systems in any cloud provider, engineers must include a detailed estimate of costs of the new system. They must understand the long-term costs of the new system, including service, storage, and usage costs. Poor setup choices, lax account security, and lack of planning for resource cleanup can ruin a successful project with unplanned expensive costs.

Microsoft Azure includes a powerful tool for estimating costs. The pricing calculator (https://azure.microsoft.com/pricing/calculator/) provides a graphical interface for collecting all the resources required for a project and generating estimates for cost based on usage. Practicing with Azure resources is the best way to learn how to judge the estimates from the pricing calculator. Business decisions involve risk and cost calculations, and this tool can help validate your decision to use a cloud architecture.

Azure resource pricing changes as new systems are added, more capacity comes online, and new versions of existing services are released. These changes tend to lower existing costs, or raise the threshold for free usage. Your agreement with Microsoft for software, services, and support can also modify the final amount billed. Some services, like Data Lake Storage, can take advantage of pre-purchased capacity at reduced rates. A knowledgeable data engineer can make a huge impact on TCO in this type of scenario. Reviewing the Azure documentation and subscribing to the Azure newsletter helps keep engineers current with changes to pricing and capabilities.

2.5.1 Event Hubs

Event Hubs pricing includes tiering, scaling, and usage costs. Event Hubs Dedicated includes everything for very high throughput for a very large price per hour. Event Hubs Basic does not include several important features, like multiple consumer groups and direct file capture, but costs about 50% less than the Standard tier. See Event Hubs pricing http://mng.bz/GdGv for specific prices. Most scenarios will use the Standard tier and include file capture for an additional cost. The primary cost decision for configuring a new Event Hub involves choosing a base number of throughput units. Generally this is two throughput units at minimum, but you should calculate the volume of data ingress to minimize throttling of any message submissions.

2.5.2 Stream Analytics

The Azure Stream Analytics cost structure consists of streaming unit usage per hour. Typical scenarios involve one to six streaming units, depending on the complexity of the queries. Each job has a fixed base cost per month, but each job can have multiple inputs and outputs. Most systems need only a single job per event hub. See http://mng.bz/zrQB for specific prices. We'll cover capacity planning for Stream Analytics in chapter 4.

2.5.3 Data Lake Storage

Azure Data Lake Storage (ADLS) pricing covers three activities: space utilization, read and write transactions, and data transfers. The storage calculation is based on monthly average file storage. Read and write transactions are inexpensive. Outbound data transfers incur charges; inbound transfers are free. Prepurchasing storage space provides a discount. See http://mng.bz/0ZwN for specific prices.

ADLS gen 2 adds tiered storage to the mix, with modified costs for space utilization and transactions. The design of the analytics system should take into account these differences in long-term costs. See pricing http://mng.bz/K5Bj for specific prices.

For most scenarios, storage follows compute in terms of cost. Balancing tiered access cost savings with latency requirements adds to the complexity. However, hot and cool tiers have the same latency. Most data should be shifted to the cool tier within a month. ADLS gen 2 reduces costs significantly. Because of the cost savings, for most projects you'll want to use ADLS gen 2, or plan a migration from gen 1 to gen 2.

2.5.4   *Data Lake Analytics*

Azure Data Lake Analytics (ADLA) cost structure consists of analytics unit usage per hour. Prepurchasing unit-hours provides a discount. See http://mng.bz/9A57 for specific prices.

Any ADLA job will run with a single analytics unit at 100% efficiency, but most jobs can take advantage of parallel processing to shorten the duration of the job. Data engineers can help determine the optimum allocated units for a particular job. They can also plan for monthly usage and assist in prepurchasing unit-hours.

For example, suppose a job imports two files, aggregates the data, and writes a summary file.

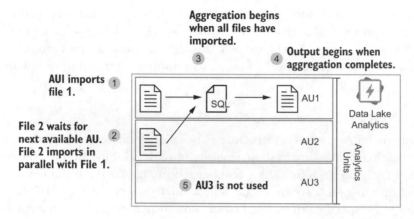

Figure 2.10   Parallel processing in Azure Data Lake Analytics jobs with multiple analytics units

This job can run with one, two, or more analytics units doing the processing. Figure 2.10 shows a job that uses 2 AUs but has been allocated 3AUs. The third AU is not used.

1 Using one unit, both files will import sequentially, the aggregation step will execute, and finally the summary file will be written.
2 Using two units, both files will import in parallel, then the aggregation step will execute, then the summary file will be written.
3 Using three or more units will run just like using two units. A job will use *at most* one unit per file, but usually processes multiple files per unit. Any extra units beyond two will incur charges for the duration of the job without doing any work.

Each analytics unit allocated to the job incurs charges for the duration of the job. In the best case, a job that takes four hours with one AU would take two hours with two AUs, and one hour with four AUs. All three runs would cost the same: 4hr*1AU = 2hr*2AU = 1hr*4AU = 4AUhrs. In reality, jobs are not entirely parallel, and analytic units will be idle for some portion of the job. The optimization work determines how much parallelization can be achieved for which portion of the job, and then balances the requirements for total job duration with minimizing cost. We'll look more closely at optimizing ADLA jobs and costs in chapter 7.

2.5.5 SQL Database

Three flavors of SQL Database are available in Azure. Azure SQLDB provides a PaaS SQL Server database with scalable processing throughput and storage. You can use it with a single database, multiple databases pooling resource consumption, and even a virtual instance of a SQL Server. SQLDB offers the lowest-cost tiers, as well as higher tiers for better performance and storage. Performance and storage costs are bundled.

Azure Stretch Database shards your on-premise database by attaching a cloud database and handling multi-database queries. This allows storage expansion at lower costs. Stretch Database costs include processing engine and storage. Storage costs are approximately the same rate as premium Blob Storage.

Azure Hyperscale Database moves storage to a separate engine in Azure Storage, allowing unlimited storage. Costs for Hyperscale include the processing engine, storage, and any read replicas added. Read replicas cost approximately two-thirds of the full instance. Storage costs are approximately two-thirds of the premium Blob Storage rate.

2.5.6 Data Factory

Two versions of Data Factory are available. Data Factory gen 1 is a configuration-driven service using JSON files to define the various endpoints, data movements, and transforms in each job. Data Factory gen 2 builds on gen 1, providing a GUI for building the JSON configurations. Calculating the ongoing costs involves several variables. These variables fall into two main categories: data operations and orchestration. Data operations charge for the duration of copy events between source and sink. A synthetic usage metric called a *data movement unit (DMU)* measures the duration of data activities and meters the movement rate. DMU usage is billed per hour. For gen 2, Azure adds charges for both read/writes and monitoring operations against entities like a dataset or list of pipeline activities.

Jobs which move data between cloud resources are more expensive than moving from on-premises to cloud. Orchestration charges cover executions of the Integration Runtime, both in the cloud and on-premises. Charges are lower for executing more jobs in the cloud, or executing longer-running jobs on-premises.

To formulate a recommendation, plan for the most cost-effective scenario which accomplishes the project requirements. For example, 10 jobs running for 10 seconds each minute would be more expensive than a single job that runs 4 hours each day. There would be more data operations and more jobs would be run. In Figure 2.11, multiple short pipelines cost more than a single pipeline running for a longer period.

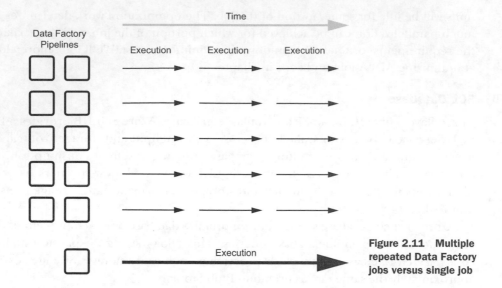

Figure 2.11   Multiple repeated Data Factory jobs versus single job

NOTE   We'll look more closely at Data Factory setup and configuration in chapter 10. Setting up the self-hosted Integration Runtime (IR) will clarify the differences between cloud and on-premises IR functions.

Summary

- Using highly abstract cloud services reduces setup and maintenance time, but limits options. You pay to shift maintenance and support of the underlying services to Microsoft.
- Microsoft Azure offers several well integrated services that can combine to form an analytics processing system. Connecting multiple resilient services together forms a resilient cloud-native application.
- Every Azure service must have a name. Designing an effective naming convention makes managing resources easier.
- Calculating costs requires estimating the volume and size of the data collection. Each kind of service charges for usage and storage differently.

General storage with
Azure Storage accounts

This chapter covers

- Creating a storage service
- Setting up an Azure Storage Blob Storage
- Configuring file access in Blob Storage

In the previous chapter you explored some services provided by Microsoft Azure: Event Hubs, Stream Analytics, Data Lake, Data Lake Analytics, and SQL Database. You saw at a high level how these services can work together to create an analytics system.

This chapter begins showing you how to design and set up these services to lay the foundation of an analytics system. The first step is learning how to implement a storage system that is secure and scalable using Azure Storage accounts.

Durable storage serves both input and output for your analytics system. You can integrate your existing applications and third-party software with file-based transports. The comma-separated values (CSV) format has long been used to export data from applications. More recently, Extensible Markup Language (XML) and JavaScript Object Notation (JSON) provide greater structure for data interchange. All three formats are stored in plain text files. When delivered as exports from existing systems, these formats provide sources for data processing.

After processing, they can hold the output of user queries. Figure 3.1 shows examples of durable storage as sources in the Batch layer, and outputs from the Speed and Serving layers.

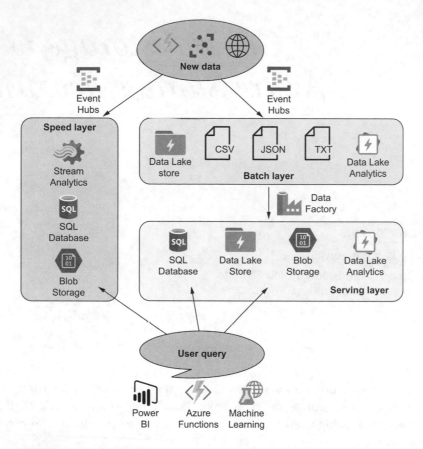

Figure 3.1   Lambda architecture with Azure PaaS services

Azure Storage accounts provide several types of durable and transient storage. The first we'll look at, Blob Storage, is a cheap and resilient service for storing any kind of file. A number of services in Azure integrate directly with Blob Storage, including Event Hubs, Stream Analytics, and Cloud Shell. Blob Storage will be used as part of your analytics system. Let's look at how Azure Storage accounts run Blob Storage, and other types of storage too.

> **TIP**   You can find the code listings online in the GitHub repository for this book at https://github.com/rnuckolls/azure_storage.

3.1   Cloud storage services

Azure Storage is Microsoft's first cloud storage service. It provides multiple specialized types, of essentially key/value stores: queues, blobs, tables, file shares. Key/value pairs store data in a flat hierarchy. The key is used for lookup, and the value stores simple or complex data. Blob Storage and file shares have a particularly large value, and a key that looks like a file path. Tables are standard key/value stores. Queues store ID and text fields. Azure Storage also provides backing for virtual machine (VM) disks in Azure VMs.

- Blob Storage stores files as byte collection blobs, with a programmatic command interface.
- Files service stores files, with a Server Message Block (SMB) protocol interface. Use this service for network shares.
- Queue service stores messages in a queue for sequential programmatic retrieval.
- Tables service stores collections of key/value pairs, with unique IDs.

Suppose the Finance and Operations departments want a joint file archive that can be used with multiple Azure services. Users and systems from each department will upload files to the archive. Access to upload files for one department must not allow reading files from the other department. You need to design and implement an appropriate access scheme in a Storage account that satisfies these requirements. How can you accommodate this request?

3.1.1   Before you begin

The scenarios in the next section use a security group from Azure Active Directory (AAD) called "Finance." If you don't want to use an existing AAD group, you should create this group in AAD. You can use the scripts in appendix A to create the users and groups required in this chapter.

3.2   Creating an Azure Storage account

Azure offers multiple methods for creating new resources, including Azure Power-Shell, Resource Manager (ARM) templates, and the Azure portal. Though PowerShell and ARM templates allow you to more easily automate your activities in Azure, the Azure portal presents a lower bar to entry. This chapter uses examples from both the Azure portal and PowerShell scripts to demonstrate procedures and features in Azure.

> **NOTE** You should already be familiar with the Azure portal and have a subscription. If not, please visit https://azure.microsoft.com/en-us/free/ to sign up for a free month. You will need an email address and a credit card to create a subscription.

Setting up an Azure Storage account requires a few pieces of information common to all Azure services, including a subscription, name, location, and resource group.

- A subscription groups services together for access control and billing.
- A resource group groups related services together for management.

- A location assigns services to a regional data center.
- Names are globally unique identifiers within the specific service.

It also requires some options specific to Azure Storage.

- Selecting the "Premium" performance tier provisions solid state drives in Azure Storage, but limits the service to page blobs such as VM disks. The "Standard" tier supports all types of Azure Storage services.
- Selecting your account kind provides backward compatibility for existing implementations of the Blob Storage or general-purpose storage services.
- The contents of an Azure Storage account can be replicated for increased redundancy. Options are available for single data center redundancy (LRS), multi-data center redundancy (ZRS), and multi-region, multi-data center redundancy (GRS) with read access (RA-GRS). See section 3.2.3 later in this chapter for more details.

3.2.1   *Using Azure portal*

Use the following steps to create a new Storage account with these options. Figure 3.2 shows the Azure portal interface for creating a Storage account.

1   In the Azure portal, click the Create a Resource menu or the Add button on the Storage accounts blade. This opens the Create Storage Account blade. You can also browse directly to http://mng.bz/awDB.

2   Choose a subscription. The default will be the oldest subscription, if you have access to more than one.

3   Choose a resource group. (See appendix A for instructions if you haven't created one.)

4   Choose a name ("[XYZ]deveastus2"). The Storage account name must be lowercase alphanumeric, between 3-24 characters, and globally unique.

5   Choose a location. Azure Storage are available in all regions; choose one close to you. Keep Azure resources that interact in the same region to minimize network latency. You may choose a region to match your user base, as some governments restrict movement of data outside their zone of control.

6   Choose the default Standard performance level. Premium is only for VM disks.

7   Choose the default kind, StorageV2. This is the latest version, and there are no benefits to using the previous version for new projects.

8   Choose the LRS replication type, or leave the default RA-GRS. (LRS costs less than RA-GRS.)

9   Choose the Hot access tier. This minimizes costs for your tutorial usage. The Cool tier and Archive tier include a minimum storage duration cost for each file. Access tiering allows you to balance content retrieval latency with cost.

10   Review your choices and create the Storage account.

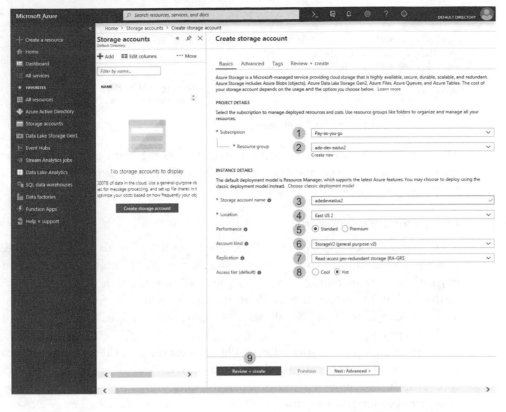

1. Use the same subscription for related resources.
2. Use the same resource group for related resources.
3. Name must be alphanumeric only.
4. Keep related resources in the same location for best performance.
5. Premium is only for VM disks.
6. Leave the default StorageV2.
7. Redundant storage incurs higher costs.
8. Choose Cool if you will rarely access these files.
9. Review, and then create the Storage account in two steps.

Figure 3.2   Creating a Storage account

3.2.2   *Using Azure PowerShell*

The `New-AzStorageAccount` command creates a new Storage account. The `SkuName` parameter selects the replication type. Possible values include Standard_LRS, Standard_ZRS, Standard_GRS, Standard_RAGRS, Standard_GZRS, Standard_RAGZRS, Premium_LRS, and Premium_ZRS. Premium SKUs are used with VM disk creation. The parameter `EnableHttpsTrafficOnly` with a value of 0 disables HTTPS traffic, but you shouldn't do this. Storage account requests are limited to HTTPS only by default. Execute the script in listing 3.1 in Azure PowerShell.

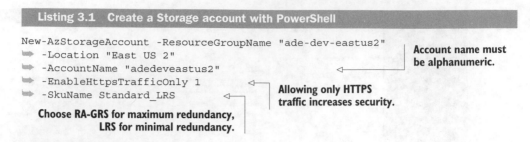

Listing 3.1   Create a Storage account with PowerShell

```
New-AzStorageAccount -ResourceGroupName "ade-dev-eastus2"
     -Location "East US 2"
     -AccountName "adedeveastus2"
     -EnableHttpsTrafficOnly 1
     -SkuName Standard_LRS
```

Account name must be alphanumeric.

Allowing only HTTPS traffic increases security.

Choose RA-GRS for maximum redundancy, LRS for minimal redundancy.

This PowerShell script will return an error if a Storage account by that name exists. With your new Storage account in place, you should consider backup and disaster recovery options for the data stored there.

3.2.3   *Azure Storage replication*

A common working space for collaboration probably needs to be highly available. Picking a location near your users' physical location will reduce network latency over the Internet. Azure Storage provide some flexibility in configuration to allow for differing availability requirements. Your Storage account contents can be replicated to multiple locations. Figure 3.3 shows files replication in a local data center and to secondary regions.

At minimum, three copies of each file are kept in the local data center. *Local redundant storage* (LRS) uses only the local data center. *Zone redundant storage* (ZRS) replicates contents to another data center in the same region. *Geo-redundant storage* (GRS) replicates contents to a separate region. *Read-access geo-redundant storage* (RA-GRS) replicates contents to a separate region, and allows read access. Adding replication to Azure Storage gives your applications redundancy, and raises their cost and complexity. This redundancy increases the storage price.

> **NOTE**   For the latest pricing details, see http://mng.bz/gg4E.

Microsoft chooses the region pairing, and when to declare a region unrecoverable and failover to the secondary region.

- Regions are separated physically, with at least 300 miles between paired regions' data centers.
- Regions are paired geographically, to comply with data residency requirements.
- Paired regions receive updates sequentially, to minimize downtime and effects of adverse outcomes due to updates.

> **NOTE**   See http://mng.bz/7XEV for the latest list of paired regions.

For greater control or shortened recovery times, you may wish to backup data to a second Storage account in a separate region using a tool like AzCopy. You can find an introduction to AzCopy in section 3.3.4 later in this chapter.

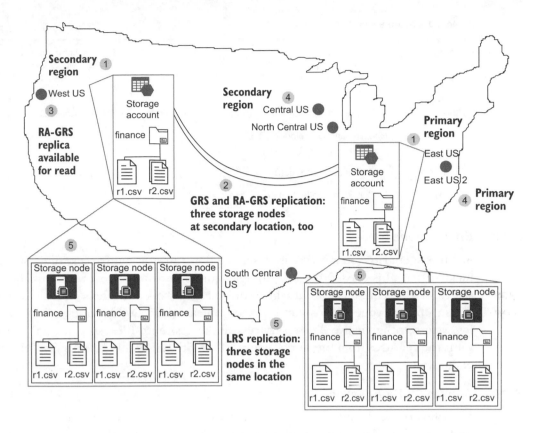

Figure 3.3 Storage account replication to multiple zones

IMPORTANT   Microsoft maintains Azure data centers in locations around the world. Every Azure service you create is available in at least one location. Some services, like Azure Storage, can run in any Azure location. Not all services are available in all locations. For best performance, keep services which need to connect to each other in the same location.

3.3 Storage account services

Azure Storage provides cheap cloud storage options, including services targeted at NoSQL data, queues, and VM disks. Storage accounts consist of five services: files, blobs, disk, queues, and tables. Table 3.1 shows what each of the services offer.

Table 3.1 Azure storage containers

Type	Feature	Limitation
Files	SMB interface for file shares; high throughput; folder-file hierarchy	TB scale files and shares
Blobs	Global replication; high throughput; flat-file hierarchy	PB scale storage
Disk	High throughput; folder-file hierarchy	Attached to VM; no access outside VM
Queues	Message store; no hierarchy	Messages only
Tables	NoSQL store; collection-item hierarchy	Table items only

3.3.1   Blob storage

For this scenario, you want to use a service that can store and access files. Since you want to use this service for file storage, queue and table stores are out. For disk stores, a dedicated VM would be required to access the files. This requirement doesn't match your low cost directive, so you can eliminate this option. In an analytics system, other native Azure services will access these files, so you don't need or want the features from file or disk stores. Blob Storage would be most useful for this example.

3.3.2   Creating a Blobs service container

In order to use the new Storage account for Blob Storage, you need to create a *container*. All blob files reside within a container. A container works just how it sounds. It's a logical grouping of a set of objects, in this case files. Because you want to store text files in this Storage account, you won't be setting up a queue, table, or disk container. You have no need to enable remote file share access to the log files, so you don't need a file service.

1 In the Azure portal, browse to the Azure Storage Account blade. One approach is to click the All Services blade, filter to Storage accounts, and click the Storage Accounts icon.
2 Click your newly created Azure Storage service "[XYZ]deveastus2".
3 In the Storage account, under Blobs Service, click Blobs to show the Blobs blade.
4 Click the Container button to add a new container. Figure 3.4 shows the New container blade.
5 Enter *finance* as the container name. The name must be lowercase alphanumeric (including hyphens), between 3-63 characters, and unique in the Storage account.
6 Leave the default Public access level Private. Other access levels allow read or read and list access to the container by anonymous public users.
7 Click OK to create the container.

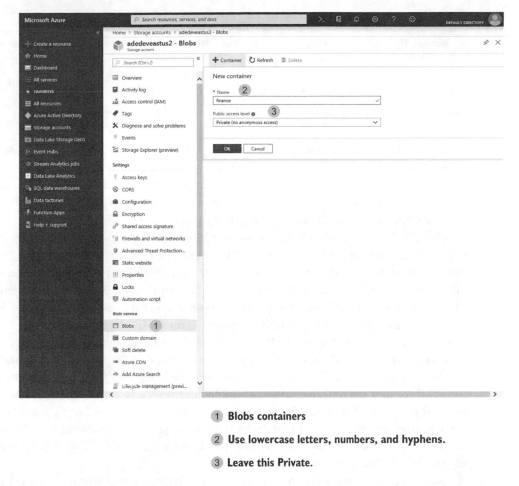

① **Blobs containers**

② **Use lowercase letters, numbers, and hyphens.**

③ **Leave this Private.**

Figure 3.4   Creating a Blob container

You can now use the Azure portal or other tools to copy the files into the Finance container.

3.3.3   *Blob tiering*

Azure Storage containers should be configured for each use case. Access tiering in Blob containers allows you to balance content retrieval latency with cost. For example, cheap long-term archival of files is a common use case. Which tier would best suit this? A hot tier provides the fastest retrieval; use a warm/cool tier for slower retrieval, or a different cost structure. A cool tier would be the least expensive for long term storage, but may have long retrieval times and additional retrieval fees. Table 3.2 lists the Blob access tiers.

Table 3.2   Azure Storage Blob access tiers

Access Tier	Latency	Storage cost	Access cost	Minimum period
Hot	Milliseconds	Highest	Lowest	N/A
Cool	Milliseconds	Middle	Middle	30 days
Archive	< 15 hours	Lowest	Highest	180 days

Tiering options are available when targeting General purpose v2 or Blob storage. These kinds allow you to change the blob access level between Hot, Cold, and Archive levels, to better manage your costs. You can choose only Hot and Cool as the default tier for the Blob container. New blobs are only created at the Hot or Cool tier. You can also set blobs to the Archive tier on a per-blob basis.

Use the Azure portal, Azure Storage Explorer, or the Azure SDK to change a blob tier to Hot, Cool, or Archive. Moving a blob from the Cold or Archive tiers to another tier incurs a prorated charge, if the minimum storage period has not been met. Deleting a blob from the Cold or Archive tiers incurs a prorated charge, if the minimum storage period has not been met. Moving a blob from Hot to Cool, Cool to Archive, or Hot to Archive tiers incurs write operation charges. Moving a blob from Archive to Cool, Cool to Hot, or Archive to Hot incurs read operation charges.

Frequently accessed files, or files for systems that need fast performance, prioritize low latency over price. For frequently accessed or transitory files, you would choose the Hot tier as a default. Some use cases, like archival storage, need to write once and be read rarely. In this case, price would rank higher than latency, so you would choose the Archive tier. First copy the blobs to Blob Storage with a default at the Hot tier, to prevent an initial retention period charge. Then shift the blobs to the Archive tier with your selected tool.

Now that you have some perspective on the cost of using Storage account Blobs, let's look at how you can move files to the storage containers.

3.3.4   Copy tools

Now that you've created a Storage account and a blob container for the Finance department, you can start copying the files. Figure 3.5 shows four options for tools to copy files. The Azure portal provides a web-based interface for uploading and downloading files. AzCopy is a command-line tool from Microsoft for copying files to and from Storage account services, including Blobs and Files. Azure Data Factory (ADF) uses cloud scheduling and on-premises integration to copy data. (You can read about ADF in chapter 10.) Azure Storage Explorer provides a desktop GUI interface for uploading files to multiple Azure services, including Azure Storage.

Each tool has its benefits.

- The Azure portal is available without an install.
- AzCopy can be used for automated file copying without user interaction.

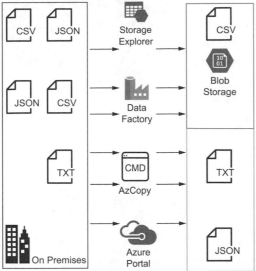

Figure 3.5   Blob Storage copy tools

- File copying with ADF can be included in multi-step workflows, and integrate with other Azure services.
- Storage Explorer provides an easy to use GUI and tracks the status of actions.

STORAGE EXPLORER

Azure Storage Explorer has a flexible authentication process. It can authenticate to Azure Storage using Azure Active Directory (AAD), shared access signature (SAS) tokens, or the storage keys themselves. You'll see more about access controls for Azure Storage later in this chapter. Figure 3.6 shows Storage Explorer connecting with multiple types of authentication. You can use drag-and-drop to upload and download files, or use the buttons in the toolbar.

AZCOPY

AzCopy works well for simple copies. Both Storage Explorer and AzCopy allow you to copy files into new folders. AzCopy uses wildcard matching to select files for copying.

Listing 3.2   Command line log shipping with AzCopy

```
"C:\Program Files (x86)\Microsoft SDKs\Azure\AzCopy\azcopy"
    /Source:C:\csvLogs\aa /Dest:https://abc.
    blob.core.windows.net/project-abc/v1/v1.1
    /destkey:==StorageKey== /Pattern:"ch*.csv" /Y
```

Plan for version of files

/Y switch for suppressing acknowledgments

① Use the account key to connect to a Storage account. All resources and services are accessible.

② Use a shared access signature to connect to a Storage account. Only resources and services in the SAS are accessible.

③ Connect to Data Lake with your Azure Active Directory (AAD) user.

④ AAD user provides access to Storage account resources and services based on role. Nearly all roles grant read access.

⑤ Storage Explorer interprets the folder structure of the files in a Storage account Blob service.

⑥ Use Storage Explorer to change Access Tier: Hot, Cool, and Archive.

⑦ Store many file types with recognized MIME types.

Figure 3.6   Storage Explorer configured to connect to Azure Storage with access keys and SAS tokens.

AzCopy, as a command-line application, can be scheduled to run automatically. AzCopy includes many options for selecting files to include, and configuring the output commands.

- Omitting the /Pattern option copies all files in the selected folder.
- The /S option recursively copies sub-folders and their files.

- Blobs are assigned a MIME type of `application/octet-stream` during upload by default. Add the option `/SetContentType` to have AzCopy assign the MIME type of the blob based on the file extension. AzCopy comes with most MIME types preconfigured in the AzCopyConfig.json file, which is located in the AzCopy directory.
- For copies of the same file type, or to override the configured MIME type, add option `/SetContentType:[MIME-type]` to explicitly set the type.
- By default, an operation journal is output at %LocalAppData%\Microsoft\Azure\ AzCopy\AzCopy.jnl. This file tracks the progress of the execution, and AzCopy can use it to restart the process if there is a problem. This file is deleted upon successful completion.
- Add the option `/V` to output a verbose log file at %LocalAppData%\Microsoft\ Azure\AzCopy\AzCopy\AzCopyVerbose.log.

Listing 3.3 Setting specific MIME type with AzCopy

```
"C:\Program Files (x86)\Microsoft SDKs\Azure\AzCopy\azcopy"
➥ /Source:C:\csvLogs\aa /Dest:https://abc.
➥ blob.core.windows.net/project-abc/v1/v1.1
➥ /DestKey:==StorageKey== /Pattern:"ch*.csv" /XO /Y
➥ /SetContentType:text/csv
```

/XO switch to exclude older files from copy when present in the target folder.

Pattern is copying CSV files, so set MIME type to CSV.

See http://mng.bz/emnv for download instructions. You can read more about file versioning and data drift in chapter 4.

3.3.5 Queues

Azure Storage accounts also support a basic queuing service. Queuing services fill an important role in applications, forming a buffer between front-end and back-end processes.

Queues are used for many purposes, but they all accomplish the same goal: they add a holding area for objects to await processing. People and cars both wait in queues to be serviced; imagine waiting in line for a bank teller, or in a car wash. In the digital realm, almost any type of electronic object can be stored in a queue, to await further processing. Examples include page requests on a web server or outbound messages on an email server. In this section we'll refer to objects in queues as *messages*.

A system implementing queues needs three components: incoming messages, a message storage service, and a message servicer. A *message* can be as simple as a text completion signal "Done" or as complex as a serialized JSON object. Simple message queues store the entire message in the queue. More complex message queues store the message in separate storage, and hold a reference to the message in the queue. For example, the JSON object in listing 3.4 is less than 150 bytes and could be stored in a queue in its entirety.

> **Listing 3.4 Sensor object JSON message**

```
{
  "Player":"abera101",
  "Node":12,
  "NodeValue":100.2,
  "EventTime":"2020-04-05T13:15:1947365Z"
}
```

The *storage system* can be implemented as an in-memory list or stack, rows in a text file, multiple text files, rows in a database, and so on. Azure provides several *queueing services*, including the Azure Queue service and Service Bus queues. Finally, *servicers* retrieve messages from the queue and do some work on or with them. One or more instances of a computer program retrieve messages from the queue when present, and when work on previous messages has completed.

Queues are described by the scheduling of message retrieval. For example, *first-in-first-out* (FIFO) queues push the messages into a tube. New messages go in one end; the oldest messages come out the other end first (figure 3.7).

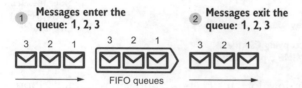

Figure 3.7 First-in-first-out queue

Last-in-first-out (LIFO) queues resemble a stack of items; you add or remove items from only the top of the stack (figure 3.8).

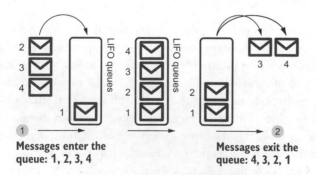

Figure 3.8 Last-in-first-out queue

Other approaches to message retrieval include *priority* scheduling and *longest-wait* scheduling. Priority queuing, like premium ticket boarding at an airline departure gate, assigns a priority to the queued object. The server, such as the airline employee, must take higher-priority queued objects first. This can be accomplished with separate queues for each priority. Longest-wait scheduling covers more complex scenarios, where multiple steps are required to clear a queue. The Azure Queue service is a FIFO queue, but does not guarantee ordering. Regardless of the approach, queues provide a method for allowing wait time and ordering retrieval.

In this chapter, you'll see how queues work by using an Azure Queue service.

WHEN INPUT RATE EXCEEDS OUTPUT RATE

Imagine a direct processing system where a single message generator produces 100 messages per hour, and a single message servicer processes 100 messages per hour. The rate of production and servicing are equal. When messages are produced faster than they are processed, the system can't work at optimal efficiency. To increase the efficiency of a direct processing system, you can increase capacity to handle the submission rates at all times, including spikes; decrease the submission rate; or you can drop submissions. Figure 3.9 compares these three approaches.

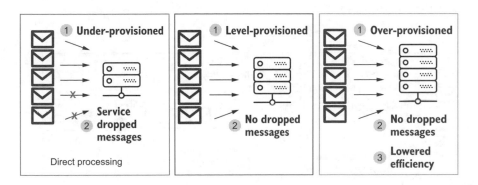

Figure 3.9 Over-provisioning prevents dropping submissions.

If dropping submissions is not an option, and the system needs to optimize the load and handle spikes in submission rates, a new element needs to be introduced between the submissions and processing steps. This element is a queue.

QUEUE-BASED LOAD LEVELING

A system using a queue can run with submission rates lower than the maximum processing rate, with processing rates higher than the maximum submission rate, or with both rates equal. What happens when there's a spike in submissions? If the message servicer cannot keep up with the rate of submissions, the queue message count grows. Once the spike in submissions ends, the queue message count reduces.

When the rate of submissions varies over time, the number of messages in the queue ebbs and flows. This system of processing has the following characteristics:

1 The input rate does not match the output rate.
2 The total input rate equals the total output rate over a given time frame.

3 Inputs and outputs operate on discrete elements.

4 The input does not need to wait on the output to complete.

With these characteristics, this system benefits from a queue.

- A queue decouples the submission rate from the processing rate.

- A queue shifts wait times from the submitter to the queue itself.

- With a queue, the servicer processes messages at a predictable rate until the queue is empty, regardless of the submission rate.

This pattern of varying submission rate with steady processing rate is called *queue-based load leveling*. With this pattern, you can optimize the provisioning of submitters and servicers by matching the average submission rate to the processing rate for a given time period. This also brings the benefit of smoothing the output of the system over time. With queue-based load leveling, you can capture all the submissions in the queue and process them at a rate subsequent services can handle, even if those services cannot handle a spike in submissions. You can see load leveling depicted in figure 3.10.

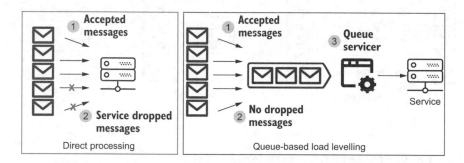

Figure 3.10   Queue-based load leveling prevents dropping submissions.

Queues can be used in many scenarios where the rate of incoming submissions varies significantly. Browser requests to a web server highlight the variable nature of event submissions. End users can request content from the server at any time. A web page could see huge spikes in traffic from a popular news story or recommendation by an influential source. Web servers can handle several requests at a time, but at a high enough request rate, some requests will have to wait for processing.

Microsoft Internet Information Services (IIS) provides a metric for the size of HTTP service request queues, to monitor request rates and diagnose long wait times. For other applications, your system will need to manage its own queue.

Earlier in the chapter, you created an Azure Storage account. The Storage account provides a management layer for services including Blob, File shares, the key-value Table, and Queues. All of these services provide different interfaces to key-value stores, including queues. A key-value store is simply a set of data (the value) with a unique identifier (the key). You use the key to retrieve the value. The Queues service stores messages. Let's look at how to create one in Azure.

3.3.6 Creating a queue

For the next season of the Jonestown Sluggers, the corporate IT group will begin sending data to your analytics system for further processing, during the games. One or more users will submit stats using a new app. The first set of stats to be implemented will cover pitching. To support this, you need to create an endpoint in Azure to accept the incoming stats and hold them for processing. How can you accommodate this?

The first iteration of the pitching stats includes a game ID, pitcher ID, time of the pitch, speed and type of the pitch, and whether the pitch was a strike.

Listing 3.5 Pitch statistic

```
{
    "Game":"JNT202004080",        ◁─┐  Home team code, year,
                                       month, day of game
    "Pitcher":"abera101",         ◁──    Pitcher code
    "InningPitch":"05T25",        ◁──┐
    "Speed":100.2,                    Fifth inning, top of
    "Type":"Fastball",                inning, 25th pitch
    "Result":"B"
}
```

From the description, you don't yet know what the processing will be. Because you know this data is being submitted to your Lambda analytics system, you should plan to store the data for later batch processing, and allow for near real-time processing too. Because there will be multiple submitters, and later multiple streams of data, you need an ingestion endpoint that can handle multiple simultaneous inputs. To minimize complexity and cost, you should choose a single endpoint and a single processor. You can handle the ingestion endpoint with an Azure Storage queue and a bit of code.

With queue-based processing, the processing technology is disconnected from the outside-facing endpoint, the queue. Requests enter the queue, and processors read from the queue. The submitting application and processing application only need to know the queue endpoint and the data definition for messages stored in the queue. The processing application can be updated or replaced without changes or interruption to the submitting application. Figure 3.11 shows a queue-based processing solution for the pitching statistics.

Let's create a queue and write some code to implement this functionality.

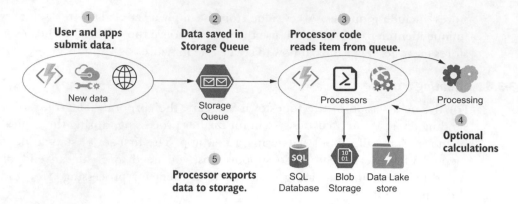

Figure 3.11   Queue-based processing reduces the size of processors.

AZURE STORAGE QUEUE CREATION

Earlier in this chapter, you created an Azure Storage account and added a Blob Storage container. (If you haven't created the Storage account yet, refer to section 3.2 for creation details.) You can use the same Storage account to host the Queue service too. Create the queue using the Azure portal by following these steps:

1   In the Azure portal, browse to the Storage account blade, and select the Storage account you created earlier.
2   In the Overview blade, click the Queues service.
3   On the Queues blade, click the Queue button to create the new queue.
4   Choose a name for the queue, consisting of lowercase letters, numbers, and hyphens, less than 63 characters long.
5   Click OK to create the queue.

You can also create the queue with Azure PowerShell. The `New-AzStorageQueue` command creates a new Storage account queue. You need to supply a name for the new queue, and a context object describing the Storage account to use. The context object is stored as a variable in PowerShell. Execute the following script (listing 3.6) in PowerShell, with Azure PowerShell enabled.

Listing 3.6   Create new Azure Storage queue using PowerShell

```
$account = Get-AzStorageAccount -ResourceGroupName "ade-dev-eastus2"
    -AccountName "adedeveastus2"
New-AzStorageQueue -Name "pitcherstats" -Context $account.Context
```

New queue name   **Azure Storage account
                                                            to hold the queue**

Creating an Azure Storage queue is quick; the underlying storage and interface has already been provisioned. Now that you have a queue, you can add some data.

WRITING TO THE QUEUE

Azure PowerShell also integrates the Azure SDK for .NET. This means you can create .NET objects and execute methods right from PowerShell. Listing 3.7 is a script that populates the new queue, using the Azure SDK to submit queue messages. The script gets the queue context using `Get-AzStorageAccount` and then gets an instance of the queue using `Get-AzStorageQueue`. Then it runs a loop 30 times. Each loop creates a JSON text string with randomized data, then adds the JSON to a new queue message object. The PowerShell `New-Object` command creates an in-memory object of the type specified by the `TypeName` parameter, in this case a CloudMessageQueue. The CloudMessageQueue object submits the message to the Azure queue using the `Add-MessageAsync()` function.

Listing 3.7 Generate pitcher stats messages

```
$account = Get-AzStorageAccount -ResourceGroupName "ade-dev-eastus2" -
    AccountName "adedeveastus2"
$queue = Get-AzStorageQueue -Name "pitcherstats" -Context $account.Context

for($i = 0; $i -lt 30; $i++)              ◁──  The number of iterations doesn't
{                                              matter, it's just a method for
$game = "JNT202004080"                         generating multiple examples.
$pitcher = "abera101"
$inning = Get-Random -Minimum 0 -Maximum 10    ◁──            The Get-Random
$pitch = Get-Random -Minimum 0 -Maximum 110                  method generates
$inningPitch = $inning.ToString("D2") + "T" + $pitch.ToString()   values greater
$speed = Get-Random -Minimum 75 -Maximum 110                than or equal to
$type = switch (Get-Random -Minimum 1 -Maximum 4) {         the -Minimum
  1 {"FA"; break}                                           parameter, and
  2 {"CU"; break}                                           less than the
  3 {"KN"; break}                                           -Maximum
}                                                           parameter.
$result = switch (Get-Random -Minimum 0 -Maximum 3) {
  0 {"B"; break}
  1 {"S"; break}
  2 {"F"; break}
}                                              Pipe the array out to a
                                               minimal JSON object.
$message = @{Game=$game; Pitcher=$pitcher; InningPitch=$inningPitch;
    Speed=$speed; Type=$type; Result=$result} | ConvertTo-Json -Compress  ◁──
$queueMessage = New-Object -TypeName
    Microsoft.Azure.Storage.Queue.CloudQueueMessage
    -ArgumentList $message                     ◁──  Fully qualified
$queue.CloudQueue.AddMessageAsync($QueueMessage)     CloudQueueMessage .NET
}                                                    type used.
```

The message body can be any UTF-8 data format, including base-64 encoded binary data. Using a JSON-serialized text string is a common method to store complex objects in queue messages. The queue servicer can deserialize the message contents and use the schema to assist in processing. Now that you've added some messages to the queue, you can use several technologies to retrieve them.

READING FROM THE QUEUE

The following script reads messages from the new queue, using the Azure SDK. The script gets an instance of the queue. Then it runs a loop while the hasMessage state is true. Once no more messages are retrieved from the queue, the hasMessage state is set to false, and the loop ends. Deleting the retrieved message is the final step, as shown in listing 3.8.

Listing 3.8   Retrieve pitcher stats

```
$account = Get-AzStorageAccount
    -ResourceGroupName "ade-dev-eastus2"
    -AccountName "adedeveastus2"
$queue = Get-AzStorageQueue -Name "pitcherstats"
    -Context $account.Context

$hasMessage = $TRUE
while ($hasMessage)
{
$queueMessage = $queue.CloudQueue.GetMessageAsync()
if ($queueMessage.Result -is
    [Microsoft.Azure.Storage.Queue.CloudQueueMessage])
{
Write-Host $queueMessage.Result.AsString
$queue.CloudQueue.DeleteMessageAsync
    ($queueMessage.Result.Id,$queueMessage.Result.popReceipt)
$queueMessage = $null
}
else { $hasMessage = $FALSE }
}
```

A WHILE loop iterates over the code, checking for true at the start of each iteration.

Check the message retrieval using type check -is.

Messages in Storage account queues must be deleted to be removed from the queue.

Clear the message to prepare for the next iteration.

Write the contents of the message to screen. Actual work with the message would be done at this point.

> **NOTE**   You can create this same pattern of create client, read message, process message, and delete message in other compiled languages that use the Azure SDK.

Even with the simplicity of the Azure Queue service, there are still configuration options and limitations that influence how you work with the queue. In the next section, you'll see more about the read-lock-delete pattern of message processing in the Azure Queue service.

3.3.7   *Azure Storage queue options*

The Queue service implements a locking feature on message read. A message is *dequeued*, or more exactly leased, for 30 seconds by default. You can extend the lease as needed in your servicer code by calling the client `UpdateMessage` command. While a message is locked, a subsequent request for a message will retrieve the next message in line. A dequeued message must be deleted to be removed from the queue, or it will remain in the queue until its expiration date passes. This means when messages fail to complete processing before the lease expires, they return to the queue for another attempt at processing. The returned message can then be processed again. However, the returned message might be processed after a message that arrived to the queue later. The Azure Queue service does not guarantee processing order. A default expiration of one day in the future is added to new messages, but can be set up to seven days.

> **TIP** The Azure Queue service messages have a maximum size of 64 KB. Azure Service Bus queues handle message sizes up to 256 KB. If you need larger-sized messages, you can save the contents to a blob and reference the blob URL in the message body.

The Azure Queue service provide a simple endpoint for writing and reading messages from a queue. The Queue service's main strength, its simplicity, also limits its use to systems with developer support. Developers must write code to manage the logic for writing, reading, and deleting messages.

Once you've created the Storage account, created a container and queue, and copied some files, you'll be prepared to set up multiple storage services and multiple Storage accounts on demand. Creating Azure Storage accounts is one of the basic skills needed to store data files in Azure. The AAD user account that created the Storage account becomes the owner and has full permissions to administer the resource. If you are the sole admin for your business, this may be sufficient. For most use cases, additional users are given access following service creation. Giving access to users expands the usefulness of storage services. Let's look at methods for allowing secure access to the storage services.

3.4   Storage account access

You have created a Storage account and Blob Storage. But the service is not useful for anyone else in its current state. In order for others to use it, you need to define, plan, and implement an *access scheme*. An access scheme defines who is allowed to access resources and what they are allowed to access. In order to provide secure access, you'll look at how the file hierarchy of the Storage account influences its security model. Then you'll see how to plan and implement file access by working through an access scenario. By the end of this section, you'll be able to configure secure file access for a Storage account.

3.4.1   *Blob container security*

Returning to our earlier example, the Finance and Operations departments want a joint file archive that can be used with multiple Azure services. Users and systems from each department will upload files to the archive. Access to upload files for one department must not allow reading files from the other department. You need to design and implement an appropriate access scheme in a Storage account that satisfies these requirements. How can you accommodate this request?

Up to this point, the Azure Storage you've created have been accessible only by the owner, you. Now you need to broaden access to include other users. This scenario applies the principle of least privilege by restricting access to each department's files and folders to members of that department. By working through this scenario, you'll learn some approaches to configure security controls on Azure Storage and Data Lake stores.

3.4.2   *Designing Storage account access*

Storage accounts have two security boundaries: at the account level, and the container level. Storage accounts use AAD RBAC for authentication to the entire account, and alternately access keys for authentication to the Storage account or individual containers. AAD authentication and authorization only confers access to management functions of the Storage account. Key-based authorization can be granted for the Storage account, all containers, by container type, or for specific actions on a container. How do you set up a Storage account so that you have a common file location but still restrict access to certain files?

You can create two Blob containers in the Azure Storage account, one for each department. Separate Secure Access Signature (SAS) tokens for each department would be used to control access. SAS tokens incorporate the access keys for authorization. Using a single Azure Storage account relies on SAS tokens; giving a department access via AAD RBAC would give that department access to all the Blob containers.

Or you can create two Azure Storage accounts, with a single Blob container each. Each department would have access to their respective Storage account and any containers within it via AAD authorization. This approach doesn't quite meet the requirements of a "joint file archive," but you can access multiple Storage accounts with various tools and Azure services.

Let's create a single Storage account with two Blob containers, one for each department. You can refer back to figure 3.12 for more instructions.

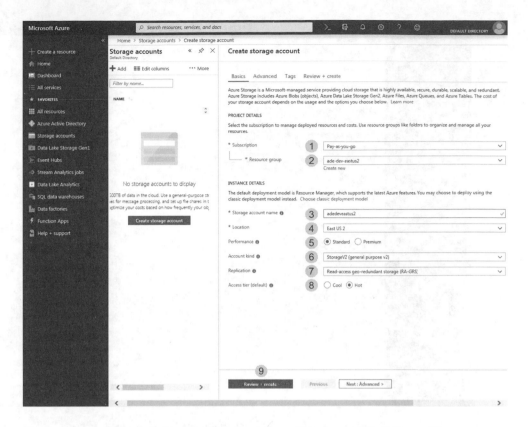

1. **Use the same subscription for related resources.**

2. **Use the same resource group for related resources.**

3. **Name must be alphanumeric only.**

4. **Keep related resources in the same location for best performance.**

5. **Premium is only for VM disks.**

6. **Leave the default StorageV2.**

7. **Redundant storage incurs higher costs.**

8. **Choose Cool if you will rarely access these files.**

9. **Review, and then create the Storage account in two steps.**

Figure 3.12   Creating a Storage account

Now create two Blob containers using the Azure portal.

1 In your Storage account, click Containers under Blob Service to show the Blobs blade.

2 Click Container to show the New Container wizard. Figure 3.13 shows the New container blade.

3 Enter "finance" for the Name.

4 Leave the Public Access Level at the default, Private.

1. **Blobs containers**
2. **Use lowercase letters, numbers, and hyphens.**
3. **Leave this Private.**

Figure 3.13   Creating a Blob container

5   Click OK to create the container.
6   Repeat for the "operations" container.

The Storage account is ready for you to add access controls.

HIERARCHY STRUCTURE IN AZURE STORAGE BLOB CONTAINER

When you create a Storage account, you also need to create a container in order to do anything useful. The container is the root of the file hierarchy for Blobs and Files, so it must be present in order to address any files. Both Files and Blobs emulate a folder structure, and have an addressable URL like https://ABCDEF.blob.core.windows.net/ABCDEFcontainer/ABC/DEF/123.csv. Clicking the blob in the Azure Portal container Overview blade brings up the blob's properties window, which displays the blob's URL.

As the owner of the Storage account, you have full access to all files in the Blobs and Files containers via your AAD user. You can assign role-based access to other AAD users too, and grant them access at the Azure Storage account level. This access covers all services in the Storage account, including Blobs and Files containers. You can use the Azure Portal to configure the roles.

1 Click Access Control (IAM) in the Azure Storage Service blade to show the Access Control blade. Figure 3.14 shows the Access Control blade.

2 Click Add Role Assignment to show the Add Role Assignment blade.

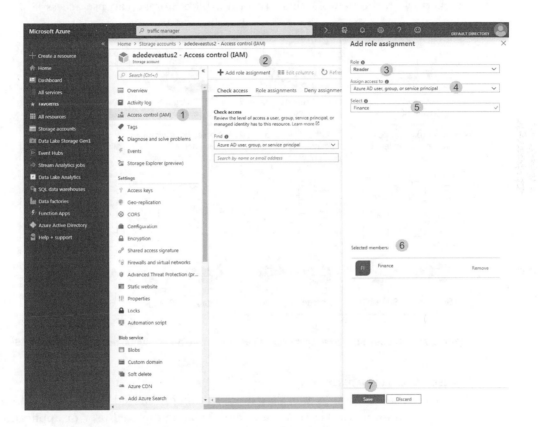

① Access control defines what you can do to the service, and is required for minimal access to the stored files.

② Click Add role assignment to give new permissions.

③ Owners have full control, Contributors nearly as much, and Readers just read.

④ Use Azure AD groups for easiest management. Other options are Azure service-to-service authorization.

⑤ Start typing to filter the list.

⑥ Click on a security user or group to select.

⑦ Save your new role assignment.

Figure 3.14   Assigning AAD group to Azure Storage service roles

3 Select Reader for the Role.

4 Select the default—Azure AD User, Group, or Service Principal—to Assign access to. Other options allow authorization by Azure services.

5 Click the Finance group to select the group.

6 Click Save to add the role assignment.

But you can't set access permissions on a folder. Blobs and Files set access permissions at the container level. Blobs allow individual file access permissions as well, via a SAS token. The Files service uses access keys to set access permissions. Permissions are checked when the network share is set up. Blob Storage can use access keys or SAS tokens to set permissions. Figure 3.15 describes the various access schemes.

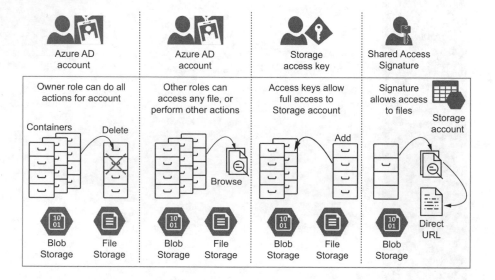

Figure 3.15   Access Storage account resources with Azure AD accounts, access keys, and SAS

SHARED ACCESS SIGNATURES

A *SAS token*, also known as a *SAS key*, is a URI-friendly hashed string derived from the Storage account access key. It is generated by an authorized user or application for distribution to an end user. The SAS token provides granular access to Storage account resources, like Files and Blob containers.

A SAS token has multiple properties which define the access granted.

- *Start and end dates* provide a limited window for access.
- A *set of permissions* grant actions to the user.
- A *stored access policy* serves as a reusable and easily revocable container for permissions.
- SAS tokens can be generated for the entire Storage account, service container, or individual files.

SAS tokens at the container level must be created using the Azure REST API or Azure PowerShell module. There isn't a method in the Azure portal to specify the policy when creating a SAS token. You can use Azure PowerShell to create a container-level token with a 24-hour effective window by providing these options:

- The name of the service container
- A valid start date
- A valid expiration date
- The Azure Storage account containing the service container, as context
- The permissions for the SAS token

The `New-AzStorageContainerSASToken` command creates the SAS token on a specific container, and returns the value interactively. Set the SAS token permissions using the `Permission` parameter, passing a combination of (a)dd, (r)ead, (w)rite, (c)reate, (d)elete, and (l)ist. This command requires you to specify a Storage account to target using the `Context` parameter. The `New-AzStorageContext` command retrieves a Storage account context by name.

Listing 3.9 Create shared access signature for container

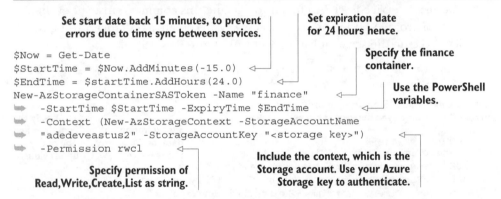

Set start date back 15 minutes, to prevent errors due to time sync between services.

Set expiration date for 24 hours hence.

Specify the finance container.

Use the PowerShell variables.

```
$Now = Get-Date
$StartTime = $Now.AddMinutes(-15.0)
$EndTime = $startTime.AddHours(24.0)
New-AzStorageContainerSASToken -Name "finance"
    -StartTime $StartTime -ExpiryTime $EndTime
    -Context (New-AzStorageContext -StorageAccountName
    "adedeveastus2" -StorageAccountKey "<storage key>")
    -Permission rwcl
```

Specify permission of Read,Write,Create,List as string.

Include the context, which is the Storage account. Use your Azure Storage key to authenticate.

Add the option `-FullUri` to return the full URL to the Azure Storage container. The default expiration is one hour after the start time. Any valid date will work, as long as it's after the start time.

STORED ACCESS POLICY

Stored access policies allow you to create a common reference for multiple SAS tokens. SAS tokens generated from the policy use the permissions and time frame specified in the policy. Editing or deleting the policy updates the SAS tokens. This feature is not available with individual SAS tokens. The stored access policy applies only to containers.

To create a new stored access policy for a container, you must choose a container, a name, and a permission set. Create and write permissions allow uploading files; read and list permissions allow viewing the contents. SAS tokens should have a start and expiry time, but you can remove access after a set time by adding a start and end time to the associated policy. Using shorter duration SAS tokens will improve security by minimizing how long compromised keys can be used. You can also revoke tokens by modifying the associated policy.

To create an access policy, use the `New-AzStorageContainerStoredAccessPolicy` command. Execute the script in listing 3.10 in a window with Azure PowerShell to create a policy named `AddFiles` on the Finance container. The script connects to the Storage account where you created the Finance container service.

Listing 3.10   Create a Storage account stored access policy

Create a policy named AddFiles. Specify permission of Read,Write,Create,List as string.   **Include the context, which is the Storage account.**

```
New-AzStorageContainerStoredAccessPolicy -Container "finance"
    -Policy "AddFiles" -Permission rwcl
    -Context (New-AzStorageContext -StorageAccountName
    "adedeveastus2" -StorageAccountKey "<storage key>")
```

Use the Azure Storage key to authenticate.

You can create a container-level SAS token using a policy with the `New-AzStorage-ContainerSASToken` command. Pass the `Policy` parameter with the policy name. You can use a service-level SAS token to execute this command instead of the root service key, to avoid exposing the root access key. To create a SAS token using the access policy, execute the script in listing 3.11 with Azure PowerShell.

Listing 3.11   Create SAS with access policy

Set start date back 15 minutes, to prevent errors due to time sync between services.

Set expiration date for 24 hours hence.   **Specify the container and the policy set up previously.**

Use the PowerShell variables.

```
$Now = Get-Date
$StartTime = $Now.AddMinutes(-15.0)
$EndTime = $startTime.AddHours(24.0)
New-AzStorageContainerSASToken -Name "finance" -Policy "AddFiles"
    -StartTime $StartTime -ExpiryTime $EndTime
    -Context (New-AzStorageContext -StorageAccountName
    "adedeveastus2" -StorageAccountKey "<storage key>")
    -FullUri
```

PowerShell returns the value of the SAS immediately, and adds the URL of the Storage account and container.   **Include the context, which is the Storage account. Use the Azure Storage key to authenticate.**

Using PowerShell variables enables you to reuse values in a session. It also makes your script easier to read, by shortening the lines. Listing 3.11 can be executed multiple times, each time returning a new signature and expiration. Make sure you have created the stored access policy before trying to create a SAS tied to it.

TIP Add Immutable blob storage policy to a Blob container to prevent *any* modifications to files in the container, even for the Owner role. You can add an Immutable blob storage policy using the Access policy blade of the specific

Blob container in the Azure portal. It does not need to be attached to a SAS token to be effective.

Now that you've learned how to create the Storage account and access keys, you can create useful storage services. In this scenario, you explored securing access in Azure Storage. While it's possible to create discrete security configurations in a single Storage account, creating SAS tokens relies on an external service for authorization. Ongoing usage of the Storage account with SAS tokens requires the client to renew the keys periodically. Alternately, using separate Storage accounts provides clear security boundaries, but create difficulties in addressing the stored files without switching contexts.

3.5   *Exercises*

The following exercises can help you internalize the new features introduced in this chapter. You should be able to create Blob containers and queues, and provide secure access to them.

3.5.1   *Exercise 1*

Your department wants to use Storage account Blobs to archive application logs. Access to the archive will be infrequent, and the archive must minimize cost. Which two options for the Blob container should you choose?

1 Cold tier
2 Archive tier
3 LRS replication
4 GRS replication
5 BAK replication

SOLUTION

1 The Cool tier costs less than the default Hot tier. There isn't a Cold tier.
2 The Archive tier is the most cost effective option for long-term storage, but it does have a minimum storage term.
3 LRS replication is the most cost effective option for replication. LRS maintains copies only in the local data center.
4 GRS replication is a more costly option for replication than LRS. GRS maintains copies in multiple data centers.
5 There is no BAK replication option.

3.5.2   *Exercise 2*

A user requests access to a Storage account Blob container to upload a few files. A Storage account administrator returns a SAS token to the user shortly thereafter. The next day, the user complains that they can't upload files to the container. Select all potential causes.

1 The Azure region where the Storage account is located is experiencing an outage.
2 The Storage account has been deleted.
3 The Blob container has been deleted.
4 The SAS token has expired.
5 The user's password has changed.

SOLUTION
Answers 1 through 4 are possible.

1 Azure regions occasionally have outages. Internet connectivity problems can also prevent access.
2 Storage accounts can be deleted at any time, if there isn't a retention policy in place.
3 Blob containers can be deleted at any time, if there isn't a retention policy in place.
4 The default timeout for a SAS token is one hour.
5 The user's account is not connected to the SAS token used for access. The user's account is only used for access if they are an owner of the Storage account.

Summary

- Azure Storage consists of several services. Blob Storage provides cost effective storage in the cloud. The Queue service provides simple messages queues.
- Microsoft provides several tools for copying files into Azure Storage, each with a strong use case. Pick the tool that works for the task at hand.
- Queues disconnect input rate from processing rate. Both rates can be scaled independently.
- Azure Storage account access is granted at the Storage account level using AAD. Granular access at the container/service level is granted using access keys. Shared access signatures grant access at the container/service level and the blob level. The access control method will influence your choice of a single Storage Account or multiple.

Azure Data Lake Storage

This chapter covers

- Setting up a Data Lake store
- Configuring file access in Data Lake Storage
- Understanding and planning for data drift

In the last chapter, you learned how to work with a fundamental Azure service, the Storage account. Storage accounts provide nearly unlimited storage for many Azure services, with high throughput and high redundancy. Storage accounts also host other file-based services, such as file shares and queues.

In this chapter, you'll learn about another storage service, Azure Data Lake Storage (ADLS). You'll create a Data Lake store and learn how to structure your data lake to increase maintainability and security. You'll learn how this service supports other Azure services through Azure Active Directory authentication. This will be the central service around which you construct the analytics system.

ADLS resembles a local file system, with folders and files. Azure Active Directory (AAD) controls access to folders and files, with assignable read/write/execute permissions. ADLS provides the primary storage backbone for the master data set, a source of data for batch layer processing. ADLS also stores batch analysis artifacts, including the report files that make up the output of the Serving layer (see figure 4.1).

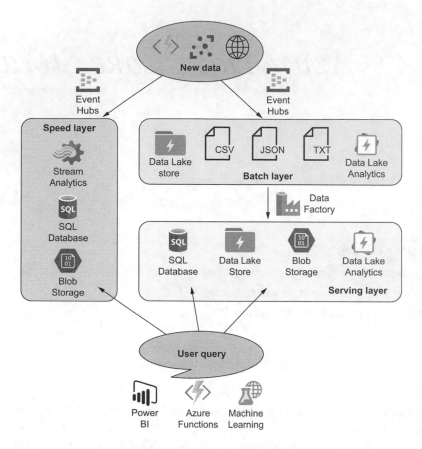

Figure 4.1   Lambda architecture with Azure PaaS services

Massive storage in ADLS allows for massive data, feeding massive batch jobs. ADLS builds on Hadoop and the Hadoop Distributed File System (HDFS). Hadoop manages storage and data retrieval across a horizontally-scalable cluster of data nodes. ADLS provides security management and integration with other Azure services while abstracting Hadoop commands. ADLS provides a familiar interface over a complex system.

Let's see what's involved in creating a Data Lake store.

TIP   You can find the code listings in the GitHub repository for this book at https://github.com/rnuckolls/azure_storage.

4.1 Create an Azure Data Lake store

Setting up an ADLS store requires some information common to all Azure services, including a subscription, name, location, and resource group.

- A *subscription* groups resources together for access control and billing.
- A *resource group* groups resources together for management.
- A *location* groups resources into a regional data center.

IMPORTANT By default, all files in ADLS are encrypted at rest. You should leave the management of the encryption keys to the service unless you have a system in place to manage them.

4.1.1 Using Azure Portal

Here's how to create a new ADLS store.

1 In the Azure portal, use the Create a Resource menu to open a New Data Lake Storage Gen1 blade, or use the All Services menu and filter on Data Lake Storage Gen1. Or you can go directly to the New Data Lake Storage Gen1 blade at https://portal.azure.com/#create/Microsoft.AzureDataLakeStore. Figure 4.2 shows the New Data Lake Storage Gen1 blade.

2 Choose a name ("[XYZ]deveastus2"). The name must be lowercase alphanumeric, between 3-24 characters, and globally unique. Read more about Azure service naming conventions in chapter 3.

3 Choose a subscription. The default will be the oldest subscription, if you have access to more than one.

4 Choose a resource group. (See appendix A for instructions if you haven't created one.)

5 Choose a location. ADLS stores are not available in all regions; choose one close to you. Keep resources that interact in the same region to minimize network latency. You may choose a region to match your user base, as some governments restrict moving data outside their zone of control.

6 Choose a pricing package, or leave the default, Pay-as-you-go. This minimizes costs for your tutorial usage. In a production system, reserving storage up front provides discounts. See http://mng.bz/6AXy for more information.

7 Choose an encryption management scheme, or leave the default, Enabled. To use a self-managed key, you will need to create an Azure Key Vault and an encryption key.

8 Create the Data Lake store.

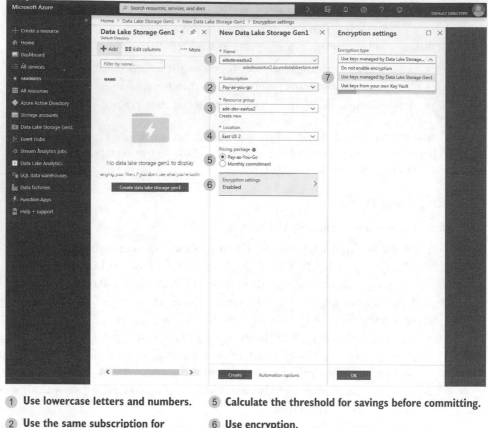

① Use lowercase letters and numbers.

② Use the same subscription for related resources.

③ Use the same resource group for related resources.

④ Keep related resources in the same location for best performance.

⑤ Calculate the threshold for savings before committing.

⑥ Use encryption.

⑦ Unless you have established key management systems, let the service manage the keys.

Figure 4.2   Creating a Data Lake store

4.1.2   *Using Azure PowerShell*

You can also create an ADLS store via Azure PowerShell. Use the `New-AzDataLake-StoreAccount` command to create it. The command takes the resource group, location, and a name for the new ADLS store. You can disable file encryption by passing `DisableEncryption`, or specify an encryption scheme using the `Encryption` parameter. `Encryption` takes ServiceManaged or UserManaged as a value. User-managed encryption require the use of Azure Key Vault, which you'll learn more about in chapter 10. Access Azure PowerShell by visiting Azure Cloud Shell at https://shell.azure.com/, or clicking the >_ header menu in the Azure portal.

Listing 4.1   Create new Data Lake store

```
New-AzDataLakeStoreAccount -ResourceGroupName "ade-dev-eastus2"
➥ -Name "adedeveastus2" -Location "East US 2"
➥ -Encryption "ServiceManaged"
```

This script will return an error if an ADLS store by that name exists, or if ADLS is not available in the selected region. ADLS is not available in all regions, so it's a good idea to select a region that supports ADLS before creating the rest of your services, to keep all services in the same region. This lowers the latency of network communication between services.

You can also specify some other options during setup. You can add key/value pairs called *tags* to help locate the service later. If you know your storage size, you can pre-purchase storage at a discounted rate, using the `Tier` parameter. Possible values for the `Tier` parameter include Consumption, Commitment1TB, Commitment10TB, Commitment100TB, Commitment500TB, Commitment1PB, and Commitment5PB.

Listing 4.2   Create a new Data Lake store with options

```
New-AzDataLakeStoreAccount -ResourceGroupName "ade-dev-eastus2"
➥ -Name "adedeveastus2" -Location "East US 2"
➥ -Tag @{User="ADE";}          ⊲        Create a tag called
➥ -Tier Commitment1TB          ⊲        User with value ADE.
```

Pre-purchase 1 TB of storage each
month and save 12% over basic rate.

Add a tag for management of resources. This is especially useful when browsing the All Resources blade in the portal, because you can filter the list of resources using the tags you have provided. Use a consumption plan, until you've calculated your monthly storage needs. You can purchase a plan at any time. Pre-purchasing capacity lowers costs, bringing them closer to that of Storage account Blobs.

> **TIP**   If you know how much data you will store in the Data Lake, purchasing capacity in advance can save you money. Once your storage level passes a threshold close to your commitment, you can reduce your spending. For example, if you are archiving more than 900 GB of log files, purchasing 1 TB of capacity will cost less than paying as you go. Overages are calculated at the standard rate of $0.039/GB.

Creating Storage accounts and ADLS stores are basic skills for storing data files in Azure. The AAD user account that created the Storage account becomes the owner and has full permissions to administer the resource. If you are the sole admin for your business, this may be sufficient. For most use cases, additional users are given access following service creation. Giving access to users expands the usefulness of storage services. Let's look at methods for allowing secure access to the storage services.

4.2   *Data Lake store access*

You created the ADLS store, but the service is not useful for anyone else in its current state. Only you, the owner, can access it. For others to use it, you need to define, plan, and implement an *access scheme.*

4.2.1   *Access schemes*

The Finance and Operations departments want a joint file archive that can be used with multiple Azure services. Users and systems will upload files from each department. Access for uploading files for one department must not allow reading files from the other department. You need to design and implement an access scheme in a Data Lake store that satisfies these requirements. How can you accommodate this request?

An *access scheme* defines who can access resources and what they are allowed to access. *Authentication* encompasses validating the identity of the entity making the request. *Authorization* matches authorized entities with the actions they can perform. Authentication for ADLS is handled by AAD.

AAD is Microsoft's cloud-based identity and access management service. It provides sign-on services and account management for Office 365, the Azure portal, and other applications. AAD can use directory synchronization to allow on-premise and cloud applications to use the same account. Authentication is handled at the user level; authorization can be set for users and groups.

Authorization for ADLS actions is defined in two ways. For managing the service, role-based access controls (RBAC) allow or deny access to tasks like deleting the ADLS store, assigning roles to users, and purchasing reserved storage. For managing file and folder access, access control lists (ACLs) define granular access. The ACLs use standard Read (R), Write (W), and Execute (X) permissions. To see how these two authorization approaches work, you'll look at the security model for ADLS. Then you'll see how to plan and implement the folder hierarchy and file access. By the end of the section, you'll be able to configure secure file access for ADLS.

LEAST PRIVILEGE

Up to this point, the ADLS stores you've created have been accessible only by the owner, you. Now you need to broaden access to include other users. The Principle of Least Privilege states that "a subject should be given only those privileges needed for it to complete its task."[1] This scenario applies the principle by restricting access to a department's files and folders to members of the department. By working through this scenario, you'll learn some approaches to configure RBACs and ACLs on ADLS.

---

[1]   Michael Gegick and Sean Barnum. "Least Privilege." Cybersecurity and Infrastructure Security Agency CISA, September 14, 2005. http://mng.bz/mBny.

4.2.2 *Configuring access*

How do you set up your new ADLS store to have a common file location but still restrict access to certain files? You need separate folders for Finance and Operations, with access and default ACLs specific to each department.

ROOT FOLDER ACLs

Folders get an *access ACL* and a *default ACL*. Files get an access ACL only. Folder and file access is not inherited; each folder and file contains its permissions list in metadata. The access ACL determines access for the folder or file itself. The default ACL determines the access ACL for files created in the folder and the default ACL for child folders.

Access ACLs can be set using the Access blade of a file or folder in the Data Explorer blade of an ADLS store, in the Azure portal. Default ACLs can be set using the Advanced blade in the Access blade of a folder in the Data Explorer blade, in the Azure portal. The Advanced blade also lets you apply ACLs to child folders.

New folders created in the ADLS store's root folder "/" copy the ACLs from the root folder. When the ADLS store is first created, the root folder has a unique access ACL and default ACL. The AAD account used to create the ADLS store is assigned the root folder owner role. Since you are the creator, you are the root folder owner by default. A security group, with an all-zero GUID, is assigned to the root folder owner role, to satisfy a requirement that folders must have a group owner. This null security group does not permit access and should be replaced with a valid group. This ensures access to the folders and files in case access via the creator account is lost. You'll replace the owner group in the next section.

ROOT FOLDER OWNER

Assigning ownership and access and default ACLs to the root folder creates the broad outlines of your access scheme. If you don't have an AAD user and group, see appendix A for a PowerShell script to create them.

Azure uses AAD extensively for user and service authentication. You should already be familiar with the Azure portal and using AAD for authentication and authorization to Azure services. Listing 4.3 shows an Azure PowerShell script for creating a new user and security group, and assigning the user to the group. The script uses the commands New-AzADUser, New-AzADGroup, and Add-AzADGroupMember. The new user command requires a display name, a mail name, a principal name which is an email address, and a password. The security group command requires a display name and a mail name. The group membership command requires both member and group identifiers: either user principal name or ID, and group display name, object, or ID. You need to construct a UserPrincipalName using one of the AAD registered domains. For a personal Azure account, use your signup email without the top-level domain, and append .onmicrosoft.com. For example, if creating an AAD user for techuser@azuredomain .com, the UserPrincipalName is techuser@azuredomain.onmicrosoft.com.

Execute these lines with Azure PowerShell to create the user and group membership.

Listing 4.3 New AAD user and group

Use the secure password.   **Prompt for a password for the new user.**

```
$SecureStringPassword = Read-Host -Prompt "Enter password" -AsSecureString

$User = New-AzADUser -DisplayName "Tech User"
  -Password $SecureStringPassword -MailNickname "techuser"
  -UserPrincipalName "techuser@azuredomain.onmicrosoft.com"

$Group = New-AzADGroup -DisplayName "Technical Operations"
  -MailNickname "TechOps"

Add-AzADGroupMember -MemberObjectId $User.Id
  -TargetGroupObjectId $Group.Id
```

Get the ID from the variable $User, from the new user command.

Build the principal name from MailNickname and your AAD registered domain.   **Get the ID from the variable $Group, from the new group command.**

This PowerShell script will return an error if a group by that name exists. The new user and security group have no access to the ADLS store at this time, but allow authentication to Azure and the various services. Next, you'll give the group, and through it the user, access permissions in the ADLS store.

NOTE If you are using an Azure subscription without a corporate Active Directory, then your domain will be some variation of the email you used to sign up with Azure. You can find this value by going to the AAD Overview blade. The domain is listed above the header Default Directory. It is also listed in the Custom Domain Names blade.

Now you've created a user and a security group in AAD using PowerShell. You can use them when securing the ADLS store's root directory. Set the owning group to the TechOps group using the Azure portal.

1 In the Azure portal, use the All Services menu and filter on Data Lake Storage Gen1 to show the Data Lake Storage Gen1 blade.
2 Select your Data Lake store to display the Overview blade.
3 In the Overview blade, click Data Explorer.
4 In the Data Explorer blade, click Access. Figure 4.3 shows the Access blade.
5 In the Access blade, verify that "/ (Folder)" is displayed below the header, indicating you have selected the root folder.
6 In the Owners section, click the group 00000000-0000-0000-0000-000000000000.
7 In the Access Details blade, click Change Owning Group. This opens an AAD search blade.
8 In the Select User or Group blade, search for and select the TechOps AAD group, and click Select.

You can also set the owning group on the ADLS store root folder "/" with PowerShell. The `Set-AzDataLakeStoreItemOwner` command sets the owner for a folder. The

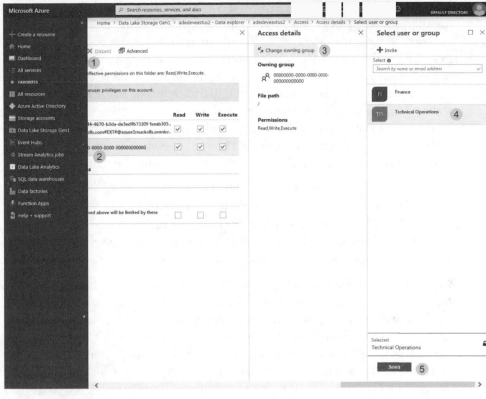

1 Browse into root folder and click Access.

2 Click the null security group.

3 Click "Change owning group."

4 Select a security group from Azure Active Directory.

5 Click "Select" to commit change.

Figure 4.3 Assigning owning group to Data Lake store folder

`Account` parameter specifies the name of the ADLS store you wish to update. The forward-slash character following `Path` parameter indicates the root folder. This PowerShell script changes the security group owner, passing in the ID of the "Technical Operations" AAD group. Execute this line in PowerShell Core with the Azure PowerShell module loaded.

Listing 4.4 Set Data Lake owner

```
Set-AzDataLakeStoreItemOwner -Account "adedeveastus2"    Group owner instead
 -Path / -Type Group                                      of user owner.
 -Id (Get-AzADGroup -DisplayName "Technical Operations").Id

                                            Get the security group ID.
```

`Get-AzADGroup` returns a security object, which has an ID property. Instead of in-lining the group object lookup, you could include the GUID directly.

Next, set a fallback access ACL for non-owners on the root folder. This ACL has Read (R) and Execute (X) permissions. Without this ACL, non-owner AAD users will not be able to list the folder structure from the root folder. Users with access to specific files can access them directly via URL, in the form adl://adedeveastus2.azuredat-alakestore.net/file.csv. You can find this path under Properties for the file in the Azure portal Data Explorer blade. As an alternative, you could apply specific ACLs for AAD groups as they are added to the Data Lake service and give access to one or more folders in the store. Try setting the fallback ACL using the Azure portal.

1 In the Overview blade of the Data Lake service, click Data Explorer.
2 The Data Explorer blade opens in the root folder.
3 Add a file and folder list ACL for everyone on the root folder by clicking Access, then checking the Read and Execute boxes under Everyone Else.
4 Click Save to set the ACL on the root folder.

You can also set the ACL using PowerShell. The `Set-AzDataLakeStoreItemAclEntry` command takes full words as values for its `Permissions` parameter. Values include None, Execute, Write, WriteExecute, Read, ReadExecute, ReadWrite, and All. The `AceType` parameter defines the type of ACL to add: User, Group, Mask, or Other. Other sets the ACL for "everyone else"—users and groups that don't have a specified permission. Mask applies to all users and groups, and the folder and file owning group. The owning group is set when a folder or file is created. For ADLS service owners, a default mask ACL on the root "/" folder gives owners access to all files and folders. Execute this line with Azure PowerShell to set the default ACLs.

Listing 4.5   Set Data Lake default access entry

```
Set-AzDataLakeStoreItemAclEntry -AccountName "adedeveastus2"
 ➡ -Path / -AceType Other -Permissions ReadExecute        ⟵┐
```
         Use AceType Other to set the "everyone else" ACL. ┘

IMPORTANT   Make sure that one of your first steps is assigning a valid security group to the service owner role and root folder owning group when configuring security. If your AAD account gets locked out or removed, users in the owning group can still access the Data Lake folders. This rationale applies to the service owner role as well. The service owner role can view all data in the store, but the root folder owning group cannot manage the Data Lake service, unless they have more than Reader role. You can choose different security groups for different roles. For instance, your organization's Technical Operations group can manage a Data Lake service as an owner, while the Analytics or Architects group can be the root folder owning group.

4.2.3 *Hierarchy structure in the Data Lake store*

Storing lots of data in cloud storage enables users to apply analysis over the data. Lowering the implementation effort for new data collection often means accepting unprocessed or uncurated data sets, which then need transformation and data cleansing to prepare them for consumption. Having a designated landing zone for the initial data marks a clear distinction between the original and processed data files. You'll look more closely at planning folder hierarchies in section 4.3.1.

NEW INBOUND FILES FOLDER

Now that you have the root folder in better shape, let's add a top-level folder named Staging. The Staging folder is a target for storing unprocessed data. Finance and Operations will deposit files in subfolders under Staging. This Staging folder will inherit the owners assigned to the root folder on creation. You will also add an ACL to allow users to list any files and view the Staging folder itself. Without this fallback ACL, non-owner users will be unable to browse the folder hierarchy. Use the Azure portal to create the folder and set the ACL.

1. Create the Staging folder by clicking New Folder and enter the name `Staging`.
2. Click on the new Staging folder to browse it.
3. Add a file and folder list ACL for everyone by clicking Access, then checking the Read and Execute boxes under Everyone Else.
4. Click Save to set the ACL on the Staging folder.

This ACL will only give access for the Staging folder. Subfolders will belong to their respective groups, and general access won't be provided. You'll look more closely at this folder structure in section 4.3.1.

FINANCE AND OPERATIONS FOLDERS

In order to secure separate access to the Operations and Finance folders, you'll need users and groups in AAD. You can create these using the Azure portal or Azure PowerShell. Here is an Azure PowerShell script for creating a new Finance user, a new security group, and assigning the user to the group. This script uses the same commands that were used to set the root folder ACLs. Execute these lines in PowerShell with the Azure PowerShell module loaded.

Listing 4.6   Finance AAD user and group

Use the secure password.   **Prompt for a password for the new user.**

```
$SecureStringPassword = Read-Host -Prompt "Enter password" -AsSecureString   ⊲

$User = New-AzADUser -DisplayName "Finance User"
    -Password $SecureStringPassword -MailNickname "financeuser"
    -UserPrincipalName "financeuser@azuredomain.onmicrosoft.com"   ⊲

$Group = New-AzADGroup -DisplayName "Finance"
    -MailNickname "Finance"
```

Build the principal name from MailNickname and your AAD registered domain.

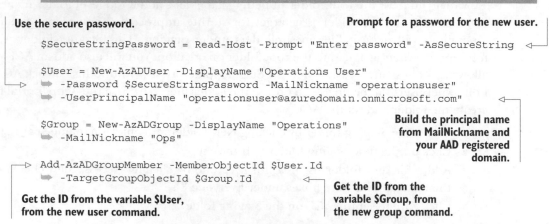

Here is an Azure PowerShell script for creating a new Operations user, a new security group, and assigning the user to the group.

Execute these lines in PowerShell with the Azure PowerShell module loaded.

Listing 4.7   Operations AAD user and group

Now that you've set up access to the Staging folder, create Finance and Operations folders under Staging in the same way. For these folders, assign a Read, Write, Execute (RWX) ACL to the Finance and Operations AAD groups, respectively.

Figure 4.4 shows how to set the ACLs on a folder. Use the Azure portal to create the folders and set the ACLs.

1 Create the department folder for Finance under Staging.
2 Click on the new Finance folder to browse the folder.
3 Click Access to show the Assign Permissions blade, then click Add to configure the ACL.
4 For Select User or Group, select the Finance group.
5 For Select Permission, check the Read, Write, and Execute boxes under Permission.
6 Select This Folder and All Children.
7 Under Add As, select An Access Permission Entry and a Default Permission Entry. This will set the permission on the folder and the inherited permission on any new files.
8 Click Ok to set the ACL on the Finance folder.
9 Repeat this process for Operations folder.

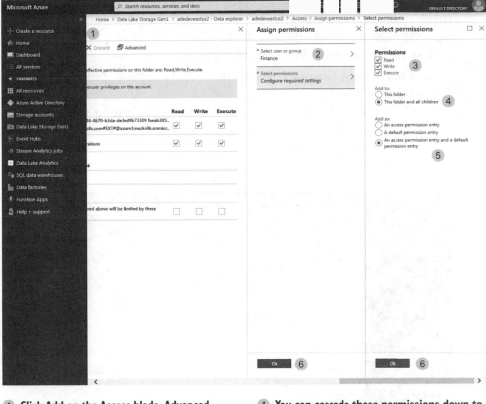

① **Click Add on the Access blade. Advanced lets you modify child permissions.**

② **Select an Azure Active Directory security group or user.**

③ **Choose Read and Execute for folder listing, or all three for full control.**

④ **You can cascade these permissions down to existing child files and folders.**

⑤ **Set permission on only existing files and folders (access), on new files and folders when created (default), or both.**

⑥ **Click Ok twice to commit the permissions.**

Figure 4.4   Assigning ACLs to a Data Lake store folder

DATA LAKE STORE AUTHORIZATION

If your end users will only use command-line tools to copy files, then you can manage the ADLS store using ACL permissions only. If they will use the Azure portal, Power-Shell, or Storage Explorer, then one more step is required. You need to give access via RBAC permissions to any AAD user or group using the folders.

Many built-in roles are available. The Owner role has full control of the ADLS store. The Contributor role has full control, except for assigning access via RBAC permissions. The Reader role allows read-only access to management data, and access to interact with storage via tools. You can read about the security controls at http://mng.bz/5a9Z.

Every AAD user or group that needs to access the ADLS store must have at least the Reader role. To complete the setup of the two departments' folders, you need to assign the Reader role to the two AAD groups.

Use the Azure portal to configure the roles.

1   Click Access Control (IAM) in the Data Lake Service blade to show the Access Control blade.

2   Click the Add Role Assignment or Add button within the Add a Role Assignment container to show the Add Role Assignment blade. Figure 4.5 shows the Add Role Assignment blade.

3   Select Reader for the Role.

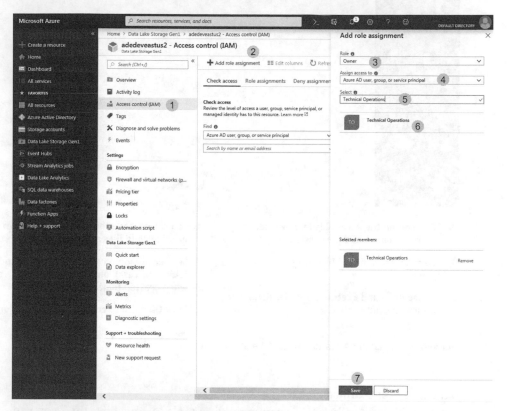

① **Access control defines what you can do to the service and is required for minimal access to the stored files.**

② **Click Add role assignment to give new permissions.**

③ **Owners have full control, Contributors nearly as much, and Readers just read.**

④ **Use Azure AD groups for easiest management.**
Other options are Azure service-to-service authorization.

⑤ **Start typing to filter the list.**

⑥ **Click on a security user or group to select.**

⑦ **Save your new role assignment.**

Figure 4.5   Assigning AAD group to Data Lake service roles

4 For Assign Access To, select the default: Azure AD User, Group, or Service Principal. Other options allow authorization by Azure services.

5 Start typing `Finance` in the Select input to filter the list of AAD users.

6 Click the Finance group to select the group.

7 Click Save to add the role assignment.

The Data Lake service owner role gives access to all the content, as well as management functions for the ADLS store. As an owner, you can assign other AAD users as owners too. These owners, and other Data Lake service roles, are separate from the root, sub-folder, and file owners.

The Finance and Operations departments now have a joint file archive to store data for analysis. The initial process for setting up the data lake had four steps:

1 Creating the ADLS store.

2 Configuring default security.

3 Creating the subfolders for each department.

4 Configuring the folder security for each department.

In the next section, you'll build on the initial root folder with a plan for data use, management, and governance. The plan materializes in a folder structure.

4.3 Storage folder structure and data drift

Data lakes provide unstructured storage and access controls for users and tools to perform analysis on stored data. This generates business value from the collected data. For this reason, it's important that the data be of high quality and easy to locate. You've seen how a folder structure and access controls can define what actions are allowed. This is one mode of data governance. Segregating unfiltered data from reviewed, corrected, enhanced, or otherwise processed data is another mode. In this section, you'll see how applying a structure from the start provides data governance and assists users. This structure helps your users understand and locate the data they need.

The Jonestown Sluggers head office manages the home stadium for the team. Finance has years of vendor sales data. They would like to store this data in your new data lake for analysis. The data is stored in CSV files in multiple folders and with different schemas. You want to ensure that the data is accessible and can be found by analysts. How can you accommodate this request?

4.3.1 Hierarchy structure revisited

Earlier in this chapter you created root-level folders to solve the immediate requirement for storing data, without much structure beyond that necessitated by ADLS. Now you're going to look at an approach to structuring folders which provides a usage pattern for analysis. You already created a Staging folder in the root folder of the ADLS store. Now you'll take this folder construction further.

Documenting a storage area, especially a data lake, is more than just taking notes to support it. Data files need attributes like source, type, quality, and date. These attributes help users to find the data they need. You can provide these attributes at a basic level using a combination of folder structure and file naming conventions.

> **TIP**   Azure offers a service called Data Catalog. This service stores metadata on multiple sources of data, including files and folders in ADLS stores. Data Catalog is covered briefly in the final chapter of this book. You can find more information with Microsoft's introduction to Data Catalog at http://mng.bz/oR2M.

ZONES FRAMEWORK

Imagine splitting your data lake into multiple sections, or *zones*, based on the level of processing and/or transformation required. An initial zone would be a place for external services and users to upload unprocessed data. You created this zone when you created the Staging folder in the previous section. The next zone stores validated and slightly processed files for long-term access, without further modification. This is the Raw zone. The third zone allows storage of ad hoc query output, as well as other files used when creating new data investigations. This is the Sandbox zone. The last zone stores production query output for business use. This is the Curated zone.

In a production ADLS store, analytics and automation systems handle data movement into and between zones. Sources of business data, like application logging, user behavior tracking, and IoT data, flow into the Staging zone. Azure services like ADF and ADLA copy, clean, transform, and enrich data before outputting files to the Raw zone. Analysts use tools like ADLA to generate data files in their Sandbox folder. Finally, analysts and data engineers use these same tools to create final data sets in the Curated zone for end user queries. Figure 4.6 shows the layout of the zones framework, with the flows of data between the zones.

> **NOTE**   You can read about creating and using ADLA jobs in chapter 7. You'll hear more about data movement in chapter 10 on data integration with ADF.

STAGING ZONE

Let's look at the Staging zone. This zone is for initially loading files into the data lake. Access to files and folders in the Staging zone should be limited to systems loading the data. Often these files need some type of processing before they can be used. Combining multiple small files into larger files for long-term storage would happen here. Distributed processing systems work most efficiently with fewer, larger files. Another example would be personally identifiable information (PII) cleansing. Files in the Staging zone should not be expected to remain long. Taking the design and structure from listing 4.6, here are a set of PowerShell commands to set up these folders for the zone framework. Execute listing 4.8, listing 4.9, listing 4.10, and listing 4.11 using a PowerShell client with Azure PowerShell loaded to set up the folders.

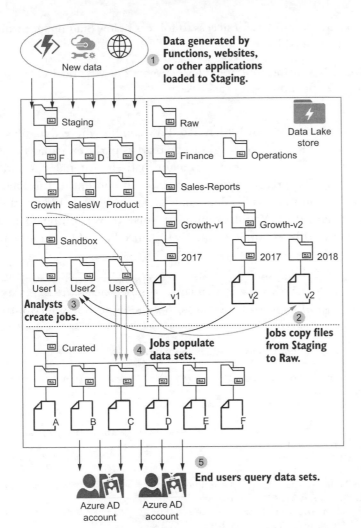

Figure 4.6 shown with the following labels:

1. Data generated by Functions, websites, or other applications loaded to Staging.

Staging
F D O
Growth SalesW Product

Sandbox
User1 User2 User3

Analysts 3 create jobs.

Curated
A B C D E F

Raw
Finance Operations
Sales-Reports
Growth-v1 Growth-v2
2017 2017 2018
v1 v2 v2

Data Lake store

2. Jobs copy files from Staging to Raw.

4. Jobs populate data sets.

5. End users query data sets.

Azure AD account   Azure AD account

Figure 4.6   Folder structure with zones framework

Listing 4.8   Set up a Data Lake store Staging folder

```
New-AzDataLakeStoreItem -AccountName "adedeveastus2" -Path "/Staging" -Folder
New-AzDataLakeStoreItem -AccountName "adedeveastus2" -Path "/Staging/Finance"
    -Folder
New-AzDataLakeStoreItem -AccountName "adedeveastus2" -Path "/Staging/DevOps"
    -Folder
New-AzDataLakeStoreItem -AccountName "adedeveastus2" -Path "/Staging/
    Operations" -Folder
New-AzDataLakeStoreItem -AccountName "adedeveastus2" -Path "/Staging/Finance/
    Growth" -Folder
New-AzDataLakeStoreItem -AccountName "adedeveastus2" -Path "/Staging/Finance/
    SalesW" -Folder
New-AzDataLakeStoreItem -AccountName "adedeveastus2" -Path "/Staging/Finance/
    Product" -Folder
```

Remember to return and set an ACL for access to folders below Staging, according to product or department ownership.

> **TIP**   ADLA performs best using splittable files between 250 MB and 1 GB. See http://mng.bz/6QWZ for more best practices.

RAW ZONE

Staging files are destined for the Raw folder. The Raw zone is where data files go to die. In the Raw zone, content of all types waits to be read as part of an analytics job or other request. Files in the Raw zone should remain in their original state, without modification or updating. To preserve this state, access to content in the Raw zone should be limited to read-only access for data analysts. Collections of data in the Raw zone can suffer from data drift. You'll examine the use of versioning to mitigate effects of data drift later in this section. Execute these Azure PowerShell commands to set up the folders.

Listing 4.9   Set up a Data Lake store Raw folder

```
New-AzDataLakeStoreItem -AccountName "adedeveastus2" -Path "/Raw" -Folder
New-AzDataLakeStoreItem -AccountName "adedeveastus2" -Path "/Raw/Finance"
    -Folder
New-AzDataLakeStoreItem -AccountName "adedeveastus2" -Path "/Raw/Operations"
    -Folder
New-AzDataLakeStoreItem -AccountName "adedeveastus2" -Path "/Raw/Finance/
    Sales-Reports" -Folder
New-AzDataLakeStoreItem -AccountName "adedeveastus2" -Path "/Raw/Finance/
    Sales-Reports/Growth-v1" -Folder
New-AzDataLakeStoreItem -AccountName "adedeveastus2" -Path "/Raw/Finance/
    Sales-Reports/Growth-v2" -Folder
New-AzDataLakeStoreItem -AccountName "adedeveastus2" -Path "/Raw/Finance/
    Sales-Reports/Growth-v1/2017" -Folder
New-AzDataLakeStoreItem -AccountName "adedeveastus2" -Path "/Raw/Finance/
    Sales-Reports/Growth-v2/2017" -Folder
New-AzDataLakeStoreItem -AccountName "adedeveastus2" -Path "/Raw/Finance/
    Sales-Reports/Growth-v2/2018" -Folder
```

> **WARNING**   Many data exploration techniques rely on finding outliers. Cleaning and normalizing data at the Raw stage could remove valuable data. Consider storing even data rows that fail Staging processing in "Error" folders adjacent to the data files.

SANDBOX ZONE

The Sandbox zone is an open area where data analysts can process files. It allows uploading of new data and creating multiple versions of combined data files as new data products are developed. Use this zone as a testing space for developing processing routines. The data can be minimally or majorly processed in the Sandbox. Access to content in the Sandbox zone should be unrestricted for each user. This zone does not serve data to end users. Execute these Azure PowerShell commands to set up the folders.

Listing 4.10 Set up a Data Lake store Sandbox folder

```
New-AzDataLakeStoreItem -AccountName "adedeveastus2" -Path "/Sandbox" -Folder
New-AzDataLakeStoreItem -AccountName "adedeveastus2" -Path "/Sandbox/User1"
    -Folder
New-AzDataLakeStoreItem -AccountName "adedeveastus2" -Path "/Sandbox/User2"
    -Folder
New-AzDataLakeStoreItem -AccountName "adedeveastus2" -Path "/Sandbox/User3"
    -Folder
```

You can skip setting up user folders in the Sandbox zone until you have users ready to do analysis. Remember to secure each user folder with appropriate ACLs.

CURATED ZONE

The Curated zone holds output from analytics jobs run against data files in the Raw zone. This data has been processed, preparing it for use by end users. A common use case would be exploration with visualization tools by business users. Access to content in the Curated zone should be limited to read-only access for business users and tools, and write access for data analysts and jobs creating the data sets. Execute these Azure PowerShell commands to set up the folders.

Listing 4.11 Set up a Data Lake store Curated folder

```
New-AzDataLakeStoreItem -AccountName "adedeveastus2" -Path "/Curated" -Folder
New-AzDataLakeStoreItem -AccountName "adedeveastus2" -Path "/Curated/FolderA"
    -Folder
New-AzDataLakeStoreItem -AccountName "adedeveastus2" -Path "/Curated/FolderB"
    -Folder
New-AzDataLakeStoreItem -AccountName "adedeveastus2" -Path "/Curated/FolderC"
    -Folder
```

These are the top-level zones that should be set up in the Data Lake store. These are community best practice, not a specific Microsoft recommendation. Figure 4.7 shows a hierarchy scheme using the zones approach.

In each zone, data files are sorted by department, source, and type. Sorting often includes a date of ingestion, or loading, into the ADLS store. The folder hierarchy of the Raw zone typically follows that of the Staging zone, but can vary depending on file aggregation or data drift controls. The Sandbox zone can be constructed using folders per user, rather than being broken up by department and source. Data sets in the Curated zone have a business case, and frequently combine data from multiple sources. The Curated zone can be constructed using folders per business unit, project, or along security boundaries.

Later chapters will walk through the processes that move data between folders, create new data files, and return data to the end user. When you use a folder hierarchy and enforce it with security controls, you reduce the likelihood of your data lake becoming a data swamp.

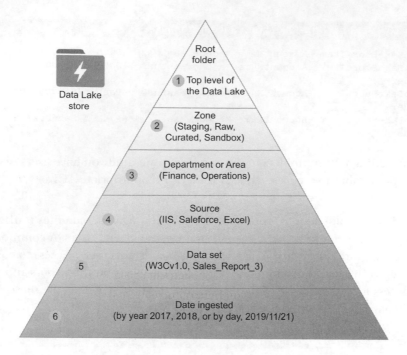

Figure 4.7   Azure Data Lake folder hierarchy

4.3.2   *Data drift*

When the structure of the data storage format changes over time, this is *data drift*. "Data drift exists in three forms: structural drift, semantic drift, and infrastructure drift."[2] The set of fields contained in a data file can increase or decrease over time. This is *structural drift*. The content of each field can contain new values with the same meaning, or new meaning. This is *semantic drift*. And the systems generating, housing, or processing the data may change, leading to entirely different formats. This is *infrastructure drift*. Since computing systems change over time, data drift is a natural part of operating computer systems. Data drift causes problems with data analysis, because two sets of data structures representing the same type of content must be handled differently.

Data drift can be managed using folder structure and naming conventions. Segregating data files with differing structures prevents breaking changes to existing analysis processes. Thoughtful naming conventions provide direction for finding the correct data sources and matching the import logic to the structure and schema. Because later analysis must take into account these changes in the data itself, you should plan from the beginning ways to clearly identify the changes.

---

[2]   Girish Pancha. "Big Data's Hidden Scourge: Data Drift." CMSWire.com. April 8, 2016. http://mng.bz/oPX2.

MITIGATING DATA DRIFT IN ZONES

Now consider a folder hierarchy using the zones framework. Finance has years of vendor sales data, stored in CSV files in multiple folders and with different schemas. To store the vendor sales data, you have several options for folder structures. The files can be loaded directly into the Curated zone, if this data has been validated and aggregated. But this scenario states that the files will be used for analysis. In this case, the files can land in the Staging zone and be validated, cataloged, and moved to the Raw zone by an automated process. Alternatively, the Finance team could load the vendor sales data directly into the Raw zone. But how will you deal with differing schema in the data files?

The framework spreads out from the root and our four zones to numerous, more targeted folders. This organizes the files contained and conveys details about the files. Figure 4.8 depicts the zones framework as a pyramid.

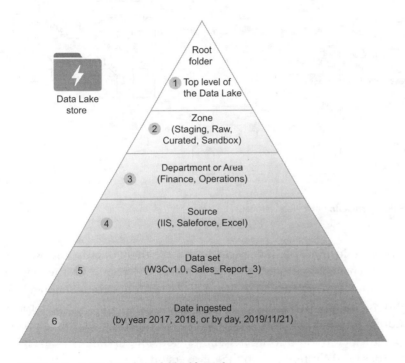

Figure 4.8   Azure Data Lake folder hierarchy

Because the likelihood of data drift increases with time, you should incorporate versioning into your plan. Versioning the files allows analytics jobs to process files with the same schema in the same way, or to use different processes with differing schema.

Analytics jobs read from folders in the Raw zone hierarchy, which now includes four folder levels, defining:

1 The originating department or area
2 The source

3 The data set

4 A version of the file within

The folder naming convention matters less than the principle of segregation: an analytics job can read all the files in a single folder, and be guaranteed that their schema match. This hierarchy adds description to the files, and versioning mitigates the effects of data drift. Figure 4.9 shows this folder structure laid out.

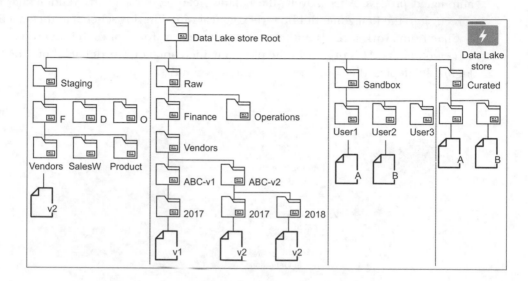

Figure 4.9   Folder structure with file versions

With this structure in place, Finance can bulk load their data in the Raw zone. If needed, you can create an automated process to migrate data from the Staging zone Vendors folder into Raw. Finance would load new vendor data into Staging, but would need to notify you of any change in schema. Otherwise, you may need to rely on failure notifications or other processes to detect the data drift. For your part, you will need to create the new folder for the new file version, and update any data movement and analytics jobs to add references to the new version.

With the zones framework, versioning by file folder works in any of the four top zones: Staging, Raw, Sandbox, or Curated. The zone structure provides flexibility around your implementation, especially at the lowest levels. Figure 4.8 shows a hierarchy scheme using ingestion date as the lowest level. This works well in a slowly changing environment, with little data drift, and analysis bounded by date ranges. This structure benefits from automated processing to create the folders and copy the files, especially when including month and day folders. Consider some other lower-level folder variations.

- How granular are the data files? Will they be combined by week or month to improve efficiency? Try segregating by file version.

- How great is the volume? Will the files need to be divided into smaller files by day, hour, or minute? Try a year, month, day folder structure.
- Does a single department generate a single format, like images or XML? Try segregating at the Source level by format, then by project set.
- How rapidly does the data drift? It's easiest to modify the folder structure at the bottom, rather than at the zone, department, or source level.

TIP Many data lakes collect data sources from third parties. Consider adding a "Third-Party" or individual third-party folders at the Department level of the zones framework.

With the zones framework, you have a model for minimizing the impact of data drift in your ADLS store. It also provides a method for managing your ADLS store's security structure. With these attributes in mind, you can create an ADLS store to serve your analytics system well.

4.4   Copy tools for Data Lake stores

Several Microsoft tools operate within Azure, copying files between services. Keeping the data transfer in Azure, rather than downloading and uploading files, minimizes network egress charges. Network transfers within an Azure data center are faster than across the Internet. ADLCopy is a command-line tool for copying files from Storage accounts to ADLS stores and between ADLS stores. ADLA can perform the same functions as ADLCopy. (You can read more about ADLA in chapter 7.) Azure Data Factory (ADF) uses cloud scheduling and Azure runtimes, including ADLA, to copy data between services. (You can read about ADF in chapter 10.) You can even export files directly from SQL Data Warehouse to ADLS. Chapter 3 discussed copying files into Storage accounts. Figure 4.10 adds two more options for tools to copy files to Azure storage services.

Each tool has a strong use case.

- The Azure portal is available without an install.
- ADLCopy can be used for automated file copying without user interaction.
- File copying with ADF can be included in multi-step workflows and integrated with other Azure services.
- Storage Explorer provides an easy-to-use GUI and status tracking of actions.
- ADLA can retrieve data during processing jobs.

4.4.1   Data Explorer

You can use the Azure portal to manage files and folders in ADLS, including uploading files and setting access permissions. Data Explorer is a blade within the ADLS Service Management blade in the Azure portal. You can access it from the Overview blade, or via Data Lake Storage Gen1 > Data Explorer in the left menu.

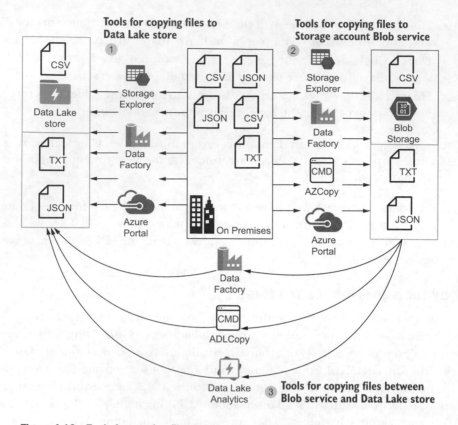

Figure 4.10   Tools for copying files between storage services

To set up a new folder in the Staging zone for the ABC vendor, follow this example.

1 In the All Services blade, enter "Data Lake Storage Gen1" in the filter and select the Data Lake Storage Gen1 service type to see your ADLS stores. Click on the ADLS store you created in the previous section, "[XYZ]deveastus2".

2 In the Overview blade of the ADLS store, click Data Explorer.

3 Browse to the /Staging/Finance folder.

4 In the Data Explorer blade, click New Folder.

5 Name the folder *Vendors*. Folder names can be any string of characters that are valid in a URL.

6 Click the Vendors folder to browse to it.

7 In the Data Explorer blade, click New Folder.

8 Name the folder *ABC*.

9 Click the ABC folder to browse to it.

10 Click Access to assign permissions to the folder.

11 Click Upload to view the Upload Files blade.

12 Click the folder icon to open a File Select dialog.

13 Select your files and click Open to begin uploading them to the ABC Data Lake folder.

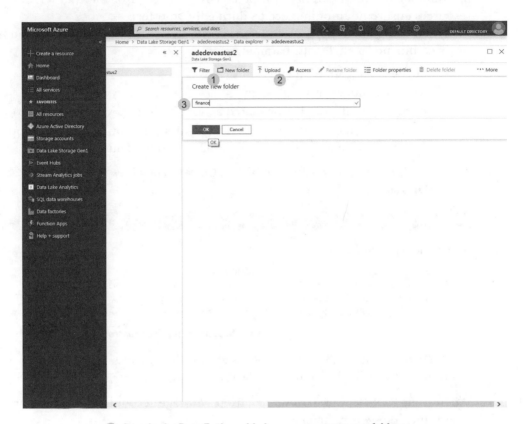

① **Once in the Data Explorer blade, you can create new folders.**

② **You can upload files. Browse into the target folder first.**

③ **Name can be any string of characters that can be URL-encoded.**

Figure 4.11 Creating a new folder in Data Lake store

4.4.2 *ADLCopy tool*

ADLCopy is a command-line tool for copying files between Storage accounts and ADLS stores and between ADLS stores. It doesn't copy files from on-premises stores to an ADLS store. Because the file copy occurs between storage systems in Azure, Azure resources are used to execute the copy, eliminating Internet bandwidth and single system constraints. You can download ADLCopy at https://aka.ms/downloadadlcopy.

The copy can run in standalone (shared) mode or ADLA (dedicated) mode. With standalone mode, Azure executes the job using available shared resources for ADLS. With ADLA mode, you configure the transfer to use dedicated resources and tweak the number of analytics units to balance cost and speed of the transfer. Dedicated resources ensure no throttling occurs during the transfer.

When using ADLCopy in standalone mode from a Storage account to an ADLS store, commands include four parameters:

- Source is the path to the files.
- Dest is the target of the file copy.
- Sourcekey is the root key or shared access signature key. (see chapter 3)
- Pattern is a regex pattern to match the files for copying. Pattern is optional, and not supplying a pattern will copy all files in the Source path.

The following listing shows the use of ADLCopy to copy files from a Storage account to an ADLS store.

Listing 4.12   ADLCopy transfer standalone

Replicating the folder structure

```
"C:\Program Files (x86)\Microsoft SDKs\Azure\ADLCopy\adlcopy"
    /Source https://abc.blob.core.windows.net/project-abc/v1/v1.1
    /Dest adl://abc.azuredatalakestore.net/iislogs/v1/v1.1/
    /SourceKey ==StorageKey== /Pattern "ch*.csv"
```
Use file patterns for finer control.

NOTE   See section 4.3.1 earlier in this chapter for a discussion of folder hierarchies and versioning in the data lake.

When using ADLCopy in ADLA mode from a Storage account to an ADLS store, commands include six parameters:

- Source is the path to the files.
- Dest is the target of the file copy.
- Sourcekey is the root key or shared access signature key. See chapter 3 for more details.
- Pattern is a regex pattern to match the files for copying. This is optional, and not supplying a pattern will copy all files in the Source path.
- Account is the name of the ADLA to use for executing the copy job.
- Units specifies how many analytics units to use for the job. See chapter 7 for a discussion of ADLA analytics units.

The following listing shows the use of ADLCopy to copy files from a Storage account to an ADLS store, using your existing ADLA to execute the job.

Listing 4.13 ADLCopy transfer with ADLA

Implement change in hierarchy by targeting new folder.

```
"C:\Program Files (x86)\Microsoft SDKs\Azure\ADLCopy\adlcopy"
➥ /Source https://finance.blob.core.windows.net/datalakeload/p-abc/
➥ /Dest adl://abc.azuredatalakestore.net/staging/finance/p-abc-v1.2/
➥ /sourcekey ==StorageKey== /Pattern "tv*.csv"
/Account dedeveastus2 /Units 2
```

Use file patterns for finer control.

Add ADLA account after file name pattern, use 2 parallel workers.

When using the ADLA account, the `Pattern` switch must be placed before the `Account` and `Units` switches. Unattended copy executions are possible. On first execution, ADLCopy prompts for Azure credentials. These are saved in the %AppData%\ADLCopy\TokenCache.dat file. This file will then provide authentication for scheduled executions of ADLCopy. You'll need to add the Storage account and ADL account as a data source in ADLA, if not already attached. You can read more about ADLA in chapter 7.

4.4.3 *Azure Storage Explorer tool*

Azure Storage Explorer provides a desktop GUI interface for uploading files to multiple Azure services, including Storage accounts. Azure Storage Explorer can also connect to ADLS stores using AAD. MIME types are identified by file extension. Figure 4.12 shows Storage Explorer connecting with multiple types of authentication. You can use the drag-and-drop function to upload and download files, or use the individual function buttons in Storage Explorer. Download Azure Storage Explorer at http://mng.bz/nzNK.

> **NOTE** Data Explorer and other Azure services don't create sub-folders automatically, but copy files only. Other tools, like Storage Explorer or ADLCopy, will copy files and folder structure. Creating folders yourself, and carefully planning the structure of your folder hierarchy, will help keep your data lake from turning into a data swamp!

With an Azure Data Lake store at your disposal, you are ready to capture data and begin data analysis. Using the zones framework will help you keep your data lake under control. The following chapters will show you how to set up more services in Azure, run real-time and batch processing, and automate your system.

1 Use the account key to connect to a Storage account. All resources and services are accessible.

2 Use a shared access signature to connect to a Storage account. Only resources and services in the SAS are accessible.

3 Connect to Data Lake with your Azure Active Directory (AAD) user.

4 AAD user provides access to Storage account resources and services based on role. Nearly all roles grant read access.

5 Storage Explorer interprets the folder structure of the files in a Storage account Blob service.

6 Use Storage Explorer to change Access Tier: Hot, Cool, and Archive.

7 Store many file types with recognized MIME types.

Figure 4.12   Storage Explorer configured to connect to Storage accounts with access keys and SAS keys

4.5 Exercises

The following exercises can help you internalize the new features introduced in this chapter. You should be able to create a Data Lake store and configure access.

4.5.1 Exercise 1

Which of these commands will create a new ADLS store without prompting for additional info?

1. `New-AzDataLakeStoreAccount -ResourceGroupName "ade-dev-eastus2"`
2. `New-AzDataLakeStoreAccount -ResourceGroupName "ade-dev-eastus2" -Name "adedeveastus2"`
3. `New-AzDataLakeStoreAccount -ResourceGroupName "ade-dev-eastus2" -Name "adedeveastus2" -Location "East US 2"`
4. `New-AzDataLakeStoreAccount -ResourceGroupName "ade-dev-eastus2" -Name "adedeveastus2" -Location "East US 2" -Encryption "ServiceManaged"`

SOLUTION

When using the `New-AzDataLakeStoreAccount` command, resource group, account name, and region are required. If the selected ADLS store name doesn't exist, options 3 and 4 will not prompt for additional input. Azure PowerShell will prompt for user input for text values when the parameters are absent.

4.5.2 Exercise 2

The Operations team has installed a data collection application called *Vacuum* connected to the shop floor machines. They will schedule a daily export for three data types: machine start and stop times, machine amperage draw, and operator inputs. Each file name will include the type, year, month, and day. Devise a folder structure to store each data set.

SOLUTION

1. Because this is a new data feed, start the folder structure in the /Staging folder.
2. This data set has a clear department owner. Use a new or existing folder for Operations at /Staging/Operations.
3. This data set is generated by an application named Vacuum, so create the third-level folder for this application at /Staging/Operations/Vacuum.
4. Three data sets are listed, each potentially having their own schema and uses. Create a folder for each data set. It is up to you if you add a discriminator for version to the folder name, add a folder beneath it, or disregard the version until a new version of the schema is released. You can create a folder for each data set, like /Staging/Operations/Vacuum/operating_times.
5. With a single file per day, you have options for the depth of your folder structure. Segregating files by year and month aligns with typical monthly reporting schedules. The exporting process typically handles creating new folders as needed,

but you can start the structure to give guidance and ensure correct ACLs are in place. The lowest level of folders should look like /Staging/Operations/Vacuum/ operating_times/2019/03.

Summary

- ADLS is a petabyte-scale storage service which provides a hierarchical folder structure over HDFS. This structure provides fine-grained access control.
- AAD is used to secure files and folders in Azure Data Lake stores, which reduces management.
- Dividing the ADLS store into zones creates a structure necessary to control usage. This helps support user access to data.
- Planning for data drift during creation of ADLS folders provides clear guidance for later accommodating the changes. This helps users work with data in multiple schemas.

Message handling with Event Hubs

5

This chapter covers

- Creating an Event Hub
- Configuring partitions and throughput units
- Saving messages to disk
- Accessing Event Hubs

In the previous chapters, you learned about services that can store the potentially limitless volumes of data generated by modern applications. These services support the speed and batch layers of the Lambda architecture. Data storage forms both sources and outputs for data, and queries to answer user questions.

In this chapter, you'll learn about another Azure data source. Event Hubs exposes a high-throughput endpoint for ingesting and serving *event messages*. Events messages record the activities of modern applications as a time-based series of event data. *Producers* generate event messages, and *consumers* process event messages. Event Hubs forms the bridge between the two. In this way, Event Hubs decouples the producers from the consumers. By decoupling ingestion from consumption, Event Hubs allows multiple producers to communicate with multiple consumers.

5.1   How does an Event Hub work?

An Event Hub ingests messages from applications. It records the details of each message in a journal and saves the message data for retrieval. The message data can be simple or complex. The Event Hub serves messages on request. Each message consumer records the last message read in the journal. Multiple consumers can read from the same journal of messages.

Messages are retained in the journal until the retention period elapses and are not removed during retrieval. This means multiple consumers can read from the same journal, and a single consumer can read from the journal multiple times. This differs from the Azure Queue service, where messages are deleted on successful processing. Replaying messages from the journal allows reprocessing of events, and having multiple consumers allows different processing to happen on the same data set. Extending the retention period lets us revisit our old data in the future.

Applications submit messages to Event Hubs via an API using HTTPS, Advanced Message Queuing Protocol (AMQP), or the Apache Kafka protocol. HTTPS is the industry standard for secure Internet web communication. AMQP messages are an industry standard for message queuing. Kafka is an open-source option for hosting a high-throughput message endpoint. The Kafka protocol is an open standard. If you don't want to manage a Kafka cluster, you could use Event Hubs in a namespace using Kafka. One example would be using an Event Hub as the message ingestion point for a Databricks cluster. All protocols require a fully qualified domain name (FQDN) endpoint to submit messages to. In Event Hubs, this is called the *Event Hubs namespace*.

The Event Hubs namespace can be thought of as the gateway or load balancer for one or more Event Hubs. It lets applications use common connection strings to access multiple Hubs for sending and receiving. It also allows you to create SAS keys that grant access to read and write to the Hubs in the namespace. By acting as a gateway in front of your Event Hub, the namespace can route traffic to a second Hub if there is a regional outage.

> **NOTE**   Although this scenario could easily fit with an IoT Hub deployment, for the purposes of submitting event data to Azure, Event Hubs and IoT Hubs are functionally equivalent.

Let's see how Event Hubs work by collecting data for a new scenario.

> **TIP**   You can find the code listings in the GitHub repository for this book at https://github.com/rnuckolls/azure_storage.

5.2   Collecting data in Azure

For the next season of the Jonestown Sluggers, the IT group is piloting a biometric monitoring program during practice and home games. All of the players have sensors integrated into their uniforms, recording data multiple times per second and submitting to your analytics system. The development team wants to send the data to Azure for processing. To support this initiative, you need to create an endpoint in Azure to accept the incoming stats and hold them for processing. Later work will add real-time stats analysis and batch analysis.

To collect data from one or more sources, you can proceed with four general tasks.

1 Define your data schema.
2 Define your collection endpoint.
3 Generate your data.
4 Submit data to the endpoint.

Figure 5.1 shows these steps using Azure services as endpoints.

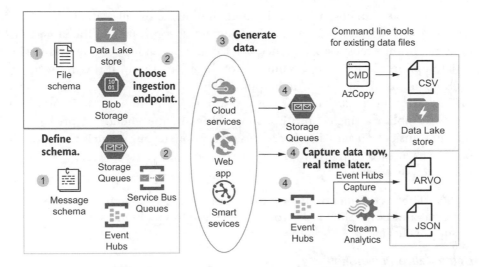

Figure 5.1 Data collection from multiple sources to multiple targets

Collecting data from devices works the same way as collecting from software. Because the data collection will occur in real-time, let's choose a message schema, like that used for pitching stats. A file schema would be better suited to batch processing.

For the first iteration of the biometric stats, include a player identifier, sensor identifier, the value read, and the sensor read time, as shown in the following listing.

Listing 5.1 Player statistics

```
{
    "Player":"abera101",            ◁—  Player identifier
    "Node":12,
    "NodeValue":100.2,                                      ISO 8601
    "EventTime":"2020-04-05T13:15:1947365Z"   ◁—   datetime format
}
```

With a data format defined, you can move on to setting up the collection endpoint. To route traffic to an Event Hubs service, you need a FQDN. Each Event Hub relies on a namespace. Because of this, Event Hubs can take advantage of some redundancy and recovery features. It also means you must create the namespace before creating an Event Hub.

5.3   Create an Event Hubs namespace

Event Hub namespaces host an Internet-routable endpoint for message submission to an Event Hub. The endpoint provisions throughput capacity for Event Hubs in the namespace. This capacity is allocated and priced using *throughput units*, an allotment of bandwidth and message rate that controls the input and output of messages through your namespace and Hubs.

Namespaces can host up to 20 throughput units, across all of the Event Hubs in the namespace. You may need more than one namespace to handle the largest ingestion pipeline, but for most uses, a namespace can handle multiple Event Hubs. The Auto-Inflate option will increase the number of throughput units if the traffic approaches the maximum for ingestion or output. When using Auto-Inflate, set the maximum throughput units to 20. This ensures you won't lose incoming data if the throughput rate rises above a single unit. Enabling retries by the client can prevent data loss during transient outages, like ServerBusyException, if your usage is very sporadic. You pay for each throughput unit provisioned, even if the ingestion rate does not require that much throughput.

> **TIP** The maximum number of throughput units available through the Azure portal and PowerShell is 20. You can increase this to 40 units by submitting a support ticket.

5.3.1   Using Azure PowerShell

You can use Azure PowerShell to create an Event Hubs namespace. The `New-AzEventHubNamespace` command creates the namespace. This command takes multiple parameters: a name, resource group, location, performance tier, and throughput level. `NamespaceName` defines part of the routable Event Hub URL. The namespace name must be alphanumeric and hyphens, end with a letter or number, and be globally unique. Read more about Azure service naming conventions in chapter 3. `SkuName` accepts Basic or Standard as values. The Standard tier adds Auto-Inflate scaling for longer message retention, more connections, geo-disaster recovery, and more control over writing to the queues. `SkuCapacity` accepts an integer from 1-20 for the number of throughput units. You can also enable Auto-Inflate by adding `EnableAuto-Inflate` and providing a value for `MaximumThroughputUnits`, between 1-20. Add `EnableKafka` to use the Kafka protocol in this namespace.

Run listing 5.2 in Azure PowerShell to create a namespace. Access Azure PowerShell by visiting Azure Cloud Shell at https://shell.azure.com/, or clicking the >_ header menu in the Azure portal.

Listing 5.2   Create a new Azure Event Hub Namespace using PowerShell

Standard tier, 1 throughput unit.

```
New-AzEventHubNamespace -ResourceGroupName "ade-dev-eastus2"
    -NamespaceName "ade-dev-eastus2-hubs" -Location "East US 2"
    -SkuName "Standard" -SkuCapacity 1
    -Tag @{User="ADE";}
    -EnableAutoInflate
    -MaximumThroughputUnits 5
```

Enable automatic scaling of throughput units. Required when using MaximumThroughputUnits.

Tag this resource with ADE to aid in searching.

Limit scaling to a maximum of 5 throughput units.

You can use the Azure portal to create a new Event Hubs namespace too. The Create Namespace blade is located at https://portal.azure.com/#create/Microsoft.EventHub. With both methods, you need to select the throughput units for your namespace.

5.3.2   Throughput units

You can increase the throughput of your Event Hubs by adding more throughput units, with some conditions. Starting with a single throughput unit minimizes your hourly cost. The maximum ingestion rate of a single throughput unit is 1 MB per second and up to 1000 ingestion events per second. The maximum output rate of a single throughput unit is 2 MB per second and up to 2000 messages per second. With Auto-Inflate enabled, your ingestion endpoint won't stop accepting new messages when the first ingestion limits are reached. Some consumers, or readers, cannot run in parallel against an Event Hub and are limited to a single throughput unit on the output side. We'll cover high-output parallel readers in the next chapter, with Stream Analytics. For now, you can monitor the incoming rates of messages and bytes on the namespace's Overview blade in Azure portal.

> **WARNING**   There is no "Auto-Deflate" for throughput units. Be sure to monitor your Event Hub namespace for throughput usage, and scale down when usage returns to a lower volume.

An Event Hub namespace hosts an endpoint in a single datacenter and region. To enable greater fault tolerance, the namespace offers routing of event submissions to a secondary datacenter during an outage.

5.3.3   Event Hub geo-disaster recovery

Azure services run in multiple data centers, regions, zones, and on multiple continents around the world. Even with the distributed nature of the execution and resilient design of Azure services, outages can occur. You should plan how you will recover from short and long outages in Azure services. As part of a disaster-recovery plan, you may want to set up redundancies and fail-over paths between Azure services. Event Hubs makes this fairly painless with *geo-disaster recovery routing*.

To have a failover endpoint to mitigate downtime, you need to add a second Event Hubs namespace and connect the primary and secondary namespaces via an alias. The alias is a routing FQDN, which routes incoming messages to the active Event Hubs namespace. Figure 5.2 shows the flow of messages in Event Hubs when using a geo-disaster recovery alias.

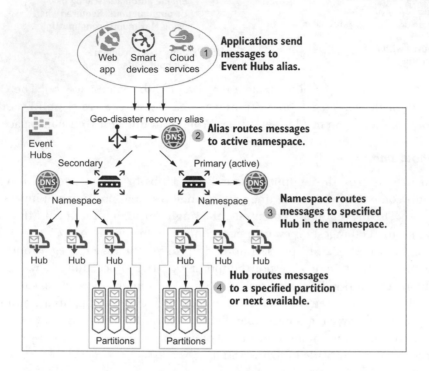

Figure 5.2   Routing messages with Event Hubs Geo-disaster recovery alias

You can create the geo-recovery alias using Azure PowerShell. The command `New-AzEventHubGeoDRConfiguration` creates the alias using two existing Event Hub namespaces. You provide the alias using the `Name` parameter, along with the resource group to store the metadata. Both namespaces need to run on at least the Standard tier. You can change the tier of an existing Event Hubs namespace on the Overview blade of the Azure portal, by clicking the Pricing Tier link. You can pair an Event Hubs namespace with a namespace in any other supported Azure region. Using namespace zone redundancy restricts the available locations to regions in the United States, Europe, and Southeast Asia. Because the routing alias will be the FQDN used in your connection strings, choose a name that is region-neutral and that conveys the use of the namespaces.

The script in listing 5.3 does the following:

- Creates a second Event Hubs namespace
- Creates a routing alias
- Assigns the primary and secondary namespaces

Execute this script in Azure PowerShell. Access Azure PowerShell by visiting Azure Cloud Shell at https://shell.azure.com/, or clicking the >_ header menu in the Azure portal.

Listing 5.3   Create a secondary Azure Event Hub namespace and alias using PowerShell

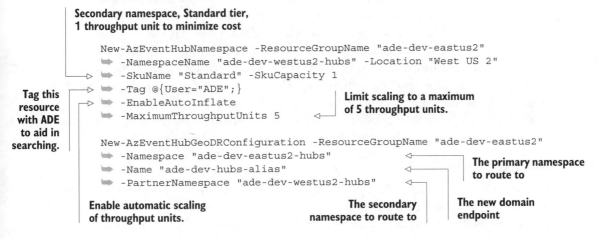

5.3.4   *Failover with geo-disaster recovery*

In the event of a long-term regional outage of Event Hubs, you would change the primary namespace from the failed region to the functional one. The failover does not happen automatically: you initiate it. After you initiate the failover, event messages collection resumes in the new primary namespace. If and when the failed namespace comes online, it will then be the secondary.

> **TIP**   Geo-disaster recovery works to recover parts of your analytics system from a regional disaster. You should ask yourself a few questions before using it, including the following:
>
> - How often can you expect to use the failover?
> - How quickly can you update your systems to use a new Event Hubs namespace?
> - Can you re-create the rest of the analytics system on short notice?

If you can tolerate several hours of downtime for the ingestion endpoint, you probably don't need to use a geo-disaster alias. If you can easily update your systems with a new Event Hubs endpoint address, you don't need to use a geo-disaster alias. If you can re-create your Event Hubs and update your systems easily, then you can create a new Event Hubs namespace when needed, and forgo the expense of running a secondary namespace. Automation is your friend.

With at least one namespace created, you can create an Event Hub. The Event Hub contains the journal that records messages. Both the namespace and an Event Hub are required for a complete endpoint.

5.4   Creating an Event Hub

The Event Hub provides only a few options, but they have a big impact on usability. These include the duration of message retention, partition count, and automatic output to durable storage. Because the data and journal entry for each message are recorded in durable storage, data accumulates in the Event Hub. Each Event Hub includes a set amount of storage with the cost of the throughput unit. Once this included storage is consumed, you can allow the oldest messages to be removed or pay for extra storage to extend the retention period. Each partition represents a parallel path for ingesting and consuming messages. With Event Hubs Capture, you can output the message data to accessible storage without needing a consuming application. You'll see more about each of these options later in this section.

5.4.1   Using Azure portal

In the Azure portal, you first choose the namespace, then add an Event Hub. The Event Hub name must be alphanumeric and hyphens, periods, or underscores, and begin and end with a letter or number. You must select a message retention period between one and seven days. Message retention sets a minimum duration for storing messages, and at least one day of message retention is provided at no extra cost.

You need to provide a partition count value too. Choose a partition count that matches your use case. The partition count controls the maximum parallel consumers that can process messages simultaneously. The minimum is two, which allows for redundancy in the system. Even though there can be 26 players on the baseball roster, you don't need to set the partition count to 26. Use two partitions instead. Higher partition counts are needed for much larger throughput demands. Capture automatically saves messages to Azure Storage or Data Lake Storage. Leave Capture disabled. You'll configure it later.

> **TIP** Additional partitions do not increase the cost of the Event Hub namespace, but they can negatively affect downstream performance if the number of messages does not require high throughput.

5.4.2   Using Azure PowerShell

You can also create the Event Hub by using Azure PowerShell. The `New-AzEventHub` command creates an Event Hub. You need to provide a name, resource group, location, and the namespace connected to the Event Hub. Use the `MessageRetentionInDays` parameter to specify the message retention period and `PartitionCount` to set the number of partitions. Run the following script (listing 5.4) to create the Event Hub with two partitions and message retention of one day.

Listing 5.4   Create Event Hub

```
New-AzEventHub -ResourceGroupName "ade-dev-eastus2"
-NamespaceName "ade-dev-eastus2-hubs" -Name "biometricstats"
  -MessageRetentionInDays 1          One day of message retention
  -PartitionCount 2                  (storage) included in the
                                     throughput unit rate
  Up to 32 partitions can be divided
  between the throughput unit rate.
```

Because the throughput units are set at the namespace level, you can add more Event Hubs to the namespace without extra charges. Remember that throughput units are split among the Event Hubs in the namespace. There is a maximum of 10 Event Hubs per namespace. Let's look at some of the ways you can configure the Event Hub.

> **TIP**   If you want to prepare for a failover event and have created a secondary namespace, you can reuse this script to create a secondary Event Hub. Change the NamespaceName to "ade-dev-westus2-hubs", or the name you used for the secondary namespace. There is no ongoing charge for adding an Event Hub (without Capture enabled) to the namespace, only for the throughput units. (The resource group can be reused for both East US 2 and West US 2 resources for simplicity.)

With a namespace and Event Hub, the last thing needed to write messages to Event Hubs is an access key.

5.4.3   *Shared access policy*

A Shared Access Signature (SAS) key is required to access an Event Hub. Creating an Event Hub namespace generates a new key policy named RootManageSharedAccessKey. The default access policy gives full control to the service. This policy includes a primary and secondary SAS key. You can view the policy keys in the Azure portal in the Event Hubs Namespace > Shared Access Policies blade.

You can view the keys and connection string for a particular policy using Azure PowerShell too. Use the `Get-AzEventHubAuthorizationRule` command to list the access keys for an Event Hub namespace. By default, RootManageSharedAccessKey is included, allowing full access to the service. Execute the following PowerShell script (listing 5.5) to see the available rules.

Listing 5.5   Get Event Hub namespace default policy

```
Get-AzEventHubAuthorizationRule -ResourceGroupName ade-dev-eastus2
  -NamespaceName ade-dev-eastus2-hubs
Get-AzEventHubKey -ResourceGroupName ade-dev-eastus2          The Event Hub
  -NamespaceName ade-dev-eastus2                              namespace
  -AuthorizationRuleName RootManageSharedAccessKey     The policy name
```

With the namespace, Event Hub, and access key, you can give the development team access to the new Event Hub. Later in the chapter you'll see more details about configuring SAS policies, and see an example script for writing to the Event Hub. Now let's look more closely at the inner workings of the Event Hub.

5.5   Event Hub partitions

An Event Hub behaves like a multi-lane highway where all cars obey the speed limit. Figure 5.3 shows messages as cars on a highway. From a single on-ramp, a car on the highway can run in any lane, and lanes can separate from the highway at any point. Each Event Hub comes with a minimum of two partitions, the lanes of the highway. Event Hubs have throughput units and partitions for managing throughput, the throughput unit functioning as a speed limit. Messages submitted earlier are retrieved first, but retrieval can begin from any point of the journal. A single consumer can service all partitions, or multiple consumers will divide the partitions between them automatically.

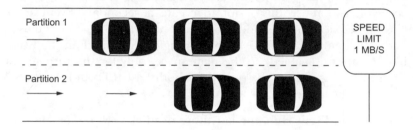

Figure 5.3   Partitioned Event Hub runs at throughput unit rate.

An outage of a single partition does not cause the Event Hub to become unavailable. Because an Event Hub has multiple partitions serving a single entry point, any partition can handle any inbound message. Event Hubs was designed around this requirement. An extra partition-serving process is kept warm on the Event Hub to take over a failed partition. This extra partition supports the high availability of the Hub as part of its hourly rate. For your two-partition Event Hub, there are actually three processes running, with one at idle.

5.5.1   Multiple consumers

Event Hubs implements the message storage differently from Azure Queue service. With the Queue service, each message is an individual file. With Event Hubs, each message is written to a common log and read from the same log. Consumers read messages not yet flagged as read from the log, selecting the next batch of messages belonging to the partition they service.

Event Hubs provides a method for multiple consumers to read from the same log and track the read messages separately. Each Event Hub includes a single *consumer group* named $Default. This consumer group identifies which consumers read from the journal and use the same checkpoint to identify the last read message. For Basic tier namespaces, only the default consumer group is allowed. For Standard tier, you can add multiple consumer groups and allow multiple application consumers to read the same Event Hub messages.

5.5.2 Why specify a partition?

If you want to specify a specific order of processing for a set of messages, then specify a partition. All the messages in that partition will be processed by the same consumer, because only one consumer from a consumer group reads from a partition. This ensures consistency in the state of related messages. For example, Stream Analytics can group messages in a specific partition together when making calculations and can use multiple consumers to read multiple partitions.

5.5.3 Why not specify a partition?

Unassigned messages are assigned a partition, round-robin style. Assigning messages to a specific partition can cause message count skew between partitions, which can slow processing in heavily used partitions. If messages are tied to a specific partition, then any outage with the partition will prevent the ingestion endpoint from accepting those messages. Event Hub partitions can go offline for a number of reasons. Processes will be shifted or created to bring the partition back online, but during the outage, submissions will fail. If high availability is more important than consistency in processing, then allow the Event Hub to manage the message partition.

Figure 5.4 shows a comparison of assigned messages to unassigned messages.

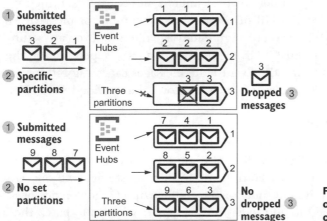

Figure 5.4   Partitioned queues can be highly available or highly consistent.

When defining partitions on your messages, adding retry logic to your code can keep partition outages from causing message loss.

5.5.4   *Event Hubs message journal*

These separate partitions all read from the same message tracking source, the journal. Every message coming into the endpoint is recorded to the journal, along with its partition. In figure 5.3, you can think of the journal as a list of vehicle makes and models, with the partitions representing which vehicle is in which lane. Event Hubs uses Blob Storage behind the scenes to serve the log file for the partition consumers. Remember from chapter 3 that Azure Storage services are backed by multiple stores for high availability. Thus message ingestion and storage are both protected from network outages.

5.5.5   *Partitions and throughput units*

Event Hubs implements a partitioned journal, with at least two partitions in every Event Hub. When submitting messages to the Event Hub, you can choose to use the first available partition. The Event Hub will distribute messages evenly among the partitions. If you choose a partition for a message, then the Event Hub will send those messages only to that partition.

Each partition can only utilize a single throughput unit. Your ingestion and output rates may never reach the maximum of a single throughput unit. Using the default of two partitions, only two throughput units can be used, even if more partitions are available. When creating an Event Hub, a valid practice is to choose the number of partitions based on the expected maximum throughput rate.

Using a log impacts message retention in an interesting manner. One day of message retention defines at most a full day's worth of messages in the log. At 1 MB per second per throughput unit per day, that yields 60 sec × 60 min × 24 hrs, or 86400 MB of messages. At 1,000 messages per second per throughput unit per day, that yields 60 sec × 60 min × 24 hrs × 1,000, or 86.4 million messages if each message is 1 KB. Once the log reaches 86400 MB or the equivalent number of messages, the oldest messages are deleted. When you configure message retention, you are setting the storage limit for messages to 86400 MB × (number of days). Depending on the size and volume of messages entering the Event Hub, messages can be stored for days, weeks, or months. You pay for the storage of messages over the provided 86400 MB.

5.6   *Configuring Capture*

When creating or configuring an Event Hub, you may choose to enable Capture. Capture creates discrete files from batches of Event Hub messages. This allows you to save the messages from your Event Hub queue to durable storage without writing additional code. To add equivalent functionality to the Azure Queue service or Service Bus queues, you would need to add logic to your queue servicers to batch the messages, authenticate to the storage service, and write the files. Capture provides a codeless method for generating files for batch processing.

When enabling Capture, you can choose an output folder in Blob Storage or Data Lake Storage. You control the batch size by setting a maximum time window between

1 and 15 minutes and a maximum size window between 10 MB and 500 MB. You can choose to skip outputting a file if no messages are received in the time window. In general, larger files perform better in batch processing, so choosing larger windows is preferable. These settings can be modified at any time.

5.6.1 File name formats

When configuring the Capture function, you will choose a folder pattern using all of the following parameters:

- Namespace
- EventHub
- PartitionId
- Year
- Month
- Day
- Hour
- Minute
- Second

You are free to organize the parameters in any order. The last parameter will form all or part of the file name. For example, the following pattern emphasizes filenames over granular folders.

```
{Namespace}/{EventHub}/{Year}/{Month}/{Day}/{Hour}/{EventHub}_{PartitionId}_
{Year}_{Month}_{Day}_{Hour}_{Minute}_{Second}.avro
```

The ingestion rate for your Event Hub can affect how you design the folder pattern. A single throughput unit provides a maximum ingestion rate of 1 MB per second. With a maximum of a single throughput unit per partition, multiple files per minute can be generated, but no more than 1 file per second per partition. At this rate, with 32 partitions, you could generate 230,400 files per hour if your size window is 10 MB, or 4,608 files for a 500 MB window size. Review your expected ingestion rate against the folder pattern to keep the file count per folder below 1,000. Using more than 1,000 files becomes difficult to manage with Storage Explorer.

5.6.2 Secure access for Capture

When you choose Blob Storage as the destination for your captured files, security is handled by the Event Hub during Capture setup. The Capture setup retrieves the root access key from the Storage account and stores it for access. If needed, the specified Blob Storage will be created.

> **WARNING** You may reset the root access key for an Azure Storage account. This will cause Capture to stop saving files to any Blob Storage in the Storage account. Remember to refresh the connection between the Event Hub and the destination Blob Storage when this happens.

When you choose Data Lake Storage, you must configure access before enabling Capture. You must assign access permissions for `Microsoft.EventHubs` to the folder structure that will store the Capture data. Event Hubs uses this service principal to identify itself to other Azure services. Assign Execute (X) permission to the folder hierarchy, from the root folder to the folder that holds the Capture pattern results. Then add Read (R), Write (W), and Execute (X) permissions to that holding folder and all subfolders by default. (See chapter 4 for details on assigning file and folder permissions in Azure Data Lake Storage.)

The following Azure PowerShell script creates a new Zones Staging folder for collecting statistics and sets the necessary permissions for Event Hubs. The script will prompt to overwrite the folder if present. You learned about the zones framework in chapter 4. The final step applies the permissions over any existing folders and files. Run this script in Azure Cloud Shell https://shell.azure.com/ for the most consistent PowerShell experience.

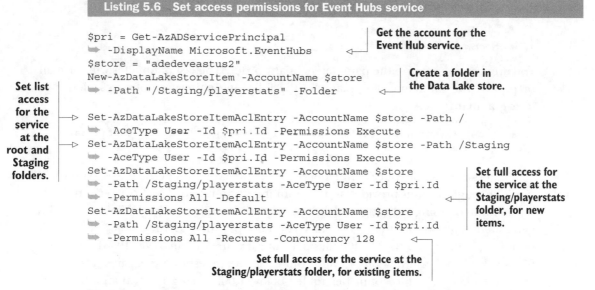

Listing 5.6   Set access permissions for Event Hubs service

```
$pri = Get-AzADServicePrincipal          ← Get the account for the
    -DisplayName Microsoft.EventHubs          Event Hub service.
$store = "adedeveastus2"
New-AzDataLakeStoreItem -AccountName $store    ← Create a folder in
    -Path "/Staging/playerstats" -Folder          the Data Lake store.

Set-AzDataLakeStoreItemAclEntry -AccountName $store -Path /
    AceType User -Id $pri.Id -Permissions Execute
Set-AzDataLakeStoreItemAclEntry -AccountName $store -Path /Staging
    -AceType User -Id $pri.Id -Permissions Execute
Set-AzDataLakeStoreItemAclEntry -AccountName $store
    -Path /Staging/playerstats -AceType User -Id $pri.Id
    -Permissions All -Default          ← Set full access for
Set-AzDataLakeStoreItemAclEntry -AccountName $store          the service at the
    -Path /Staging/playerstats -AceType User -Id $pri.Id          Staging/playerstats
    -Permissions All -Recurse -Concurrency 128          folder, for new items.
```

Set list access for the service at the root and Staging folders.

Set full access for the service at the Staging/playerstats folder, for existing items.

The `-Recurse` and `-Concurrency` parameters are used to apply permissions to existing child folders and files. The recursion does not apply to permissions using the `-Default` parameter, which sets permissions on new folders and new files in the current folder.

5.6.3   *Enabling Capture*

You can use the Azure portal to enable Capture on an Event Hub, either at creation or at a later time. You'll need to choose values for four options:

- Time window
- Size window
- Blob Storage or Data Lake Storage for a storage provider
- Filename and file path for the files

Here's how to enable Capture:

1   In the Azure portal, use the All Services menu and filter on Event Hubs to show the Event Hubs blade.

2   Select the Event Hubs namespace that routes messages for the Event Hub to view the Overview blade.

3   On the left, under Entities, click Event Hubs to open the Event Hubs blade for the namespace.

4   Select the Event Hub you want to enable Capture for ("biometricstats") to open its blade. Figure 5.5 shows the Capture configuration blade.

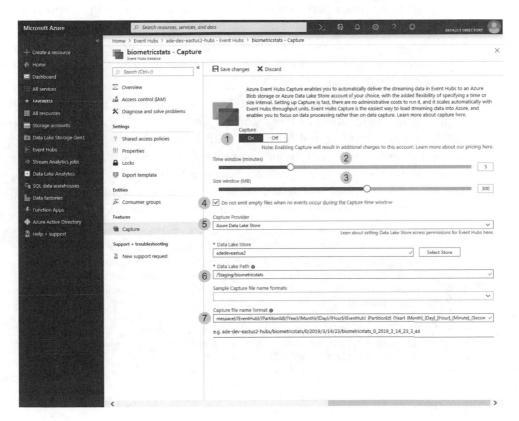

1   Toggle On to reveal options.

2   Maximum time window between saving files is between 1 minute and 15 minutes.

3   Maximum size window is between 10 MB and 500 MB.

4   Check to prevent creation of empty files after the maximum time window has passed.

5   Select Azure Storage or Azure Data Lake Store.

6   Path begins with / and does not need final /.

7   This is a free-text field, but you must use all available parameters at least once.

Figure 5.5   Creating a new Event Hub with Azure portal

5   On the left, under Features, click Capture to show the Capture blade.

6   Select On if Capture is set to Off.

7   Select a Time Window of 5 minutes.

8   Select a Size Window of 300 MB.

9   Enable the option Do Not Emit Empty Files. Leave this disabled if you want a consistent number of files using time window segmentation.

10 Select Azure Data Lake Store as the Capture provider.

11 Enter the name of your Data Lake ("[XYZ]deveastus2") in the Data Lake Store field.

12 Enter the folder path you used to set up folder security in the previous section (listing 5.6).

13 Select a naming convention from the Sample Capture File Name Formats field, or provide your own in the Capture File Name Format field. See section 5.6.1 for more details.

The PowerShell script in listing 5.7 enables Capture using the maximum time and size values, with a destination of Blob Storage. The `Get-AzEventHub` command retrieves the Event Hub object to enable Capture. `Get-AzStorageAccount` retrieves the Storage account to use. `New-Object` creates a property object for setting all the Capture configuration values. Finally, `Set-AzEventHub` saves the changes to the Event Hub object. The script uses the folder pattern described in section 5.6.1 and uses Blob Storage for the provider. Run this script in PowerShell with Azure PowerShell module enabled.

Listing 5.7   Enable Capture using PowerShell

```
$eh = Get-AzEventHub -ResourceGroupName ade-dev-eastus2
    -NamespaceName ade-dev-eastus2-hubs -Name biometricstats
$storageId = (Get-AzStorageAccount -ResourceGroupName ade-dev-eastus2
    -Name adedeveastus2).Id
$eh.CaptureDescription = New-Object
    -TypeName Microsoft.Azure.Commands.EventHub.Models
    .PSCaptureDescriptionAttributes
$eh.CaptureDescription.Enabled = $true
$eh.CaptureDescription.IntervalInSeconds  = 900
$eh.CaptureDescription.Encoding  = "Avro"
$eh.CaptureDescription.SizeLimitInBytes = 524288000
$eh.CaptureDescription.Destination.Name =
    "EventHubArchive.AzureBlockBlob"
$eh.CaptureDescription.Destination.BlobContainer = "players"
$eh.CaptureDescription.Destination.ArchiveNameFormat =
"{Namespace}/{EventHub}/{PartitionId}/{Year}/{Month}/{Day}/{Hour}
/{EventHub}_{PartitionId}_{Year}_{Month}_{Day}_{Hour}_{Minute}_{Second}"
$eh.CaptureDescription.Destination
    .StorageAccountResourceId = $storageId
Set-AzEventHub -ResourceGroupName ade-dev-eastus2
    -NamespaceName ade-dev-eastus2-hubs -Name biometricstats
    -InputObject $eh
```

Annotations:
- **Time window in seconds, for a 15 minute window.** → `$eh.CaptureDescription.IntervalInSeconds  = 900`
- **Avro format** → `$eh.CaptureDescription.Encoding  = "Avro"`
- **Specify the file name format as a text string.** → `$eh.CaptureDescription.Destination.ArchiveNameFormat =`
- **This line instantiates a new Capture settings object.** → `$eh.CaptureDescription = New-Object ...`
- **Size window in bytes, for a 500 MB window.** → `$eh.CaptureDescription.SizeLimitInBytes = 524288000`
- **Using Blob Storage for storage provider** → `"EventHubArchive.AzureBlockBlob"`
- **ID of the Azure Storage account** → `.StorageAccountResourceId = $storageId`
- **Update the Event Hub, passing in the Capture settings object. Available outside of Canada.** → `-InputObject $eh`

There are two options for encoding: Avro and AvroDeflate. AvroDeflate uses zlib compression to reduce file size. AvroDeflate is not available via the Azure portal. To use Data Lake Storage, you must use the Azure portal.

> **TIP** Apache Avro is a file format for storing data with detailed schema. Because it stores data as binary blocks, you can't use a text editor to view the files: you need software to decode and edit them. Microsoft lists several options at http://mng.bz/nP4e. Chapter 8 covers using Data Lake Analytics with other services, including files generated by Event Hubs Capture.

5.6.4 The importance of time

The usefulness of timestamps on events cannot be overstated. Timestamps (and other granular date and time values) let you determine if two events occurred simultaneously or sequentially. File names, like those generated by Event Hub Capture, frequently use date and time elements. Aggregations by hour, day, and month are common. Real-time processing of event data uses a *time window function* to group events. A time window function groups events based on their relations to each other in time. They could be events occurring within 5 seconds of any other event, within a 5 minute block, within a 60 minute timeout. Queue messages can be processed out of order, but streams of messages are always read in order. Events that were delayed and arrived late need to be slotted into the stream at the correct time. You'll read more about time windows and ordering in the next chapter on Stream Analytics. For now, remember that Event Hubs adds an enqueued timestamp to every message written to the log, in addition to any event timestamps in the message data.

5.7 Securing access to Event Hubs

Security for Event Hubs covers many of the same tactics as for on-premises installations, including controlling access to hardware, the execution and behavior of applications, and who can manage the systems. These practices can be put into place for Azure resources too. Microsoft takes care of many of them as part of their cloud hosting platform. This includes physical security at Azure datacenters, patching and network security for the services that run Azure resources, and audit logging and monitoring of operations. Other practices, like using less-privileged accounts or limiting network access to systems, are left to the end user.

You can use two avenues to add security to Event Hubs.

- You can restrict the network where Event Hubs runs and what networks can connect to the Event Hubs namespace.
- You can restrict the available actions for connected clients.

Both options are configured at the Event Hubs namespace level. Azure services are already secured and monitored. However, most Azure services are created and run in a public cloud infrastructure. This means your new Event Hub and namespace can receive malicious requests designed to gain access to data or the system. To add another layer of security, you can restrict connections to your namespace with Virtual Networks and IP address filters. New Event Hubs namespaces restrict access to selected networks only. There are no networks at creation time, so you must disable this setting or add your Event Hub namespace to a Virtual Network.

Azure provides a configurable *Virtual Network* (VNet) service to allow administrators to restrict access to resources. VNets restrict network traffic between IP addresses with a gateway and firewall, much like a traditional network. VNets currently support various compute services like App Services and Virtual Machines. Distributed services like Azure Storage, SQL Database, and Event Hubs are also supported, but Stream Analytics does not integrate with VNets. Due to this, we won't discuss securing Event Hubs namespaces with VNets.

You can also secure access to an Event Hub namespace with an *IP firewall*. IP firewalls restrict access to ports at a specific IP address. The firewall is enabled at the Event Hubs namespace. You can allow connections from specific IP addresses and address ranges to the Event Hubs namespace. IP Firewall is only available for Event Hubs namespaces at the Standard level. Note that enabling the IP Firewall interferes with connections from multiple Azure services, including Stream Analytics. Due to this, we won't discuss securing Event Hubs namespaces with IP firewall.

Sending HTTPS or AMQP requests is the first step in interacting with Event Hubs. The next layer of security you may want to implement covers authentication and authorization to the Event Hub, as we'll discuss in the following section.

5.7.1   *Shared Access Signature policies*

To connect to the Event Hub namespace or Event Hub using a client, you must use a URL endpoint and a shared access key. Both are managed through Shared Access Signature (SAS) policies. Each policy includes a primary and secondary key, and a connection string for each key. Each key can be regenerated separately. This allows key rotation and resets without loss of availability.

You can view policies to copy the keys and connection strings for use in your applications. In the Event Hubs namespace, click Shared Access Policies to view any SAS policies. Every namespace comes with a default policy called RootManageSharedAccessKey. This policy is assigned all three options:

- Manage
- Send
- Listen

You can use this policy for all actions on the Event Hub namespace and Event Hubs. A better policy would separate client activities with separate policies. Some systems will write messages and only need a Send policy. Other systems will read messages, or control aspects of the Event Hub or namespace. These systems can be assigned policies appropriate to their activities.

You can create new SAS policies with the Azure portal. All you need is to name the policy and select options. SAS policies can be created at the namespace level, for use in all Event Hubs, or at the Event Hub level for the most granular control.

Use the Add function from the SAS Policies blade in the Azure portal to create a new policy. Provide a name for the policy. The name can only contain numbers, letters, hyphens, periods, and underscores. Select one or more permissions for the policy. Manage allows changing settings in the Event Hub, but does not allow sending or reading messages. Send and Listen allow sending and reading messages, respectively.

Execute the PowerShell script in listing 5.8 to see the keys and connection strings for a policy named "biometricstats-hub-writer".

Listing 5.8 Get Event Hub specific policy

```
Get-AzEventHubKey -ResourceGroupName ade-dev-eastus2      The Event Hub namespace
  -NamespaceName ade-dev-eastus2-hubs                      The Event Hub name
  -EventHubName biometricstats
  -AuthorizationRuleName biometricstats-hub-writer         The policy name
```

Now that you've created your Event Hub and added a SAS policy for access, you're ready to write messages to the Event Hub. Event Hub clients use the components of the Event Hub connection string, including the SAS policy key, to connect securely to the Event Hub. In the following section, you'll use the Event Hub and SAS policy to write messages to your Azure endpoint.

5.7.2 Writing to Event Hubs

To keep the barriers low, I've created this Event Hub process in PowerShell, rather than using C# and an IDE. The following PowerShell scripts (listings 5.9, 5.10, and 5.11) perform four main actions: create a REST API access token using the SAS policy key, create a REST request with headers, create a message in a loop, and submit the REST request.

Run these PowerShell scripts in sequence to submit 60 messages to your Event Hub. The first script creates the API access token.

Listing 5.9 Create a Shared Access Signature to Event Hubs

```
[Reflection.Assembly]::LoadWithPartialName("System.Web")     Instantiate the
  | out-null                                                  System.Web class to use
                                                              HttpUtility methods.

$key = Get-AzEventHubKey -ResourceGroupName ade-dev-eastus2
  -NamespaceName ade-dev-eastus2-hubs                         The Event Hub to
  -EventHubName biometricstats                                submit messages to
  -AuthorizationRuleName biometricstats-hub-writer
$URI="ade-dev-eastus2-hubs.servicebus.windows.net/biometricstats"

$Expires=([DateTimeOffset]                                    Use a short timeout. This limits
  ::Now.ToUnixTimeSeconds())+300                              the usage of a compromised
$SignatureString=[System.Web.HttpUtility]                     authorization token.
```

The SAS policy to use

Convert the policy key to Bytes.

Convert Bytes to a string.

```
    ⮞  ::UrlEncode($URI)+ "`n" + [string]$Expires
    $HMAC = New-Object System.Security.Cryptography.HMACSHA256
    $HMAC.key = [Text.Encoding]
    ⮞  ::ASCII.GetBytes($key.PrimaryKey)
    $Signature = $HMAC.ComputeHash([Text.Encoding]
    ⮞  ::ASCII.GetBytes($SignatureString))
    $Signature = [Convert]::ToBase64String($Signature)
    $SASToken = "SharedAccessSignature sr=" +
    ⮞  [System.Web.HttpUtility]::UrlEncode($URI) +
    ⮞  "&sig=" + [System.Web.HttpUtility]::UrlEncode($Signature) +
    ⮞  "&se=" + $Expires + "&skn=" + $key.KeyName
```

Format the Signature value as endpoint + expiration.

Hash the Signature with the policy key.

Convert the Signature string to a URL-friendly string.

Combine the string elements into the final token.

The token generated in this script expires after five minutes. You can regenerate another or increase the number of seconds. The script encrypts the URL and token timeout values to create the signature.

The format of the URL is specific to the Event Hubs REST API. The host value can be found in the selected SAS policy's `connectionstring` property. The message is converted to JSON for submission to the Event Hub. The body is formatted using the object design from listing 5.1 earlier in the chapter. Run the script in listing 5.10 in the same Azure PowerShell session as listing 5.9. This script creates a new URL for the Event Hub endpoint with a signature, then submits a new message on a new request in a loop.

Listing 5.10   Create a REST API request to Event Hubs

```
$endpoint = "https://ade-dev-eastus2-hubs.servicebus.windows.net/
⮞  biometricstats/messages" + "?timeout=60&api-version=2014-01"

$headers = New-Object
⮞  "System.Collections.Generic.Dictionary[[String],[String]]"
$headers.Add("Authorization", $SASToken)
$headers.Add("Content-Type",
⮞  "application/atom+xml;type=entry;charset=utf-8")
$headers.Add("Host", "ade-dev-eastus2-hubs.servicebus.windows.net")

$eventDate =
⮞  (Get-Date).ToUniversalTime().ToString("o")

for($i = 0; $i -lt 30; $i++)
{

#Construct body using Hashtable
$htbody = @{
    Player="abera101"
    Node=12
    NodeValue=100.2
    EventTime= $eventDate
  }
$body = ConvertTo-Json $htbody
```

The token created in listing 5.9

ISO 8601 datetime format

For loop will run 30 times

For simplicity, reuse the values for each iteration.

Stream Analytics will deserialize JSON.

```
Invoke-WebRequest -Uri $endpoint -Method POST
    -Body $body -Headers $headers
}
```

Submit the message to Event Hub with a POST method.

Message in the body, authorization token in the header

Event Hub clients can submit messages individually or in batches. The next PowerShell script expands on the last script by creating a batch of messages within the loop and sending the whole batch in a single request. The script also adds a parameter to specify the partitionId for the batch of messages. Using this script with Capture enabled, you can see all the messages collect in a single partition output file. Run the script in listing 5.11 in the same Azure PowerShell session as listing 5.9.

Listing 5.11 Create a REST API request to Event Hubs using partitions

```
$endpoint = "https://ade-dev-eastus2-hubs.servicebus.windows.net/
    biometricstats/messages" + "?timeout=60&api-version=2014-01"

$headers = New-Object
    "System.Collections.Generic.Dictionary[[String],[String]]"
$headers.Add("Authorization", $SASToken)
$headers.Add("Content-Type",
    "application/vnd.microsoft.servicebus.json")
$headers.Add("Host", "ade-dev-eastus2-hubs.servicebus.windows.net")

$eventDate =
(Get-Date).ToUniversalTime().ToString("o")
$messages =  New-Object "System.Collections.Generic.List[[String]]"

for($i = 0; $i -lt 30; $i++)
{

#Construct body using Hashtable
$partition = @{PartitionKey="3"}
$htbody = @{
    Id=(New-Guid).Guid
    Player="abera101"
    Node=(Get-Random -Minimum 0 -Maximum 40)
    NodeValue=(Get-Random -Minimum 40 -Maximum 110)
    EventTime= $eventDate
}
$messages.Add((ConvertTo-Json @{
    Body=(ConvertTo-Json $htbody)
    BrokerProperties=$partition
}))
}

Invoke-WebRequest -Uri $endpoint -Method POST
    -Body ("[" + ($messages -join ",") + "]") -Headers $headers
```

The token created in listing 5.9

ISO 8601 datetime format

For loop will run 30 times.

Use partition 3 for these messages.

A unique ID is required for each message in a batch.

Generate new data for each message in the batch.

Event Hubs uses JSON to format the batch body.

Submit the message to Event Hub with a POST method.

JSON array of messages in the body, authorization token in the header

Event Hubs focuses on reading streams of messages. In the next chapter, you'll learn how to take these streams and process them into insights in near real-time.

5.8   Exercises

The following exercises can help you internalize the new features introduced in this chapter. You should be able to create an Event Hub, choose a partition and streaming units count, and configure Capture.

5.8.1   Exercise 1

In order to create an Event Hub with automatic failover, which of the following, if any, are not required?

1 Two Event Hubs
2 Two Event Hub namespaces
3 Two namespace aliases
4 Two throughput units per Event Hub
5 Two consumer groups

SOLUTION

Geo-disaster recovery requires a single alias to use as the message ingestion endpoint. It requires two namespaces, one in each region. Each namespace requires an Event Hub, with matching names and consumer groups. The default consumer group can be used. Each namespace requires at least one throughput unit.

5.8.2   Exercise 2

Given the following rates of ingestion, how many throughput units and partitions are required to ingest 1 KB messages?

1 300 messages/sec
2 3,000 messages/sec
3 30,000 messages/sec

SOLUTION

To find the answer, you need to know the message and data allowance per throughput unit, and compare the message and data rates. The message allowance per throughput unit is 1,000 ingestion events per second, which includes message batches and single messages. The data allowance is 1 MB per second. Calculate the data rate at N messages multiplied by the average message data size.

1 This rate requires one throughput unit to handle 300 messages and 0.3 MB of message data, because the message rate and data rate are below allowances. Two partitions are the minimum per Event Hub.
2 This rate requires three throughput units to handle 3,000 messages and 3.9 MB of message data, because the message rate exceeds the allowance. Three partitions will be required to support three throughput units.

3 This rate is over the maximum allowance for 20 throughput units. This rate also exceeds the data allowance of 20 MB per second. Contact Microsoft to increase the maximum number of throughput units to 30 or more.

A batch of 1,000 1 K messages is under the maximum 1 MB per ingestion event. Thirty message batches per second will require 30 throughput units to meet the 1 MB per second data allowance. This rate would require 30 partitions as well.

One partition is required per throughput unit for maximum ingestion. You can use up to 20 throughput units per Event Hub or up to 40 by contacting support. Using 30 throughput units would require 30 partitions to support 30,000 messages per second.

5.8.3 *Exercise 3*

Given 500 1 KB messages per second entering an Event Hub, what is the largest file size you can generate with Capture? What about 1,000 1 KB messages per second?

SOLUTION

The two measures for the Capture trigger are size and time. 500 MB or 15 minutes are the largest windows.

500 messages × 1 KB × 60 seconds × 15 minutes / 1024 KB/MB = 439 MB

Therefore, a 439 MB file will be generated every 15 minutes.

1000 messages × 1 KB × 60 seconds × 15 minutes / 1024 KB/MB = 879 MB

Therefore, a 500 MB file will be generated every 8.5 minutes.

Summary

- Event Hubs accept messages via a namespace route. You can configure multi-region redundancy by using an alias for a pair of namespaces to mitigate regional outages.
- Event Hubs uses a partitioned log for storing messages. Partition count determines downstream parallelism. Multiple services can read all messages written to the message log, yielding higher processing throughput.
- Access policies define which activities are allowed for connected clients. Using separate keys makes controlling and revoking access easy.

Real-time queries with
Azure Stream Analytics

6

This chapter covers

- Creating a Stream Analytics service
- Configuring inputs and outputs
- Choosing the number of streaming units
- Writing queries using window functions
- Writing queries for parallel processing

In previous chapters you've seen examples of prep work for *batch processing*, loading files into storage, and saving groups of messages into files. Storage accounts, Data Lake, and Event Hubs set the base for building a batch processing analytics system in Azure. In this chapter, you're going to see how these services support *stream processing* too.

Stream processing covers running an operation on individual pieces of data from an endless sequence, or on multiple pieces of data in a time-ordered sequence. These two approaches are called *one-at-a-time* or *real-time* stream processing and *micro-batch* processing.

Figure 6.1 shows two queries processing a stream of data. One query checks every new data item and returns an output for each match. The other query counts how many items were submitted during a repeating time frame. The data

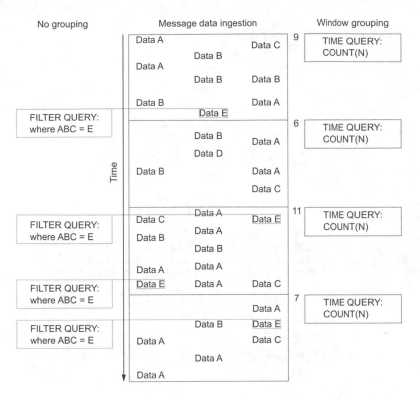

Figure 6.1 Data stream with one-at-a-time and micro-batch queries

is organized by time. Data in files from Azure Storage and messages from ingestion services like Event Hubs can both feed into stream processors. Stream processors generate results in real time rather than on demand. The query is registered once, and results are output repeatedly.[1]

> *This model is called the continuous query model, meaning the query is constantly being evaluated as new data arrives.*

> —Andrew G. Psaltis

In this chapter, you'll learn about a new Azure service, *Stream Analytics*. Azure Stream Analytics (ASA) reads data sources, executes operations over the data, and outputs results to data sinks. Stream processing generates output as input is received and query requirements are fulfilled. ASA performs the processing that drives the Speed Layer of Azure's Lambda architecture (see figure 6.2).

ASA uses Structured Query Language (SQL) to define the data operations. ASA tightly integrates with other Azure services, like Event Hubs, Azure Storage, and SQL

---

[1] Andrew G. Psaltis. *Streaming Data Understanding the Real-Time Pipeline.* Shelter Island, NY: Manning Publications, 2017.

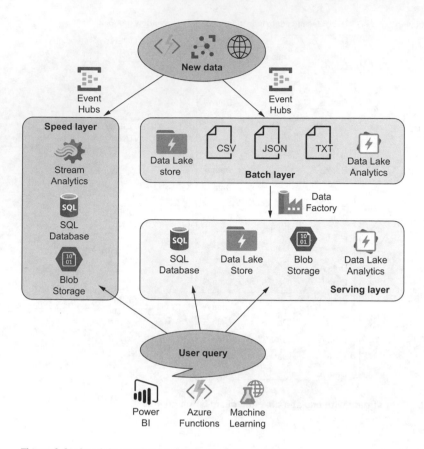

Figure 6.2   Lambda architecture with Azure PaaS services

Database (SQLDB). This means that you can spend your time writing queries to trigger data output, instead of writing code to handle the input and output connections.

To get started, let's create an ASA service and set up an input and output.

TIP   You can find the code listings in the GitHub repository for this book at https://github.com/rnuckolls/azure_storage.

6.1   *Creating a Stream Analytics service*

The Jonestown Sluggers baseball team has put biometric sensors in all players' uniforms and begins collecting data during practice and home games. The data flows into Azure using an Event Hub. You have been asked to save the stream to files in Azure Data Lake Storage (ADLS). How can you fulfill this request?

Using ASA, you can read from Event Hubs and write data to a number of targets, including ADLS. ASA can match the throughput of an Event Hub and automatically recovers from outages and network partitions. Let's look at what makes an ASA service work.

6.1.1 Elements of a Stream Analytics job

ASA instances are referred to as *jobs*. The ASA job consists of four parts:

1 Inputs
2 Transformations
3 Outputs
4 Coordination

Inputs read data into the job. This includes connections to stream sources including Event Hub, IoT Hub, and Blob Storage. Inputs can also be static reference sources, which are used for data enrichment during the transformation processing. These reference sources include Blob Storage and SQLDB.

Transformations transform input data and combine input and reference data. An ASA job contains a single query, which contains one or more transformations in the form of SQL statements. You write transformations using SQL queries.

Outputs connect the transformed data to external sinks, like storage, or queues for further processing or event triggering. Outputs include connections to file stores like Blob Storage, relational stores like SQLDB, message queues like Event Hubs, and even Azure Functions for code-driven data processing. An ASA job can have multiple outputs.

ASA jobs must coordinate data movement between inputs, transformations, and outputs. Because ASA is built on a clustered infrastructure, parallel processing can occur at each of these steps. Creating an ASA job provisions the cluster and sets up a framework to complete the steps in the processing job.

6.1.2 Create an ASA job using the Azure portal

To create an ASA job in the Azure portal, you select a name, region, resource group, and hosting environment. ASA jobs can run in the Azure cloud, but they can also be compiled and deployed to an IoT edge device. Selecting Edge for the Hosting Environment enables this feature. Finally, you'll need to choose the number of streaming units (SUs) to use in your job. An SU is a processing resource node for an ASA job. Each SU allocated to a job increases the throughput and therefore the monthly cost. Here's how to create the job in Azure portal:

1 In the Azure portal, use the All Services menu and filter on Stream Analytics jobs to show the Stream Analytics Jobs blade.
2 Click Add to open the new Stream Analytics Job blade. You can also browse to https://portal.azure.com/#create/Microsoft.StreamAnalyticsJob.
3 Choose a name ("abe-dev-eastus2-asa-biometricstats"). The name must be alphanumeric and hyphens or underscores and be less than 63 characters long.
4 Choose a subscription. The default will be the oldest subscription, if you have access to more than one.
5 Choose a resource group. (See appendix A for instructions if you haven't created one.)

6 Choose a location in the same region as your input sources. The default is East US. ASA jobs are only available in select regions at the time of writing, including in North and South America, Europe, and Asia. You can check the entire list of regions at http://mng.bz/vxj1.

7 Select 1 SU to start. You can increase the number later once you have analyzed the query load and maximum parallelization possible.

8 Click Create to create the job.

6.1.3 *Create an ASA job using Azure PowerShell*

You can also use Azure PowerShell to create an ASA job. Using PowerShell scripts to create resources allows for a repeatable process and consistent configuration across environments. Access Azure PowerShell by visiting Azure Cloud Shell at https://shell .azure.com/, or clicking the >_ header menu in the Azure portal.

Unlike creating most other Azure resources with Azure PowerShell, ASA jobs require a JSON configuration file as part of the process. This file contains general settings for the job. Because the configuration file doesn't include specific details like name and resource group, you can reuse its files for multiple jobs.

The configuration file contains location and properties elements. Choose a location value from the list of available regions for ASA, removing spaces from the name. The sku name element in properties has only one value, Standard.

Aside from the SKU, the properties array element contains settings to control event ordering and error handling. Event ordering is critical for many types of stream processing calculations. Sources for ASA are restricted to those that guarantee order of processing. We'll discuss order of message handling later in the chapter. For now, use the default values for these settings. You can see the format of the ASA job configuration file in the following listing.

Listing 6.1   ASA job configuration file

```
{
  "location":"EastUS2",
  "properties":{
    "sku":{
      "name":"Standard"          ← Standard is the only allowed value.
    },
    "eventsOutOfOrderPolicy":"Adjust",          ← Covers both late and out-of-order windows. Use Adjust or Drop.
    "outputErrorPolicy": "Stop",          ← Use Stop or Drop, like when you put out a fire. Stop = Retry.
    "eventsOutOfOrderMaxDelayInSeconds":0,
    "eventsLateArrivalMaxDelayInSeconds":5,
    "compatibilityLevel": 1.1          ← Choose 1.0, 1.1 (the default), or 1.2.
  }
}
```

NOTE   Compatibility level 1.2 introduces some changes around integration with other services, particularly when reading from sources that allow parallelization. Parallel processing is discussed later in this chapter. You can read more about these changes at http://mng.bz/4A0D.

To use Cloud Shell to create an ASA job, you will need to add the job configuration file to your Cloud Shell storage. There are two ways to do it: use the Cloud Shell upload function or create a new file with the Cloud Shell file editor.

CREATING CLOUD SHELL FILES

To upload the file, first copy the JSON from listing 6.1 into a new JSON file named "streamingjob.json" on your computer. Then log in to Cloud Shell at https://shell .azure.com/. Finally, click the Upload/Download Files button in the Cloud Shell menu and select Upload. This will open a dialog where you can select the new configuration file. The uploaded file will be stored in the Cloud Shell root folder. You can move it to another existing folder using the Move command. The file will now be available for use in PowerShell commands.

The second method involves using the editor in Cloud Shell to create a new configuration file. This method allows you to create a file in the folder of your choice. Follow these steps to create the file.

1 Open and log in to Cloud Shell in a web browser: https://shell.azure.com/.
2 Type `mkdir asa` in the window to create a folder "asa" to store the ASA job files.
3 Type `cd asa` to switch to the new folder.
4 Type `code streamingjob.json` to create a new file inside the folder.
5 Copy the JSON from listing 6.1 into the editor.
6 Press Ctrl+S/Cmd+S to save the file.
7 Press Ctrl+Q/Cmd+Q to quit the editor.

Now that you have a valid ASA job configuration file available, you can run the command to create the ASA job. `New-AzStreamAnalyticsJob` takes three parameters: the name of the job to create, the resource group for the service, and the file path for the job configuration file. Run the command in listing 6.2 using Azure Cloud Shell.

> **Listing 6.2   Create new Azure Stream Analytics job using PowerShell**

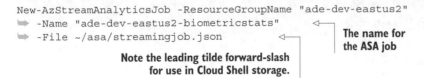

```
New-AzStreamAnalyticsJob -ResourceGroupName "ade-dev-eastus2"
➥ -Name "ade-dev-eastus2-biometricstats"          ◁─── The name for
➥ -File ~/asa/streamingjob.json          ◁──┐              the ASA job
        Note the leading tilde forward-slash
        for use in Cloud Shell storage.
```

When using Azure PowerShell, you don't configure the SUs when you configure the job. Instead you do so when configuring the transformation queries. Because of this, new ASA jobs created with Azure PowerShell use the default value of 3 SUs. If you wish to minimize cost for the ASA job at this point, you should reduce this to 1. You can do this through the Azure portal.

1 In the Azure portal, use the All Services menu and filter on Stream Analytics jobs to show the Stream Analytics Jobs blade.
2 Click the job name you want to manage.

3   Click Configure > Scale from the left navigation blade.

4   Drag the slider to the left, or change the value to 1.

5   Click Save to save the changes.

NOTE   You can also change the number of SUs using Azure PowerShell. You'll learn about creating and managing ASA job queries later in the chapter. That section includes the JSON configuration and PowerShell scripts for setting the ASA job transformations.

Now that you've created your first ASA job, you can configure inputs and outputs, to prepare it for writing transformation queries.

6.2   *Configuring inputs and outputs*

ASA jobs read unbounded data sets, transform the data, and write out the new data set or sets. You define the input sources and output sinks using tightly integrated interfaces to other Azure resources. You can't choose your own third-party or custom sources. You can choose the following *inputs*:

1   Event Hubs

2   IoT Hub

3   Blob Storage

ASA jobs also support a set of non-streaming data called a *reference input*. The reference input is a Storage account Blob file containing data in CSV or JSON format, or an Azure SQLDB query. Reference data is loaded into memory when the ASA job starts running.

You can choose from the following *outputs*:

1   Event Hubs

2   Blob Storage

3   Table Storage

4   Data Lake Storage

5   SQL Database

6   Cosmos DB

7   Azure Functions

8   Power BI

9   Service Bus queues

10   Service Bus topics

Each input and output uses a unique set of options to configure authentication, destination parameters, and batch size. Let's see how this works by configuring the ASA job to set up a *passthrough query*.

6.2.1   *Event Hub job input*

A passthrough query in this context simply takes the input fields and writes them all to the output sink without any processing. Within the ASA job, the passthrough query is made of an input and an output, tied together with SQL in a transformation. Starting with a passthrough query lets you test the inputs and outputs before creating more complicated transforms. Using a passthrough query in an ASA job, with an Event Hub input and ADLS output, gives you more control over schema drift. If you enumerate the fields in your transform, you can prevent new fields from entering long term storage prematurely. You'll add an input to the ASA job next.

CREATE AN EVENT HUB INPUT USING THE AZURE PORTAL

Once you have created your ASA job, you will need to configure inputs and outputs. In the current scenario, you are collecting data from the uniform biometric sensors using an Event Hub. To create an Event Hub input, you need to select the Event Hub and specify the connection and message format details. Here's how to do it in the Azure portal:

1. In the Azure portal, use the All Services menu and filter on Stream Analytics jobs to show the Stream Analytics Jobs blade.
2. Select your ASA job by clicking its name.
3. Click Inputs in the left navigation to open the Inputs blade.
4. Click Add to show the Input selection menu.
5. Select Event Hubs from the list of options. This displays the Event Hubs Connection Configuration blade.
6. Choose a name for the input ("input").
7. Leave the default, Select From Existing Event Hubs.
8. Select the Event Hubs namespace ("ade-dev-eastus2-hubs").
9. Select the Event Hub to read ("biometricstats").
10. Enter the consumer group to identify your stream reader, or leave blank to use the default ("$Default").
11. Choose the format, delimiter, encoding, or compression values to match the Event Hub configuration. The defaults ("JSON") match the biometricstats Event Hub.
12. Click Create to create the input.

Figure 6.3 shows the Azure portal interface for creating the input.

You need to match the settings you used for your Event Hub. This includes the access policy, consumer group, and serialization settings. Although you can use the defaults, a better practice involves creating separate access policies for each application that accesses the Event Hub. This applies to the consumer group as well, if the Event Hub runs at the Standard level and not the Basic level. At the Basic level, your Event Hub only has the $Default consumer group. Using separate consumer groups lets separate ASA

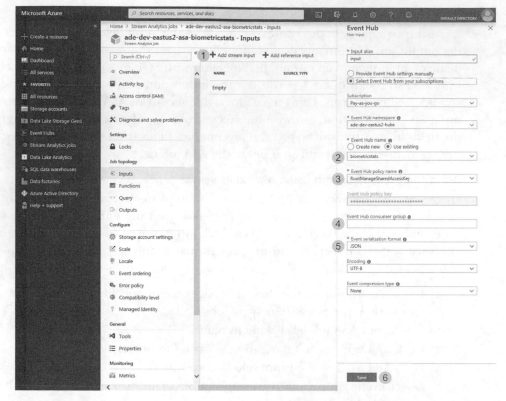

1. **Click Add stream input to show selections for Event Hub, IoT Hub, and Storage account.**

2. **Choose an existing Event Hub, or create one.**

3. **This Shared Access policy is set at the Event Hub Namespace level.**

4. **Specify a previously configured consumer group. Leave blank to use the default $Default.**

5. **Choose JSON or CSV, to match the output of your Event Hub.**

6. **Click Save to create and test the input.**

Figure 6.3   Creating a Stream Analytics Event Hubs input in the Azure Portal

jobs read the same data stream without complications, like one job updating another job's checkpoints.

> **NOTE**   See chapter 5 for more information on Event Hubs security.

CREATING AN EVENT HUB INPUT USING AZURE POWERSHELL

Like creating the ASA job with Azure PowerShell, you must reference a JSON configuration file. This file includes the input name, type, and a list of properties that configure the input source and format. The `type` element has a value of `Stream` or `Reference`. The `datasource` element defines the input's connection type and details. Possible `type` values include `Microsoft.Storage/Blob`, `Microsoft.ServiceBus/Event-Hub`, and `Microsoft.Devices/IotHubs`.

Listing 6.3 shows the configuration file for an Event Hub input. This file includes the same parameters we used for the Azure portal setup.

Listing 6.3   ASA job input configuration file

```
{
    "properties": {
        "type": "Stream",                          Event Hubs under the
        "datasource": {                            Microsoft.ServiceBus namespace
            "type": "Microsoft.ServiceBus/EventHub",   ◄─────
            "properties": {                                      Name of the Event
                "eventHubName": "biometricstats",              Hub to read from
                "serviceBusNamespace": "ade-dev-eastus2-hubs",
                "sharedAccessPolicyName": "RootManageSharedAccessKey",
                "sharedAccessPolicyKey": "==KEY==",    ◄─────
                "consumerGroupName": "$Default"    ◄─────    Replace with your
            }                                                access policy key.
        },
        "compression": {                           The $Default consumer
            "type": "None"                         group works with Basic
        },                                         and Standard level
        "serialization": {                         Event Hubs.
            "type": "Json",       ◄─────   Match the
            "properties": {                serialization of the
                "encoding": "UTF8"         Event Hub message.
            }
        }
    },
    "name": "HubsInputBiometrics",
    "type": "Microsoft.StreamAnalytics/streamingjobs/inputs"
}
```

Annotations in left margin:
- **Name of the Event Hubs namespace** → points to serviceBusNamespace
- **Name of the access policy for connecting to the Event Hub** → points to sharedAccessPolicyName

Follow these steps to save the contents of listing 6.3 to Azure Cloud Shell.

1. Open and log in to Cloud Shell in a web browser at https://shell.azure.com/.
2. Type `cd asa` to switch to the new "asa" folder. Type `mkdir asa` if the folder doesn't exist, then switch to the folder.
3. Type `code HubsInputBiometrics.json` to create a new file in the folder.
4. Copy the JSON from listing 6.3 into the editor.
5. Update the value of `sharedAccessPolicyKey` with the key value from your Event Hub policy.
6. Press Ctrl+S/Cmd+S to save the file.
7. Press Ctrl+Q/Cmd+Q to quit the editor.

Now that you have a valid input configuration file, you can run the Azure PowerShell command to create the input. `New-AzStreamAnalyticsInput` takes the resource group, ASA job name, name of the new input, and the file path for the job configuration file. Run the command in listing 6.4 using Azure Cloud Shell to add the Event Hub input.

Listing 6.4   Create a new Azure Stream Analytics job Event Hub input using PowerShell

```
New-AzStreamAnalyticsInput -ResourceGroupName "ade-dev-eastus2"
    -JobName "ade-dev-eastus2-biometricstats"
    -Name "HubsInputBiometrics"
    -File "~/asa/inputs.json"
```

The name of
the ASA job

The name
for the input

Note the leading tilde forward-slash
for use in Cloud Shell storage.

6.2.2   ASA job outputs

ASA jobs typically use a single input with one or more outputs. Later in the chapter, you'll add a second input for static reference data. The next step in setting up the passthrough query is adding an output.

You can choose from the following *outputs*:

1 Event Hubs
2 Blob Storage
3 Table Storage
4 Data Lake Storage
5 SQL Database
6 Cosmos DB
7 Azure Functions
8 Power BI
9 Service Bus queues
10 Service Bus topics

Event Hubs, Service Bus queues, and Service Bus topics are all queues that allow event-driven processing and queue-based load balancing. Azure Functions provides a serverless queue servicer, using the output from the ASA job as an intermittent event source. Blob Storage and Data Lake Storage are files stores. SQL Database is relational database. Table Storage and Cosmos DB are non-relational indexed table stores. Power BI is Microsoft's data visualization tool. These cloud services let you build advanced data processing and querying systems with ASA jobs. For now, let's start with some foundational services for your analytics system. Let's add a Data Lake Storage output and an Azure SQLDB output.

> **NOTE**   You can read more about creating and securing Blob Storage in chapter 3, and chapter 4 covers Data Lake Storage. Chapter 5 covers queues and ingesting data with Event Hubs.

CREATE AN ADLS OUTPUT USING THE AZURE PORTAL

Creating a passthrough query for your ASA job lets you save raw data for later batch processing. You provide a location for storing the raw data using Blob Storage or Data Lake Storage. Data Lake Storage is designed for large-scale batch processing, so it's a good choice. Here's how to create the Data Lake store output in the Azure portal:

1 In the Azure portal, use the All Services menu and filter on Stream Analytics jobs to show the Stream Analytics Jobs blade.
2 Select your ASA job by clicking its name.
3 Click Job Topology > Outputs in the left navigation to open the Outputs blade.
4 Click Add to show the Output Selection menu.
5 Select Date Lake Storage Gen1 from the list of options. This displays the Data Lake Store Connection Configuration blade.
6 Choose a name for the output ("adloutput").
7 Leave the default, Select Data Lake Storage Gen1 from Your Subscriptions.
8 Select the Data Lake Storage Account Name ("adedeveastus2").
9 Enter the Path Prefix Pattern ("Staging/biometricstats/v1/{date}/{time}"). The bracketed wildcards will generate a dynamic file and folder structure.
10 Change the Date format option to YYYY-MM-DD. Leave the Time format at HH, the default. Together with the Path Prefix Pattern, this will create hourly files within daily folders in the v1 sub-folder.
11 Select CSV for Event Serialization Format. CSV files consume less storage space and are easier to use in batch processing.
12 Leave Encoding at UTF-8, the default.
13 Change Authentication Mode to User Token. Click Authorize to retrieve the user token.
14 Click Save to create the output.

Figure 6.4 shows the Azure Portal interface for creating the Data Lake output.

Because of the available authentication modes, the Azure portal is the only supported interface for creating a Data Lake store output. An authorized user token can only be retrieved using the Azure portal. The ASA job's *managed identity* can only be enabled using the Azure portal.

> **TIP** To connect to the Data Lake store using the ASA job's *managed identity*, you first need to enable this feature in the ASA job, then assign permissions to the appropriate folders in the Data Lake store. In the Azure portal, in your ASA job, click Configure > Managed Identity to open the Managed Identity blade. Check the box to enable authentication with managed identity. Remember to assign the identity (W)rite and E(x)ecute permissions on the folder path. The identity will appear like a normal user, with the name of the ASA job. Refer to chapter 4 for directions on assigning permissions in ADLS and for planning ADLS store folder hierarchies. If you enable the managed identity, you can then create an ADLS output using Azure PowerShell.

PREPARE FOR ADDING SQLDB OUTPUT

Azure SQL Database (SQLDB) provides a convenient endpoint for users familiar with T-SQL. To add a SQLDB as an output for your ASA job, you first need to create it.

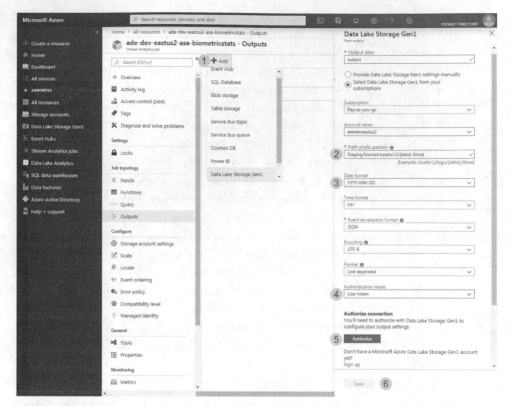

① **Click Add to show selections for Event Hub, SQL Database, and Data Lake Storage Genl.**

② **Skip leading forward slash.**

③ **Selections with forward slashes yield folders, with dashes yield filenames.**

④ **Choose User token to authenticate with your user.**

⑤ **The Authorize button opens a pop-up authentication window and will prompt for credentials if required.**

⑥ **Click Save to create and test the output.**

Figure 6.4   Creating a Stream Analytics Data Lake store output in the Azure portal

Create a SQL Server

Every SQLDB requires an Azure SQL Server as a host. To create one, you'll need to choose a resource group, name, and region, as well as an admin username and password too. You can use the PowerShell command `Get-Credential` to prompt for a secure credential when the script is executed. Run the code in listing 6.5 in Azure Cloud Shell to create the SQL Server.

Listing 6.5   Create new Azure SQL Server

The `Get-Credential` command prompts for a username and password.

```
New-AzSqlServer -ResourceGroupName "ade-dev-eastus2"
    -Location "East US 2"
    -ServerName "ade-dev-eastus2-sql"
    -SqlAdministratorCredentials (Get-Credential)
```

Choose a name for the server, according to your naming convention.

Azure SQL Servers by themselves do not accrue monthly fees. SQL Servers can be moved between resource groups and subscriptions and take any attached SQLDBs along with them. SQLDBs have three methods for billing: managed instance, stand-alone, and elastic pools. *Stand-alone* databases are separately managed and billed. *Elastic pools* group SQLDBs together for shared utilization of resources, much like a traditional SQL Server hosting multiple databases. A *managed instance* is a PaaS version of SQL Server, managing the server and database backups for you. All three types scale resources using a synthetic metric called *DTUs (database transaction units)*, or a bundle of hardware resources called a vCore. By default, new SQLDBs are created as a stand-alone databases at the lowest vCore tier. You can change this by specifying the tier with the Edition parameter. Allowed values are

- Basic
- Standard
- Premium
- DataWarehouse
- Stretch
- GeneralPurpose
- BusinessCritical

Basic, Standard, and Premium are DTU-based tiers. You can read more about provisioning SQLDBs in chapter 11.

A SQL Server without a database has few uses. You need to create a database on your new server as a target for the ASA job output.

Create a SQL Database

You can create a new SQLDB using the Azure portal or Azure PowerShell. The `New-AzSqlDatabase` command creates a new database. Pass the resource group, SQL Server name, and name of the new database. Add the `Edition` parameter to specify the database tier. Run listing 6.6 in Azure Cloud Shell to create a new SQLDB.

> **WARNING** The default tier for SQLDB is the vCore model, with monthly rates starting around $300. You may want to scale your databases to a different tier, or specify a tier during provisioning using the Edition parameter. The lowest pricing, for Standard S0 with 10 DTUs, is $0.0202/hour at the time of writing. You can find current pricing for SQLDB at http://mng.bz/9A11.

Listing 6.6   Create new Azure SQL Database

```
New-AzSqlDatabase -ResourceGroupName "ade-dev-eastus2"      The server name you
   -ServerName "ade-dev-eastus2-sql"                        chose previously
   -DatabaseName "Playerstats"
   -Edition "Basic"        Databases are not tied to a
                           particular server or region,
Set the tier to the lowest-cost tier.   and can have simpler names.
```

You'll learn more about redundancy, including cross-region replication, in chapter 11.

The new SQL Server does not allow outside connections by default. They are blocked by a firewall. This includes the query editor in the Azure portal SQLDB blade, Azure services, and SQL Server Management Studio (SSMS). In order to access the new database, you have to allow access through the firewall.

There are two types of firewall rules: one for Azure resources and one for specific IP addresses. The `New-AzSqlServerFirewallRule` command creates firewall rules on the SQL Server. This command takes the resource group and SQL server name as well as two sets of options. The `AllowAllAzureIPs` parameter creates a dynamic rule that allows Azure resources and applications to connect to the SQL Server. To add specific external IP addresses, provide a firewall rule name using the `FirewallRuleName` parameter. Include `StartIpAddress` and `EndIpAddress` to specify an IP range.

The PowerShell script in listing 6.7 will set the Allow Azure Endpoints rule and create another rule for your on-premises network. This rule will let you connect to the DB from the Azure portal query editor or your local SSMS install. If you execute the SQL statements in the following sections through Azure Cloud Shell, you won't need the on-premises rule. Run the script in listing 6.7 in Azure Cloud Shell to create the firewall rules.

> ### Listing 6.7   Create firewall rule to allow access by Azure resources

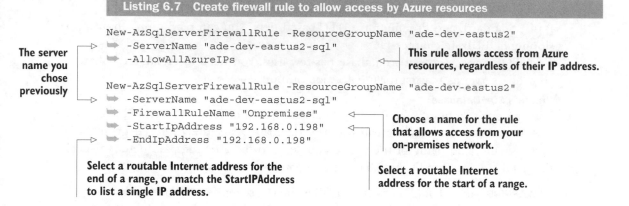

The first rule type allows all traffic from other Azure endpoints on port 1433. The second rule type allows traffic on port 1433 for specific IP addresses and address ranges. You do not have to manage the Azure endpoints rule, but you will need to update the rules if you have changing Internet IP addresses.

With the firewall rules in place, your end users can access the SQLDB. You can provide them a server name and a username and password to connect—even the admin account you used to create the SQL Server. The Azure SQL Server endpoint takes the form `tcp:[SERVERNAME].database.windows.net`. Note the use of `tcp:` preceding the SQL Server name, to force a connection over TCP.

The final step to preparing the SQLDB as an output is creating a table to store the message data. You could do this using the SQLDB Query Editor blade in the Azure portal, connecting with SQL Server Management Studio or Visual Studio, or the SQL Server

PowerShell module. Before you create the table, it's a good idea to define the table schema. This will make integration between the ASA job output and the SQLDB easier.

Biometric data definition

In chapter 5, you defined the data schema for submitting the biometric data to Event Hubs. The schema included the player ID, sensor ID, sensor value, and a timestamp. The data dictionary for the biometric data could look like table 6.1.

Table 6.1   Biometric sensor raw data

Field	Type	Byte size	Description	Source	Service
Player	String	20	abera101	Player ID	Azure Event Hub
Node	Integer	8	1	Biometric nodes ID	Azure Event Hub
NodeValue	Float	8	000.00	Sensor	Azure Event Hub
EventTime	DateTime	8	ISO 8601 00/00/0000T00:00:00	Sensor collection	Azure Event Hub

Listing 6.8 connects to the new SQLDB and runs a query. This script uses the Power-Shell command `Invoke-Sqlcmd` to execute a SQL statement. Pass the full server name with the parameter `ServerInstance`. Specify the `Database` target value. The `Credential` parameter needs a credential object, which is used to authenticate with the SQL Server and database. The `Get-Credential` PowerShell command will prompt you to enter a user and password. Use the `Query` parameter to define a SQL statement to execute.

The query creates a new table based on the data definition from table 6.1. Run the script in listing 6.8 in Azure Cloud Shell.

Listing 6.8   Create SQLDB table

The database name you chose previously

The fully qualified server name you chose previously

```
Invoke-Sqlcmd
    -ServerInstance "tcp:ade-dev-eastus2-sql.database.windows.net"
    -Database "Playerstats"
    -Credential (Get-Credential)
    -Query "CREATE TABLE Biometricstats (Player nvarchar(255), Node int,
    NodeValue decimal(5,2), EventTime datetime);"
```

Use the same credentials you used to configure the server.

Create a table to match the schema of the Event Hub message data.

Even with all of these steps to go through, you can have a fully functional SQL Server database running in a few minutes. You can further improve the setup as you load data and query the table. The SQLDB will be useful later in the chapter, for storing ASA job's complex calculations.

NOTE Event Hubs inputs add extra fields to your schema. These include `EventEnqueuedUtcTime`, `EventProcessedUtcTime`, and `PartitionId`. `Event-EnqueuedUtcTime` is a timestamp indicating when the message was accepted by the Event Hub. `EventProcessedUtcTime` indicates the read time from the queue servicer, in this case an ASA job. `PartitionId` is an integer from 0 to 31, indicating which partition holds the message. See figure 6.12 for more on `EventDate`. These fields can be used in the ASA job query and passed on to outputs. Blob inputs add a `BlobName` field, which takes the full blob path, and `BlobLastModifiedUtcTime`, which is the time the blob was uploaded.

Now that the SQLDB and raw data table have been created, you can create the ASA job endpoint.

CREATE A SQLDB OUTPUT WITH THE AZURE PORTAL

Creating ASA job outputs works much the same way as inputs. You select one of the available Azure resource types, such as SQLDB, and provide the connection and format configuration. You need to provide the SQLDB to connect to and the table to insert into. You'll need to provide a username and password with access to the database and table.

Here's how to create a SQLDB output in the Azure portal:

1 In the Azure portal, use the All Services menu and filter on Stream Analytics jobs to show the Stream Analytics Jobs blade.
2 Select your ASA job by clicking its name.
3 Click Job Topology > Outputs in the left navigation to open the Outputs blade.
4 Click Add to show the Output Selection menu.
5 Select SQL Database from the list of options. This displays the SQL Database Connection Configuration blade.
6 Choose a name for the output ("SqlOutputRaw").
7 Leave the default, Select SQL Database from Your Subscriptions.
8 Select the Database ("Playerstats").
9 Enter the Username for the connection. You can use the SQL Server admin account, or another database user.
10 Enter the Password for the user account.
11 Enter the Table Name ("Biometricstats").
12 Leave the default, Merge All Input Partitions.
13 Reduce Max Batch Count to 100. This should match your ASA job input rate per second. Double the batch size and SQLDB DTU size as the input rate doubles.
14 Click Create to create the output.

Figure 6.5 shows the Azure portal interface for creating the SQLDB output.

> **WARNING** When you create a new Azure SQL Server, you create an admin account. You can use this account for general access to all the databases on the server, but creating separate users for different applications is a better practice. You can use role-based access controls in Azure SQL Database. When you create any tables for stream data, take the opportunity to create a user, group, or role for the streaming service.

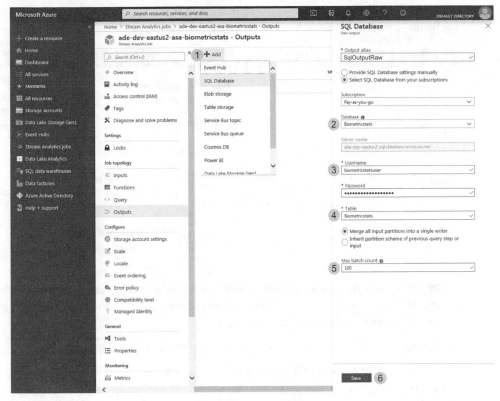

① Click Add to show selections for Event Hub, SQL Database, and Data Lake Storage Gen1.

② Choose an existing database.

③ Use a dedicated user and password for connecting to your SQL Database.

④ Enter the table name from the Database selected. This table must be created before creating the job output.

⑤ Start with a smaller batch count and increase as event volume increases.

⑥ Click Save to create and test the output.

Figure 6.5   Creating a Stream Analytics SQLDB output in the Azure portal

CREATING SQLDB OUTPUT WITH AZURE POWERSHELL

Like creating an ASA job with Azure PowerShell, you must reference a JSON configuration file. The configuration file includes the type and a list of properties. These properties configure the output source and format. The `datasource` element defines the connection type and input details. The `type` values of the datasource include `Microsoft.Storage/Blob`, `Microsoft.Sql/Server/Database`, and many others. For a SQLDB output, you provide the server, database, table, and username and password.

> **TIP** You can see the values for the various definitions of Stream Analytics outputs at http://mng.bz/QyAR.

Listing 6.9 shows the configuration file for an SQLDB output. The configuration file includes the same parameters as the Azure Portal setup.

Listing 6.9   ASA job SQLDB output configuration file

```
{
"properties":{                          Type value corresponds
    "datasource":{                         to output type.
        "type":"Microsoft.Sql/Server/Database",
        "properties":{                                          Fully qualified
            "server":"tcp:ade-dev-eastus2-sql.database.windows.net",   server name
            "database":"Biometricstats",
            "table":"Biometricstats",
            "user":"user@sampleserver",          Replace with your SQL
            "password":"****************"          Admin user, or other user
            }                                     you have created.
        }
    }                                    Replace with the relevant
}                                        user's password.
```

Name of the target database → "database":"Biometricstats",

Name of the target table → "table":"Biometricstats",

> **TIP**   Use T-SQL commands to create a new login and database user for the ASA job. You can restrict this user to write permissions, like using the db_datawriter role, if you are only using it with outputs.

Follow these steps to save the contents of listing 6.9 to Azure Cloud Shell.

1 Open and log in to Cloud Shell in a web browser at https://shell.azure.com/.
2 Type `cd asa` to switch to the new "asa" folder. Type `mkdir asa` if the folder doesn't exist, then switch to the folder.
3 Type `code SqlOutputRaw.json` to create a new file in the new folder.
4 Copy the JSON from listing 6.9 into the editor.
5 Press Ctrl+S/Cmd+S to save the file.
6 Press Ctrl+Q/Cmd+Q to quit the editor.

Now that you have a valid ASA job input configuration file, you can run the Azure PowerShell command to create the output. `AzStreamAnalyticsOutput` takes several parameters, including the resource group and ASA job to target. You assign a name to this output using the `Name` parameter. Since you exited the Cloud Shell editor still in the asa folder, you can address the configuration file with a short path. Run the command in listing 6.10 using Azure Cloud Shell.

Listing 6.10   Create new Azure Stream Analytics job SQLDB output using PowerShell

```
New-AzStreamAnalyticsOutput -ResourceGroupName "ade-dev-eastus2"
⇨ -JobName "ade-dev-eastus2-biometricstats"
⇨ -Name "SqlOutputRaw"                                    The name of
⇨ -File "~/asa/SqlOutputRaw.json"                          the ASA job
```

The name for the output

Note the leading tilde forward-slash for use in Cloud Shell storage.

ASA jobs require three things to start running: an input, an output, and a transformation. You have added an input for Event Hubs and outputs for SQLDB and Data Lake Storage. Now that you have defined inputs and outputs, you can create a query to tie them together.

6.3 Creating a job query

By default, new ASA jobs include a query with a single *transformation*. Each transformation is a SQL statement that reads from one or more inputs and writes to an output. Each step of an ASA job query is a transformation, and each job query can have one or more steps. The default query includes a working transform, with a value SELECT * INTO [YourOutputAlias] FROM [YourInputAlias]. You can view and edit the transforms in the Azure portal.

1 In the Azure portal, use the All Services menu and filter on Stream Analytics jobs to show the Stream Analytics Jobs blade.
2 Select your ASA job by clicking its name.
3 Click Job Topology > Query on the left navigation to display the Query blade.

The default query of a new ASA job includes a passthrough transform using YourInputAlias as input and YourOutputAlias as output. To use the Event Hub input and SQLDB output you setup earlier, you need to update the default query. You also need to replace the wildcard field selector with a specific field list. You can update the transforms using the Azure portal.

1 In the Azure portal, use the All Services menu and filter on Stream Analytics jobs to show the Stream Analytics Jobs blade.
2 Select your ASA job by clicking its name.
3 Click Job Topology > Query in the left navigation to open the Query blade.
4 Paste the query text from listing 6.11 into the Query window.

Listing 6.11 ASA job passthrough query transform

```
SELECT Id, NodeValue, Player, Node, EventTime, PartitionId,
EventProcessedUtcTime, EventEnqueuedUtcTime
INTO SqlOutputRaw
FROM HubsInputBiometrics;
```

To the left of the query window you'll see a list of available inputs and outputs, including any aliases you define in the Query window. Reviewing this list can help you catch misspellings in your transforms.

You can also update the query transforms using Azure PowerShell. Like creating an ASA job with Azure PowerShell, you must reference a JSON configuration file. Listing 6.12 shows the configuration file for a single transform. The file specifies the SUs value.

Listing 6.12   ASA job transformation configuration file

```
{
    "properties":{
        "streamingUnits":1,          ◁  Set the number of SUs here, instead
        "query":"SELECT                 of during the ASA job creation.
⇒          Id,
⇒          NodeValue,
⇒          Player,
⇒          Node,                     New fields
⇒          EventTime,                added by the
⇒          PartitionId,              Event Hub input
⇒          EventProcessedUtcTime,
⇒          EventEnqueuedUtcTime      INTO clause
⇒          INTO SqlOutputRaw      ◁  precedes FROM.
⇒          FROM HubsInputBiometrics;"  ◁
    }                                   INTO value matches
}                                       an output, and FROM
                                        matches an input.
```

Follow these steps to save the contents of listing 6.12 to Azure Cloud Shell.

1   Open and log in to Cloud Shell in a web browser at https://shell.azure.com/.
2   Type cd asa to switch to the new "asa" folder. Type mkdir asa if the folder doesn't exist, then switch to the folder.
3   Type code transform.json to create a new file in the new folder.
4   Copy the JSON from listing 6.12 into the editor.
5   Press Ctrl+S/Cmd+S to save the file.
6   Press Ctrl+Q/Cmd+Q to quit the editor.

Now that you have a valid ASA job transform configuration file, you can run the command to update the ASA job query. The PowerShell command New-AzStreamAnalyticsTransformation takes four main parameters: the resource group, the name of the ASA job to target, a path to the transform configuration file, and a name for the transform. Although the name is not displayed anywhere in the Azure portal, you must provide one when querying transforms using Azure PowerShell. Because a new ASA job creates a default query with a transform, PowerShell will prompt for confirmation before overwriting with the new transform. You can include the -Force parameter to override this. Run the command in listing 6.13 using Azure Cloud Shell to update the transform.

Listing 6.13   Update ASA job transformation using PowerShell

```
New-AzStreamAnalyticsTransformation -ResourceGroupName "ade-dev-eastus2"
⇒      -JobName "ade-dev-eastus2-asa-biometricstats"
⇒      -Name "Transformation"                    ◁
⇒      -File "~/asa/transform.json"           ◁
⇒      -Force                               ◁
```

The name of the ASA job → (-JobName line)

-Force option overwrites transformation without prompting.

Note the leading tilde forward-slash for use in Cloud Shell storage.

The name of the existing transformation

The query transforms do the main work of the ASA job. Once you have set up the inputs, outputs, and transformations, you can start the job.

6.3.1 *Starting the ASA job*

You have three options for specifying the starting message time for your ASA job. Different options allow you to replay the message stream in part or in whole.

- You can start at the current time.
  - Messages received after this time will be read into the ASA job.
- You can start at the last ASA job output time.
  - Messages received since that job output time will be read.
- You can start at a specific time in the past.
  - Messages received since the start time will be read.

Choose a start time based on the previous state of the processed data. Starting the ASA job at the current time works when you don't have any earlier data, or you don't want to process the older data. Starting the ASA job at the last output time allows a stopped job to pick up processing without apparent interruption to the stream. Stopping and starting the job in this manner appears as a large increase in latency in processing messages that arrived during the job stoppage. The most common reason to use this start time is because you need to update the ASA job.

The ASA job must be stopped in order to make changes to the inputs, outputs, and transforms. Once the changes are made, the ASA job can resume processing where it stopped, from a time in the past, or from the current moment. Starting the ASA job at a time in the past lets you replay the stream through the transforms in part or in full. When using Event Hubs as the input, you can replay the message stream from the earliest timestamp remaining in the log. When using Blob Storage, the job will read files with a file modified date after the job start date. Refer to section 6.5.2 for more details on message timestamps.

> **NOTE** Refer to chapter 5 for more information on Event Hubs logging.

You can start your ASA job using the Azure portal.

1. In the Azure portal, in your ASA job Overview blade, click the Start button to open the Start Job blade.
2. Select Now to start the job now, select When Last Stopped to pick up from the previous stopping point, or select Custom to select a point in time.
3. Click Start to start the job.

You can also start the ASA job using Azure PowerShell using the `Start-AzStreamAnalyticsJob` command. For this command, you need to provide the resource group, name of the ASA job, start mode, and, if using a custom start time, a timestamp. The `OutputStartMode` parameter accepts `JobStartTime`, `LastOutputEventTime`, or `CustomTime`. Run the script in listing 6.14 to start the job with a custom time.

Listing 6.14   Start an ASA job using PowerShell

```
Start-AzStreamAnalyticsJob -ResourceGroupName "ade-dev-eastus2"         The name of
    -Name "ade-dev-eastus2-asa-biometricstats"              <──────────  the ASA job
    -OutputStartMode "CustomTime"                  <──┐
    -OutputStartTime "2019-06-01T00:00Z"      <──┐      Select a custom
                                                 │      start time.
              Set the start time in the past.    │
```

The first time you start your ASA job with Azure PowerShell, you must select either
`JobStartTime` or `CustomTime` for the `OutputStartMode` parameter. You can't use
`LastOutputEventTime` for the first start. Wait until the ASA job has successfully started
at least once before using this option.

6.3.2   *Failure to start*

Your ASA job might not start. You may have problems with an input. For example, you
may have created an input with an incorrect endpoint name or address. Or you may
have an output with the same situation. In both cases, use the Azure portal to check
the Activity Log.

   You can show the Activity Log blade in the Azure portal by clicking Activity Log on
the left, when viewing your ASA job. Job start failures will be listed under Operation
Name, with an event severity of Error. You can also retrieve the Activity Log for a given
resource using Azure PowerShell. Listing 6.15 shows a script which returns status
messages for a set number of failed events. The script retrieves the `ResourceId` of a
specified resource, like an ASA job, using the `Get-AzResource` command and
resource name. It then calls `Get-AzLog` to retrieve log records with status Failed.
Run listing 6.15 in Cloud Shell to get any failed event log messages for the resource
ade-dev-eastus2-asa-biometricstats.

Listing 6.15   Reading failure messages in an ASA job using PowerShell

```
                                              The name of the ASA job
ResourceId    (Get-AzLog -ResourceId (
of the ASA        Get-AzResource -Name "ade-dev-eastus2-asa-biometricstats"   <──┘
job      └──>   ).ResourceId
                -Status "Failed" -MaxRecord 5      <──┐  Limit to most recent
              ).Properties         <──┐                 5 failed activities.
                                      │
          Show the properties, which
    contains the status messages.
```

Once you have corrected any problems with your inputs, outputs, or transformations,
you can start your ASA job. This is a good time to submit some events to your Event
Hub. Stream data will begin flowing through the inputs to the transforms to the outputs. If all parts are configured properly, events submitted at the Event Hub will be
read by your ASA job and written out to the SQLDB and the Data Lake store folder. If
there is a problem with an input or output, an alert icon will display in the ASA job
Overview blade.

6.3.3 *Output exceptions*

Once your ASA job starts and data has been submitted, your job may experience errors. The causes of errors are many and varied, ranging from disabled AAD accounts and security access changes, to schema changes in database tables, to service outages. One of your jobs as a data engineer will be to monitor your ASA jobs for errors.

An alert icon displays in the Azure portal's ASA job Overview blade whenever there is an error reading or writing to the inputs or outputs. You can view the status by clicking the icon. You can also view any status messages for a specific input or output. Open the Inputs or Outputs blade by clicking Job Topology > Inputs or Outputs on the left. Then click the specific input or output displaying the icon, to view any status messages.

ASA jobs come with a retry policy for output data errors. Retrying failed output batches is enabled by default. In some scenarios, you may value reduced latency over consistency. When you maintain a second path for collecting the raw data, the streaming data may only be valuable for near real-time calculations. In this case, your users can rely on the batch processing to provide consistency. You can disable the output retry policy using the Azure portal.

1 In the Azure portal, use the All Services menu and filter on Stream Analytics jobs to show the Stream Analytics Jobs blade.
2 Select your ASA job by clicking its name.
3 Click Configure > Error Policy on the left to show the Error Policy blade.
4 Set the Action to Drop to disable the retry policy.

Even with experience, starting an ASA job without errors is one of the most challenging parts of using ASA. By creating a passthrough query from your input to a file-based output, like Data Lake Storage or Blob Storage, you can more easily verify the fields and data provided by the input. Together with a wildcard SQL statement, like `SELECT * FROM`, you can output to fields and values without restrictions on matching data schemas. In the next section, you'll learn to write more complex transforms. Starting with a file-based output can make writing your own transforms easier.

6.4 *Writing job queries*

The Jonestown Sluggers baseball team is collecting biometric data from sensors in players' uniforms. The manager would like to get a real-time estimate of the pitcher's fatigue. Rather than an output of the last pitch thrown, the manager wants to compare the last pitch's power with the average of the most recent pitches. The development team wants you to save the calculations to a SQL Server database. How can you fulfill this request?

The ASA job query provides the logic powering the work. Inputs deliver raw data to the query transforms, and outputs deliver transformed data to consumers. The logic can be simple, as you saw in the passthrough query from the previous section. Or it can be as complicated as batch transformation, leveraging external code bases and batch windows of varying durations and periods. In the following sections, you'll build queries using built-in aggregations and functions, and enhance the raw data with static sources and functions developed by Microsoft. You'll start by using window functions to slice the data stream into micro-batches, to highlight the strengths of this approach. These queries, and the ASA jobs running them, support the Lambda architecture Speed layer by providing low latency processing and query access to the raw data. Let's start by looking at the feature that makes stream processing special: the *time window*.

6.4.1   Window functions

Streaming data enters the ASA job as a single message, followed by another, then another, with no fixed end. Thus, the ASA job query initially only sees a set of one. Time windows allow the ASA job to keep track of other data in the stream. You can think of the data entering the ASA job as fish in a river. A fisherman can cast a net across the river and catch all the fish, one at a time, or the net can let some fish pass. Using a time window is like leaving the net across the river for a while and then looking at all the fish that were caught. Let's see how time windows can be used to pull comparisons from past data.

WRITING WINDOW QUERIES

To use a time window in the query transforms, you need to define the shape of the time window and its relationship to the data. Time windows have a start time and a duration, and can begin and repeat on a set cycle, or start on receipt of a new message. Some types of time windows can overlap, whereas others run sequentially with each message in only one window. How do you decide which to use?

USING BIOMETRICSTATS EVENT HUB DATA

To create the ASA job transform, you'll want to define the data you want to collect, the calculations to be done, and any time windows which must be used to collect the data. In this scenario, you should return the pitcher ID, the value relating to the last pitch, and the average of the last several pitches. You need to filter the data for only the pitcher, and limit the metrics to fastball pitches. Let's assume the pitcher is Player abera101, node 12 is a sensor on his right arm, and values for node 12 greater than 80 indicate a fastball was thrown. Using the schema for the biometric data you used in table 6.1, a data row for the pitches could look like the following listing.

Listing 6.16   Player statistics

```
{
  "Player":"abera101",          ⟵— Player identifier
  "Node":12,
  "NodeValue":100.2,                              ISO 8601
  "EventTime":"2020-04-05T13:15:1947365Z"   ⟵—  datetime format
}
```

You saw this schema describing biometric sensor data in chapter 5. You also used PowerShell to submit messages to an Event Hub, which were then saved using Event Hub Capture. If you still have the Event Hub, you can begin the ASA job and replay those events, which will then flow through to your ASA job. This will provide data for use in the following queries. You can return to chapter 5 and run the PowerShell scripts to generate new messages.

Going by Major League Baseball stats, on average a pitcher throws 15 pitches during a 20 minute inning. About half the pitches thrown are fastballs.[2] When selecting a time window, keep in mind that results are only output at the end of the window. Waiting an entire inning doesn't seem very useful for getting immediate feedback. Reducing the window to 2.5 minutes, or 150 seconds, would track approximately four pitches by one pitcher. Let's look at how time windows can be used to calculate the data in these 150-second windows.

TIME WINDOW TYPES

Time windows in ASA transforms have a start time and a duration, and contain event messages.

Table 6.2 Time windows

Type	Start	Duration	Events Description
Tumbling	After previous window	Fixed	Events contained in only one window
Hopping	After fixed time	Fixed	Events can be contained in multiple windows.
Sliding	With each new event	Fixed	Always contains at least one event.
Session	With first event after period of no events	Variable; less than a maximum duration + two periods without events	Events contained in only one window; always contains at least one event.

Tumbling windows

Figure 6.6 describes the first type of time window, the *tumbling window*. As time passes from left to right, messages are submitted to the ASA job. Each transform that uses a time window collects the message data from that window.

The first tumbling window starts at the ASA job start time, and when its duration elapses, a new window starts. When data arrives at the ASA input, at regular or irregular intervals, it goes into the current window. Each message falls in only one window. The SQL calculation using a window includes only the messages in that window.

First, look at calculating the 150 second average. Using a tumbling time window, you define the duration of the window as 150 seconds. You first list the fields you need, including Player, Node, and the AVG() aggregate function on the Value field, with a SELECT clause. Next, use the HubsInputBiometrics input from our Event Hub to define the transform source table. Setting the TIMESTAMP BY parameter on the FROM clause to `EventTime` puts the data in order. Next, list the data restrictions using a WHERE clause. Finally, roll up the fields using a GROUP BY clause, including the `TumblingWindow()` function. This function takes two parameters: time units and

---

[2] John Walsh. "Fastball, slider, change-up, curveball—an analysis." *The Hardball Times.* https://tht.fangraphs .com/fastball-slider-changeup-curveball-an-analysis/.

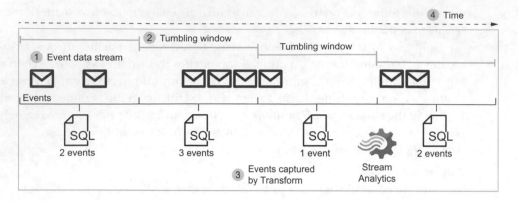

Figure 6.6   Relating tumbling time windows to data stream

duration. Pass second for the units and 150 for the duration. You should end up with a SQL statement like the following listing.

Listing 6.17   Implementing the pitcher fastball transform with tumbling window

```
SELECT Player, Node, AVG(NodeValue) AS AvgValue
FROM HubsInputBiometrics TIMESTAMP BY EventTime
WHERE Player = 'abera101' AND Node = 12 AND NodeValue > 80
GROUP BY Player, Node, TumblingWindow(second, 150)
```

In order to deliver the data as designed, you need to return the current value as well as calculate the average over the past 150 seconds. To do so, you can join two tables. For ASA job transforms, the inputs are the available tables. You can also construct *Common Table Expressions* (CTEs) for the transform steps in the ASA job query. Each CTE can be run in parallel with the SELECT statement.

Because the data you want is all in one input (HubsInputBiometrics), you can use that input joined to a CTE to do the aggregation. Wrap the average pitch speed calculation in a CTE and join it with another SQL statement that retrieves the current pitch. First we take our SQL from listing 6.17 and give it an alias. Next, first list the fields from the input, referring to them by their own alias. Add an OUTPUT clause for an output. Next, define the transform source table using the HubsInputBiometrics input. Put the data in order sorted by EventTime, as with the CTE. Add an alias to the HubsInputBiometrics table. Define an Inner Join to the CTE table, using the Player and Node as match criteria. Joins in ASA jobs require the DATEDIFF function, so add a DATEDIFF criteria with a 150-second duration, to match the tumbling window. Finally, list the data restrictions using a WHERE clause. You should end up with a SQL statement like the following listing.

Listing 6.18   Implementing the pitcher fastball transform with tumbling window

```
WITH PitchAverage AS (
SELECT Player, Node, AVG(NodeValue) AS AvgValue
```

```
FROM HubsInputBiometrics TIMESTAMP BY EventTime
WHERE Player = 'abera101' AND Node = 12 AND NodeValue > 80
GROUP BY Player, Node, TumblingWindow(second, 150)
)
SELECT a.Player, a.NodeValue, b.AvgValue
INTO SqlOutputPitcher
FROM HubsInputBiometrics a TIMESTAMP BY EventTime
INNER JOIN PitchAverage b
ON a.Player = b.Player
AND a.Node = b.Node
AND DATEDIFF(second, a, b) BETWEEN 0 AND 150
WHERE a.NodeValue > 80
```

With this transform, you get your first output after 150 seconds have elapsed from the job start time. After that, all event messages that match the pitcher and fastball criteria will emit the transform fields to the output, using the latest 150 second time window. This seems like a good start, but the updates could come sooner after the pitch. With a time window of only a few minutes, there may not be many fastballs thrown in the window. Let's see what the updates look like using more frequent updates but a longer time window.

Hopping windows

Figure 6.7 shows the next type of time window, the *hopping window*. As time passes from left to right, messages are submitted to the ASA job. Each transform that uses a time window collects the message data from that window.

Whereas tumbling window frequency is determined by duration, hopping windows let you set the repeat time independently of the window length. The time hop doesn't need to be a factor of the duration. Hopping windows can occur more frequently than

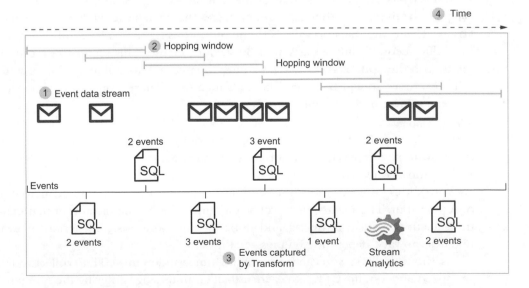

Figure 6.7   Relating hopping time windows to data stream

tumbling windows, when the time hop is less than the duration, or less frequently, when the time hop is greater than the duration. This leads to better sampling from the data stream. Setting the time hop equal to the duration yields a tumbling window.

As with listing 6.18, you can wrap a hopping time window in a CTE to collect your average speed and join the CTE with each fastball event message entering the ASA job. The `HoppingWindow()` function takes three parameters: time units, duration, and hop. Pass `second` for the units, `300` for the duration, and `30` for the hop. Change the `DATEDIFF` to a 300 second duration, to match the hopping window. The `JOIN` and `WHERE` clauses otherwise remain the same. You should end up with a SQL statement like the following listing.

> **Listing 6.19 Implementing the pitcher fastball transform with hopping windows**

```
WITH PitchAverage AS (
SELECT Player, Node, AVG(NodeValue) AS AvgValue
FROM HubsInputBiometrics TIMESTAMP BY EventTime
WHERE Player = 'abera101' AND Node = 12 AND NodeValue > 80
GROUP BY Player, Node, HoppingWindow(second, 300, 30)
)
SELECT a.Player, a.NodeValue, b.AvgValue
INTO SqlOutputPitcher
FROM HubsInputBiometrics a TIMESTAMP BY EventTime
INNER JOIN PitchAverage b
ON a.Player = b.Player
AND a.Node = b.Node
AND DATEDIFF(second, a, b) BETWEEN 0 AND 300
WHERE a.NodeValue > 80
```

With this transform, you can get your first output after 300 seconds have elapsed from the job start time. After that, all event messages that match the pitcher and fastball criteria will emit the transform fields to the output, using the 300-second time window. Each 300 second window starts after 30 seconds elapse. This seems like an improvement, with the updates coming sooner after the pitch. With a time window of multiple minutes, there should be several fastballs included. There's one more time window that can deliver outputs even sooner.

Sliding windows

Figure 6.8 describes the next type of time window, the *sliding window*. As time passes from left to right, messages are submitted to the ASA job. Each transform that uses a time window collects the message data from that window.

With sliding time windows, the window starts when an event message arrives at the ASA job input. This means there will be one time window for each event that matches the selection. Unlike tumbling and hopping time windows, the period of window updates can vary, depending on message times.

As with listing 6.18, you can wrap a sliding time window in a CTE to collect your average speed and join the CTE with each fastball event message entering the ASA job. The `SlidingWindow()` function takes two parameters: time units and duration. Pass `second`

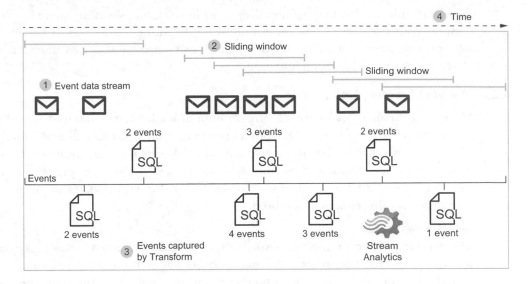

Figure 6.8   Relating sliding time windows to data stream

for the units and `300` for the duration. This covers about 25% of an inning. Set the `DATEDIFF` to 300 seconds, to match the sliding window. The `JOIN` and `WHERE` clauses otherwise remain the same. You should end up with a SQL statement like the following listing.

Listing 6.20   Implementing the pitcher fastball transform with sliding window

```
WITH PitchAverage AS (
SELECT Player, Node, AVG(NodeValue) AS AvgValue
FROM HubsInputBiometrics TIMESTAMP BY EventTime
WHERE Player = 'abera101' AND Node = 12 AND NodeValue > 80
GROUP BY Player, Node, SlidingWindow(second, 300)
)
SELECT a.Player, a.NodeValue, b.AvgValue
INTO SqlOutputPitcher
FROM HubsInputBiometrics a TIMESTAMP BY EventTime
INNER JOIN PitchAverage b
ON a.Player = b.Player
AND a.Node = b.Node
AND DATEDIFF(second, a, b) BETWEEN 0 AND 300
WHERE a.NodeValue > 80
```

With this transform, you get your first output after 300 seconds have elapsed from job start time and at least one matching event has been submitted. With this time window, a window update will be emitted for each fastball that is recorded. The average will be calculated over any fastballs recorded in the previous 300 seconds, even if there is only one.

As you can see, choosing the best time window depends on your use case. Time windows with regular periods, like tumbling and hopping time windows, give consistent results. In this way, the aggregation they provide resembles short, frequent batch processing. Your users may prefer intermittent results with extremely short latency. ASA jobs provide another type of function that does comparisons across time: Anomaly Detection Machine Learning functions.

6.4.2 *Machine learning functions*

Machine Learning (ML) covers a broad range of mathematical disciplines and computer science topics. Luckily, ASA jobs let you take advantage of a well established type of ML analysis without having to learn it all. ASA jobs include Anomaly Detection functions to detect spikes, dips, and anomalous values. They can provide a sliding value of deviation from the data stream. They can also emit updates when the function's return value crosses a threshold.

ANOMALY DETECTION

The Anomaly Detection functions work differently than the time window aggregations you've seen so far. Instead of collecting event messages, these functions analyze message data and return a judgment about each event. They return this judgment as two values: a Boolean integer signifying if the event data is anomalous and a real number score indicating how far from the norm the value lies. A lower score indicates greater deviance. Instead of the end user comparing pitch speeds to determine a drop in output, now the Anomaly Detection functions can do that work.

The Anomaly Detection functions use a continuous training model. Because you are using these functions in an ASA job, they get the benefit of an unending stream of data for training. But the functions need training before they can be effective. This means the underlying ML algorithm can detect deviations from the norm, but it doesn't know what is normal for your data until it processes a large enough set of data. When you configure the function in your ASA job transform, you define the time window so that the ML algorithm gets enough data to determine the norm. Once the first window has passed, the model is trained, and the function can issue judgments on each event message.

USING MACHINE LEARNING ALGORITHMS

To put this into practice, let's update the fastball example to use an Anomaly Detection function. The function is added to an ASA job query transform, like other SQL functions. Two functions are available: `AnomalyDetection_SpikeAndDip()` and `AnomalyDetection_ChangePoint()`. SpikeAndDip detects spikes and dips in values. ChangePoint detects anomalies, but does not classify them. SpikeAndDip takes five regular parameters and two optional parameters. ChangePoint takes the same parameters as SpikeAndDip, but drops the `Mode` parameter. SpikeAndDip is well suited for detecting drops in pitch speed in our example.

To configure the functions, you need to set which field to analyze, how long to gather data (training), and how much data to collect to get a normal range of values. Next you need to set a threshold for the difference judgment. The ML algorithm calculates a value from 0 to 100, indicating how similar the analyzed value is to the norm.

Highly similar values can rate above 95, with little better than chance rating below 50. Tuning the threshold to prevent false alarms is part of the testing process. Provide an identifier field if you want to analyze multiple similar fields at once. In baseball, there is only one pitcher at a time on the mound, but you may want to track the relief pitchers in the bullpen separately. Finally, assign any filter expression to the WHEN clause. It works like a WHERE clause on a SELECT statement. The following listing shows the function call definition outside of a SQL statement.

Listing 6.21   Structure of Anomaly Detection function

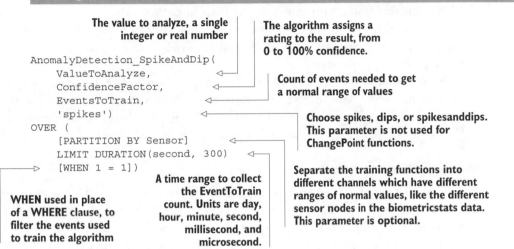

To create the ASA job transform, you still use a CTE to wrap the function, but the CTE makes it easier to retrieve function output. The CTE will return the relevant fields to output and run the Anomaly Detection function. Use a 90% confidence factor and collect 15 pitches. Pass minute for the units and 40 for the duration. You'll want a longer time frame to collect enough event data. This duration covers about two innings. Pitches are collected if Node equals 12 and Value is greater than 80. Limit the transform to emit output when events are flagged as anomalies. You should end up with a SQL statement like the following listing.

Listing 6.22   Implementing the pitcher fastball transform with Machine Learning

```
WITH PitchAnomaly AS (
SELECT Player, Node, CAST(NodeValue AS FLOAT) AS NodeValue,
AnomalyDetection_SpikeAndDip(CAST(NodeValue AS FLOAT), 90, 15, 'dips')
OVER (
PARTITION BY Player
LIMIT DURATION(minute, 40)
WHEN Node = 12 AND NodeValue > 80
)
AS ADValues
FROM HubsInputBiometrics
)
```

```
SELECT Player, NodeValue,
CAST(GetRecordPropertyValue(ADValues, 'Score') as FLOAT) AS Score
INTO SqlOutputPitcher
FROM PitchAnomaly
WHERE CAST(GetRecordPropertyValue(ADValues, 'IsAnomaly') AS BIGINT) = 1;
```

The field returned by the Anomaly Detection functions is a complex object with two properties. Use `GetRecordPropertyValue` to read a particular value. Pass the Anomaly Detection function return value and the property name to `GetRecordPropertyValue` to read the value.

With this transform, you can get your first output after 40 minutes have elapsed from job start time and 15 pitches have been collected. After that, all matching event messages since the start will emit the transform fields to the output, using the latest training group of 15 pitches.

Window functions and Anomaly Detection functions both take advantage of the streaming nature of data in ASA jobs. With them you can capture snapshots of data from an ever-changing set of micro-batches. We'll look at scheduled batches with window functions and Machine Learning algorithms in later chapters.

6.5   *Managing performance*

There are two primary concerns for managing performance of ASA jobs: keeping up with input rates and reducing latency. ASA jobs can scale resources with a simple adjustment, but often you need to adjust the job query to take advantage of the additional resources. Let's take a look at how ASA jobs manage resources.

6.5.1   *Streaming units*

Azure uses *streaming units* (SUs) to control the amount of processing resources available to handle imports, transformations, and outputs. ASA jobs charge based on the number of SUs selected. Starting with a single SU minimizes your hourly cost for Stream Analytics. Not all jobs can utilize more than a single SU.

Stream Analytics uses partitions in the inputs and outputs to divide the stream data. This division allows parallel processing of the input, output, and transformation steps. Each transformation step in the job query must use `PARTITION BY` to take advantage of the partitioning. Processing is then spread across the allocated SUs.

> **NOTE** Compatibility level 1.2 for ASA jobs removes the `PARTITION BY` requirement for matching parallel processing on inputs. See the description of compatibility level earlier in the chapter (section 6.1.3).

The underlying cluster nodes for an ASA job support up to six SUs each. When you allocate more than six SUs to your ASA job, more nodes are allocated for each block of six SUs. Partitioned data processing steps are spread across multiple nodes, using up to six SUs per partition. You must use partitioned inputs and outputs to utilize more than one node per step. The processing steps are defined in the query transforms, which you saw earlier in the chapter. Non-partitioned processing steps only run on a single node. However, separate steps can run on separate nodes, if more than six SUs are allocated.

The inputs and outputs also influence how many SUs an ASA job can use. Event Hub inputs and outputs use full nodes, up to the number of partitions in the Event Hub. Figure 6.9 compares partitioning of inputs and outputs with provisioned SUs. Recall from chapter 5 that every Event Hub uses at least two partitions. SQL Server, Blob Storage, and Data Lake Storage outputs also support writing partitioned from multiple ASA nodes.

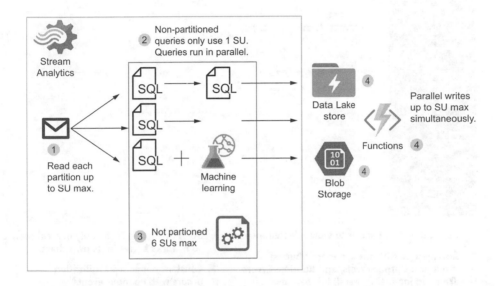

Figure 6.9 Partitioned data flow in Stream Analytics

Monitor the SU utilization to determine when to add more SUs. You can check this stat using the Metrics blade of the ASA job. There, you can view current or historical data on the job's performance. Figure 6.10 shows the Metrics blade with three metrics selected.

1 Click General > Metrics link in the left navigation.
2 In the Metric selection area above the grid, select Metric SU % Utilization from the Metric drop down.
3 Monitor the values shown during typical usage.
   a When SU % Utilization is above 70%, add more SUs.
   b When SU % Utilization is below 30%, reduce the number of SUs.

You can select 1, 2, or 3 SUs incrementally. When selecting more than 3 SUs, they're allocated in blocks of 6, corresponding to another full cluster node. You can select 6, 12, 18, and higher numbers of SUs in blocks of 6. For small to medium ASA jobs with

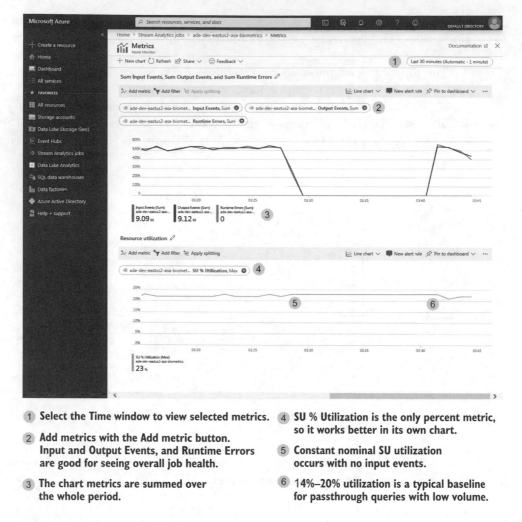

1. **Select the Time window to view selected metrics.**

2. **Add metrics with the Add metric button. Input and Output Events, and Runtime Errors are good for seeing overall job health.**

3. **The chart metrics are summed over the whole period.**

4. **SU % Utilization is the only percent metric, so it works better in its own chart.**

5. **Constant nominal SU utilization occurs with no input events.**

6. **14%–20% utilization is a typical baseline for passthrough queries with low volume.**

Figure 6.10   Monitoring SU % utilization in ASA

several discrete transformations, it may be more cost-effective to run multiple ASA jobs, reading from a single source. Then each ASA job would perform a specific function, outputting to a separate sink.

6.5.2   *Event ordering*

ASA jobs support micro-batch processing over time-dependent data. Time-dependent data contains one or more timestamps. At a basic level, a single timestamp contains a date and time. Common uses for timestamps include the message creation time and submission time. Although creation and submission times should be nearly the same, occasionally submission lags behind creation. For example, connections to an Event Hub from the on-premises network may be unavailable. In this case, the best practice is to repeat sending the message until the submission succeeds. In this situation, the creation and submission timestamps can vary significantly. Figure 6.11 shows how time assignment can vary between processing steps.

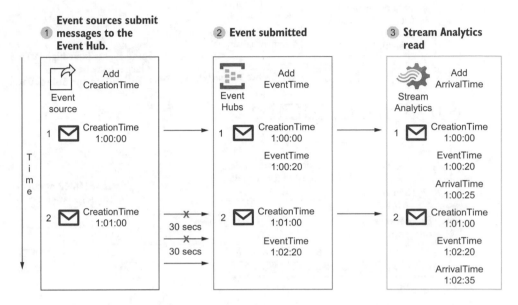

Figure 6.11   Event time assignment in data stream

When a message arrives late to a set of streaming data, the data is either valuable or not.

- If the data is no longer valuable, you can drop it.
- If the data is valuable, and you are processing one-at-a-time, you can proceed with processing the data.
- If the data is valuable, and you are processing micro-batches, you need to pause the batch that should include the late data until it arrives and can be included. Figure 6.12 describes how data submissions, ASA jobs, and job queries relate to advancing time.

When you have defined your query with a time window transformation, you start processing your data in micro-batches. The time window sets the boundaries for the data used in the batch. You define the window for the ASA job by setting the timestamp in the transforms. Because message data timestamps invariably differ from the submission time, you should consider a strategy to deal with the variability.

ASA jobs support three methods for handling data with time sequence errors.

- Wait for late data and include it.
- Include early data in the stream.
- Correct out-of-order data.

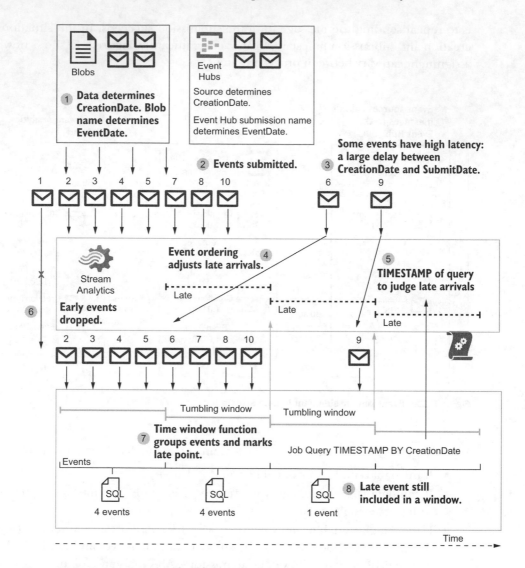

Figure 6.12   Event ordering in ASA data stream

Message data with a timestamp before the submission time is *late data*. Message data with a timestamp after the submission time is *early data*.

By default, ASA jobs collect up to five minutes of data ahead of your selected job start time, which allows the job to include early data in the stream for processing. This five-minute lead time is not configurable. Early data before this window is not included in the data stream.

Also by default, ASA job queries collect five extra seconds of data beyond the timestamp window, to account for system latency. This wait period provides the query transaction with an automatic pause for each transaction window. Because most message timestamps are defined before submission, most message data would be classified as late data. The late arrival window can and should be adjusted to account for any expected latency. For example, clock time drift on unmanaged systems generating data can cause timestamps to be early or late by minutes to hours. You can extend this wait up to 20 days. Of course, by that point the stream processing done by the job can hardly be called "real-time." Extending the wait time for late data increases the job's memory usage as well as the latency of each transaction.

ASA jobs can detect out-of-order timestamps in the data stream. Message data is out-of-order if sorting by timestamp or submission time results in different sequences. Message data can be late, out-of-order, or both. By default, transactions do not wait for out-of-order data. You can increase this wait period up to 60 minutes. Extending the wait time for late data increases the memory usage as well as the latency of each transaction. Figure 6.13 shows the Event Ordering blade in the Azure portal.

① **Range of variability in transmitting message.**

② **The job will rearrange events into order, based on ORDER BY clauses in the job query.**

③ **Change the specified date to the latest acceptable date, or drop the message.**

④ **Save the changes.**

Figure 6.13   Adjusting variable time in ASA job

For example, let's look at the behavior of timestamps given a set of late and out-of-order windows. The job query uses a transaction with a 10-second window function. You can read more about window functions in the section on writing job queries.

- The late window is set to 60 seconds.
- The out-of-order window is set to 20 seconds.
- The out-of-bounds policy is set to adjust. In table 6.3, you can see how these configurations affect the transaction window.

Table 6.3   Late and out-of-order message data

Order	Message time (mm:ss)	Submission time (mm:ss)	Timestamp (mm:ss)	State	Adjustment	Reason
1	01:00	01:00	None	On-time	Dropped	Outside five minute early window
2	01:33	01:34	None	Late	Dropped	Outside five minute early window
-	-	-	07:00	Job start	-	-
3	07:00	07:01	07:00	Late	No change	Within late window
4	07:03	07:10	07:03	Late	No change	Within late window
5	07:02	07:12	07:02	Late, out-of-order	No change	Within late window, within out-of-order window
6	07:12	07:15	07:12	Late	No change	Within late window
6	07:17	07:16	None	Early	Dropped	Early submission
7	07:07	07:29	07:09	Late, Out-of-order	Timestamp set to maximum out-of-order window	Within late window, beyond out-of-order window
8	07:09	08:15	07:15	Late, Out-of-order	Timestamp set to maximum late window	Beyond late window, beyond out-of-order window

ASA jobs calculate the state of each piece of message data by comparing the timestamp with the submission time. The data source provides the submission time, and the ASA job logs the most recent submission time. If the timestamp falls outside the window specified for late or out-of-order messages, one of two things can happen. You can choose to drop the message data from the stream and not process it, or you can adjust the message timestamp to the submission timestamp, minus the value of the state window. You can adjust the late data window, out-of-order window, and handling policy in the Azure portal. These options do not affect the job pricing. Use these steps to configure your ASA job.

1 In the Azure portal, use the All Services menu and filter on Stream Analytics jobs to show the Stream Analytics Jobs blade.
2 Select the Stream Analytics job you want to manage.
3 Click Configure > Event Ordering from the left navigation blade.
4 Choose a late message window, from 0 seconds to 20 days.
5 Choose an out-of-order window, from 0 seconds to 60 minutes.
6 Choose an out-of-bounds handling policy, of Adjust or Drop.
7 Click Save to save the changes.

Your late and out-of-order windows will reflect the latency and recovery mechanisms in your data generators. For example, if you have an on-premises application with retry logic that resubmits failed messages for up to five minutes, you should increase both windows to five minutes or more. Conversely, if you consume job outputs every minute, messages more than one minute late would have little value after that minute passed. If they still have value, setting the late window to one minute with an Adjust policy will include the late messages during the minute they are submitted, but will increase the latency while waiting for late messages.

6.6 Exercises

6.6.1 Exercise 1

Determine if each ASA job query can use more than six SUs. Each query uses an Event Hub with two partitions and a Data Lake output.

Listing 6.23   Exercise 1a

```
SELECT Player, Node, AVG(NodeValue) AS AvgValue
INTO SqlOutputPitcher
FROM HubsInputBiometrics TIMESTAMP BY EventTime
WHERE Player = 'abera101' AND Node = 12 AND NodeValue > 80
GROUP BY Player, Node, TumblingWindow(second, 150)
```

Listing 6.24   Exercise 1b

```
SELECT Player, Node, AVG(NodeValue) AS AvgValue
INTO SqlOutputPitcher
FROM HubsInputBiometrics TIMESTAMP BY EventTime
PARTITION BY PartitionId
WHERE Player = 'abera101' AND Node = 12 AND NodeValue > 80
GROUP BY Player, Node, TumblingWindow(second, 150)
```

Listing 6.25   Exercise 1c

```
WITH PitchAnomaly AS (
SELECT Player, Node, CAST(NodeValue AS FLOAT) AS NodeValue,
AnomalyDetection_SpikeAndDip(CAST(NodeValue AS FLOAT), 90, 15, 'dips')
OVER (
PARTITION BY Player
```

```
LIMIT DURATION(minute, 40)
WHEN Node = 12 AND NodeValue > 80
)
AS ADValues
FROM HubsInputBiometrics
)
SELECT Player, NodeValue,
CAST(GetRecordPropertyValue(ADValues, 'Score') as FLOAT) AS Score
INTO SqlOutputPitcher
FROM PitchAnomaly
WHERE CAST(GetRecordPropertyValue(ADValues, 'IsAnomaly') AS BIGINT) = 1;
```

SOLUTION

Exercise 1a consists of one transform with no CTEs, and the transform does not use PARTITION BY, so it can use up to six SUs.

Exercise 1b uses PARTITION BY, so this query can use up to 12 SUs.

Exercise 1c consists of a transform with a CTE, so it can use up to 12 SUs. Because the CTE step does not partition by the same key as the Event Hub input (PartitionId), this step can only use up to 6 SUs. Because the SELECT step does use PARTITION BY, this step can only use up to 6 SUs.

6.6.2   Exercise 2

You want 100 hopping window calculations each hour. Which of these options will give you that count?

1   TumblingWindow(second, 150)
2   HoppingWindow(hour, 100)
3   HoppingWindow(hour, 1, 100)
4   HoppingWindow(second, 300, 36)

SOLUTION

The correct choice is option 4. Option 1 uses a tumbling window. You can configure a hopping window to behave like a tumbling window, but not vice versa. Option 2 does not include the required hop value. Option 3 uses a 1-hour time window and hops forward 100 hours. Option 4 uses a 5-minute window and hops every 36 seconds.

Summary

- When using Azure PowerShell to create ASA jobs, a configuration file is required. You can create and reference these config files from Azure Cloud Shell. This method of configuration makes automating the configuration process more difficult.
- You can start using real-time processing in ASA jobs by creating a passthrough query. The passthrough query provides an easy channel for saving Event Hub streaming data to multiple storage options.

- Starting the ASA job tests the configuration of your inputs, outputs, and transforms. Passing the tests ensures the streaming calculations work correctly. ASA jobs provide exception logs when components fail to assist with troubleshooting.
- ASA job transforms analyze data over given time ranges. ASA jobs provide data collection functions which advance through the time ranges in multiple ways. These let you collect data over time without specifying an end.

Batch queries with Azure Data Lake Analytics

7

This chapter covers

- Writing job queries using U-SQL
- Creating U-SQL jobs
- Creating a Data Lake Analytics service
- Estimating appropriate parallelization for U-SQL jobs

In the last chapter, you used Azure Stream Analytics as a source for raw data, using a *passthrough query*. The passthrough query takes incoming data and passes it to the output, in this case files in Azure Data Lake Storage (ADLS). Figure 7.1 shows this use of Stream Analytics in parallel with the serving layer.

This is the latest example of prep work for *batch processing*, which includes loading files into storage and saving groups of messages into files. Azure Storage accounts, Data Lakes, and Event Hubs services set the base for building a batch processing analytics system in Azure. With files in the ADLS store, you're ready to start doing batch processing.

In this chapter, you'll learn how to use Azure Data Lake Analytics (ADLA) to run analysis over data stored in semi-structured files. ADLA powers the batch processing pillar of the Lambda architecture. Figure 7.2 shows ADLA as the focus of

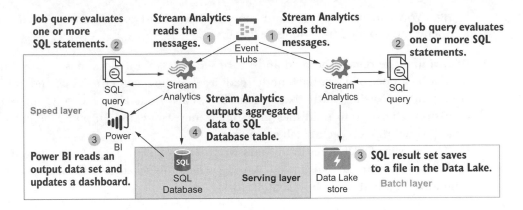

Job query evaluates one or more SQL statements. 2

Stream Analytics reads the messages. 1

Event Hubs

Stream Analytics reads the messages. 1

Job query evaluates one or more SQL statements. 2

SQL query

Stream Analytics

Stream Analytics outputs aggregated data to SQL Database table.

Stream Analytics

SQL query

Speed layer

Power BI 3

Power BI reads an output data set and updates a dashboard.

4

SQL Database

Serving layer

Data Lake store

SQL result set saves to a file in the Data Lake. 3

Batch layer

Figure 7.1   Lambda architecture with Azure PaaS Speed layer

the batch layer. ADLA uses Azure's unbounded fast storage and readily available processing nodes to make analyzing file-based data sets as easy as analyzing relational database data sets.

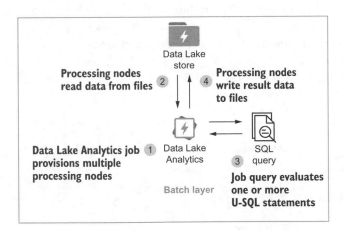

Data Lake store

Processing nodes read data from files 2

4 Processing nodes write result data to files

Data Lake Analytics job provisions multiple processing nodes 1

Data Lake Analytics

SQL query

3

Job query evaluates one or more U-SQL statements

Batch layer

Figure 7.2   Lambda architecture with Azure PaaS Batch layer

ADLA jobs read data files, filter the data, execute calculations, and output new data sets to files. You define a list of files to read, which make up a file set. The list can be a single file, an array of files, or a wildcard declaration to select multiple files and folders. ADLA jobs define the read, write, filter, and calculation operations with the *U-SQL* language, a unique coding language that combines aspects of SQL and C#.

U-SQL blends SQL and C# syntax to define a batch job. A compiler transforms this definition into a set of commands that can be executed in parallel on separate nodes. This job then executes on one to hundreds of nodes, to process a nearly unlimited amount of data. This follows the *sharding* cloud design pattern.

TIP You can read more about the sharding cloud pattern in Microsoft's documentation at http://mng.bz/0Zy6.

By dividing the data to be read and processed across multiple nodes, the overall job duration can be reduced. Each node reads a set of the data in the batch and performs commands according to the batch definition. Each node also takes advantage of the data store sharding to read files in parallel, increasing throughput. This horizontal scaling is defined on each batch execution.

The power of ADLA lies in this massive scalability. The U-SQL language is the tool to define your data analysis in ADLA and harness this scalability. Before we start running jobs, we need to see how U-SQL works.

TIP You can find the code listings in the GitHub repository for this book at https://github.com/rnuckolls/azure_storage.

7.1 U-SQL language

The biometric data is now flowing into your ADLS store and is available for analysis. The development team would like to view summary reports of the data, with the average node value, grouped by player, node, and day. The data is collected by the Event Hub and saved in ADLS in folder /Staging/biometricstats/v1. How can you fulfill this request?

ADLA U-SQL jobs read data files, transform data, and write out data in a batch. They can read and write data files from ADLS stores or Blob Storage. Figure 7.3 shows a job which reads multiple files from an ADLS store and writes multiple files to an ADLS store.

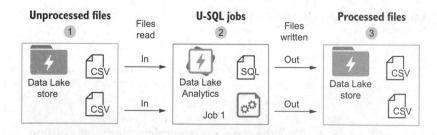

Figure 7.3   Reading and writing data files with ADLA

U-SQL defines loading, filtering, and calculations on data with *rowsets*. A rowset describes the output of a data operation: either a load or a calculation. Each rowset works a bit like an object class, with properties and dynamic read and calculate operations. Each step of the batch job is a rowset calculation.

Rowsets are generated from data from the files listed in the job or as results from calculation on other rowsets. The calculations are defined as expressions describing the shape of the data output, rather than the row-by-row operations to perform. This makes U-SQL a declarative language like T-SQL. The statements defining the operations are collected into a U-SQL script, which is loaded and compiled in a U-SQL job. The compiler transforms the script into the row-by-row operations to perform.

> **IMPORTANT** The job compilation makes it tricky to debug the intermediate calculation results. The evaluation isn't complete until the job is complete. In practice, this means you get the output of the U-SQL job at the end or not at all. Developing U-SQL scripts can be an iterative process, with each step generating an output file.

Each U-SQL job builds a unique application, with the U-SQL script defining the work. To build this application, the U-SQL script describes four elements.

1 A file reader, called an *extractor*, matched to the type of files being read
2 A file writer, called an *outputter*, matched to the type of file being written
3 A set or list of files to read and a list of files to write
4 A set of calculations to perform on the data

With these four elements, you can build complex transformations. By combining file selectors, extractors, expressions, and outputters, you can define analysis jobs that run over small and large amounts of data. A U-SQL script is a file with a .usql extension that contains U-SQL commands. You upload the script to a new job via the Azure portal, Azure PowerShell, or another tool like Azure Data Factory. Let's look at each element before putting them together in a U-SQL script.

7.1.1 Extractors

Extractor expressions define a file read operation. ADLA includes three extractors by default: CSV, TSV, and Text. You define a read operation using the EXTRACT command, which has four parts:

1 A rowset variable assignment
2 A schema definition
3 A FROM clause
4 A USING clause

The FROM clause uses a file set to list the file or files to read. The file set can be a string file path or a string variable. The USING clause declares a new instance of the extractor class, with the specific type. Listing 7.1 shows a typical Extractor expression, reading a single file defined in a variable, with the CSV extractor.

Extractors implement schema-on-read functionality. You define the field order and field type to be read in the EXTRACT expression. The extractor reads the file and does a conversion for you. U-SQL uses the underlying C# Type.Parse() function to do the conversions.

The U-SQL statements in listing 7.1 contains six important U-SQL syntax rules.

1. `DECLARE` begins a variable declaration.
2. Variable names begin with the @ sign.
3. Standard C# types are available for variables.
4. `String` and `DateTime` types enclose their values in double-quotes; integers don't.
5. Row set names also begin with the @ sign.
6. All U-SQL statements end with a semicolon.

Listing 7.1   CSV EXTRACT statement

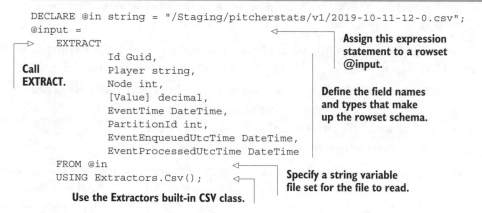

```
DECLARE @in string = "/Staging/pitcherstats/v1/2019-10-11-12-0.csv";
@input =
    EXTRACT
            Id Guid,
            Player string,
            Node int,
            [Value] decimal,
            EventTime DateTime,
            PartitionId int,
            EventEnqueuedUtcTime DateTime,
            EventProcessedUtcTime DateTime
    FROM @in
    USING Extractors.Csv();
```

Call EXTRACT.

Assign this expression statement to a rowset @input.

Define the field names and types that make up the rowset schema.

Specify a string variable file set for the file to read.

Use the Extractors built-in CSV class.

The `EXTRACT` command creates a rowset variable that can then be modified using expressions or written to a new file with an *outputter* class.

7.1.2   *Outputters*

Outputters write the rowsets to files in Data Lake Storage. ADLA includes three outputters by default: CSV, TSV, and Text. You define an output operation using the `OUTPUT` command, which has three parts: a variable assignment, a `TO` clause, and a `USING` clause. `OUTPUT` references a rowset to write out. The `TO` clause uses a file path to list the file to write. The file set can be a string file path or a string variable. Declare a new instance of the outputter with `USING`. Listing 7.2 shows two outputter expressions, writing a single file to a file path defined in a variable or inline, with the CSV and TSV outputters.

Listing 7.2   CSV OUTPUT statement

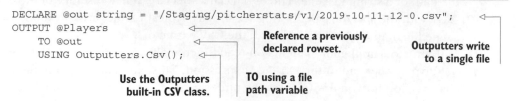

```
DECLARE @out string = "/Staging/pitcherstats/v1/2019-10-11-12-0.csv";
OUTPUT @Players
    TO @out
    USING Outputters.Csv();
```

Reference a previously declared rowset.

Outputters write to a single file

Use the Outputters built-in CSV class.

TO using a file path variable

```
OUTPUT @Players
    TO "/Raw/pitcherstats/v1/pitcher/2019-10-11-12-0.tsv"          ←⌐  A full path
    USING Outputters.Tsv();          ←⌐  Use the Outputters        ⌐  to a file
                                         built-in TSV class.
```

Outputters use the schema of the referenced rowset. Outputter file paths can use relative paths to the default ADLS store, or direct paths to ADLS stores or Blob Storage. File selector variables work with outputters too, but are limited to a single line.

7.1.3   File selectors

File selectors define the list of files read by the extractor. The simplest form specifies a single file by path and filename. The FROM clause of the extractor function takes a string, string variable, or string array as an input, to select the files to read. The following statement creates a variable selecting a single file.

```
DECLARE @in string = "/Staging/pitcherstats/v1/2019-07-01-13-0.csv";
```

You build these variables as inputs to an extractor function. The text gets parsed by the extractor function before being used to read the files. Because of this, you can instruct the extractor with special syntax.

For example, you can pass in a wildcard for a portion of the file or folder name. The wildcard uses braces {} to delineate the parsed portion. Using /Staging/ pitcherstats/v1/{*}.csv for a selector selects all CSV files in the /Staging/pitcher-stats/v1 folder.

```
DECLARE @in string = "/Staging/pitcherstats/v1/2019-07-01-{*}.csv";
```

The wildcard braces format can extract values from the filepath too, including filename and dates. Dates are commonly used for folder and filename syntax, which makes extracting the date a straightforward example. The extracted value(s) becomes an extra field in the file schema available in the read expression. For example, add a field named filedate of type DateTime and one named filename of type string to your expression schema. The {filedate:yyyy}, {filedate:MM}, {filedate:dd}, and {filename} wildcards parse the specified portions of the file path during each file read and include the value in the rowset field.

```
DECLARE @in string = "/Staging/pitcherstats/v1/
➥ {filedate:yyyy}-{filedate:MM}-{filedate:dd}-{filename}.csv";
```

In this example, a field called filedate is constructed during file read. When the extractor uses this @in variable, it parses the filenames found in the folder path v1, collects the data for filedate, and adds a new filedate field to each row read from each file. Table 7.1 shows the field values from two filenames using this wildcard format.

Table 7.1   Constructing a field from file name

File name	filedate field	filename field
/2019-11-01-aa.csv	2019-11-01T00:00:00.0000000Z	aa
/2019-11-02-cc.csv	2019-11-02T00:00:00.0000000Z	cc

NOTE   You can use multiple wildcards in input file paths, but only one wildcard is allowed in an output file path. Using {*} in the output file selector will output the ID of the vertex writing the file. You can read more about vertexes later in this chapter.

The DECLARE command creates a new variable of the specified C# type. All variables are constants in U-SQL. You can't change the value once declared, unless you use the EXTERNAL keyword. The DECLARE EXTERNAL @variable declaration allows the variable to be declared twice.

```
DECLARE EXTERNAL @Year int = 2019;
// Year = 2019
```

This allows tools to inject their own parameters into the U-SQL script. If you don't inject a variable parameter, the script will use the original value as a default. The injected variable parameters are added to the beginning of the U-SQL job by the tool that submits the job. The EXTERNAL keyword on a variable, following the same variable without the keyword, prevents the subsequent value from being set. This pattern works like IF NOT EXISTS([variable]), short-circuiting the variable declaration.

```
DECLARE @Year int = 2020;              ◁─┐ Injected variable
DECLARE EXTERNAL @Year int = 2019;     ◁─┐ Original script
// Year = 2020                              variable declaration
```

Using an injected variable parameter looks like the following listing.

Listing 7.3   Using injected variables

```
--Start of file--
DECLARE @Year int = 2020;              ◁─┐ Injected variable

DECLARE EXTERNAL @Year int = 2019;     ◁─┐ Overridden
// Year = 2020                              variable
...
--End of file--
```

NOTE   You'll work with injecting variable parameters into U-SQL jobs in Azure Data Factory, when you configure automation and scheduling for your analytics system. The Azure Data Factory pipeline will submit your job file to ADLA. You can read more about Azure Data Factory in chapter 10.

7.1.4   Expressions

Expressions create and transform rowsets using the data read by the extractors. An expression can create new calculated columns, join multiple rowsets, and filter and group rows, as you would with other SQL languages. An expression references a previously declared rowset or defines one with a row enumeration.

Use the SELECT statement to create an expression. When adding a calculated column, use the connector AS to provide a name for the field. Expressions end with a semicolon.

Listing 7.4 shows an example of creating a rowset using enumeration. An enumerated rowset generates a set of rows using a parenthetical list of comma-separated field values. The list of field values is given a name, using the AS connector, and a set of field names. The following defines a rowset with three rows, then defines a second rowset based on the first, including an aggregation column.

> **Listing 7.4   Building rowset with expressions**

```
@PlayerList  =                          ← Rowset 1 name,
    SELECT * FROM                         preceded by @ sign
        (VALUES
            ("abera101", 13, 15.0, new DateTime(2019,9,30) ),     ← C# format
            ("abera101", 13, 18.0, new DateTime(2019,9,30) ),       for types
            ("jstro102", 4, 220.10, new DateTime(2019,10,10) )
        ) AS
            D( Player, Node, NodeValue, EventTime );    ← Column names
                                                          for rowset
    @Players =
        SELECT Player,              ← SELECT fields to
        Node,                         include in rowset
        AVG(NodeValue) AS AvgValue,    ← Calculated columns must
        EventTime                        include AS [columnName]
        FROM @PlayerList
        GROUP BY Player, Node, EventTime;    ← Statement ends
                                               with semicolon
```

Rowset 2 name → `@Players`

FROM Rowset 1 → `FROM @PlayerList`

These are just two examples of the expressions you can write. Expressions in U-SQL can become quite complicated and benefit from advanced knowledge of SQL. But don't let that stop you! The ADLA compiler will help optimize the job, and you can refactor and rerun jobs. Remember, maintaining the original data files is one of the key tenets of Lambda architecture. As long as you follow this tenet, you can execute batch jobs again and again without risk to the data.

Much of the challenge in using ADLA jobs and U-SQL involves structuring a working U-SQL script. Let's overcome that by writing a job.

7.2   U-SQL jobs

Now that you've seen what's in a U-SQL script, let's go through the steps for creating one. The most basic U-SQL jobs read and write files with a *passthrough query*. The passthrough query doesn't change the data it processes, nor does it read or interpret the file schema. Three common use cases for ADLA passthrough queries are moving files, splitting and combining files, and transforming file formats. This type of U-SQL job can be structured with three steps: read file to memory, create rowset, and write rowset to file.

For the biometric data scenario, you'll want a script that's a bit more complicated. This script will apply a schema to a rowset during file read and then use that rowset as a source for an aggregation operation. This type of U-SQL script can be structured with four steps: read file to memory, create rowset, create aggregation, and write rowset to file. Let's look at each step.

7.2.1 *Selecting the biometric data files*

Reading files in a U-SQL script uses the `EXTRACT` command and a file selector. As you recall from chapter 4, the files for your analytics systems are stored in ADLS and arranged according to the zones framework. First, let's make sure some files are available.

Make sure you have a Data Lake store available. (You can review chapter 4 for instructions on creating a Data Lake store if needed.) The biometric data schema was introduced in chapter 5, and new files were saved to the ADLS store using Stream Analytics in chapter 6. The biometric file schema has the following fields:

1 `Id`: String
2 `Player`: String
3 `Node`: Integer
4 `NodeValue`: Decimal
5 `EventTime`: DateTime
6 `PartitionId`: Integer
7 `EventEnqueuedUtcTime`: DateTime
8 `EventProcessedUtcTime`: DateTime

The following listing shows the first two rows of an example file.

> **Listing 7.5   Player biometrics stats file**

```
Id,Player,Node,NodeValue,EventTime,PartitionId,
➥ EventEnqueuedUtcTime,EventProcessedUtcTime
89f324ef-1927-4ae9-b610-7570e8e24e4d,mjone101,13,20.79,
➥ 2019-07-11T01:19:21.1357084Z,2,2019-07-11T01:19:24.5087084Z,
➥ 2019-07-11T01:19:24.5897084Z
```

Include a header row. Upload three copies of the file to your Data Lake store. For this example, the values don't matter. You can duplicate the same file three times.

> **TIP**   This file format was generated from data submitted to an Event Hub and written to Data Lake Storage with Stream Analytics. You can retrieve a file for your job with 100 K rows in this format from the GitHub repository for this book at http://mng.bz/XPv1.

You can also get a simple C# project for creating multiple large files in this format at http://mng.bz/yylo.

For this scenario, the data is stored in your ADLS store. This file selector path includes folders and the filename itself. You'll see later in the chapter how you can read files from alternate ADLS stores and Blob Storage.

Using the EXTERNAL clause for file selectors allows you to reuse the U-SQL script in the future. The file selector variable uses a braced wildcard to select all files in the v1 folder with a CSV extension. If you inject a file selector path with a tool like ADF, you can modify the path to reference other folders or specific files that share the same schema. The following listing demonstrates building a file selector variable.

> **Listing 7.6 Declaring file path variables with wildcards**

```
DECLARE EXTERNAL @in string = "/Staging/biometricstats/v1/{*}.csv";
```

The filename must include the file extension. Because you're passing a wildcard in the file selector, the extractor will read all three files in the folder and combine the file rows into the extractor rowset.

7.2.2 Schema extraction

Extractor expressions use the file selector variable. The extractor has four parts: a rowset variable assignment, a schema definition, a file set selection statement, and an extractor configuration.

- The rowset variable references the rows extracted from the file set.
- The schema definition defines the fields in the rowset for the expression.
- The file set selection identifies the files.
- The extractor configuration allows you to match the particulars of the files you are reading.

The schema definition for the extractor follows the EXTRACT command. List the name of the field and the C# type. The name cannot be all uppercase and does not need to match the file header. The schema field order does need to match the file field order. It's critical to include all of the fields in the file in the EXTRACT expression. If you don't, none of the rows will be read. Add virtual fields before or after the file fields. These would include any wildcard values extracted from the file set selector.

The built-in CSV, TSV, and Text extractors can accept input parameters to match the specific file format. Table 7.2 lists the parameters and their defaults.

The CSV and TSV extractors are derived from the Text extractor and use a set of defaults for the parameters. The delimiter should be a single Unicode character, but you'll need to use a special code for some special characters such as tab (\t), newline (\n), or carriage return (\r). The CSV extractor uses a comma (,) as delimiter, and TSV uses \t for tab.

Table 7.2   Extractor parameters

Parameter	Possible Values	Default	Description
delimiter	Any Unicode character	,	
encoding	Encoding.[ASCII], Encoding.BigEndianUnicode, Encoding.Unicode, Encoding.UTF7, Encoding.UTF8, Encoding.UTF32	Encoding.UTF8	
escapeCharacter	Any Unicode character, or unset	null	
nullEscape	Any string	null	A string that represents null
quoting	true, false	true	Field values wrapped in double-quotes ignore delimiters.
rowDelimiter	Any string of length 1	\r\n and \r and \n	\r\n is a special case
silent	true, false	false	Skip rows with errors in parsing, or use null for field conversion failures.
skipFirstNRows	Any Integer	0	
charFormat	string, uint16	uint16	Controls serialization of Unicode char values

Listing 7.7 shows the extractor expression for the biometric data files using the CSV extractor. Because the file includes a header row, use the parameter skipFirstNRows to skip the header.

Listing 7.7   Using a CSV extractor

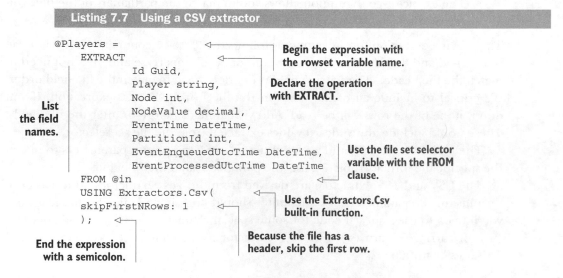

```
@Players =
    EXTRACT
        Id Guid,
        Player string,
        Node int,
        NodeValue decimal,
        EventTime DateTime,
        PartitionId int,
        EventEnqueuedUtcTime DateTime,
        EventProcessedUtcTime DateTime
    FROM @in
    USING Extractors.Csv(
        skipFirstNRows: 1
    );
```

Begin the expression with the rowset variable name.

Declare the operation with **EXTRACT**.

List the field names.

Use the file set selector variable with the **FROM** clause.

Use the Extractors.Csv built-in function.

End the expression with a semicolon.

Because the file has a header, skip the first row.

With the @Players rowset defined, you can create another rowset expression to do the required aggregation.

7.2.3 Aggregation

U-SQL supports many of the familiar SQL aggregate functions, including SUM, COUNT, AVG, MAX, MIN, STDEV, and VAR. Use these functions in a U-SQL expression to generate a new field. This new field must have a name assigned. You'll see more about aggregate expressions in chapter 8. In this scenario, the report description requires the average node value, grouped by player, node, and day. Listing 7.8 shows a U-SQL expression setting a new rowset variable, using the @Players rowset from the previous section.

> **Listing 7.8 Calculations in a U-SQL expression**

```
@DailyAgg =
    SELECT  Player,
            Node,
            EventTime.ToString("d") AS AvgDate,      ◄─── Use a C# DateTime.ToString
            AVG([Value]) AS Average                        format output to get a
    FROM @Players                                          simple date.
    GROUP BY Player, Node, EventTime.ToString("d");  ◄─── Provide a name for
                                                           the aggregate field.
```

Calculations done in U-SQL expressions can be as complicated as necessary. You can add multiple expressions, each building on previous expressions, to build complex conversions and calculations.

7.2.4 Writing files

An outputter expression uses a file selector variable or a string filepath to define the file target. The outputter has three parts: a rowset variable assignment, a file set selection statement, and an outputter configuration.

- The rowset variable references the rows extracted from the file set.
- The file set selection identifies the file to write.
- The outputter configuration allows you to set the particulars of the files you are writing.

The built-in CSV, TSV, and Text outputters can accept input parameters to set a specific file format. Table 7.3 lists the parameters and their defaults.

Use the OUTPUT command to write out a rowset. Provide the rowset variable following OUTPUT. The TO clause defines the file target for the write, using a string or file set variable. The USING clause specifies the outputter class to use and enumerates any configuration parameters. Listing 7.9 shows the U-SQL expressions to write the @DailyAgg rowset from the previous section to a CSV file, using a file set variable.

Table 7.3   Outputter parameters

Parameter	Possible values	Default	Description
delimiter	Any Unicode character	,	
dateTimeFormat	Any string	O	C# DateTime formatting codes
encoding	Encoding.[ASCII], Encoding.BigEndianUnicode, Encoding.Unicode, Encoding.UTF7, Encoding.UTF8, Encoding.UTF32	Encoding.UTF8	
escapeCharacter	Any Unicode character, or unset	null	
nullEscape	Any string	null	A string that represents null
quoting	true, false	true	Field values wrapped in double-quotes ignore delimiters.
rowDelimiter	Any string of length 1	\r\n	\r\n is a special case
charFormat	string, uint16	uint16	Controls serialization of Unicode char values
outputHeader	true, false	false	

Listing 7.9   Using a CSV outputter

OUTPUT command begins the file write expression.

```
DECLARE EXTERNAL @out string = "/Curated/biometricstats/v1/daily_value_avg.csv";

OUTPUT @DailyAgg
    TO @out
    USING Outputters.Csv(outputHeader: true);
```

Using a file selector variable

Include the rowset columns as a header row in the file.

Writing the file is the last step for this U-SQL job. U-SQL scripts can be stored as text files with a .usql file extension. The following listing shows the entire U-SQL script for the biometric data aggregation query.

Listing 7.10   U-SQL aggregation query script

```
DECLARE EXTERNAL @in string = "/Staging/biometricstats/v1/{*}.csv";

@Players =
    EXTRACT
        Id Guid,
        Player string,
        Node int,
```

```
            NodeValue decimal,
            EventTime DateTime,
            PartitionId int,
            EventEnqueuedUtcTime DateTime,
            EventProcessedUtcTime DateTime
    FROM @in
    USING Extractors.Csv(
    skipFirstNRows: 1
    );

@DailyAgg =
    SELECT
        Player,
        Node,
        EventTime.ToString("d") AS AvgDate,
        AVG(NodeValue) AS Average
    FROM @Players
    GROUP BY Player, Node, EventTime.ToString("d");

DECLARE EXTERNAL @out string =
➥ "/Curated/biometricstats/v1/daily_value_avg.csv";

OUTPUT @DailyAgg
    TO @out
    USING Outputters.Csv(outputHeader: true);
```

You can use this script to create a new job in ADLA. In order to do that, you need to create the ADLA service.

7.3 *Creating a Data Lake Analytics service*

ADLA services manage execution of U-SQL scripts for batch processing. ADLA services access ADLS stores via the user executing the job and Blob Storage through a Storage account key. The service keeps track of previous job executions, letting you review instructions, file contents, and performance. The service does not schedule jobs, however. You can read more about scheduling U-SQL jobs in chapter 10.

There is no charge for the ADLA service itself. U-SQL jobs are billed on consumption, which is the total run time for the job multiplied by the number of nodes, at the hourly node rate. You'll learn more about processing nodes later in the chapter. The U-SQL job also stores job management data, compiled U-SQL job code, and custom User Defined Function (UDF) code in the default Data Lake store. These stored files incur monthly costs, but are usually negligible compared with the overall cost of ADLS storage.

> **NOTE** ADLA currently bills jobs at a rate of $2 (USD) per hour per node. You can see the latest Azure Data Lake Analytics pricing at http://mng.bz/K5l0.

7.3.1   *Using Azure portal*

Creating an ADLA service in the Azure portal requires the standard selections of name, region, and resource group. You also need to select the default ADLS store and a pricing package. The pricing package allows you to pre-purchase, on a monthly basis, a number of job processing node hours at a discount. Here's how to create the job in the Azure portal:

1 In the Azure portal, use the All Services menu and filter on Data Lake Analytics to show the Data Lake Analytics resource. Click Data Lake Analytics to show the resource blade.

2 Click Add to open the new Data Lake Analytics blade. You can also browse to https://portal.azure.com/#create/Microsoft.AzureDataLakeAnalytics.

3 Choose a subscription. The default will be the oldest subscription, if you have access to more than one.

4 Choose a resource group. (See appendix A for instructions if you haven't created one.)

5 Choose a name ("adedeveastus2"). The ADLA service name must be lowercase alphanumeric and be between 3 and 24 characters long.

6 Choose a location in the same region as your input sources to minimize egress charges and latency. The default is East US 2. ADLA services are only available in select regions at the time of writing, including Central US and East US 2, North Europe, and West Europe. You can check the entire list of regions at http://mng.bz/MdND.

7 Choose an existing ADLS store from the list of stores or create a new store using the Create New link.

8 Select the default Pricing package, Pay-as-You-Go. Monthly commitments can reduce spending in production, but are not needed unless you expect more than 100 hours of processing in a month.

9 Click Review + Create to create the service.

The ADLA is ready to accept new U-SQL jobs to execute.

7.3.2   *Using Azure PowerShell*

Using PowerShell scripts to create resources gives you a repeatable process and consistent configuration across environments. You can access Azure PowerShell by visiting Azure Cloud Shell at https://shell.azure.com/, or click the >_ header menu in the Azure portal.

Creating an ADLA service in the Azure portal requires the standard selections of name, region, and resource group. You also need to select the default ADLS store and a pricing package. Creating the service with Azure PowerShell offers more options than with Azure portal. With the Azure PowerShell command, you can also adjust policy limits and storage growth. Let's take a closer look at these options.

ADLA MANAGEMENT DATA

ADLA maintains a set of artifacts for each U-SQL job, including the compiled code generated from the U-SQL script and the details of the job execution. These are stored in job folders within the system root folder in the default ADLS store for the ADLA account. The `QueryStoreRetention` parameter lets you modify the artifacts' retention period. The default is 30 days. With this parameter, you can increase or decrease how long these folders are kept and so change the storage cost in the ADLS store or reduce the clutter of old jobs in ADLA. The amount of space taken by this folder is negligible compared with the large amount of data files in a production ADLS store.

LIMITS ON JOB EXECUTION

You can adjust the limits on the number of jobs and maximum Analytics Units (AU) available for the service. An AU refers to the processing node used to run a U-SQL job in ADLA. The jobs policy's `MaxJobCount` parameter sets the maximum number of simultaneous U-SQL jobs that can be run. The default maximum is three. The AU policy's `MaxAnalyticsUnits` parameter sets a maximum number of AU available to all jobs combined. The default maximum is 32. These limits help control spending, but can restrict larger jobs from using the maximum number of resources. These two policies can also be changed after service creation using the Azure portal and the Azure PowerShell command `Update-AzDataLakeAnalyticsComputePolicy`.

RESERVE CAPACITY

You can choose from multiple levels of commitment plans, once you have established your base monthly consumption level. These plans allow you to pre-purchase Analytics Unit-Hours for use during the month, at a reduced rate. There are nine levels, including the "Pay-as-You-Go" Consumption plan:

- Consumption
- Commitment100AUHours
- Commitment500AUHours
- Commitment1000AUHours
- Commitment5000AUHours
- Commitment10000AUHours
- Commitment50000AUHours
- Commitment100000AUHours
- Commitment500000AUHours

Use the `Tier` parameter to set the commitment plan. Listing 7.11 shows a PowerShell script for adding a commitment plan to an ADLA service. Use the `Set-AzDataLakeAnalyticsAccount` command to modify an existing ADLA. The parameters for this command are the same as for `New-AzDataLakeAnalyticsAccount`. Changing an ADLA service in Azure PowerShell requires the name of the ADLA service and the optional parameter to change.

> **Listing 7.11   Adding a monthly commitment to your ADLA service with Azure PowerShell**

```
Set-AzDataLakeAnalyticsAccount -Name "adedeveastus2"
    -Tier "Commitment100AUHours"
```

You can run the script in listing 7.12 to create the ADLA service.

> **Listing 7.12   Creating a new ADLA service with Azure PowerShell**

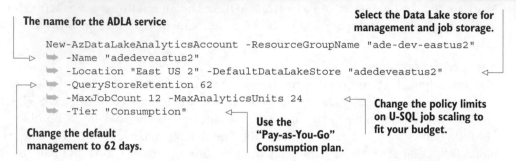

The name for the ADLA service

Select the Data Lake store for management and job storage.

```
New-AzDataLakeAnalyticsAccount -ResourceGroupName "ade-dev-eastus2"
    -Name "adedeveastus2"
    -Location "East US 2" -DefaultDataLakeStore "adedeveastus2"
    -QueryStoreRetention 62
    -MaxJobCount 12 -MaxAnalyticsUnits 24
    -Tier "Consumption"
```

Change the default management to 62 days.

Use the "Pay-as-You-Go" Consumption plan.

Change the policy limits on U-SQL job scaling to fit your budget.

Once the ADLA service has been created, you can submit U-SQL jobs.

7.4   *Submitting jobs to ADLA*

There are multiple methods for submitting U-SQL jobs for execution in ADLA. You can use the Azure portal directly, pass a U-SQL file via an Azure PowerShell command, submit a job using an Azure Data Factory (ADF) pipeline, or run a job remotely through Visual Studio. You can read about ADF pipelines in chapter 10.

> **TIP**   Working with U-SQL jobs in Visual Studio requires Azure Data Lake Tools for Visual Studio, a separate download. You can learn how to submit U-SQL scripts via Visual Studio at Microsoft's website: http://mng.bz/aRW9.

7.4.1   *Using Azure portal*

Submitting jobs with the Azure portal is the easiest way to get started. The portal interface lets you create a new job from scratch, upload saved U-SQL files, and edit U-SQL scripts before submitting the job. Here's how to create the job in the Azure portal:

1   In the Azure portal, use the All Services menu and filter on Data Lake Analytics to show the Data Lake Analytics resource. Click Data Lake Analytics to show the resource blade.

2   Select the ADLA service ("adedeveastus2") that will run the U-SQL job, to open the service Overview blade.

3   Click New Job to open the New Job blade.

4   Choose a name ("Sensor Aggregate"). The name can be any combination of alphanumeric and punctuation characters.

5   Choose one Analytics Unit for this first run. The default is one. You'll see later in the chapter how to scale AUs for the job.

6 Copy/paste the contents of listing 7.10 into the job body window or type the expressions.

7 Click Submit to submit the job to the ADLA cluster.

Figure 7.4 shows the Azure portal interface.

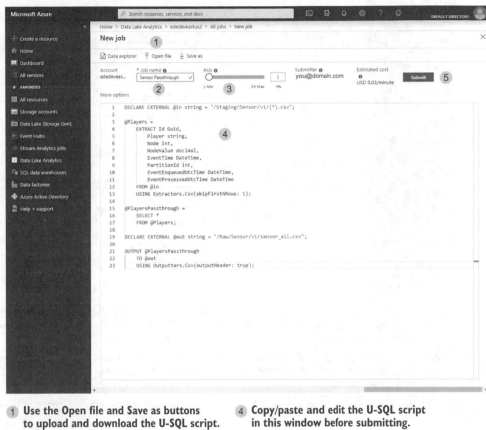

① **Use the Open file and Save as buttons to upload and download the U-SQL script.**

② **Choose a meaningful name.**

③ **Use slider or text box to select the number of Analytical Units for the job.**

④ **Copy/paste and edit the U-SQL script in this window before submitting.**

⑤ **Click Submit to compile and execute the job.**

Figure 7.4   Creating a new U-SQL job with the Azure portal

The job will be submitted for parsing and compiling. If these are successful, the job will begin processing. If not successful, the job window will display an error message and diagnostic information to help correct the problem. Once processing is complete, you can review the job output and the specifics of the execution. Figure 7.5 shows an example of a completed job. You can leave the New Job blade at any point after submitting and the job will continue.

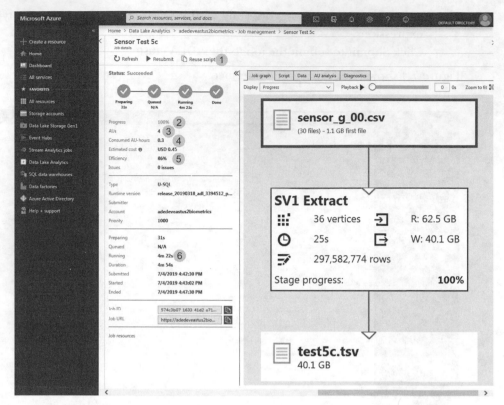

1. **Run the job again or make a copy of the entire job with an opportunity to edit the script before submission.**

2. **The amount complete increases as the job executes, but is not a reliable method for estimating total time.**

3. **The number of AUs selected for this job.**

4. **The total processing AU-hours spent determines cost. This number totals all AUs selected over the execution time.**

5. **Greater amounts of data are processed more efficiently. Too many AUs for the amount of data lowers efficiency. Aim for >70% efficiency.**

6. **Total running time determines cost and is less than job duration.**

Figure 7.5   U-SQL job result details

7.4.2   *Using Azure PowerShell*

As when creating ASA jobs with Azure PowerShell, U-SQL jobs require a file as part of the submission process. This file contains the instructions for the job. You can see the contents of the aggregation query script in the following listing.

Listing 7.13   U-SQL biometric aggregation query script

```
DECLARE EXTERNAL @in string = "/Staging/biometricstats/v1/{*}.csv";

@Players =
    EXTRACT
```

```
        Id Guid,
        Player string,
        Node int,
        NodeValue decimal,
        EventTime DateTime,
        PartitionId int,
        EventEnqueuedUtcTime DateTime,
        EventProcessedUtcTime DateTime
    FROM @in
    USING Extractors.Csv(
    skipFirstNRows: 1
    );

@DailyAgg =
    SELECT
        Player,
        Node,
        EventTime.ToString("d") AS AvgDate,
        AVG(NodeValue) AS Average
    FROM @Players
    GROUP BY Player, Node, EventTime.ToString("d");

DECLARE EXTERNAL @out string =
➡ "/Curated/biometricstats/v1/daily_value_avg.csv";

OUTPUT @DailyAgg
    TO @out
    USING Outputters.Csv(outputHeader: true);
```

Use the Azure PowerShell `Submit-AzDataLakeAnalyticsJob` command to submit the job. Set the `Account` parameter to the name of the ADLA account to run the job, and set `Name` to the job name. Pass the name of the U-SQL script file using `ScriptPath`. The `AnalyticsUnits` parameter sets the number of AUs, up to the maximum number allowed in the ADLA.

To use Cloud Shell to create a U-SQL job, you will need to add the U-SQL file to your Cloud Shell storage. Save the contents of listing 7.13 to a file named /adla/dailyagg.usql. There are two ways to do it: use the Cloud Shell upload function or create a new file with a Cloud Shell file editor.

> **NOTE** If you've forgotten how to do this, see section 6.1.3 "Creating Cloud Shell files" in chapter 6 for directions.

The script in listing 7.14 returns a job object with the current status of the job. If not enough AUs are available, or the maximum number of jobs are currently executing, the new job will be queued for execution.

Listing 7.14 Create a Data Lake Analytics job

**The U-SQL job name will be displayed in the Azure portal
and when querying the list of jobs via Azure PowerShell.**

```
Submit-AzDataLakeAnalyticsJob -Account "adedeveastus2"
➡ -Name "Sensor Daily Agg"
```

➥ `-ScriptPath "~/adla/dailyagg.usql"`   ◄───┐ **Note the tilde forward-**
➥ `-AnalyticsUnits 1`   ◄───┐   **slash in the file path in**
  Specify the number of Analytics   **Cloud Shell.**
  Units. If unsure, start with one.

Once the daily aggregation job completes, you'll have a new CSV file in the ADLS store to give to the development team. You can grant them access to the curated ADLS folder or transfer the CSV file another way. We'll look at scheduling U-SQL jobs in chapter 10 and copying data in chapter 12.

7.5   Efficient U-SQL job executions

U-SQL jobs in ADLA are made up of expression statements, collected as a script, submitted to the ADLA cluster as a job, and stored in U-SQL files. To manage a batch processing analysis system with ADLA, you must choose the number of AUs for each job. To improve the ROI on each job, you should learn how to balance the job duration with the cost. You should also ensure you aren't using more AUs than necessary, by reviewing previous jobs and estimating how many AUs you'll need for future jobs.

7.5.1   Monitoring a U-SQL job

You can check the status of a U-SQL job using the Azure portal. Browse to the ADLA Overview blade and click Data Lake Analytics > Job Management. This will display a list of submitted jobs and their current status.

   You can check on the job using the Azure PowerShell command `Get-AzDataLakeAnalyticsJob` to get the latest info. Use the `Name` parameter to search for the job you submitted named "Sensor Daily Agg." If you know the JobId, you can use that. The following listing shows these two approaches.

Listing 7.15   Checking status of a Data Lake Analytics job

```
$jobId = (Get-AzDataLakeAnalyticsJob -Account "adedeveastus2"
➥  -Name "Sensor Daily Agg" -Top 1).JobId
Get-AzDataLakeAnalyticsJob -Account "adedeveastus2" -JobId $jobId    ◄───┐
```

                              Use Top parameter to return most recent job.

The output of `Get-AzDataLakeAnalyticsJob` is a formatted object with various properties.

```
ErrorMessage        :
Properties          : Microsoft.Azure.Management.DataLake.
➥  Analytics.Models.USqlJobProperties
JobId               : 762531a0-b8e6-4345-91cb-0e321c7ac0b0
Name                : Sensor Daily Agg
Type                : USql
Submitter           : user@domain.com
DegreeOfParallelism : 1
Priority            : 1000
SubmitTime          : 7/27/19 8:14:07 PM +00:00
```

```
StartTime              : 7/27/19 8:14:47 PM +00:00
EndTime                : 7/27/19 8:24:14 PM +00:00
State                  : Ended
Result                 : Succeeded
```

You can monitor the job status using the State property of the returned object.

- A value of Running indicates the job has compiled and is executing.
- A value of Ended, with a Result value of Succeeded, indicates a completed execution.

To determine the cost, take the difference between the EndTime and StartTime in hours, multiplied by the DegreeOfParallelism, and by $2 (USD) per hour. For example, a U-SQL job that ran 4,500 seconds (1.25 h) with a DegreeOfParallelism of 10 would cost approximately $25. In order to understand if this cost can be reduced for the next execution, let's look more closely at how ADLA processes jobs.

7.5.2 Analytics units

ADLA provides access to a pool of U-SQL job processors, along with a compiler and job monitor. These services form the *ADLA cluster*. New jobs are created with a U-SQL script and one or more processing nodes to run on.

The processing node is called an *Analytics Unit* (AU). Each AU is an entirely managed node, with a fixed set of CPU and memory. Each AU runs for the entirety of the job, running the next available processing step that makes up the job. A processing step is called a *vertex*.

7.5.3 Vertexes

The job script is sent to a compiler, which generates anywhere from a few to many thousands of vertexes per job, depending on the number, size, and type of files, and number of expressions. Individual vertexes are distributed across the available processing nodes, or AUs. ADLA manages job creation, compilation, vertex scheduling, and monitoring for you.

When you submit a U-SQL job to ADLA, you define the job name, U-SQL script, and the number of processing nodes available for the job. The U-SQL job processes through multiple steps:

1. A new job is created. ADLA checks the maximum simultaneous job count and maximum AU count per job.
2. If other jobs are running, and not enough AUs are available for the job, the job is queued until other jobs complete and release enough AUs.
3. The job starts by allocating the requested AUs and compiling the U-SQL script. ADLA checks the U-SQL for syntax errors and compiles the code into vertexes.
4. Job execution and billing begins. Parallelizable steps (vertexes) are distributed among available processing nodes (AUs).

5 Job execution completes once the last vertex has completed processing. The monitoring node updates the final job status and saves the job's performance profile.

You can see how the ADLA cluster distributes the work in figure 7.6.

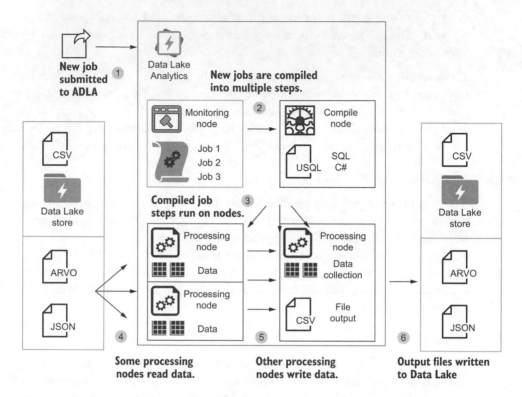

Figure 7.6 Data flow through the ADLA cluster

Some vertexes can be run in parallel and some must wait for previous steps to complete. Suppose a U-SQL job is defined to import two 100 MB files, aggregate three columns, and write a single output file. This should have four vertexes: one for each file import, one for the aggregation, and one for the file output. You can run this U-SQL job with one, two, three, or more AUs. With one AU, all vertexes will run sequentially on the node. With two AUs, the file imports will execute in parallel, one per AU, then the aggregation will run on one AU, then the file out will run on one AU. With three AUs or more, the file imports will execute in parallel, one per AU, then the aggregation will run on one AU, then the file out will run on one AU. The third AU will not be used. Beyond two AUs, this job would be over-provisioned. Figure 7.7 shows how the processing steps are parceled out among the available nodes.

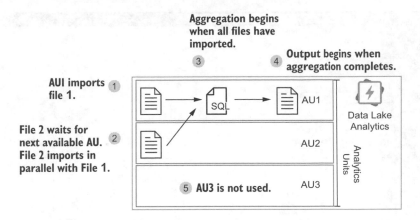

Figure 7.7   Allocating multiple AUs to a four-step U-SQL job

The available nodes are allocated and billed in terms of AU-seconds. An AU-second equates to 1 node allocated for 1 second. Thus 10 AU-seconds equates to one node allocated for 10 seconds, 2 nodes for 5 seconds, or 10 nodes for 1 second. Each job is billed in AU-hours for the nodes allocated for the duration of the job, regardless of how many vertexes are executed by the node.

> **WARNING**   U-SQL jobs include reading and writing to the associated Data Lake store. The output files are also stored there. Thirty days of job management data are stored by default. The activity, data files, and management files also incur charges, separate from the job execution rate, in AU-hours.

Figure 7.8 show the results of a successful job run in the Azure portal.

Management and compile processing time are not billed. The single node runs all vertexes sequentially until the job is complete. U-SQL job execution with one AU will only reach 100% efficiency if at least 1 GB of data is read. Allocating more than one AU (node) will lower the overall job efficiency, because few U-SQL jobs can break every expression into parallel steps. Allocating more than one AU will decrease the job duration in most cases. The ADLA compilation step reviews the job files for size and count, analyzes the expressions in the script, and divides the work into vertexes.

> **NOTE**   Azure Data Lake Store Gen1 runs on the Hadoop Distributed File System. Large files are broken into blocks of 250 MB each, called *extents*. ADLA vertexes can read a single large file from the Data Lake in parallel, each vertex assigned up to four 250 MB extents. This makes the vertexes most efficient when reading files close to 1 GB. Files smaller than 250 MB are read with a single vertex.

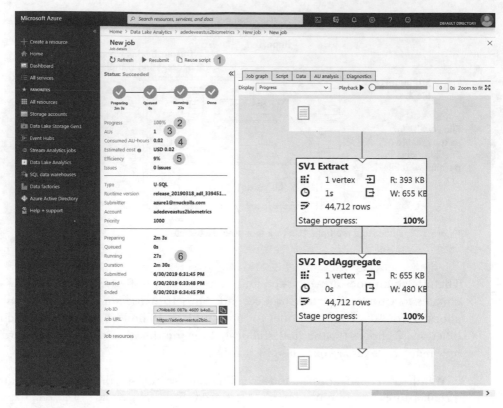

1. **Run the job again or make a copy of the entire job with an opportunity to edit the script before submission.**

2. **The amount complete increases as the job executes, but is not a reliable method for estimating total time.**

3. **The number of AUs selected for this job.**

4. **The total processing AU-hours spent determines cost. This number totals all AUs selected over the execution time.**

5. **Larger files are more efficient than smaller files. Too many AUs on the job lowers efficiency. Aim for for >80% efficiency.**

6. **Total running time determines cost and is less than job duration.**

Figure 7.8   **U-SQL job result details**

7.5.4   *Scaling the job execution*

Determining the optimal number of AUs for the first execution of a new U-SQL script is more of a guess than a calculation. Judging the total number of vertexes and the degree of parallelism for any step is complicated, until the ADLA compiler has analyzed the job and the execution is complete.

Figures 7.9 and 7.10 show the results of multiple U-SQL job runs with varying file sizes, counts, and AU allocations. To check basic read and write efficiency, a *passthrough*

U-SQL script was used to read the files and write a single output file without any intermediate calculations.

Listing 7.16   A simple passthrough expression

```
@PlayersPassthrough =
    SELECT *
    FROM @Players;
```

Four U-SQL passthrough query scripts were executed with the following files selected:

- 10 files of 113 MB
- 100 files of 113 MB
- 10 files of 1157 MB
- 30 files of 1157 MB

The four U-SQL scripts were executed six times each, doubling the number of AUs with each job run, from 1 to 32. The total execution time and efficiency were plotted against the number of AUs for the job run. Figure 7.9 shows the efficiency of various file counts and file sizes, at varying levels of parallel execution.

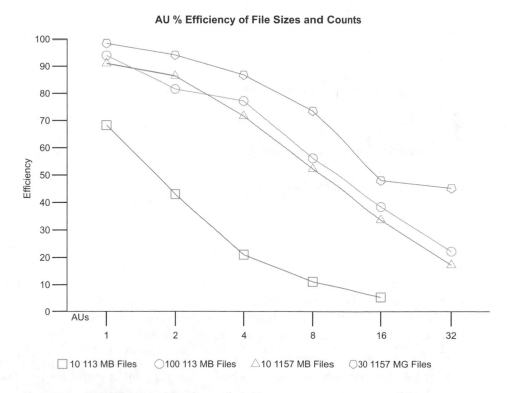

Figure 7.9   AU %Efficiency of file sizes and counts

The job efficiency ratings show how much of the overall execution time used all allocated AUs. Figure 7.9 shows that file overhead has a significant impact for small sets of small files. You can see the jobs don't reach peak efficiency until they read more than 10 GB of data.

Figure 7.10 shows the execution time in seconds for the same file counts and file sizes.

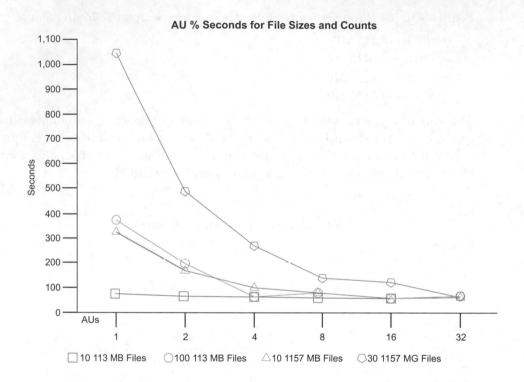

Figure 7.10   AU Seconds for file sizes and counts

You can see that parallelization with multiple AUs can decrease job time significantly as the amount of data read increases. Roughly, for each 8 GB of total files read, the job will benefit from an increase in AU allocation. Most batch jobs benefit from optimizing the number of AUs for subsequent executions. For some jobs, you can scale back the number of AUs without significantly increasing execution time.

Here are a few guidelines you can use for the first run.

- File count doesn't matter.
- If job duration doesn't matter, choose 1 AU. It will cost the least to execute the job.

- Calculate 1/8th of the total GB of data read into the job and round up to the next whole number. Using that number for your initial AU count will reduce the job duration for a relatively small increase in cost.
- Don't use more AUs than the total number of GB of data to be read in the job.

Getting skilled at estimating the available parallelization will help you balance cost with producing output in the desired timeframe.

7.6 Using Blob Storage

Suppose a third-party has delivered a list of ball players to a Storage account in Blob Storage. The file is a tab-separated text file with multiple fields and a header row. The development team would like to retrieve the list of active players from the file and write it as a CSV file in the ADLS store. How can you fulfill this request?

U-SQL jobs can perform all of these steps. File selectors can target files in Blob Storage, extractors can read multiple formats and combine multiple files, and outputters can write CSV files.

7.6.1 Constructing Blob file selectors

For this scenario, the data is stored in a Storage account Blob. The path to files in Blob Storage requires a protocol and URI structure.

The Blob Storage path starts with the "wasb://" protocol, which targets Blob Storage using the HTTPS protocol. The path uses an Azure Storage account and Blobs container format:

```
wasb://[blob container name]@[Storage account name]/[filename]
```

The file selector variable in listing 7.17 uses string compilation to combine elements. This allows elements to be injected into a string. @fileprefix defines part of the file name and gets injected into the Blob Storage path along with the wildcard element. This path includes the Storage account name (adedeveastus2), the Blob container for the files (biometricstats), the path structure in the container, and the file extension with a wildcard for the filename. You can use the same wildcard pattern as for Data Lake store paths. The following listing demonstrates building a file selector variable.

Listing 7.17 Declaring Blob file path variables with wildcards

```
DECLARE EXTERNAL @fileprefix string = "Player";
DECLARE @in string = String.Format("wasb://biometricstats@adedeveastus2/
➥ Staging/Players/{0}{1}.txt", @fileprefix, "{*}");
```

The extractor will add .blob.core.windows.net to the Storage account name, if not included. The filename must include the file extension. Because you're passing an asterisk wildcard in the file selector, the extractor will read any files starting with the file prefix player with a TXT extension in the Blob Storage container, and combine the rows into the extractor rowset.

IMPORTANT   Files in Blob storage are case-sensitive.

Make sure you have an Azure Storage account and Blob store available. To read from the Blob store with this file selector, you'll need to have a file available in the Blob store.

NOTE   You can review chapter 3 for instructions on creating a Storage account and Blob store.

Listing 7.18 shows the first two rows of a sample tab-separated file with the following schema:

1 `PlayerId`: String
2 `PlayerName`: String
3 `TeamName`: String
4 `TeamPosition`: String
5 `PositionStart`: DateTime
6 `PositionEnd`: DateTime

Listing 7.18   Player team stats file

```
"PlayerId"    "PlayerName"    "TeamName"    "TeamPosition"    "PositionStart"
➥ "PositionEnd"
"abera101"    "Arnold Berathal"    "Jonestown Sluggers"    "Pitcher"    2010-
    07-11T00:00:00.0000000Z
➥ 2020-07-11T00:00:00.0000000Z
"jstro102"    "John Strong"    "Poplar Bats"    "Second Base"    2010-07-
    11T00:00:00.0000000Z
```

Create a file named /Staging/Players/PlayerDetails.txt with these fields, with multiple rows, and upload to your Blob store (adedeveastus2/biometricstats). Include a header row.

TIP   You can retrieve a file for use in your job from the GitHub repository for this book at http://mng.bz/gyZ8.

The file selector provides the path to the files, but not the authorization for ADLA to access them. For that, you must add an additional data source to ADLA.

7.6.2   *Adding a new data source*

In order to read files from Blob Storage in your job, ADLA needs access to the Storage account Blob service. Initially, ADLA has access to only the Data Lake store that was selected during creation. In order to access other stores, you need to add them as new data sources.

USING AZURE PORTAL

The following describes how to create one in the Azure portal:

1 In the Azure portal, use the All Services menu and filter on Data Lake Analytics to show the ADLA blade.

2 Select the ADLA service that needs the new data source to view the Overview blade.

3 Click Data Lake Analytics > Data Explorer to open the Data Explorer blade.

4 Click Add Data Source to open the New Data Source dialog.

5 Choose a Storage type, from Azure Data Lake Storage Gen1 or Azure Storage.

6 Under Selection Method, choose Select Account.

7 Choose the correct subscription, if you have access to more than one.

8 Choose an existing account from the Azure data source list.

When adding a data source through the Azure portal, the Add Data Source dialog handles credentials for Blob Storage. Connections to Data Lake stores from ADLA occur at the job level. Each job will be submitted by an authorized AAD entity, either a user account or a service principal for a service like Azure Data Factory. ADLA passes credentials to the Data Lake store for the user executing the jobs. For jobs connecting to Blob Storage, ADLA uses the stored access key for the data source.

USING AZURE POWERSHELL

You can also add the Storage account to your ADLA service via Azure PowerShell. Use the `Add-AzDataLakeAnalyticsDataSource` command to add the service. Set the `Account` parameter to the name of the ADLA service to update, `Blob` to the Storage account name, and `DataLakeStore` to the ADLS store name. When connecting to a data source in a Storage account, you must provide an access key using the `AccessKey` parameter. You can retrieve this key from the Storage account. Add the resource group of the new data source, if different from the ADLA, using `ResourceGroupName`. Listing 7.19 shows an example of adding Blob Storage from a separate resource group to the ADLA service and a Data Lake store from the same resource group.

> **Listing 7.19   Add Storage account Blob Storage**

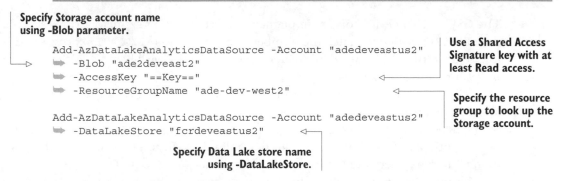

Specify Storage account name using -Blob parameter.

```
Add-AzDataLakeAnalyticsDataSource -Account "adedeveastus2"
    -Blob "ade2deveast2"
    -AccessKey "==Key=="
    -ResourceGroupName "ade-dev-west2"

Add-AzDataLakeAnalyticsDataSource -Account "adedeveastus2"
    -DataLakeStore "fcrdeveastus2"
```

Use a Shared Access Signature key with at least Read access.

Specify the resource group to look up the Storage account.

Specify Data Lake store name using -DataLakeStore.

Now you can create a U-SQL script to read from the data source.

7.6.3 Filtering rowsets

To read the tab-separated text file, you can use the generic Text extractor. You can provide any or all of the parameters. For a tab-separated file, you'll use the `delimiter` parameter to specify `\t`, the tab character.

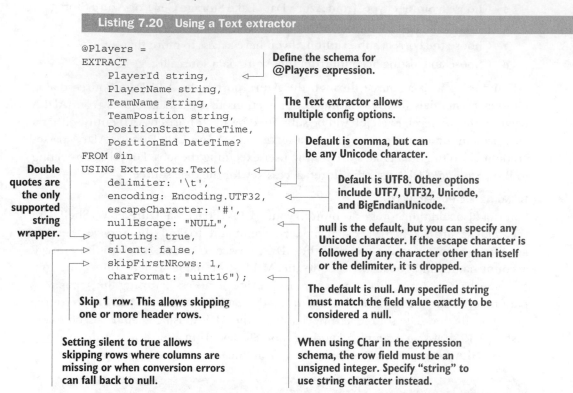

Listing 7.20 Using a Text extractor

```
@Players =
EXTRACT
    PlayerId string,
    PlayerName string,
    TeamName string,
    TeamPosition string,
    PositionStart DateTime,
    PositionEnd DateTime?
FROM @in
USING Extractors.Text(
    delimiter: '\t',
    encoding: Encoding.UTF32,
    escapeCharacter: '#',
    nullEscape: "NULL",
    quoting: true,
    silent: false,
    skipFirstNRows: 1,
    charFormat: "uint16");
```

Define the schema for @Players expression.

The Text extractor allows multiple config options.

Default is comma, but can be any Unicode character.

Default is UTF8. Other options include UTF7, UTF32, Unicode, and BigEndianUnicode.

null is the default, but you can specify any Unicode character. If the escape character is followed by any character other than itself or the delimiter, it is dropped.

The default is null. Any specified string must match the field value exactly to be considered a null.

Double quotes are the only supported string wrapper.

Skip 1 row. This allows skipping one or more header rows.

Setting silent to true allows skipping rows where columns are missing or when conversion errors can fall back to null.

When using Char in the expression schema, the row field must be an unsigned integer. Specify "string" to use string character instead.

The CSV and TSV extractors are implementations of the Text extractor, with a specific delimiter. It's critical to match the number of columns in the EXTRACT expression with the fields in the file. If they don't match, none of the rows will be read. If the row has *null* values, use a nullable field type.

U-SQL scripts can contain multiple expressions, to transform rowsets. Extractors and outputters don't use filters, but SELECT rowset operations can. The filter is a mix of SQL WHERE clause and C# comparison and equivalency operators. For example, use `!= null` instead of IS NOT NULL to filter out null values. In this case, we want the filter to include rows where the PositionEnd date is *null*.

This operation assigns the name @CurrentPlayers to the SELECT query expression rowset. Expressions can become as complex and numerous as necessary to complete the calculations. The following query expression returns the list of players currently on a team.

Listing 7.21 U-SQL filter expression

```
@CurrentPlayers =
SELECT
    PlayerName AS Name,          ◄──── Capitalize AS to provide an
    TeamName AS Team,                  alternate column name.
    TeamPosition AS Position
    FROM @Players                      Use C# equality instead        Group by column
    WHERE PositionEnd == null   ◄───── of SQL null equality.          names instead of
    GROUP BY PlayerName, TeamName, TeamPosition;   ◄────────────────  aliases.
```

The U-SQL expressions resemble SQL statements in most regards. You can see more similarities and differences in later chapters.

For this scenario, the job should output comma-separated values to the file. Listing 7.22 shows the expression for writing a rowset using the Text outputter. The outputter uses the rowset expression from listing 7.21 for the data source. The target is a CSV file in the Data Lake store, in the Raw folder. Because the input files included a header row, you need to write a header row in the output file. The Text outputter supports this based on the fields defined in the rowset expression. The CSV and TSV outputters are implementations of the Text outputter, using the defaults and a comma or tab character as the delimiter, respectively.

Listing 7.22 Using a Text outputter

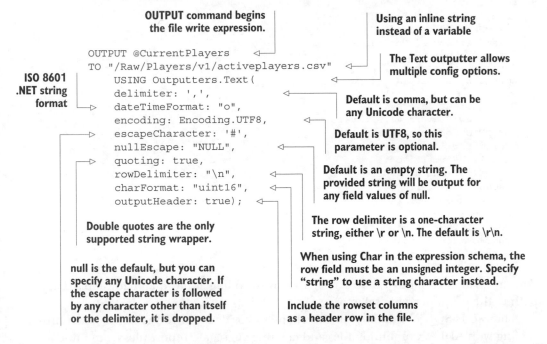

```
                    OUTPUT command begins                    Using an inline string
                    the file write expression.               instead of a variable

              OUTPUT @CurrentPlayers       ◄────
              TO "/Raw/Players/v1/activeplayers.csv"  ◄────  The Text outputter allows
                  USING Outputters.Text(                     multiple config options.
ISO 8601          delimiter: ',',
.NET string       dateTimeFormat: "o",    ◄────────────      Default is comma, but can be
format            encoding: Encoding.UTF8,                   any Unicode character.
                  escapeCharacter: '#',   ◄────────────      Default is UTF8, so this
                  nullEscape: "NULL",     ◄────────────      parameter is optional.
                  quoting: true,
                  rowDelimiter: "\n",     ◄────────────      Default is an empty string. The
                  charFormat: "uint16",   ◄────────────      provided string will be output for
                  outputHeader: true);    ◄────────────      any field values of null.

              Double quotes are the only                     The row delimiter is a one-character
              supported string wrapper.                      string, either \r or \n. The default is \r\n.

              null is the default, but you can               When using Char in the expression schema, the
              specify any Unicode character. If              row field must be an unsigned integer. Specify
              the escape character is followed               "string" to use a string character instead.
              by any character other than itself
              or the delimiter, it is dropped.               Include the rowset columns
                                                             as a header row in the file.
```

Listing 7.23 shows the complete U-SQL script for reading a file from Blob Storage. The script uses parameters on the extractor and outputter to match the file specifications.

Listing 7.23   U-SQL script to list players

```
DECLARE EXTERNAL @fileprefix string = "Player";
DECLARE @in string = String.Format(
➡ "wasb://biometricstats@adedeveastus2/Staging/Players/{0}{1}.txt",
➡ @fileprefix, "{*}");

@Players =
EXTRACT
    PlayerId string,
    PlayerName string,
    TeamName string,
    TeamPosition string,
    PositionStart DateTime,
    PositionEnd DateTime?
FROM @in
USING Extractors.Text(
    delimiter: '\t',
    encoding: Encoding.UTF8,
    escapeCharacter: '#',
    nullEscape: "NULL",
    quoting: true,
    silent: false,
    skipFirstNRows: 1,
    charFormat: "uint16");

@CurrentPlayers =
SELECT
    PlayerName AS Name,
    TeamName AS Team,
    TeamPosition AS Position
    FROM @Players
    WHERE PositionEnd != null
    GROUP BY PlayerName, TeamName, TeamPosition;

OUTPUT @CurrentPlayers
    TO "/Raw/Players/v1/APlayers.csv"
    USING Outputters.Text(
    delimiter: ',',
    dateTimeFormat: "o",
    encoding: Encoding.UTF8,
    escapeCharacter: '#',
    nullEscape: "NOTHING",
    quoting: true,
    rowDelimiter: "\n",
    charFormat: "uint16",
    outputHeader: true);
```

You can write files out to a Blob service too, by providing a fully-qualified Blob storage path to the outputter's file selector.

The two U-SQL jobs defined in this chapter provide an introduction to batch processing with ADLA. Combining files and creating aggregate report files from raw data may be all you need to do. You'll get to see more complex batch processing in chapters 8 and 9.

7.7 Exercises

7.7.1 Exercise 1

Given this list of files, write a file selector which includes only files of type CSV with "12" in the name.

- /sales/nj/park1/2012-01-08-receipts.csv
- /sales/nj/park1/2012-01-09-receipts.csv
- /sales/nj/park1/2013-01-12-receipts.csv
- /sales/nj/park1/2014-01-09-receipts.csv

SOLUTION

More than one wildcard can be used for extractor selectors. This selector will include the first three files.

```
DECLARE @in string = "/sales/nj/park1/{*}12{*}.csv";
```

7.7.2 Exercise 2

Using the following list of files and the given U-SQL script, how many AUs would you choose for your first job submission, to get an acceptable cost/speed ratio?

Filename	File size	File type
balls1.csv	855 MB	CSV
balls2.csv	655 MB	CSV
balls3.csv	565 MB	CSV
balls4.csv	995 MB	CSV
balls5.csv	755 MB	CSV
balls6.csv	602 MB	CSV
balls7.csv	677 MB	CSV
balls8.csv	822 MB	CSV
balls9.csv	599 MB	CSV
balls10.csv	765 MB	CSV
balls11.csv	752 MB	CSV
balls12.csv	678 MB	CSV
balls12.csv	681 MB	CSV
balls12.csv	854 MB	CSV
balls12.csv	644 MB	CSV
balls12.csv	589 MB	CSV

```
DECLARE EXTERNAL @in string = "/balls/balls{*}.csv";

@Balls =
    EXTRACT Id Guid,
        BallWeight decimal,
        BallManu string,
        BallSource int,
        BallUse DateTime
    FROM @in
    USING Extractors.Csv();

@BigBalls =
    SELECT
        Id,
        BallWeight,
        BallSource
    FROM @Balls
    WHERE BallWeight > 5.5
    GROUP BY Id, BallWeight, BallSource;

DECLARE EXTERNAL @out string = "/balls/bigballs.csv";

OUTPUT @BigBalls
    TO @out
    USING Outputters.Csv(outputHeader: true);
```

SOLUTION

Because the total size of the files to be read is just over 11 GB, you can use two AUs for the first run and get a significant reduction in execution time for little additional cost. You can use the 1/8th total size rule to calculate the number of AUs.

Summary

- U-SQL scripts use a mix of SQL and C# to define processing steps. The steps read, transform, and write data.
- U-SQL includes built-in classes for reading and writing text files. These classes let you focus on the data transforms instead of file manipulation at scale.
- Data Lake Analytics jobs can read from Data Lake stores and Blob Storage. This allows ADLA jobs to move data between services.
- Data Lake Analytics compiles U-SQL scripts into jobs that can be run in parallel. You can scale the amount of parallelization to balance your need for speed versus minimizing cost.

U-SQL for complex analytics

In the last chapter, you learned how to create an Azure Data Lake Analytics (ADLA) account and how to build and run simple jobs. In this chapter, you'll build on that knowledge by writing more complex queries. Because U-SQL scripts compile into C# programs, you can use many C# features within U-SQL expressions.

- You'll compare methods of structuring U-SQL for reuse, including creating indexed data stores in the U-SQL Catalog.
- You'll use C# language features to replace and extend features of SQL.
- You'll see how to reap benefits from previous jobs by reusing outputs and repeatedly reusing U-SQL scripts.

Let's get started by prepping some data for repeated use.

> **TIP**   You can find the code listings in the GitHub repository for this book at https://github.com/rnuckolls/azure_storage.

8.1   *Data Lake Analytics Catalog*

ADLA uses the attached Data Lake store for more than reading and writing files. It offers a structured interface for querying reusable rowsets via a database catalog. The catalog provides a few features for creating and running ADLA jobs, including the following:

- A database and table-naming convention
- Indexes for faster query performance
- Partitioned data for faster query performance
- Reusable rowsets across U-SQL jobs, without extractor expressions or file selectors

The ADLA catalog lets you collect and access U-SQL databases. U-SQL databases can collect and access database objects, including tables, views, functions, and stored procedures. You can then access these in your U-SQL scripts in ADLA jobs. You can view the databases in the catalog using the ADLA Data Explorer in the Azure portal. Browse to the ADLA service and choose Data Lake Analytics > Data Explorer blade. Figure 8.1 shows this tool.

> **WARNING**   Although you can use U-SQL databases the same way you use SQL Server databases, they aren't interchangeable. Indexed tables, SELECT queries using joins, views, and table-valued functions all work similarly. But you won't find common table expressions, temp tables, or SSMS.

The ADLA catalog is created when you set up your ADLA account, in the form of a folder in the default Data Lake store named *catalog*, containing data files and schema metadata. The initial files define the *master* database. The files for any U-SQL database you create will be stored in this folder.

The ADLA catalog does nothing by itself; it only provides a file and folder structure for U-SQL databases. Let's build a database of useful objects to help our users query data in the Data Lake store.

8.1.1   *Simplifying U-SQL queries*

Suppose you have a group of users who want to write queries against some data files in your Data Lake store. If these users are developers and want to learn U-SQL, you can give them access to ADLA and let them write their own jobs. What if these users only know SQL? You can build an interface for them using a U-SQL database.

Using a U-SQL database, with tables and views, gives your users a familiar syntax to query the backend data in the ADLS store. The users can be shielded from the added complexity of file imports. Let's create a database and objects using the biometric sensor data from chapter 7.

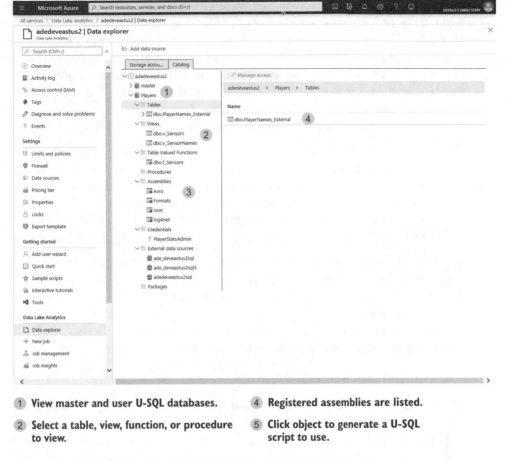

① **View master and user U-SQL databases.**   ④ **Registered assemblies are listed.**

② **Select a table, view, function, or procedure**   ⑤ **Click object to generate a U-SQL**
   to view.   **script to use.**

Figure 8.1   ADLA Data Explorer showing the U-SQL database objects

8.1.2   *Simplifying data access*

The Jonestown Sluggers are trying out uniforms with biometric sensors and collecting data in the Data Lake store. Some analysts want to access the data and add sensor names to the reports they generate. The sensor data is stored in your Data Lake
store.

U-SQL DATABASE

Because these analysts will write queries using the same set of data files repeatedly, you
can use some U-SQL database features to simplify writing the queries. You can build
one or more reusable objects in a U-SQL database.

The U-SQL catalog for your ADLA account comes with the *master* database. All
U-SQL scripts start with a reference to this database, so by default any U-SQL script
can access objects within it. You can place new objects in the master database, which

makes them easy to access. However, creating objects here restricts your ability to manage data access and prevents removing objects at the database level. For example, if you want to limit access by department, you can place related objects in a department-specific U-SQL database and grant access to that department. In another case, you could create a U-SQL database for use by consultants doing data analysis. You can load the required data into the database, and when the project is completed, clean up the temporary data and artifacts by removing the database. These scenarios are difficult to accomplish using the master database. You'll find additional benefits to using a U-SQL database later in the chapter.

> **IMPORTANT**   Always create at least one U-SQL database in your ADLA account. This keeps all the database objects together and makes managing the database objects, including granting access and deletions, much safer. Always use a `USE DATABASE [Database];` command in your scripts when working with U-SQL databases.

You use a U-SQL script in an ADLA job to create a database. In this case, the U-SQL script contains only expressions and does not read or write files. You load the script into a job like any other. You need to run the script only once, and the database will persist. You can configure access after the database is created. The syntax for creating the database is familiar. Use 'IF NOT EXISTS' when creating a database to confirm it doesn't already exist, as in the following statement:

```
CREATE DATABASE IF NOT EXISTS Players;
```

It's also easy to just drop the database if it already exists, shown in the following statement. This pattern removes a current database and replaces it with an empty one. Be careful with this, because any objects created in the existing database will be deleted.

```
DROP DATABASE IF EXISTS Players;
CREATE DATABASE Players;
```

Once you've created the database, you can view it in the Azure portal.

Here's how to configure access to the U-SQL database in the Azure portal:

1 In the Azure portal, use the All Services menu and filter on Data Lake Analytics to show the ADLA blade.
2 Select the ADLA service where you created the database to view the Overview blade.
3 Click Data Lake Analytics > Data Explorer to view the Data Explorer blade.
4 The left navigation window contains two nodes: a folder hierarchy for the account and a catalog hierarchy for the account. Expand the Account Catalog node, and click on the new database.
5 Click the Manage Access button to open the Access blade.
6 Click the Add button in the Access blade to add access to Active Directory users and groups.

Now that you have the database container, you can add other objects. You have three options for reusing file import code: a U-SQL view, a table-valued function, or a U-SQL table. All of these need data to be useful. Two data files are provided for use with these objects. You can get the biometric sensor file from the GitHub site for this book at http://mng.bz/eQrG. Save this file in your Data Lake store as /Staging/Sensor/v1/sensor_00.csv. The biometric sensor naming file is also on GitHub at http://mng.bz/pBMR. Save it in your Data Lake store as /Raw/Sensor/v1/SensorNames.txt.

> **TIP** The biometric sensor file has 100 K rows containing player and sensor IDs, and sensor values with timestamps. This schema was generated from data submitted to an Event Hub and written to Data Lake store with Stream Analytics.
>
> You can also get a simple C# project for creating multiple large data files in this format in the repository at http://mng.bz/OMdj.

U-SQL VIEW

U-SQL views offer a means to encapsulate U-SQL extractor and query expressions. You can think of this as moving a block of code into a separate function, where the database is the class, and the function returns a rowset. U-SQL views define a rowset, either as a SELECT command from a U-SQL table, a value array, or as an EXTRACT command from files. Create a view using CREATE VIEW [viewname], and remove a view using DROP VIEW [viewname]. You can include the IF EXISTS option to check if it exists before execution. The following listing shows the script for a view which reads from the sensors file.

Listing 8.1 U-SQL view for sensors file

```
USE DATABASE Players;
DROP VIEW IF EXISTS v_Sensors;        ⟵  Drop view first to
CREATE VIEW v_Sensors   ⟵               replace an existing view.
    AS
EXTRACT Id Guid,              No need to check for
        Player string,       existence immediately
        Node int,            following DROP VIEW
        NodeValue decimal,   command
        EventTime DateTime,
        PartitionId int,
        EventEnqueuedUtcTime DateTime,
        EventProcessedUtcTime DateTime
    FROM "/Staging/Sensor/v1/sensor_00.csv"
    USING Extractors.Csv(skipFirstNRows: 1);
```

Views operate much like expression variables, but the logic for populating the rowset is saved in the U-SQL database for use across ADLA jobs. You can reuse the view in U-SQL scripts by fully qualifying its name, in the form [Database].[Schema].[Name]. You can also add a USE [Database] statement to shorten the object names in the script. U-SQL databases include the dbo schema by default. New database objects are added using the dbo schema unless a different schema is included in the object at creation. The following listing shows a U-SQL script using the new view and outputting the rowset to a new file.

Listing 8.2   Query the U-SQL view for sensors file

```
@view = SELECT * FROM [Players].[dbo].[v_Sensors];    ◁────  This expression uses the
                                                              fully qualified view name.
OUTPUT @view
    TO "/Sandbox/User1/Players.dbo.v_Sensors.tsv"     ◁────  Write out the rowset into
    USING Outputters.Tsv();                                   your user sandbox folder.
```

At this point, your users can access the sensor data, but not the sensor names. You can add a second view to provide access to the names in the same way you created the sensor data view.

Listing 8.3   U-SQL view for SensorNames file

```
USE DATABASE Players;
DROP VIEW IF EXISTS v_SensorNames;
CREATE VIEW v_SensorNames
    AS
EXTRACT Id int,
        NodeName string
    FROM "/Raw/Sensor/v1/SensorNames.txt"
    USING Extractors.Tsv();
```

You can manage this same set of Sensor names with a SELECT ... FROM VALUES rowset. The VALUES operator specifies an array object as the data source, instead of a U-SQL table, rowset variable, or extractor function. When you create row data with VALUES, you don't need to upload or read data from files. The rowset gets compiled with the ADLA job, and you don't have to wait for the file read during job execution.

Creating the SELECT ... FROM VALUES rowset uses a specific syntax to create the row array. The array is a comma-separated list of parenthesis-delimited comma-separated field values. The array is then declared as a rowset with field names. Each row is within parentheses: (1, "abc") is a row with an integer of value 1 and a string with value abc. The rowset declaration VALUES (a,b), (a,b) is wrapped in parentheses too. The column name declaration uses the AS {alias}({fieldName},{fieldName}); clause, following the rowset declaration. The entire expression looks like SELECT * FROM (VALUES (a,b), (a,b)) AS X(A,B);. You can see how this works as an alternative to using an EXTRACT statement for the sensor names file in the following listing.

Listing 8.4   U-SQL view using VALUES table

```
USE DATABASE Players;
DROP VIEW IF EXISTS v_SensorNames;
CREATE VIEW v_SensorNames
    AS
SELECT *                        The VALUES clause and rows
FROM (VALUES      ◁────         are wrapped in parentheses.
```

```
(1,"Heartrate"),
(2,"Pulse"),
(3,"Temperature Chest"),
(4,"O2"),
(5,"Left Pectoralis"),
// Shortened for readability
(38,"Right Metatarsal Pressure"),
(39,"Unused"),
(40,"Unused")
) AS r(Id,NodeName);
```

Each row is wrapped in parentheses, contains all fields separated by commas, and is separated from subsequent rows by a comma.

The rowset alias is unused, but the field name list is required.

The table schema can be declared implicitly, as in listing 8.4, or the field types can be declared explicitly. The explicit declaration looks like `AS r(Id int, SensorName string)`. Now you have two views to extract some complexity from the analysis queries. Let's look at how you use these views in a U-SQL query.

U-SQL JOIN

With two views, you have two separate rowsets. With U-SQL, you use a `JOIN` clause in a `SELECT` statement to connect two rowsets into one. Five types of joins are available in U-SQL:

- INNER JOIN
- OUTER JOIN
- CROSS JOIN
- SEMIJOIN
- ANTISEMIJOIN

`INNER JOIN` and `OUTER JOIN` work like their T-SQL counterparts. `CROSS JOIN` joins every row of the first rowset with every row of the second rowset. `SEMIJOIN` includes every row in the first rowset that has at least one matching row in the second rowset. `ANTISEMIJOIN` includes every row in the first rowset that has no matching rows in the second rowset. Except for `CROSS JOIN`, all joins use the `ON` clause to define the match or matches between individual fields in the rowsets. Listing 8.5 shows the use of an `INNER JOIN` to add the sensor name to the list of sensor values by joining two views. The join clause uses the C# equality operator `==` to match the fields.

When using a join clause, you must provide an alias for each rowset in the expression, in the form `[ObjectName] AS [alias]`. Aliases can contain letters and numbers, and must start with a letter. The `AS` operator is a reserved word. All reserved words in U-SQL are all capitals, and only reserved words can be all capitals. Make sure your aliases include at least one lowercase letter or a number.

Listing 8.5 Query the U-SQL views for sensors with sensor names

```
@view = SELECT s.Id, s.Player, s.Node, sn.NodeName, s.NodeValue, s.EventTime
    FROM [Players].[dbo].[v_Sensors] AS s
    INNER JOIN [Players].[dbo].[v_SensorNames] AS sn
    ON s.Node == sn.Id;
```

Fully qualified view name

Match two fields in the join clause with ==.

AS sn clause to add alias

```
OUTPUT @view
    TO "/Sandbox/User1/Players.dbo.v_Sensors.tsv"
    USING Outputters.Tsv();
```

If you wanted, you could even bundle the two view expressions in listing 8.5 into a third view. Views are useful for single expression reuse.

At this point, you can hand over the script from listing 8.5 to your users and let them query the data. But perhaps you want to simplify the expressions further, or add more functionality to the data lookup. If you want to reuse multiple expressions, you can use a table-valued function.

U-SQL TABLE-VALUED FUNCTIONS

Table-valued functions (TVF) extend the view wrapper for reusing U-SQL expressions. TVFs add three extra features beyond the view:

1 Optional parameters
2 A returned `TABLE` definition
3 A `BEGIN ... END` wrapper for multiple expressions

By using parameters, you can extract logic flow from your analysis scripts, read data from different files or folders, or move `WHERE` clauses into routines for consistent use. The TVF can contain far larger blocks of logic than views, by combining multiple expressions in a chain.

You create a TVF with the `CREATE FUNCTION [functionname]` command and remove it with `DROP FUNCTION [functionname]`. You can include the `IF EXISTS` option to check if it exists before execution.

The TVF can include one or more parameters by adding a parenthetical set of variable declarations. These variables are available for use in the TVF. `CREATE FUNCTION [f_Name] (@ID int = 0)` shows the first part of the command, specifying an integer parameter named `@ID`. The `@ID` variable has a default value set, so the parameter will be optional when using the TVF. Separate multiple parameters with commas.

TVFs must define a return variable as a `TABLE` type. This type includes a field definition schema very similar to a table variable in T-SQL. Use the clause `RETURNS @result TABLE()` to define the return variable. Add each field with a name and type, separated by commas, within the parentheses. A typical variable with an integer and string fields looks like `RETURNS @result TABLE(Id int, Result string)`.

The body of the TVF is defined by the clause `AS BEGIN ... END;` which wraps the data processing expressions. The TVF body can have any number of expressions. The last expression must assign the `RETURNS` variable to an expression that returns the fields for the `TABLE()`. For instance, for a return clause of `RETURNS @result TABLE(Id int, Result string)` the last expression would include the `Id` and `Result` fields.

```
BEGIN
--expressions omitted for brevity
@result = SELECT Id, Result FROM @rows;
END;
```

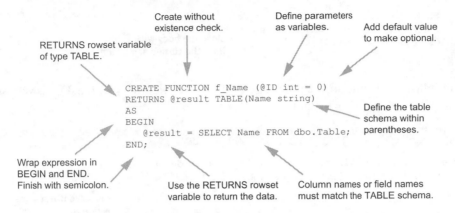

Figure 8.2 Table-valued function description

Figure 8.2 shows an example of the entire TVF U-SQL creation script.

Expressions in a TVF can read from the same sources as any other U-SQL script, including value rowsets, EXTRACT statements, views, tables, and other TVFs.

The following listing shows the script for a view that reads from the sensors file.

Listing 8.6 U-SQL function for sensors file with sensor names

```
USE DATABASE Players;
DROP FUNCTION IF EXISTS f_Sensors;          No need to check for existence
CREATE FUNCTION f_Sensors ()                immediately following DROP
RETURNS @result TABLE(                      FUNCTION command
    Id Guid, Player string, Node int, NodeName string,
    NodeValue decimal, EventTime DateTime)          Define the six fields of
    AS                                              the sensor values with
BEGIN                                               name result.
@sensors = EXTRACT         Start the body
        Id Guid,           with BEGIN.
        Player string,
        Node int,
        NodeValue decimal,
        EventTime DateTime,
        PartitionId int,
        EventEnqueuedUtcTime DateTime,
        EventProcessedUtcTime DateTime
    FROM "/Staging/Sensor/v1/sensor_00.csv"
    USING Extractors.Csv(skipFirstNRows: 1);

@sensorNames = EXTRACT
        Id int,
        NodeName string            Use the              Match the field
    FROM "/Raw/Sensor/v1/SensorNames.txt"    RETURNS    names of the
    USING Extractors.Tsv();                  variable for  rowset with field
                                             the last rowset  names of the
@result = SELECT                             expression.   TABLE variable.
        s.Id, s.Player, s.Node, sn.NodeName, s.NodeValue, s.EventTime
```

Drop view first to replace an existing TVF.

```
      FROM @sensors AS s
      INNER JOIN @sensorNames AS sn
      ON s.Node == sn.Id;                        Close the body with END;.
END;                                             Note the closing semicolon.
```

The following listing shows the usage of the TVF. The query with a TVF is very similar to a query using a view or table.

```
@view = SELECT s.Id, s.Player, s.Node, sn.NodeName, s.NodeValue, s.EventTime
     FROM [Players].[dbo].[f_Sensors]() AS s;              No parameters needed,
                                                           but parentheses are
OUTPUT @view                                               required
     TO "/Sandbox/User1/Players.dbo.f_Sensors.tsv"
     USING Outputters.Tsv();
```

Putting parameters within the parentheses adds options for the behavior of the TVF. For example, suppose you want to add a new field to the sensor file. This is an example of structural drift, and it can break reading and import processes. You need an approach to handle changes to analytics processes dealing with these files.

   In order to read both the eight-field and nine-field schemas, you could create separate views or functions for each schema version. This can be cumbersome when multiple schemas are in use or the schemas change frequently. This book recommends that the folder structure for the sensor file follows the zones framework, including a level for versioning. Creating a function with a version parameter makes managing the data extracts easier.

   The first version of the TVF reads the sensor file from the version 1 folder, /Staging/Sensor/v1/sensor_00.csv. The second version reads from both version 1 and version 2 folders and uses the version parameter to switch between them.

   First, add a parameter for the version to the CREATE clause. CREATE FUNCTION [f_Sensors] (@version string = "v2") shows the first part of the command, specifying a string parameter named @version. The @version variable has a default value set, so the parameter will be optional when using the TVF. Unless specified with the version parameter, the TVF will return data from the version 2 file set.

> **NOTE**   You can read more about the zones framework and data drift in chapter 4. For this chapter, we will use two versions of the sensor file with different schemas. Each version will have its own folder under the file set folder. You can retrieve three files, with 100 K rows in this format, for use in your job at http://mng.bz/YrQj, sensor_02.csv, and sensor_03.csv. Save these files to your Data Lake store in /Staging/Sensor/v2/sensor_01.csv, /Staging/Sensor/v2/sensor_02.csv, and /Staging/Sensor/v2/sensor_03.csv.

You can structure your TVF to allow targeting folders when reading data files, based on a parameter. For the sensor files, you can write the expressions with different queries, based on the differences between versions. This calls for an IF ... THEN ... ELSE statement.

U-SQL supports one selection statement for logic, the IF statement. Given two versions of the sensor files, one including the new field "NodeType", you can structure your TVF to support both. You can chain multiple ELSEIF statements together with IF to handle multiple options.

The IF statement looks like a blend of the SQL and C# versions. It combines a series of expressions ending with semicolons, but without brackets or parentheses.

```
IF @version == "v2" THEN
    --EXTRACT FROM v2;
ELSE
    --EXTRACT FROM v1;
END;
```

For three or more options, you can add multiple selections using ELSEIF clauses before the final ELSE.

```
IF @version == "v3" THEN
    --EXTRACT FROM v3;
ELSEIF @version == "v2" THEN
    --EXTRACT FROM v2;
ELSE
    --EXTRACT FROM v1;
END;
```

Now let's make a new script to handle both versions. First, add an optional version parameter to the TVF. This parameter will be used to determine which schema version and file location to use, with a default value indicating the latest version. Adding a default value makes the TVF easier to use and provides a measure of self-documentation.

```
CREATE FUNCTION f_Sensors (@version string = "v2")
```

Next, update the RETURNS clause to include the new field. TVFs return a single TABLE type. Because the new schema includes an extra field, it must be added to the TABLE type.

```
RETURNS @result TABLE(
    Id Guid, Player string, Node int, NodeType string,
    NodeName string, NodeValue decimal, EventTime DateTime)
```

The addition of the new field implies all other versions of the rowset will include the field, even if the file schema did not contain it. You will need to decide on a value for this new field for these schemas: a null, default, or lookup value. For this example, provide a value of Unknown. In this example there are only two versions. You can cover them both with a single IF ... ELSE statement. With these defaults in place, you can write the complete U-SQL script.

Listing 8.8   U-SQL function for sensor file with sensor names and versioning

```
USE DATABASE Players;
DROP FUNCTION IF EXISTS f_Sensors;
CREATE FUNCTION f_Sensors  (@version string = "v2")
RETURNS @result TABLE(
    Id Guid, Player string, Node int, NodeType string,
    NodeName string, NodeValue decimal, EventTime DateTime)
AS
BEGIN
    IF @version == "v2" THEN          ◁───  Use the C#
    @sensors = EXTRACT                      equality ==.
        Id Guid,
        Player string,
        Node int,
        NodeType string,
        NodeValue decimal,
        EventTime DateTime,
        PartitionId int,
        EventEnqueuedUtcTime DateTime,
        EventProcessedUtcTime DateTime
        FROM "/Staging/Sensor/v2/sensor_{*}.csv"     ◁───  With multiple files,
        USING Extractors.Csv(skipFirstNRows: 1);           use a wildcard {*}
                                                           to read all files.
    ELSE
    @sensorLoad = EXTRACT
        Id Guid,
        Player string,
        Node int,
        NodeValue decimal,
        EventTime DateTime,
        PartitionId int,
        EventEnqueuedUtcTime DateTime,
        EventProcessedUtcTime DateTime
        FROM "/Staging/Sensor/v1/sensor_00.csv"
        USING Extractors.Csv(skipFirstNRows: 1);

    @sensors = SELECT
        Id, Player, Node, "Unknown" AS NodeType, NodeValue,
        EventTime, PartitionId, EventEnqueuedUtcTime, EventProcessedUtcTime
        FROM @sensorLoad;
    END;

@sensorNames = EXTRACT
        Id int,
        NodeName string
    FROM "/Raw/Sensor/v1/SensorNames.txt"
    USING Extractors.Tsv();

@result = SELECT
        s.Id, s.Player, s.Node, s.NodeType,
        sn.NodeName, s.NodeValue, s.EventTime     ◁───  Include new
    FROM @sensors AS s                                   field in the
    INNER JOIN @sensorNames AS sn                        return rowset.
    ON s.Node == sn.Id;
END;
```

Planning for data drift ensures the data in your Data Lake store remains accessible to your end users. Using views and TVFs lets you abstract some of these changes away. Because TVFs allow parameters and multiple expressions, they are a powerful method for abstracting complexity and handling changing versions of the same data.

8.1.3 *Loading data for reuse*

U-SQL provides one more method of abstracting the data access routines in ADLA jobs: the U-SQL table. U-SQL views and TVFs read the original Data Lake store files any time they are used in a job. U-SQL tables don't read from the original files, but save the data elsewhere. U-SQL tables use a set of sorted and indexed files to make data retrieval faster. Part of creating the U-SQL table is populating and indexing the files for the table. This provides both permanence to the data schema and a method for optimizing data reads. Storage location and read optimization are the key aspects to consider when using U-SQL tables.

U-SQL TABLES

U-SQL tables provide access to a pre-defined set of data in tabular format—rows and columns—along with a pre-defined schema for the underlying data. The ADLA catalog supports two types of tables:

1 Managed
2 External

Managed tables store the schema definition, *and the table data*, in files within the catalog folders in the associated Data Lake store. External tables store the schema definition, but reference external data sources. When your data is stored in an Azure SQL Database, you can leave the raw data there and configure read access through a U-SQL external table. When your data sources are files in your Data Lake store, or your database is not located in Azure, you can use a U-SQL managed table to restructure the data storage. Figure 8.3 shows the two types of U-SQL tables.

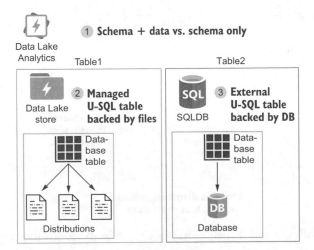

Figure 8.3 Managed versus external tables

U-SQL external tables support Azure SQL Database, SQL Data Warehouse, and Azure VM-hosted SQL Server. Chapter 9 covers integrating ADLA with external tables.

U-SQL managed tables (hereafter, *tables*) store large blocks of data organized for efficient reads and filtering. In addition, by defining schema, U-SQL tables simplify exploring the data in the Data Lake store. A U-SQL table is made up of a schema definition, a clustered index, and a backing file structure. The schema definition includes the table name, the field names and types, and a distribution method for storing the data rows across multiple files. This differs from the schema-on-read pattern, where you define the field order and field type in the EXTRACT expression. Every table must have an index and a distribution method. Let's look at details of creating a table.

CREATING A U-SQL TABLE

Creating a table uses the CREATE TABLE command. The command includes the table name. You can also include the IF NOT EXISTS option. You supply the list of fields as parameters to the command.

With the list of fields, you must include an index definition, which takes the form INDEX [name] CLUSTERED([Field] ASC/DESC). U-SQL tables only support clustered indexes. The CLUSTERED option takes a comma-separated list of one or more fields, with an ordering description.

CREATE TABLE also requires the DISTRIBUTED BY option. You must select an algorithm for distributing the data rows across the backing files, and one or more fields from the field list as a parameter for the algorithm. Listing 8.9 shows the script for creating a U-SQL table for the sensor file, which you have already loaded into your Data Lake store in /Staging/Sensor/v2/. The script adds an index on the Node and EventTime fields. It uses the HASH distribution algorithm on the Node field, which distributes rows with the same values as the Node field to the same backing file.

Listing 8.9   Create U-SQL table with hash distribution

```
USE DATABASE Players;
CREATE TABLE IF NOT EXISTS SensorData
(
    Id string,                          ⟵──  Define the table
    Player string,                            schema to match
    Node int,                                 the target file.
    NodeType string,
    NodeValue decimal,
    EventTime DateTime,
    PartitionId int,                                    Define a clustered
    EventEnqueuedUtcTime DateTime,                      index using one or
    EventProcessedUtcTime DateTime,                       more columns.
    INDEX idx_SensorData CLUSTERED(Node ASC, EventTime ASC)   ⟵──
)
DISTRIBUTED BY HASH(Node);       ⟵──  Choose a distribution method,
                                       with HASH as the default.
```

You can read more about indexes and distribution algorithms in the following sections.

TABLE STRUCTURE

Because U-SQL tables are basic structures, built on top of unstructured data files, creating objects requires a bit more thought than the typical relational database. Defining the table structure is the most important aspect of U-SQL table usage. Using the right table structure reduces the overall data read by eliminating entire segments of data. This is a form of *predicate pushdown,* and using it reduces the time and cost of running ADLA jobs.

Predicate pushdown isn't a set of code, but an approach to processing filters in SQL statements. A filter (predicate) can be evaluated in memory on the full dataset. Predicate pushdown seeks to evaluate the filter by limiting the amount of data read from storage to only that matching the filter. U-SQL tables enable this by distributing data rows into separate files with one or more keys.

TIP One way to harness predicate pushdown in ADLA jobs is by using conventions for naming and structuring the extracted files, like new folders each month or {year}-{month}-{day}-XYZ file naming conventions. This way, you can reduce the number of files and rows read into memory during the job. You can structure U-SQL EXTRACT expressions to target a relevant segment of data files for a job. Fewer files and fewer rows means fewer vertexes to run and shorter run times. You can read more about Data Lake Storage structure in chapter 4 and ADLA jobs in chapter 7.

TABLE DISTRIBUTIONS

The data stored in a U-SQL table is spread across two or more segments, called *distributions,* to aid in parallel reads and segment eliminations. Each distribution gets a set of the overall table data and is stored in a separate file or files.

Every U-SQL table must have a key for use in distributing the data rows. Each key value is assigned to a distribution according to an algorithm. The algorithms are listed in table 8.1.

Table 8.1 Distribution algorithms

Algorithm	Description	Use	Typical key field
Round-robin	Distributes all rows evenly across all segments	For unique identifiers, or data that heavily reuses a subset of values in the key field	Unique identifier
Range	Splits the values of the key into discrete ranges, and distributes the rows to segments with other rows in the same range	Good for date keys, and numeric data in known ranges	Cost, date, size
Hash	Hashes the key, and puts rows with the same key in the same segment	For data that reuses the values of the key field equally, and when you want to eliminate segments based on a category	Foreign keys

Figure 8.4 depicts distribution keys and methods for three different data sets for three different tables. The first table is designed around searching for data based on the PRICE field. The second is a lookup table with descriptions. The third would be used in queries joining and filtering on the CODE field.

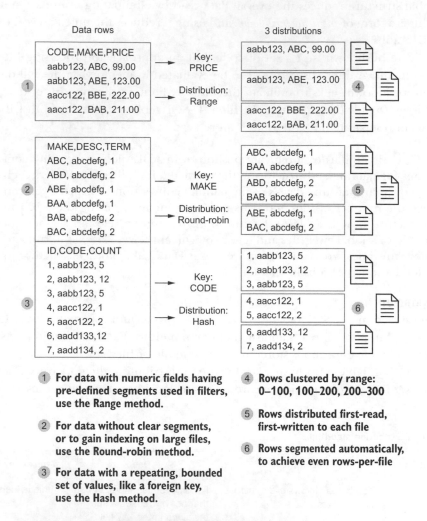

1. **For data with numeric fields having pre-defined segments used in filters, use the Range method.**

2. **For data without clear segments, or to gain indexing on large files, use the Round-robin method.**

3. **For data with a repeating, bounded set of values, like a foreign key, use the Hash method.**

4. **Rows clustered by range: 0–100, 100–200, 200–300**

5. **Rows distributed first-read, first-written to each file**

6. **Rows segmented automatically, to achieve even rows-per-file**

Figure 8.4   ADLA table distributions using different methods

The set of data in each distribution is determined by the key and the number of distributions on the table. Figure 8.5 shows distribution files on separate U-SQL tables. Each table defines the number of distributions used. The number of distributions can be chosen automatically or manually.

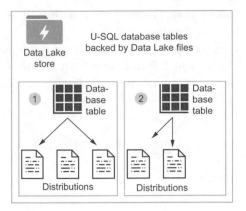

1. **U-SQL table with three distributions, three files**

2. **U-SQL table with two distributions**

Figure 8.5   ADLA table distributions structure

CHOOSING A DISTRIBUTION KEY

The segmentation of the data is driven by the distribution key. This key is one or more fields that are included in the table. In general, the key should be chosen based on the intended query usage. For lookup tables where a single row is used with a join, the unique identifier for the join is a good distribution key. For lookup tables where multiple rows are returned by the query, a field representing a foreign key is a good choice, when used with the *hash* distribution method. For data tables not reliant on joins, but that are used with WHERE clauses to define ranges like "greater than" or "between," use a field that represents a continuous set of values, like a date field or integer.

Each distribution file that makes up the U-SQL table should be no greater than 2 GB. Based on the expected table size, you can choose to set the distribution count for the table during creation. This calculation for N number of distributions follows:

(byte size of a single row) * (average row count per unique key) * (number of unique keys) / $N <= 2$ GB

For example, you could have 100 files, each with 1 M rows of 1 KB length, with 256 unique values in a potential key. You would calculate your number of distributions as:

(1 KB * (100 * 1000000 / 256) * 256) / 2 * 1048576 KB $<= N, N >= 48$

If you have most of the data to be loaded into the table when you start, you can allow the U-SQL job to calculate the number of distributions for you. The compiler chooses a distribution count from the list of 2, 10, 20, 60, 120, 240, 480 to meet the 2 GB target. To use this automatic calculation, choose a representative set of data for the initial load.

You don't want to use a data set that consists primarily of rows for a few unique identifiers, which you are then using for your distribution key.

You can retrieve the distribution key info using an Azure PowerShell command. `Get-AzDataLakeAnalyticsCatalogItem` will give you information about any U-SQL catalog item. The `-ItemType` parameter specifies the type of object from a set. Table 8.2 lists the allowed types.

Table 8.2   Catalog object types

Type	Description
Database	Container for U-SQL objects
Schema	dbo
Assembly	Custom C# code
Table	Schema metadata over data files
TableValuedFunction	TVF
TableStatistics	Data on U-SQL table's contents
ExternalDataSource	Connection info for external tables
View	Reusable Extractor expression
Procedure	Like a TVF, but does not return a rowset
Secret	Passwords
Credential	Connection info for external tables
Types	Custom C# types
TablePartition	Data on U-SQL table partitions

The `-Path` parameter uses the fully qualified object name, with the database, schema, and object name elements, and returns an object with several properties. To get the distribution info, target the `.DistributionInfo` property.

Listing 8.10   Table distribution information via Azure PowerShell

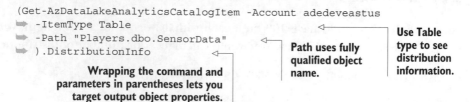

```
(Get-AzDataLakeAnalyticsCatalogItem -Account adedeveastus
   -ItemType Table
   -Path "Players.dbo.SensorData"
   ).DistributionInfo
```

Wrapping the command and parameters in parentheses lets you target output object properties.

Path uses fully qualified object name.

Use Table type to see distribution information.

The `.DistributionInfo` property output looks like the following example.

```
Type Keys           Count DynamicCount
---- ----           ----- ------------
   2 {Player, Node}    10            0
```

If your data grows too large for the 480 2 GB distributions, or you want to load and/or delete large segments of data at once, U-SQL tables offer partitions too.

TABLE PARTITIONS

In addition to the required distributions that store the data rows, tables can also divide rows among file partitions. U-SQL table partitions provide a coarser, more manual method of segmenting the rows in a table. File partitions allow larger table capacity and more options for predicate pushdown during queries.

Both table distributions and partitions reduce overall file reads for U-SQL queries, when using filters matching the segmentation keys. Using tables this way trades additional storage cost for reduced ADLA job costs, because the file reads are reduced significantly. Converting a data set originally segmented for one type of query (or undifferentiated) into a segmentation matching another query type is a strong use case for U-SQL tables. Figure 8.6 describes the process of predicate pushdown using U-SQL table partitions or distributions. Including the distribution or partition key in the WHERE clause lets the ADLA job compiler use the table structure to limit file reads to distributions that contain the key values 1, 2, or 3.

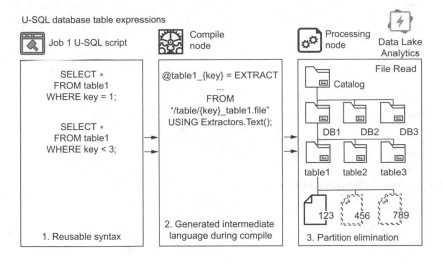

Figure 8.6   ADLA table partitions data elimination

NOTE   The intermediate language is not U-SQL, but the U-SQL EXTRACT expression is illustrative of the process.

When adding partitions to a U-SQL table, each partition's rows are distributed to files by the table distribution key, and all have the same partition key value(s). When partitioning is used, the underlying files backing the distributions are segmented further, grouped by the chosen partition key. Because of this, U-SQL tables don't allow the partition key to be the same field as the distribution key, or be included in the table index. The U-SQL table doesn't need to be partitioned, but if it will be, this must be done at table creation. During table loading, data will be added to a backing file based on the partition key value and the algorithm for the distribution key. As with files backing an unpartitioned table, file management is handled for you. Figure 8.7 demonstrates the hierarchy of segmentation with U-SQL tables.

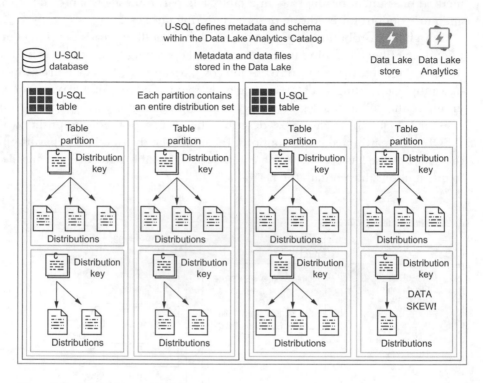

Figure 8.7   ADLA table partition structure

To create a table with partitions, include the PARTITIONED BY [field] parameter in the table creation expression. Listing 8.11 shows the expression for *SensorData*, modified for partitioning. In this case, the table is designed around queries that filter on players and sensor nodes.

Listing 8.11   Create a U-SQL table with a specific partition

```
USE DATABASE Players;
DROP TABLE IF EXISTS SensorData;
CREATE TABLE IF NOT EXISTS SensorData
(
    Id Guid,
    Player string,
    Node int,
    NodeType string,
```

```
       NodeValue decimal,
       EventTime DateTime,
       PartitionId int,
       EventEnqueuedUtcTime DateTime,
       EventProcessedUtcTime DateTime,
       INDEX idx_SensorData CLUSTERED(Node ASC, EventTime ASC)
)
PARTITIONED BY (Player)
DISTRIBUTED BY HASH(Node);
```

When planning to use partitions in U-SQL tables, consider both data loading and querying. U-SQL table loading works best when all the data in the partition is loaded during one or a few loads. Inserting data into existing U-SQL tables, either partitioned or not, creates delta files instead of appending to the original files. Read performance can begin to degrade after a few rounds of insertions. You may want to structure your partitions around the frequency of your data loads, to minimize this fragmentation. U-SQL includes a way to reorganize the underlying files to rectify this if it does occur. The REBUILD option on the ALTER TABLE command shifts data around in the backing files to make data reads from fewer files. This is an example of a U-SQL script with no file output.

```
ALTER TABLE [TableName] REBUILD;
```

Alternately, you may want to select partition key values that match different use cases for the data, such as years, clients, states, or other top-level divisions. This type of partitioning works well when the data products have been defined and you are optimizing the production system.

Before loading data into partitioned tables, you need to create the partitions. Each partition holds one value of the key. You need to generate a list of values for the field used to partition the table. This can be done by requesting the list from the data owners, or by running a U-SQL script over the data, grouping by the field in question. Once you have the list, create a U-SQL script containing the partitioning operations.

Creating partitions uses the ALTER TABLE command. Use the option ADD PARTITION to add a partition, or DROP PARTITION to drop a partition. Adding or dropping a partition takes the key value as a parameter, of a type matching the partition key. You can also include IF NOT EXISTS when adding partitions, and IF EXISTS when dropping partitions, which will prevent errors when executing the command. In most cases, you would not drop an existing partition before adding a new partition of the same value. Listing 8.12 shows the U-SQL script for adding the first partitions to the SensorData table, using string values.

Listing 8.12 Changing a U-SQL table

```
USE DATABASE Players;
DECLARE @partition string = "mjone101";
ALTER TABLE SensorData
ADD IF NOT EXISTS PARTITION (@partition);
```

```
DECLARE @partition2 string = "pharv102";
ALTER TABLE SensorData
ADD IF NOT EXISTS PARTITION (@partition2);
```

WRITING TO A U-SQL DATABASE TABLE

What happens if you load data to a partitioned table, but haven't created partitions for all the key values? The ADLA job will fail. Partitions for the key values must be created manually. There must be at least one partition added to the table before you can load data to a table created for partitioning. If there isn't a matching partition for all data rows, U-SQL provides an option for INSERT statements to handle this. You can drop the rows that don't match, or provide a catch-all partition. Add ON INTEGRITY VIOLATION IGNORE after the field definition to drop the row, or ON INTEGRITY VIOLATION MOVE TO PARTITION ([partition]) to write the row to the selected partition. Include a partition for unmatched values when you create the initial partitions. You must set a value for this partition but it doesn't matter what you choose, as long as it isn't in the partition key value set. The following listing shows an example for adding an unmatched key partition to the SensorData table.

Listing 8.13   Add unmatched partition to U-SQL table

```
USE DATABASE Players;
DECLARE @partitionx string = "playerx";
ALTER TABLE SensorData
ADD IF NOT EXISTS PARTITION (@partitionx);
```

With this extra partition, if you add ON INTEGRITY VIOLATION MOVE TO PARTITION ("playerx") to the INSERT statement, Player field data that doesn't match an existing partition will be loaded into the playerx partition.

Listing 8.14   Using INTEGRITY VIOLATION MOVE in a U-SQL table
---

```
USE DATABASE Players;

@sensors = EXTRACT
        Id Guid,
        Player string,
        Node int,
        NodeType string,
        NodeValue decimal,
        EventTime DateTime,
        PartitionId int,
        EventEnqueuedUtcTime DateTime,
        EventProcessedUtcTime DateTime
    FROM "/Staging/Sensor/v2/sensor_{*}.csv"
    USING Extractors.Csv(skipFirstNRows: 1);

INSERT INTO SensorData
(Id,Player,Node,NodeType,NodeValue,EventTime,
➥  PartitionId,EventEnqueuedUtcTime,EventProcessedUtcTime)
ON INTEGRITY VIOLATION MOVE TO PARTITION ("playerx")
SELECT * FROM sensors;
```

Inserting data into U-SQL tables updates the clustered index.

TABLE INDEXES

Every U-SQL table must have a clustered index, and there can be only one index per table. The clustered index organizes the rows within each distribution. The index is the row order within the distribution's backing files. The clustering key doesn't need to be unique. Because the distribution key is usually used as a predicate of the query reading from the table, including the key as an index field is a good idea. For instance, for tables with low ratio of rows per key value, rows for multiple key values can be stored in the same backing files. Therefore, adding the key field to the table index can reduce read times. The clustered index orders the rows within the backing files, and the U-SQL compiler can use the index to read only sub-sections of the file. You can create a *covering index*, which includes your expected query filters. The index can't be removed or changed once created. You will need to drop, then create and load the table to use a different index.

READING DATA FROM TABLES

To get the data back out of the table, you can use a regular rowset expression, with a fully qualified table name.

```
@sensorNames = SELECT * FROM [Players].[dbo].[SensorNames];
```

8.2   *Window functions*

U-SQL *window functions* segment the rowset by a selected field's value. Each row is segmented based on the specified field or fields. The number and size of segments is handled by the window function. In this way, it is similar to the GROUP BY clause that also handles the number and size of the output buckets. They differ in that GROUP BY reduces the number of rows in the resulting rowset to the number of unique values in each bucket, whereas the window function maintains the rows.

In U-SQL scripts, the OVER () clause is used with the selected aggregation function to generate a new field, or as part of a calculation. U-SQL includes the standard functions COUNT, SUM, MAX, MIN, STDEV, and AVG. You can't use the window function in the same expression as a GROUP BY clause.

For example, you might want to include the average of the NodeValue field for each row of the sensor data file, and then use it to calculate the difference between the row's value and the average. You can do this with a window function.

```
@counts =
    SELECT
        s.Player,
        s.Node,
        s.NodeValue,
        AVG(s.NodeValue) OVER () AS NodeValueAvg
        FROM [Players].[dbo].[f_Sensors]("v1") AS s;
```

```
OUTPUT @counts
    TO "/Sandbox/User1/SensorData/Window1.tsv"
    USING Outputters.Tsv();
```

In this case, no field was specified for the window, so the average is calculated over the entire rowset, and each row has the same value for the average.

```
"Player","Node","NodeValue","NodeValueAvg"
"mjone101",13,20.79,255.5399421
"mjone101",13,20.79,255.5399421
"mpete101",7,160.74,255.5399421
"mpete101",7,160.74,255.5399421
"pharv102",29,411.90,255.5399421
```

You may want a more targeted average to use in the calculation. In this case, include the field or fields that would define unique segments. When defining window function segmentation, fields with discrete values work better than numerical fields with continuous values. For example, both the `Node` and `NodeValue` are numbers, but the `Node` values represent discrete objects while the `NodeValue` is a measurement on an scale. The following script calculates the average for the entire rowset, for each Player, and for each combination of Player + Node. Put a `PARTITION BY [field]` clause inside the `OVER ()` clause to specify the fields to create the window segments.

```
@counts =
    SELECT
        s.Player,
        s.Node,
        s.NodeValue,
        AVG(s.NodeValue) OVER () AS NodeValueAvg,
        AVG(s.NodeValue) OVER (PARTITION BY s.Player) AS NodeValuePlayerAvg,
        AVG(s.NodeValue) OVER (PARTITION BY s.Player, s.Node) AS
    NodeValuePlayerNodeAvg,
        (s.NodeValue - (AVG(s.NodeValue) OVER (PARTITION BY s.Player,
    s.Node))) AS NodeValueDiff
        FROM [Players].[dbo].[f_Sensors]("v1") AS s;

OUTPUT @counts
    TO "/Sandbox/User1/SensorData/Window2.tsv"
    USING Outputters.Tsv();
```

For each field using a windowed aggregation function, the calculation is performed on the aggregate field on all rows in the window. The resulting value is applied to each row. You can see the segmentation of rows in figure 8.8, with a changing aggregation value.

Running the previous script with multiple aggregate windows over the sensor data generates the following rows.

```
"Player","Node","NodeValue","NodeValueAvg","NodeValuePlayerAvg",
"NodeValuePlayerNodeAvg","NodeValueDiff"
"mjone101",13,20.79,255.5399421,255.36,256.28,-235.49
"mjone101",13,20.79,255.5399421,255.36,256.28,-235.49
```

```
"mjone101",14,448.08,255.5399421,255.36,255.64,192.43
"mpete101",7,160.74,255.5399421,255.94,259.17,-98.43
"mpete101",7,160.74,255.5399421,255.94,259.17,-98.43
"mpete101",8,383.95,255.5399421,255.94,258.87,125.07
"pharv102",26,94.81,255.5399421,255.29,261.67,-166.86
"pharv102",29,411.90,255.5399421,255.29,268.30,143.59
// significant digits reduced for clarity
```

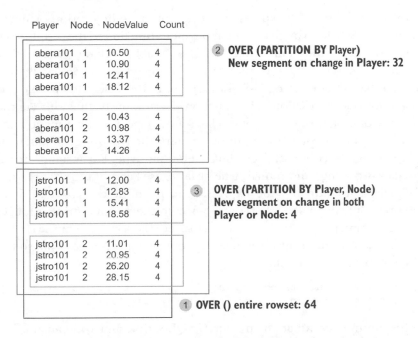

Figure 8.8   Segmenting rowset with OVER () window function

You can see that the three averages are consistent over their windows, but change as the windows change. The U-SQL compiled code calculates the windows of the entire rowset, each player, and each player-node.

For this example, we used built-in functions to add new fields to rowsets, and evaluated them for each row. Let's see how this works when you add your own functions using C#.

8.3   Local C# functions

You can build a new field using C# code too. You can build a C# expression within a U-SQL expression by naming the output, using the AS operator. In this example, the field NumberTwo is created by adding 1 to field NumberOne.

```
@numbers = SELECT
    NumberOne,
    (NumberOne + 1) AS NumberTwo
    FROM @rows;
```

You can use built-in C# functions to process values. This example uses the C# conditional operator ? to generate a field with one of two string values.

```
@numbers = SELECT
    NumberOne,
    NumberOne > 100 ? "Large" : "Small" AS NumberSize
    FROM @rows;
```

What if you want to use a C# expression more than once in a script, or need more complex code? U-SQL lets you define an anonymous function in the script, assign it to a variable, and call the function as needed. The variable declaration takes the form: `DECLARE @Xyz Func<input type,output type> = (input) => {code;};`. By now, you should be familiar with declaring U-SQL variables. In this case, the variable is of type `Func`, a C# anonymous function. The function declaration begins with `Func<type>`, which accepts one or more C# types. The return type for the function must be defined. If there are one or more input parameters, the type for each parameter will be listed, separated by commas, preceding the output type. For instance, for a function that takes two strings and returns true or false, use `Func<string, string, bool>`. Add an equals sign = and put the expression in parentheses (). We're defining a lambda expression: `(inputs) => {}`. For instance, to check if one string is longer than another, use `(string1, string2) => { return string.Length(string1) > string.Length(string2);}`. The return value of the comparison > is a boolean, so the complete U-SQL expression looks like:

```
DECLARE @LongerThan Func<string, string, bool> = ((string1, string2) =>
{return string.Length(string1) > string.Length(string2);});
```

Declare this anonymous function in your U-SQL script, and you can use it in any rowset expression. Calling the function in a rowset expression look like:

```
DECLARE @LongerThan Func<string, string, bool> = ((string1, string2) =>
{return string.Length(string1) > string.Length(string2);});

@Strings = SELECT
    String1,
    String2,
    @LongerThan(String1, String2) AS LargerString
    FROM @rows;
```

LargerString field is a boolean.

Let's look at a more complicated problem. In this example, users are querying sensor data using your new TVF. They want to compare each node value with the previous value, and add a new field showing Greater, Lesser, or Same depending on the change in value. The users haven't been able to do this themselves, and have asked for your help. How will you satisfy this request?

U-SQL includes several built-in window functions. In the last section, you saw how you can use aggregation functions like AVG() to evaluate row values. These functions return the same value for every row in the window. There's another set, called analytic functions, that can return a new value for each row in the window. Table 8.3 lists these functions.

Table 8.3 Analytic functions

Function	Name	Description	Parameters
CUME_DIST	Cumulative distribution	Ranked position of value within the ordered window	None
PERCENTILE_CONT	Percentile	Percentile of continuous distribution of values within the window	Double, percentile to calculate
PERCENTILE_DISC	Percentile	Percentile of discrete distribution of values within the window, matching a value in the window	Double, percentile to calculate
FIRST_VALUE	First value	Returns the first value from the ordered window	None
LAST_VALUE	Last value	Returns the last value from the ordered window	None
LEAD	Leading value	Returns the specified offset value ahead of the current row	Field type, field; Integer, offset; Field type, default value
LAG	Lagging value	Returns the specified offset value before the current row	Field type, field; Integer, offset; Field type, default value
PERCENT_RANK	Relative rank	Rank between 0 and 1 of the current value within the window	None

The LAG() function returns the field value from a preceding row. LAG() and LEAD() take three parameters: a field to read, the number of rows move forward or back, and a default value if no row is found. Passing a field of NumberOne, an offset of two rows, and a default of 100 looks like LAG(NumberOne, 2, 100). LAG() and LEAD() use the OVER() window option to define the row order, but do not use a partitioning value like other functions. The returned value can be NULL if a row is not present at the offset or the field value is NULL. The returned value is based on the position of the current row and offset row, instead of performing a calculation. The OVER() option contains an ORDER BY statement with the ordering fields. Using a LAG() function for field Number-One, an offset of 1, and a default of 0, the entire expression looks like:

```
@numbers = SELECT
    NumberOne,
    LAG(NumberOne, 1, 0) OVER(ORDER BY NumberOne) AS LastNumber
    FROM @rows;
```

To fulfill your end users' request, you have several options. You could add a new field to the existing TVF, or create an entirely new TVF. This would make the new field reusable, but could cut down on the use in ad-hoc queries. Or you could provide an example script, as shown in listing 8.15. Providing the inline function in a script allows it to be used in other scripts, and modified by the end user. This script passes the output of LAG() to the inline custom C# function, and includes the output of that function as a new field in the rowset. The LAG() calculation orders the rows by Player, Node, and EventTime.

Listing 8.15   Declaring an anonymous function in U-SQL

```
DECLARE @Trend Func<decimal, decimal?, string> =
((nodeValue, lastValue) =>
{
    if (nodeValue > lastValue)
    {
        return "Greater";
    }
    else if (nodeValue < lastValue)
    {
        return "Lesser";
    }
    else
    {
        return "Same";
    };
});

@counts =
    SELECT
        s.Player,
        s.Node,
        s.NodeValue,
        s.EventTime,
        LAG(s.NodeValue, 1, 0) OVER(ORDER BY s.Player, s.Node, s.EventTime)
    AS lastNodeValue,
        @Trend(s.NodeValue, LAG(s.NodeValue, 1, 0) OVER(ORDER BY s.Player,
    s.Node, s.EventTime)) AS NodeTrend
        FROM [Players].[dbo].[f_Sensors]("v1") AS s;
OUTPUT @counts
    TO "/Sandbox/User1/SensorTable/SensorData5.tsv"
    ORDER BY Player, Node, EventTime
    USING Outputters.Tsv(outputHeader: true);
```

Function accepts a decimal and a nullable decimal, and returns a string.

Name of the input parameters precedes the Lambda operator, separated by a comma.

Return a value using the return operator.

Including the LAG() function output in the field list is not required, but useful for validation.

Player, Node, and EventTime are used to define previous row.

With these inline functions, you can convert, validate, and construct many variations of the raw data using U-SQL and C#. In the next chapter, you'll learn how to create your own classes to add even more complex C# logic. The U-SQL catalog forms the container for database items, including assemblies of custom code. Now that you've seen some of U-SQL's processing capabilities, you're ready to expand on it with integrations for your own custom code and external endpoints.

8.4   *Exercises*

The following exercises can help you internalize the new features introduced in this chapter.

8.4.1   *Exercise 1*

Given a rowset containing the fields in the following extract, generate a new rowset that matches the example.

Listing 8.16   Extract

```
Id,Code,Volume,Units,Detail
1,"ABE",12,4,"<span>Test</span>"
2,"ABEF",22,2,"<span>Fourth</span>"
3,"AB",13,2,"<span></span>"
```

Listing 8.17   Example

```
Id,Desc,Sold
1,ABE:Test,48
2,ABEF:Fourth,44
3,AB,26
```

SOLUTION

This exercise requires string operators to modify the values in the Detail field. You also have to concatenate the Code and Detail fields, and check that the Detail field has a value, other than the HTML. This exercise assumes that all Detail fields use the same <span> wrapper. Your solution could look like the following script.

```
@rows =
SELECT *
FROM (VALUES
    (1,"ABE",12,4,"<span>Test</span>"),
    (2,"ABEF",22,2,"<span>Fourth</span>"),
    (3,"AB",13,2,"<span></span>")
    ) AS r(Id,Code,Volume,Units,Detail);

@newrows =
SELECT
    Id,
    Code,
    string.Format(
    "{0}{1}",
    Code,
    string.IsNullOrWhiteSpace(
        Detail.Replace("<span>", "")
        .Replace("</span>", "")) ?
            string.Empty :
            ":" + Detail.Replace("<span>", "").Replace("</span>", "")
        ) AS Detail,
    (Volume * Units) AS Sold
FROM @rows;

OUTPUT @newrows
TO "Sandbox/User1/code-units.csv"
USING Outputters.Csv(outputHeader:true);
```

This C# code could be encapsulated in an inline function as well.

8.4.2   *Exercise 2*

Given a set of data files with the following properties, choose a U-SQL database object to make reading the data easier on end users.

FILE SET A

- 600 10 M-row, 1 GB files containing application events
- New files are generated daily
- Files are stored in hierarchy Year/Month/Day
- Routine queries run daily and monthly

FILE SET B

- A 500 K-row, 100 MB file containing start and end dates for machine processes
- Ad-hoc queries that retrieve rows for a particular machineID and date

FILE SET C

- 15 200 M-row, 1 TB files containing banking transaction data
- New files are generated monthly
- Routine queries run each month for each branch

SOLUTION

For file set A, a TVF would be optimal. The TVF would allow passing year, month, and day parameters. The parameters can be used to define the file path for the EXTRACT expression.

For file set B, a view would be optimal. The file is small enough to be handled by a single vertex in an ADLA job. The overhead of loading a U-SQL table would be greater than the efficiency gains in the subsequent jobs.

For file set C, a U-SQL table with partitions would work well. Each monthly file could be loaded to daily or monthly partitions. Previous months can be deleted via partitions.

Summary

- U-SQL databases provide containers for storing reusable objects. These can be U-SQL expressions and data sets. Reuse means quicker query development.
- U-SQL tables allow optimized read access to large data sets. Data is reorganized for partition elimination, which saves time and money.
- U-SQL includes built-in functions for working with row-based data. Data values can be aggregated without reducing the number of rows returned.
- U-SQL allows custom C# functions to be inlined in rowset expressions. This allows complex data manipulations using C# statements.

Integrating with Azure
Data Lake Analytics

This chapter covers

- Using Azure Cognitive Services to enhance data
- Building user-defined functions using Visual Studio and C#
- Connecting to remote data sources

In the last chapter, you learned how to use Azure Data Lake Analytics (ADLA) to build reusable objects. You also used C# to enhance, and sometimes replace, the functions of SQL. In this chapter, you'll build on that by adding features to improve your U-SQL scripts. You'll use the Data Lake store to serve assembly files for use in ADLA jobs. You'll run Azure PowerShell and U-SQL scripts to modify the ADLA and Data Lake environments. You'll add new types of data extraction classes to ADLA, and add C# functions for modifying data. You'll also connect to external providers to add even more data with minimal effort. This extensibility is facilitated by the compiled nature of ADLA jobs.

The ADLA cluster translates each U-SQL script submitted into a .NET compiled application as a new ADLA job. This creates a new set of code to be executed on the cluster nodes assigned to the job. Because the script is compiled, each job includes a step that allows external code libraries to be included. The compiler includes SQL and .NET assemblies in every job, which lets jobs use many C# and SQL functions. Adding custom assemblies to a job works this way:

1 You submit a U-SQL script as part of an ADLA job.
   a The script defines the data sources to use and the logic to process the data.
   b The script defines any external assemblies to be included in the code.
   c The job defines the number of processing nodes to use for executing the code.
2 The job is submitted to the job compiler.
   a The compiler includes some Microsoft system assemblies and U-SQL language assemblies with the job code.
   b The compiler includes any referenced assemblies with the job code.
   c The compiler create a runtime to execute on the processing nodes.
3 The processing nodes execute the job runtime, write output files, and report progress to the monitoring node.

Figure 9.1 shows the compiler building the job code and incorporating these assemblies.

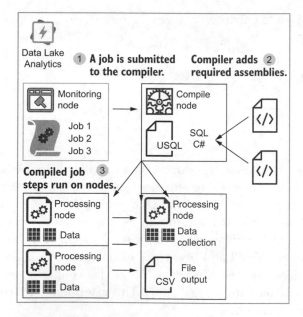

Figure 9.1   Code flow through the ADLA cluster

The U-SQL database stores data-object descriptions and provides methods for referencing data objects and compiled assemblies. You can take advantage of this by compiling your own code, registering your own assemblies in the database, and referencing those functions in your scripts. The assembly files are copied and stored in the Data Lake like other files. This allows the ADLA compiler to find them and include them in the job code.

Because ADLA has integrated access to your Data Lake, ADLA is a convenient vehicle for analyzing both structured and unstructured data stored there. By adding custom or third-party assemblies, you can expand the capabilities of ADLA's parallel processing engine. Let's look at the process by adding Machine Learning (ML) algorithms to ADLA.

> **TIP** You can find the code listings in the GitHub repository for this book at https://github.com/rnuckolls/azure_storage.

9.1 Processing unstructured data

The Jonestown Sluggers have installed time-lapse cameras around their stadium to capture information about the spectators in the stands. Each camera has a fixed view of the stands, and records one image per second. The images are uploaded to your Data Lake store for analysis. You have been asked to provide statistics on spectators' gender and age. How can you fulfill this request?

This analysis consists of two common computer-vision functions: object detection and facial recognition. Object-detection software identifies objects in an image by type and position. Facial-recognition software recognizes human faces and facial features. Both types of software are available in Azure via Cognitive Services.

9.1.1 Azure Cognitive Services

Azure Cognitive Services bundles a set of ML algorithms into APIs. Microsoft developed these algorithms using millions of iterations of content data analysis, including images, video, audio, and text data sources. The resulting algorithms are bundled into assemblies for developer use. These assemblies accept unstructured data content and return structured data about the objects in the content. The inputs include text-, image-, audio-, and video-analysis algorithms. To use the algorithms, you create Cognitive Service endpoints as resources in your Azure account. The API service endpoints are available through REST HTTP calls and through a .NET SDK library integration. Figure 9.2 shows how a system for analyzing data with Cognitive services could be structured.

To fulfill the image processing request, you could build an application to use these APIs, and send the data to it. This approach makes sense if you need immediate analysis of images. But the ADLA support team has made using Cognitive Services much easier than this. They have created a set of assemblies for using the ML text- and image-algorithms in U-SQL scripts. Using an ADLA job allows parallel processing of images without extra code complexity, and you can immediately process the output using logic in the job. The ADLA Cognitive assemblies let you analyze text and image content within ADLA jobs. You need to load and register the U-SQL Cognitive assemblies to use them in a job.

ADLA creates the U-SQL catalog with every ADLA account to maintain a container for referencing objects for reuse in U-SQL scripts. Because U-SQL is compiled at job

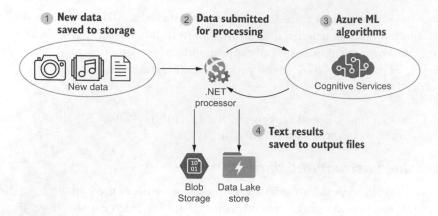

Figure 9.2   .NET integration with Cognitive services

time with external assemblies, you can use the Cognitive Services assemblies in your ADLA jobs too. First, you need to add them to your Data Lake and register them in a database within the catalog.

In the Azure portal, you can add these assemblies by adding a set of U-SQL extensions, called *Advanced Analytics*. This copies the Cognitive Services assemblies, along with language processing assemblies for R and Python, into your ADLA Data Lake. You can trigger this as follows:

1 In the Azure portal, use the All Services menu and filter on Data Lake Analytics to show the Data Lake Analytics resource. Click Data Lake Analytics to show the Resource blade.
2 Click Sample Scripts to display the Sample Scripts blade.
3 Click Install U-SQL Extensions to copy the assemblies into folder /usqlext in the default Data Lake root folder.

NOTE   The new folder inherits existing permissions from the root folder upon creation. You can learn more about Data Lake permissions in chapter 4.

The new folder contains assemblies for using Cognitive Services, Python scripts, and R scripts. Python and R are popular languages for doing large-scale data processing. The folder includes scripts for registering these assemblies within the master U-SQL database. We'll look at registering assemblies shortly.

9.1.2   *Managing assemblies in the Data Lake*

The new folder created when you install the U-SQL extensions sits at the root of your Data Lake store. Although this location is easy to reference, creating new root folders without planning for long-term usage makes your folder structure shallow like a swamp instead of deep like a lake.

As a practical design, you should structure your assembly folders much as you would your data folders—along security boundaries with versioning over time, and segmentation aligned with project or source.

TIP Defining a folder structure and using it consistently prevents your Data Lake from becoming a Data Swamp. You can read about the zones framework, a practical design for structuring your Data Lake, in chapter 4.

Using the model of the zones framework, you should design a folder structure that is narrow at the top and branches out. The basic structure should include a top-level folder to hold user code. This code can be separated into U-SQL scripts and C# assemblies. The scripts can be divided by project, database, or user, depending on your needs. Figure 9.3 shows a folder structure arranged this way.

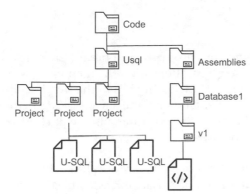

Figure 9.3 Creating the Data Lake folder structure for code

NOTE Submitting jobs to ADLA via Azure Data Factory requires the job script to be stored in Azure Storage. Because ADF will have authorized access to your ADLS store in order to execute the job, it's standard to store the script in the same ADLS store. Chapter 10 covers automating data processing with Azure Data Factory.

With this design in mind, let's move the Cognitive Services assemblies out of the /usqlext folder and into a managed structure. This structure will use the /Code/ Assemblies tree, including the registered U-SQL database and version number. You can choose where to register your assemblies. If you plan to use only one general U-SQL database, you can register all assemblies there. This makes sense if you have a limited set of users accessing ADLA, or a single ADLA project. You can use one or more user databases for security separation, or you can use the master database for common usage. Registering assemblies in the master database means the functions are available to every U-SQL script. It also means greater complexity if you want to use multiple versions of the same assemblies in different projects. Using specific user U-SQL databases aligned with projects allows for simpler versioning, but requires registering the assemblies in each new database. For these common assemblies, we'll use the master database.

Copy the files and folders from the /usqlext folder into /Code/Assemblies/master/ v1 folder. You can do this with the Azure portal, Azure Storage Explorer, or other tools. The following script shows how to move the files using Azure PowerShell. You can run it using Azure Cloud Shell. The following listing cleans up the folder structure of your Data Lake by removing the files from the previous location.

Listing 9.1   Move Cognitive assemblies in Data Lake with PowerShell

```
New-AzDataLakeStoreItem -AccountName "adedeveastus2"
    -Path "/Code/Assemblies/master/cognition/v1/" -Folder
Move-AzDataLakeStoreItem -Account "adedeveastus2"
    -Path "/usqlext/assembly/cognition/"
    -Destination "/Code/Assemblies/master/cognition/v1/"
Remove-AzDataLakeStoreItem -Account "adedeveastus2"
    -Paths "/usqlext/" -Recurse
```

WARNING   Moving assembly files after they are registered breaks the registration. U-SQL scripts referencing these registrations will return an error when submitted. You must drop and/or register the assemblies in the new location before using. You can do this at any time. Updating the assembly files, either by copying to a new versioned folder or by overwriting, also requires dropping and registering the assemblies before use.

Registering the assemblies in their new location will let you call the functions from your U-SQL scripts. It also lets the ADLA compiler locate the assembly files when compiling an ADLA job. You register an assembly by creating a new ADLA job and including the registration commands. These commands can run in a separate U-SQL script, or in the same script as your data access and processing commands.

Create a U-SQL script with the CREATE ASSEMBLY command. The command takes two parameters and has two options. You must provide a single-word name for the assembly, like CREATE ASSEMBLY [CodeName]. Specify the file path with FROM @"/folder/ file.dll". Note the @ symbol which is used to denote a literal string. You can use CREATE ASSEMBLY IF NOT EXISTS to check before creation. You can also use the DROP . . . CREATE pattern instead. The following listing registers an assembly this way.

Listing 9.2   Create file assembly

```
DROP ASSEMBLY [CodeName];
CREATE ASSEMBLY [CodeName]
FROM @"/Code/Assemblies/Database/Program/v1/CodeName.dll";
```

Last, you may need to provide associated resource files with the assembly for use by the compiler. You attach these files using WITH ADDITIONAL FILES = (path array). You define a comma separated list, contained within parentheses, of one or more files that need to be included in the compiled job when using the assembly. The following listing shows a multi-file assembly.

Listing 9.3 Create a file assembly with multiple files

```
CREATE ASSEMBLY IF NOT EXISTS [CodeName]
FROM @"/Code/Assemblies/Database/Program/v1/CodeName.dll"
WITH ADDITIONAL FILES = (
    @"/Code/Assemblies/Database/Program/v1/Code1.txt",
    @"/Code/Assemblies/Database/Program/v1/Code2.dll"
);
```

Denote the array with parentheses.

Separate each file path with a comma.

Because we have moved the Cognitive Services assemblies to a new folder, we need to register the files in the master database. The following listing shows the commands for registering the facial recognition methods.

Listing 9.4 Register Cognitive Services assemblies for face recognition

```
DROP ASSEMBLY IF EXISTS [ImageCommon];
CREATE ASSEMBLY IF NOT EXISTS [ImageCommon]
FROM @"/Code/Assemblies/master/cognition/v1/vision/common/ImageIO.dll"
WITH ADDITIONAL_FILES =
    (
        @"/Code/Assemblies/master/cognition/v1/vision/common/ImageCommon.dll",
        @"/Code/Assemblies/master/cognition/v1/vision/common/FaceSdkManagedWrap
    per.dll",
        @"/Code/Assemblies/master/cognition/v1/vision/common/libiomp5md.dll",
        @"/Code/Assemblies/master/cognition/v1/vision/common/DetectionJDA.mdl",
        @"/Code/Assemblies/master/cognition/v1/vision/common/version.cog.imgcom
    mon"
    );
DROP ASSEMBLY IF EXISTS [ImageOcr];
CREATE ASSEMBLY IF NOT EXISTS [ImageOcr]
FROM @"/Code/Assemblies/master/cognition/v1/vision/ocr/ImageOCR.dll"
WITH ADDITIONAL_FILES = (
@"/Code/Assemblies/master/cognition/v1/vision/ocr/Microsoft.Ocr.dll",
@"/Code/Assemblies/master/cognition/v1/vision/ocr/Microsoft.Ocr.xml",
@"/Code/Assemblies/master/cognition/v1/vision/ocr/MsOcrRes.orp",
@"/Code/Assemblies/master/cognition/v1/vision/ocr/version.cog.ocr"
);
```

> **NOTE** The full script can be downloaded from the GitHub site for this book at http://mng.bz/7GD9.

To register all the available services, create a new job in ADLA using the U-SQL script from the GitHub repository. All metadata actions, like creating a U-SQL database or registering assemblies, only need a single AU to run. Once the job has executed, the assemblies will be ready for use in U-SQL scripts.

By registering the assemblies, you have extended the ADLA account to support Cognitive Services data analysis. Now you can move to the next part of the request: submitting images to the assemblies in U-SQL.

9.1.3   *Image data extraction with Advanced Analytics*

U-SQL scripts can analyze many types of unstructured data, as long as an extractor is available that can read the file type. The Advanced Analytics extensions, which include the Cognitive Services assemblies, provide extractors that let you read bytes from a JPEG, for storage or further processing. With these, you can read JPEG contents, process them with the Cognitive Services algorithms, and return U-SQL rowsets.

Cognitive Services extractors work like text extractors , but each extractor defines the fields returned in its rowset output. The following table lists the output fields for each image extractor.

Table 9.1   Cognitive Services extractors

Assembly	Extractor	Fields	Description
ImageIO.dll	Cognition.Vision. ImageExtractor	ImgData (byte[])	Returns a byte array of the JPEG data
ImageOCR.dll	Cognition.Vision. OcrExtractor	RectX (float), RectY (float), Width (float), Height (float), Text (string)	Returns text from image, and location of text
FaceSdkCNN.dll	Cognition.Vision. FaceDetectionExtractor	FaceIndex (int), RectX (float), RectY (float), Width (float), Height (float), FaceAge (int), FaceGender (string)	Returns one row for each face found; each row includes the detected age and gender, and the location of the detected face
ImageTagging.dll	Cognition.Vision. ImageTagsExtractor	NumObjects (int), Tags (SQL.MAP<string, float?>)	Returns a list of identified objects in the images with a confidence score on recognition
EmotionAnalysis.dll	Cognition.Vision. EmotionExtractor	FaceIndex (int), RectX (float), RectY (float), Width (float), Height (float), Emotion (string), Confidence (float)	Returns one row for each face found; each row includes the detected emotion, a confidence vote, and the location of the detected face

NOTE   SQL.MAP<TKey,TValue> creates an array of key-value pairs. To output the field using an outputter, you first need to expand the array using CROSS APPLY EXPLODE. You can read more about this type at http://mng.bz/P1z9.

Using the image extractors works like the text extractors you saw in chapter 7. You declare a file selector, create an expression using the extractor to read the files, and write out the rowset data using an outputter. Using the Cognitive Services assemblies requires one more statement in the script: REFERENCE ASSEMBLY [XYZ]. The ADLA compiler does not include the Cognitive Services assemblies by default. Once you have registered the assemblies in your U-SQL database, you must reference them in U-SQL scripts to use their functions. Use the name you assigned when you registered the assembly.

For example, if you registered ImageIo.dll as `ImageCommon` and FaceSdkCNN.dll as `FaceSdk`, then referencing these two assemblies is shown in the following listing.

Listing 9.5 Reference Cognitive services assemblies

```
REFERENCE ASSEMBLY ImageCommon;
REFERENCE ASSEMBLY FaceSdk;
```

When processing multiple images within a folder, include the filename and path information with the extractor output. This lets you link the image to the generated metadata for later use. For instance, you could retrieve a set of images including a male face or children. Without these fields, you can't tie ML output to a specific image.

You can include filename and path data using {} in the file selector. In previous chapters, you've seen the braces used with a wildcard expression {*} to select multiple files. When used to replace a portion of the path, the braces use the wildcard expression and add the replaced portion of the path as a field in the extractor output. To return a field called `FileName` with a value of the file selected, declare a file selector variable enclosing `FileName` in braces, as follows:

```
DECLARE @in = "/Staging/Stadium/v1/camera1/{FileName}.jpg"
```

The placeholder `{FileName}` passes through the extractor using the file selector, is populated for each row, and returned as a field in the rowset. Listing 9.6 shows the syntax for processing multiple images within multiple folders, and returning the folder and filename in the rowset.

Listing 9.6 Using the FaceSdk assembly

```
USE DATABASE master;
REFERENCE ASSEMBLY ImageCommon;
REFERENCE ASSEMBLY FaceSdk;
DECLARE @in = "/Staging/Stadium/v1/{Camera}/{FileName}.jpg";
@people = EXTRACT
    Camera string,
    FileName string,
    FaceGender string
    FROM @in
    USING new Cognition.Vision.FaceDetectionExtractor();
```

Here's an example from the @people rowset executed against two files c1.jpg and c2.jpg in folders Camera1 and Camera2:

```
"Camera1","c1","Male"
"Camera2","c2","Female"
"Camera1","c1","Male"
```

Listing 9.7 shows the full U-SQL script to classify people in images by age and gender. Choose one or more images that show faces to use with the script. You can use your own images, or some from an online source, such as a stock image site or a public domain source, like the Library of Congress: https://www.loc.gov/free-to-use/.

Listing 9.7   Reading facial features from images

ImageCommon is used with all the Image processing services.

The FaceSdk assembly has the Face Detection algorithms.

```
USE DATABASE master;
REFERENCE ASSEMBLY ImageCommon;
REFERENCE ASSEMBLY FaceSdk;
DECLARE @in = "/Staging/Stadium/{Camera}/{FileName}.jpg";
@people = EXTRACT
    Camera string,
    FileName string,
    NumFaces int,
    FaceIndex int,
    RectX float, RectY float, Width float, Height float,
    FaceAge int,
    FaceGender string
    FROM @in
    USING new Cognition.Vision.FaceDetectionExtractor();

@peopleRange =
    SELECT FaceGender,
    (FaceAge >= 0 && FaceAge < 20) ? "Child" :
    (FaceAge >= 20 && FaceAge < 65) ? "Adult" :
    "Retired" AS AgeCategory
    FROM @people;
@peopleCount =
    SELECT FaceGender,
    AgeCategory,
    COUNT(FaceGender) AS CountOfPeople
    FROM @peopleRange
    GROUP BY FaceGender, AgeCategory;
OUTPUT @peopleCount
TO @"/Sandbox/User1/Stadium/peopletest.csv"
USING Outputters.Csv();
```

Read the camera portion of the path and the filename.

Three-part C# conditional expression can be expanded for more categories.

The output file looks like the following listing.

Listing 9.8   Example Cognitive Services output

```
"Female","Adult",16
"Female","Child",3
"Female","Retired",2
"Male","Adult",41
"Male","Child",1
"Male","Retired",7
```

This is one of many ways you can use ML algorithms to generate new structured data from unstructured data, like images. Used in conjunction with thoughtful folder structures and filenames, these algorithms can generate data with context to help answer new questions.

Now that you have stored, registered, and used assemblies to extend ADLA's built-in functions, you are ready to build your own. The JavaScript Object Notation (JSON) format uses key-value pairs and lists of values for data interchange. You can read more about JSON at https://www.json.org/. JSON data is typically stored in files with a .JSON extension. In the next section, you'll extend your ADLA account by adding support for JSON.

9.2 Reading different file types

The Jonestown Sluggers want to correlate weather conditions with performance metrics. Every day, the IT department will load JSON files from the NOAA weather.gov API into your Data Lake store. You have been asked to load the data into a U-SQL table, including the temperature, wind speed and direction, pressure, and relative humidity. How will you fulfill this request?

U-SQL scripts do not natively support extracting rowsets from JSON files. Using a Text extractor and parsing string would be brittle at best. You need a way to add JSON support to U-SQL scripts. Microsoft has created code for this purpose. You need to retrieve it, compile it, and register it with your ADLA account. Let's dig into the process for adding custom code libraries to ADLA.

9.2.1 Adding custom libraries with a Catalog

ADLA jobs automatically load a few assemblies when a job is compiled. These include the following namespaces:

- System
- System.Data
- System.Linq
- System.Text
- System.Text.RegularExpressions
- Microsoft.Analytics.Types
- Microsoft.Analytics.Types.Sql
- Microsoft.Analytics.Interfaces

Because these assemblies are loaded by default, you can reference them from any U-SQL script. This integration is what allows the use of C# methods like `string.Format()` and `Convert.ToInt()`.

In the last section, you saw how you can register and reference other assemblies to add even more functions to U-SQL. You can write your own assemblies and load them during compile time too. The first step is to create a U-SQL database to register the assemblies.

9.2.2 Creating a catalog database

Each ADLA account creates a U-SQL catalog in the associated Data Lake store. It also adds the master database. In the previous section, you used the master database to register the Cognitive Services assemblies. The master database allows access from any

U-SQL script, because the ADLA compiler includes its path in all jobs. Using a separate database gives greater control over registering and referencing objects, including assemblies. This includes:

- Easy removal of objects
- Options for versioning of assemblies and objects
- Providing security perimeters

In chapter 8, you learned how to create a U-SQL database. The U-SQL database groups tables, views, functions, and stored procedures, and makes them accessible in U-SQL scripts. It also contains custom assemblies registered by users. You can create a database by running an Azure PowerShell script or an ADLA job. Run listing 9.9 in the Azure Shell. It will submit a short U-SQL script to ADLA to execute.

Listing 9.9   U-SQL database creation with PowerShell

```
Submit-AzDataLakeAnalyticsJob -Account "adedeveastus2"
➥ -Name "Create DB"
➥ -Script "CREATE DATABASE IF NOT EXISTS Players;"
➥ -AnalyticsUnits 1
```

Now that you have a U-SQL database to contain the references, you can prepare your assemblies. ADLA jobs load a few assemblies by default, including one for the text extractor and outputter classes. The default `Extractors` class includes functions for reading text, TSV, and CSV files. No support is provided for JSON, XML, or Avro, but you can add it with a custom assembly.

Microsoft provides documentation and example code on GitHub for ADLA users. The Azure U-SQL repository includes example code for creating new functions and implementations for new extractors. The code is collected in a set of C# projects called the *DataFormats Samples*. These include code for working with XML, JSON, and Avro. The JSON and Avro extractors are of particular interest. JSON is used for Stream Analytics output. Avro is a semi-structured format used by Event Hubs Capture. The code is open-source and available in the Azure U-SQL GitHub repository.

9.2.3   *Building the U-SQL DataFormats solution*

So far you've saved Event Hub data directly to the Data Lake store using Capture, in Avro format. You've read JSON serialized event data using Stream Analytics, and written JSON to files in the Data Lake store. But you couldn't use the data in ADLA jobs. Now you're going to add the functionality to let ADLA jobs read JSON and Avro data. The code is in the DataFormats Samples projects.

> **IMPORTANT**   This chapter requires Visual Studio IDE to create and build some code examples. Though you can build Visual Studio solutions with only the .NET framework installed, I'll assume you have Visual Studio installed, and know how to open and build a solution. You can obtain a free copy of Visual Studio at https://visualstudio.microsoft.com/vs/community/.

Start by getting the code from the Azure U-SQL repository at https://github.com/ azure/usql. Using Visual Studio 2015 or greater, open the solution file Microsoft.Analytics .Samples.sln under /Examples/DataFormats, and build the solution. This solution contains code for Avro, XML, and JSON extractors, letting you extend the range of files that U-SQL can read. The projects use .NET 4.6.1, so loading into Visual Studio will be cleaner if that is also installed. You can upgrade the projects to a newer version if needed.

Building the project creates an assembly in the project's /bin folder, along with any assemblies for code dependencies. For the Formats project, these include Avro.dll, log4net.dll, and Newtonsoft.Json.dll. You will copy the assembly and its dependencies to the Data Lake store for use by ADLA jobs.

9.2.4 Code folders

Any custom assemblies you create must be copied to the Data Lake store and registered in a U-SQL database before use in a U-SQL script. As noted in the previous section, you should structure your assembly folders much like you'd structure your data, along security boundaries with versioning over time and segmentation aligned with project or source. Figure 9.4 shows a folder structure arranged this way.

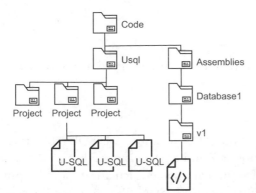

Figure 9.4   Creating the Data Lake folder structure for code

For this project, we have created a database called Players for storing related objects. Copy the DLL files from the /bin folder into /Code/Assemblies/Players/v1 folder. These files include:

- Avro.dll
- log4net.dll
- Newtonsoft.Json.dll
- Microsoft.Analytics.Samples.Formats.dll

NOTE   There are several methods for uploading, including the Azure portal Data Explorer blade. You can read more about working with files in ADLS in chapter 4.

The assemblies for Microsoft.Analytics.Interfaces.dll and Microsoft.Analytics.Types.dll are already loaded by the compiler, so you don't needed them in the folder.

The last step in preparing the assemblies is to register them with the database using a U-SQL script. The script switches context to the database, then assigns a name to the assembly file for reference. Run listing 9.10 in the Azure Shell. It submits a short U-SQL script to ADLA which registers all four assemblies.

> **Listing 9.10   U-SQL assembly reference creation with PowerShell**

```
Submit-AzDataLakeAnalyticsJob -Account "adedeveastus2"
⇒ -Name "Register Formats"
⇒ -Script "                          ← Start a new line by leaving
                                        an unclosed double quote.
CREATE ASSEMBLY IF NOT EXISTS Avro FROM    ←
⇒ `@"/Code/Assemblies/Players/Formats/v1/Avro.dll`";    Use the IF NOT
CREATE ASSEMBLY IF NOT EXISTS log4net FROM              EXISTS pattern,
⇒ `@"/Code/Assemblies/Players/Formats/v1/log4net.dll`";  with a meaningful
CREATE ASSEMBLY IF NOT EXISTS Json FROM                 name for the
⇒ `@"/Code/Assemblies/Players/Formats/v1/Newtonsoft.Json.dll`";  assembly.
CREATE ASSEMBLY IF NOT EXISTS Formats FROM    ←
⇒ `@"/Code/Assemblies/Players/Formats/v1/Players.Analytics.Samples   You can use short
    .Formats.dll`";"                                                 or fully qualified
⇒ -AnalyticsUnits 1                                                  assembly names.
```

Use backquote to escape double quote,
with a full path to the assembly file.

Now that you have the assemblies prepared, let's use them in a job to extract JSON data.

9.2.5   *Using custom assemblies*

The IT department wants you to load the JSON data into a U-SQL table; this type of request should be familiar from chapters 7 and 8. Data is stored in a particular location and format, and you need to read it, make some calculations, and output it in a specific format. To process the weather.gov API JSON files, you need access to the files, a script using a JSON extractor, and a database table.

DATA FILES

You can retrieve the forecast data directly from the weather.gov API at https://www .weather.gov/documentation/services-web-api. Use the website or a web request tool to request the files by zone and date. You can also get them from the GitHub repository for this book.

Listing 9.11 is a subset of the forecast file for November 22, 2019. The data is JSON-structured, using a schema called *JavaScript Object Notation for Linked Data* (JSON-LD). The file includes a @context array describing its contents and the definitions for decoding the data. JavaScript objects get a type definition, so we use FeatureCollection from JSON-LD. In this case, each "feature" in the features array contains a properties object, which lists the key/value pairs for the weather measurements.

Listing 9.11   Weather.gov API Observations file

```
{
  "@context": [
    "https://raw.githubusercontent.com/geojson/geojson-
    ld/master/contexts/geojson-base.jsonld",
    {
      "wx": "https://api.weather.gov/ontology#",
      "s": "https://schema.org/",
      "geo": "http://www.opengis.net/ont/geosparql#",
      "@vocab": "https://api.weather.gov/ontology#",
      "geometry": {
        "@id": "s:GeoCoordinates",
        "@type": "geo:wktLiteral"
      }
    }
  ],
  "type": "FeatureCollection",
  "features": [
    {
      "id": "https://api.weather.gov/stations/KSGT/observations/2019-11-
      22T07:56:00+00:00",
      "type": "Feature",
      "geometry": {
        "type": "Point",
        "coordinates": [
          -91.5699999,
          34.6
        ]
      },
      "properties": {
        "@id": "https://api.weather.gov/stations/KSGT/observations/2019-11-
        22T07:56:00+00:00",
        "@type": "wx:ObservationStation",
        "elevation": {
          "value": 68,
          "unitCode": "unit:m"
        },
        "station": "https://api.weather.gov/stations/KSGT",
        "timestamp": "2019-11-22T07:56:00+00:00",
        "rawMessage": "KSGT 220756Z AUTO 18011KT 10SM FEW055 BKN120 16/15
        A2994 RMK AO2 SLP137 T01610150",
        "textDescription": "Mostly Cloudy",
        "icon": "https://api.weather.gov/icons/land/night/bkn?size=medium",
        "presentWeather": [],
        "temperature": {
          "value": 16.100000000000023,
          "unitCode": "unit:degC",
          "qualityControl": "qc:V"
        },
      }                     ⟵  Items removed
    }]                          for brevity
}
```

You need to parse this JSON file and retrieve the values for temperature and other measurements.

> **TIP**   You can retrieve three example files in this format for your job at http://mng.bz/04aE.

The example files use zone MSZ010 for dates in Nov 2019. The REST API URL takes the following format.

http://mng.bz/Jxg0

Once you have retrieved the files, upload them to your Data Lake store. Using the zones framework as a guide to folder structures, create a folder in Staging to handle weather.gov files. This folder structure will let you incorporate API changes as needed, and let you target different types of data files by folder name. Copy the three example files here.

- /Staging/weather.gov/v1/observations/MSZ010/2019-11-19.json
- /Staging/weather.gov/v1/observations/MSZ010/2019-11-20.json
- /Staging/weather.gov/v1/observations/MSZ010/2019-11-21.json

U-SQL TABLE

Create a U-SQL table to store the output of the JSON extraction script. This table will make it easy for subsequent jobs to query this historical data. The table holds the values drawn from the data files. The table is structured to allow partition elimination by queries filtering on station, and for faster lookup within date ranges with an index. The measurement dates are of type `DateTime` to allow later use of C# `DateTime` functions. You can read more about creating U-SQL tables in chapter 8. Listing 9.12 shows the U-SQL script for creating the table. Execute this script as an ADLA job, using 1 AU.

Listing 9.12   Creating a U-SQL table

```
USE DATABASE Players;
CREATE TABLE IF NOT EXISTS WeatherData
(
    Zone string,
    Filename string,
    Id string,
    Station string,
    EventDate DateTime,
    Temperature decimal,
    WindSpeed decimal,
    WindDirection decimal,
    Pressure decimal,
    Visibility decimal,
    Precipitation decimal,
    RelativeHumidity decimal,
    INDEX idx_SensorData CLUSTERED(EventDate ASC)
```

```
)
DISTRIBUTED BY HASH(Station);
```

Once the U-SQL table is created and the files are in place, you can write a U-SQL script that will read the files and populate the table.

READING A JSON FILE

With the new Formats assembly registered in the Players U-SQL database, the new functions can be used in your U-SQL scripts. The assembly includes two extractor functions for processing JSON files. The first function works like a built-in text extractor; you call EXTRACT, choose the output and input files, and create the extractor class. You must instantiate this extractor with the new keyword. The following listing uses the Json-Extractor class.

Listing 9.13   Using the JSONExtractor

```
@rowset = EXTRACT
    Field1 string,
    Field2 string                     The new keyword creates
    FROM @inputFiles                  a new instance of the
    USING new JsonExtractor();    ◄── JsonExtractor class.
```

The extractor field names can come from bracketed identifiers in the file selector, or from the JSON objects in the files. For example, given a JSON file with title, weight, and color elements, the extractor can return fields named title, weight, and color. You can see this structure in listing 9.14. Assign each field a type in the extract expression, using C# conversions on the value if needed.

Listing 9.14   Example single level JSON document

```
{
  "title":"First",
  "weight": 13.6,
  "color": "Black"
},
{
  "title":"Second",
  "weight": 12.6,
  "color": "Blue"
}
```

All JSON data uses key/value pairs to structure the data elements. The key is the string preceding the colon, and the value follows the colon. This JSON example has elements only at the root level. The extractor can read them directly. You can assign the fields as type string, and convert them later if bad data is encountered during processing. The following listing shows this Extractor definition.

Listing 9.15   Example first level JSON extraction

```
@rowset = EXTRACT
    title string,
```

```
    weight decimal,
    color string
    FROM @example
    USING new JsonExtractor();
```

A CSV output of the previous rowset would yield two rows.

Listing 9.16   Example first level JSON extract output

```
"title","weight","color"
"First",13.6,"Black"
"Second",12.6,"Blue"
```

To read a multi-level JSON document with the JSON extractor, read the element with nested data as a string, and use a special function to generate a key/value pair. The value holds the nested data string. The following shows a multi-level JSON document.

Listing 9.17   Example multi-level JSON document

```
{
    "title":"First",
    "options":{
        "size":"L",
        "color":"Black"
    }
}
```

The `options` element has nested elements. Because `options` is at the root level, you can still directly extract it with the JSON extractor. The extractor in the following listing will yield a JSON string in the options field.

Listing 9.18   Example multi-level JSON extraction

```
@rowset = EXTRACT
    title string,
    options string
    FROM @example
    USING new JsonExtractor();
```

When reading a nested JSON value, the field output will be the entire nested element, rather than a single value. A CSV output of the previous rowset would yield two rows, including the header.

Listing 9.19   Example raw output from JsonExtractor

```
"title","options"
"First","{
  ""size"": ""L"",
  ""color"": ""Black""
}"
```

Though you could parse this field, the Formats assemblies include a class for handling JSON strings like this. The `JsonFunctions` class includes a function `JsonTuple()` that parses one or more elements into an array of key/value pairs. You can then retrieve the values in the array by referencing the element name. JsonTuple() takes the JSON string as a parameter, and returns an array of key/value pairs that can be addressed by the key. In the previous example, you would pass options to JsonTuple function, and you could read out the keys size and color by name.

Figure 9.5 describes the flow of data from JSON elements into rowset fields using JsonExtractor and JsonTuple. JsonExtractor reads the element value into a field with the element name. JsonTuple converts several JSON elements into a key/value array addressable by element name. You read the value using the element name in brackets ["Name"] when the rowset field is an array.

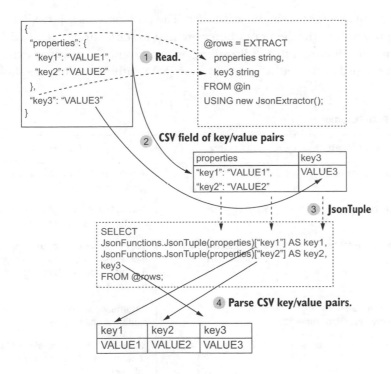

Figure 9.5   Using JsonTuple function with multi-level elements

The following example demonstrates using JsonTuple() to retrieve a value, both inline and in subsequent rowsets.

Listing 9.20   Using the JsonTuple() function

```
@rowValues = SELECT
    title AS Title,
    JsonFunctions.JsonTuple(options) AS OptionValues,
    JsonFunctions.JsonTuple(options)["size"] AS Size
    FROM @rowset;
```

```
@rowSubValues = SELECT
    Title,
    OptionValues["color"] AS Color,
    Size
    FROM @rowValues;
```

A CSV output of the two SELECT expressions yield two rows, including the header.

Listing 9.21   Example JSON extract

```
"Title","Color","Size"
"First","Black","L"
```

JsonExtractor can also take a single parameter. The parameter is a JSONPath statement defining the path to the element where you want to start extracting. Leaving this blank starts from the document root. Providing a path parameter will start extraction at the element defined in the path. Some common JSONPath definitions are shown in table 9.2.

Table 9.2   JSONPath Definitions

JSONPath	Description	Use	Output
$	Root element	$.title	Returns root element(s) named "title", in an array
.	Child element	$.options.size	Return the value of the size element which is a child of options
[]	Array elements	$.options.size.[0:1] ; $.options.size.[*]	Return the values for the first two elements named size in an array named "options"; Use * for all elements in array
@	Current element of array, used with filter	$.[?(@.color)]	Returns values of any elements that contain a child named color
?()	Filter child elements	$.[?(@.size == "L")]	Returns values of any elements that contain a child named size with a value of L

If the values you want to extract are not elements at the root, you can use the JSONPath parameter to return one or more nested elements within the file. For example, JSONPaths can be used to return elements from different levels of the same file. Figure 9.6 shows the elements returned for various JSONPath expressions.

When using JsonExtractor, the typical use for a JSONPath parameter would be to target an object with several elements one of more levels below the root, such as $.features.[*].properties in figure 9.6. Let's look at a couple of ways to parse the weather.gov data using JSONPaths.

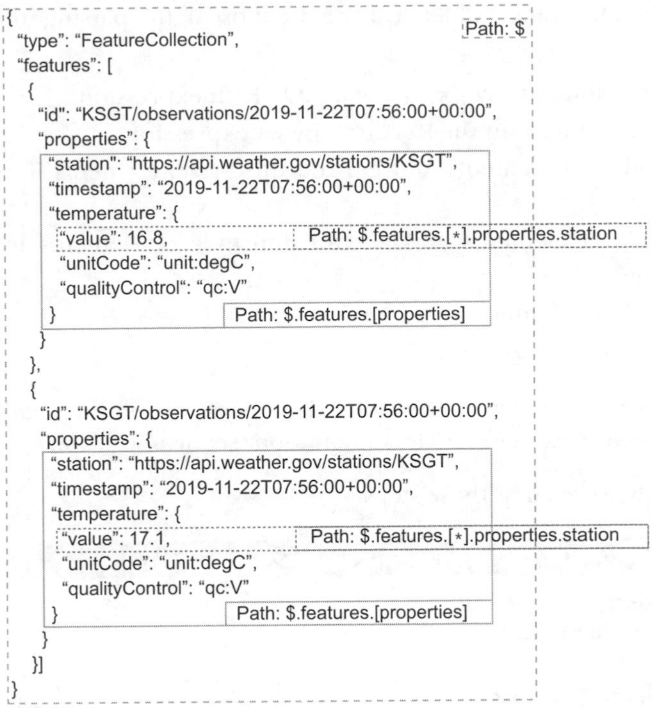

Figure 9.6   Using JSONPath expressions to select elements

TIP   Most languages support parsing JSON using JSONPath expressions. For .NET languages, the most common tool is the JSON.net assembly from Newtonsoft. This assembly is included with the Formats Visual Studio solution from earlier in this chapter, and is required by the JSONExtractor() class and other tools in this chapter.

JSON EXTRACTOR WITH NAME/VALUE PARSING

There are two differences between using the built-in text file extractors and the new JSONExtractor class: You must reference the Formats assembly in the U-SQL script, and instantiate the JSONExtractor class using the new keyword. You reference the assemblies by database and name, using the USE DATABASE [Name] and REFERENCE ASSEMBLY [Name] expressions. In this case, we're referencing the Newtonsoft JSON.net assembly and the Microsoft Sample Formats assembly (see listing 9.22). As in other .NET languages, the USING statement reduces the need to fully qualify class functions.

Listing 9.22   Referencing registered assemblies

```
USE DATABASE Players;
REFERENCE ASSEMBLY [Newtonsoft.Json];
REFERENCE ASSEMBLY [Microsoft.Analytics.Samples.Formats];
```

To extract the weather data using JSONExtractor, we'll break the parsing into several steps.

1 Get the Features elements by specifying a JSONPath expression.
2 Get the first-level elements in the EXTRACT rowset expression.
3 Parse the second-level elements and get the third-level elements in a second rowset expression.
4 Parse the third-level elements and get the fourth-level elements in a third rowset expression.
5 Parse the fourth-level elements in a fourth rowset expression.
6 Insert the data into a U-SQL table.

TIP   You can retrieve the forecast observation data directly from the weather .gov API at https://www.weather.gov/documentation/services-web-api.

The following listing shows each of these steps.

Listing 9.23   Multi-step JSON extraction using JSONExtractor

As in other .NET languages, the USING statement
reduces the need to fully qualify class functions.

```
USE DATABASE Players;
REFERENCE ASSEMBLY [Newtonsoft.Json];
REFERENCE ASSEMBLY [Microsoft.Analytics.Samples.Formats];
USING Microsoft.Analytics.Samples.Formats.Json;

DECLARE @in = @"/Staging/weather.gov/v1/observations/{Zone}/{Filename}.json";

@rows = EXTRACT
    Zone string,
    Filename string,
    id string,
    properties string
    FROM @in
    USING new JsonExtractor("features[*]");

@jsonRows = SELECT
    Zone,
    Filename,
    id AS Id,
    JsonFunctions.JsonTuple(properties)["station"] AS Station,
    JsonFunctions.JsonTuple(properties)["timestamp"] AS EventDate,
    JsonFunctions.JsonTuple(properties)["temperature"] AS TempsArray,
    JsonFunctions.JsonTuple(properties)["windDirection"] AS WindDirArray,
    JsonFunctions.JsonTuple(properties)["windSpeed"] AS WindSpeedArray,
    JsonFunctions.JsonTuple(properties)["barometricPressure"] AS PressureArray,
    JsonFunctions.JsonTuple(properties)["visibility"] AS VisibilityArray,
    JsonFunctions.JsonTuple(properties)["precipitationLastHour"] AS
      PrecipitationArray,
    JsonFunctions.JsonTuple(properties)["relativeHumidity"] AS HumidityArray
    FROM @rows;
```

Retrieve the weather file zone and filename for later storage with the file data.

The temperature value is an array of nested elements.

Get the value for station directly.

```
@jsonRows2 = SELECT
    Zone,
    Filename,
    Id,
    Station.Replace("https://api.weather.gov/stations/",string.Empty) AS Station,    ◁┐
    EventDate,
    JsonFunctions.JsonTuple(TempsArray) AS Temps,
    JsonFunctions.JsonTuple(WindDirArray) AS WindDirs,
    JsonFunctions.JsonTuple(WindSpeedArray) AS WindSpeeds,
    JsonFunctions.JsonTuple(PressureArray) AS Pressures,
    JsonFunctions.JsonTuple(VisibilityArray) AS Visibilitys,
    JsonFunctions.JsonTuple(PrecipitationArray) AS Precipitations,
    JsonFunctions.JsonTuple(HumidityArray) AS Humiditys
    FROM @jsonRows;

@splitRows = SELECT
    Zone,
    Filename,
    Id,
    Station,
    Convert.ToDateTime(EventDate) AS EventDate,
    Convert.ToDecimal(Temps["value"]) AS Temperature,
    Convert.ToDecimal(WindDirs["value"]) AS WindDirection,
    Convert.ToDecimal(WindSpeeds["value"]) AS WindSpeed,
    Convert.ToDecimal(Pressures["value"]) AS Pressure,
    Convert.ToDecimal(Visibilitys["value"]) AS Visibility,
    Convert.ToDecimal(Precipitations["value"]) AS Precipitation,
    Convert.ToDecimal(Humiditys["value"]) AS Humidity
    FROM @jsonRows2;

INSERT INTO WeatherData (
    Zone,
    Filename,
    Id,
    Station,
    EventDate,
    Temperature,
    WindDirection,
    WindSpeed,
    Pressure,
    Visibility,
    Precipitation,
    RelativeHumidity)
    SELECT * FROM @splitRows;
```

Convert the temperature nested elements into an array of key/value pairs.

Use a String.Replace function to get a more concise value for station.

Strongly-typed objects make data more precise. Done in a separate rowset expression for clarity.

Listing 9.23 outputs the parsed data rowset to a U-SQL table. You can review the script output by writing the data in the table out to a CSV file. This script satisfies the request to load the weather data to a table. This approach of using multiple rowsets for multiple nested elements can be cumbersome for deeply nested elements. The Formats assembly provides another extractor for dealing with multiple levels of nesting.

JSON EXTRACTOR WITH JSONPATH PARSING

The `MultiLevelJsonExtractor` class reads JSON files too. Like `JSONExtractor`, it requires a reference to the Formats assembly in the U-SQL script, and the class must be instantiated. `MultiLevelJsonExtractor` differs in how it reads the JSON. Rather than returning a single block of JSON, it can read multiple blocks of JSON in a single extraction. You could call it the "multi *path* JSON extractor."

If your JSON file is flat, with few nested elements, it's more efficient to write `EXTRACT` and rowset expressions with `JsonExtractor`. If your JSON file uses nested elements, or if you want to return strongly typed fields with minimal processing, scripts with `MultiLevelJsonExtractor` class are easier to write.

The `MultiLevelJsonExtractor` class takes three optional parameters. It relies on JSONPath expressions to return all specified elements from the JSON file at once. The parameters define where to find the elements to retrieve, and how to deal with missing elements.

- The first parameter `rowpath` takes a JSONPath expression defining where to start reading the file.
- The default is the JSON root element.
- The third parameter `jsonPaths` is an array of JSONPath expressions, defining the elements to return. This parameter takes zero, one, or many JSONPath expressions.

When the second parameter `bypassWarning` is `false` (the default), `MultiLevelJson-Extractor` returns errors if a JSONPath is not found. When set to `true`, it returns `null` instead.

Listing 9.24   MultiLevelJsonExtractor parameters

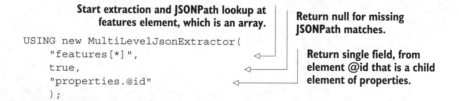

```
USING new MultiLevelJsonExtractor(
    "features[*]",
    true,
    "properties.@id"
    );
```

Start extraction and JSONPath lookup at features element, which is an array.

Return null for missing JSONPath matches.

Return single field, from element @id that is a child element of properties.

You must provide one or more fields in the `EXTRACT` expression that correspond to the expressions in the `jsonPaths` parameter. The field name must match the name of the element returned by the expression. You can specify object types other than string as well. Be aware that when `bypassWarning` is set to `true`, you need to use nullable types. `MultiLevelJsonExtractor` works like `JsonExtractor` if you don't provide any expressions for `jsonPaths`, with one caveat. You still need to provide at least one field in the `EXTRACT` expression for it to compile. The following listing shows the use of multiple JSONPaths to retrieve values from the weather file.

Listing 9.25 Multi-level extraction with MultiLevelJsonExtractor

```
USE DATABASE Players;
REFERENCE ASSEMBLY [Newtonsoft.Json];
REFERENCE ASSEMBLY [Microsoft.Analytics.Samples.Formats];
USING Microsoft.Analytics.Samples.Formats.Json;
```

As in other .NET languages, the USING statement reduces the need to fully qualify class functions.

```
DECLARE @in = @"/Staging/weather.gov/v1/observations/{Zone}/{Filename}.json";
```

Retrieve the weather file zone and filename for later storage with the file data.

```
@jsonRows = EXTRACT
    Zone string,
    Filename string,
    id string,
    station string,
    timestamp DateTime,
    temperature decimal?,
    windDirection decimal?,
    windSpeed decimal?,
    pressure decimal?,
    visibility decimal?,
    precipitation decimal?,
    humidity decimal?
    FROM @in
    USING new MultiLevelJsonExtractor("features[*]",
    true,
    "properties.@id",
    "properties.station",
    "properties.timestamp",
    "properties.temperature.value",
    "properties.windDirection.value",
    "properties.windSpeed.value",
    "properties.barometricPressure.value",
    "properties.visibility.value",
    "properties.precipitationLastHour.value",
    "properties.relativeHumidity.value");
```

temperature is the fourth item in the jsonPaths parameter. In case some readings are missing, use a nullable Decimal? type.

Using a JSONPath expression to skip a level

Return null for missing elements.

Return single field, from element station that is a child element of properties.

```
@cleanRows = SELECT
    Zone,
    Filename,
    id AS Id,
    station AS Station,
    timestamp AS EventDate,
    temperature ?? 0 AS Temperature,
    windDirection ?? 0 AS WindDirection,
    windSpeed ?? 0 AS WindSpeed,
    pressure ?? 0 AS Pressure,
    visibility ?? 0 AS Visibility,
    precipitation ?? 0 AS Precipitation,
    humidity ?? 0 AS Humidity
    FROM @jsonRows;
```

Use the null coalesce operator ?? to provide default value of 0.

```
INSERT INTO WeatherData (
    Zone,
    Filename,
```

```
        Id,
        Station,
        EventDate,
        Temperature,
        WindDirection,
        WindSpeed,
        Pressure,
        Visibility,
        Precipitation,
        RelativeHumidity)
SELECT * FROM @cleanRows;
```

The `MultiLevelJsonExtractor` class, `JsonExtractor` class, and `JsonTuple` function demonstrate the use of .NET assemblies, written in .NET languages like C#, within U-SQL scripts.

Custom assemblies extend the usefulness of U-SQL scripts and ADLA jobs. They can add many kinds of functionality to rowset processing in U-SQL scripts, such as complex string handling and data validation. This includes the Newtonsoft.Json functions, provided by the assembly you loaded in this chapter. Custom assemblies like the Microsoft Sample Formats assembly let your ADLA jobs access more types of data files. With these assemblies loaded, you can parse JSON files and take advantage of JSON data. In the next section, you'll see one more type of data source you can access in your ADLA jobs.

9.3   *Connecting to remote sources*

ADLA jobs are designed around accessing data stored in a Data Lake store or Blob Storage. But a significant amount of data is stored in relational databases. Many methods exist for exporting data from relational databases. In fact, we'll look at one method in chapter 10, using Azure Data Factory. In some scenarios it makes sense to leave the data in the database: Perhaps you want each job to use the most current data, or you don't want to invest in an automated process to extract the data on a regular basis. To support these cases, ADLA jobs can connect to external SQL Server databases and execute queries.

9.3.1   *External databases*

ADLA jobs can connect to Microsoft SQL Server databases, including Azure SQL Database (SQLDB), SQL Data Warehouse (SQLDW), and SQL Servers installed on Azure VMs. This is facilitated by two U-SQL database objects: a Data Source object and a stored credential. The Data Source defines the connection details used when querying the external database. The credential provides a secure means of storing a user and password.

CREATE A SQL SERVER
Before setting up the connections, you need to have a SQL database available. As you recall from chapter 6, you can create a SQLDB quickly with a few Azure PowerShell commands. (If you still have a SQLDB available for development purposes, you can skip to the next section and start connecting to the database.)

The first step is creating a PaaS SQL Server. You choose the resource group for the server, the server name, type, and provide the default administrator credentials. You can optionally choose the SQL Server version. At the time of writing, only `-Server-Version 12.0` is supported. Run the following listing in Azure Cloud Shell to create the new Azure SQL Server.

Listing 9.26   Create new Azure SQL Server

```
New-AzSqlServer -ResourceGroupName "ade-dev-eastus2"
    -Location "East US 2"
    -ServerName "ade-dev-eastus2-sql"           ⟵  Choose a name for the
    -SqlAdministratorCredentials (Get-Credential) ⟵ server, according to your
                                                    naming convention.
         The Get-Credential command prompts for
         a username and password interactively.
```

CREATE A SQL DATABASE

You can create a new SQLDB using the Azure portal and Azure PowerShell. The `New-AzSqlDatabase` command takes the resource group of the server, server name, and database name. You can optionally provide an edition value to set the performance tier at creation (see chapter 6 for more information). Run the following listing in Azure Cloud Shell to create a new SQLDB.

Listing 9.27   Create new Azure SQL Database

```
New-AzSqlDatabase -ResourceGroupName "ade-dev-eastus2"
    -ServerName "ade-dev-eastus2-sql"         The server name you
    -DatabaseName "Playerstats"    ⟵          chose previously
    -Edition "Basic"   ⟵             Databases are not tied to a
         Set the database to the     particular server or region,
         lowest performance tier.    and can have simpler names.
```

> **WARNING**   The default resource allocation tier for SQLDB is the vCore model, with monthly rates starting around $300.00. You may want to scale any new databases you create to a different tier, or specify a tier during provisioning using the `Edition` parameter.

ALLOW ADLA TRAFFIC

The database instance must allow connections from the ADLA servers. For Azure PaaS databases, the firewall includes an Allow All Azure IP Addresses option. The PowerShell script in listing 9.28 will set this rule and create another rule for your on-premises network. Run the script in Azure Cloud Shell to create the firewall rules.

Listing 9.28   Create firewall rule to allow access by Azure resources

This rule allows access from Azure resources,
regardless of their IP address.

```
                                                            The server
New-AzSqlServerFirewallRule -ResourceGroupName "ade-dev-eastus2"  name you chose
    -ServerName "ade-dev-eastus2-sql"              ⟵           previously
    -AllowAllAzureIPs
```

```
New-AzSqlServerFirewallRule -ResourceGroupName "ade-dev-eastus2"
   -ServerName "ade-dev-eastus2-sql"
   -FirewallRuleName "Onpremises"
   -StartIpAddress "192.168.0.198"
   -EndIpAddress "192.168.0.198"
```

The server name you chose previously

Choose a name for the rule that allows access from your on-premises network.

Select a routable Internet address for the end of a range, or match the StartIPAddress to list a single IP address.

Select a routable Internet address for the start of a range.

Once you have created the server and database and configured access, create a table named `PlayerNames`. You can do this with a PowerShell command, or with your favorite SQL Server query tool. Listing 9.29 connects to the new SQLDB and runs a query that creates a new table to hold the player names. You can see more information in chapter 6. Run the script in listing 9.29 in Azure Cloud Shell to create the table.

Listing 9.29 Create SQLDB table

```
Invoke-Sqlcmd
   -Query "CREATE TABLE PlayerNames (PlayerID int, FirstName nvarchar(255),
     LastName nvarchar(255));"
   -ServerInstance "tcp:ade-dev-eastus2-sql.database.windows.net"
   -Database "Playerstats"
   -Credential (Get-Credential)
```

Use the database you created previously.

The fully qualified server name you chose previously. Remember to prepend with tcp:

ADLA IP addresses

Azure resources rotate IP addresses as instances are brought online and offline. If you want to connect to a SQL Server running in a VM, you will need to allow ADLA access through any firewalls. Microsoft publishes a set of IP address ranges that various services use for their network connectivity. You can find the most recent list for the Public cloud at http://mng.bz/wpvq. Unfortunately, the list doesn't specifically list all services. The list for ADLA follows.

Table 9.3 ADLA IP Address Ranges

Region	IP Ranges
Europe North	104.44.91.64/27
Europe West	104.44.93.192/27
US Central	104.44.91.160/27, 40.90.144.0/27
US East 2	104.44.91.96/27, 40.90.144.64/26

9.3.2 Credentials

The U-SQL external database credential securely stores SQL Server username and passwords by encrypting them in your U-SQL database. To create an external database credential in your U-SQL database, you must use Azure PowerShell commands. Execute listing 9.30 using Azure PowerShell.

Listing 9.30   Create U-SQL credential

```
New-AzDataLakeAnalyticsCatalogCredential -AccountName "adedeveastus2"
➥ -DatabaseName "Players"
➥ -CredentialName "PlayerStatsAdmin"
➥ -Credential (Get-Credential)
➥ -DatabaseHost "ade-dev-eastus2-sql.database.windows.net" -Port 1433
```

It's up to you to manage logins and users for your Azure SQL database resources. Using non-admin users for remote access is a best practice. (See chapter 11 for configuration options for Azure SQL database users.)

9.3.3 Data Source

The CREATE DATA SOURCE command stores the connection details for the external database. It has three options to configure.

- You must provide a name for the Data Source, using alphanumeric characters and optionally underscores.
- You must specify the type of SQL Server instance you are connecting to. The value can be AZURESQLDB, AZURESQLDW, or SQLSERVER.
- You can optionally provide an existence check before executing the command (see listing 9.31).

Listing 9.31   Create Data Source for SQL Server VM with existence check

```
CREATE DATA SOURCE IF NOT EXISTS [SourceName]
FROM SQLSERVER
WITH([Options]);
```

The WITH() option can include parameters for target, credentials, and predicate push-down. The PROVIDER_STRING includes three values that are merged with the connection during database requests: Database=[DBNAME], Trusted_Connection=False, and Encrypt=True. You must provide a valid SQL database name for the Database parameter. The values for Trusted_Connection and Encrypt are just for show; they do not impact the connection. You link the U-SQL credential you created with the Data Source using the CREDENTIAL parameter.

The REMOTABLE_TYPES parameter lists the C# types for filters to be processed by the SQL Server engine. For external database queries using the Data Source, the query is parsed for WHERE filters. Any filters with a field type matching one of the types specified in the REMOTABLE_TYPES list is added to the SQL query made in the database request. This is called *predicate push-down*. (You can learn more about maximizing query performance in chapter 8.) Pushing filters to the database for evaluation often improves performance of the queries, because less data is returned from the external source. Filters with other field types are evaluated within the ADLA job after the data is returned from the database request. Removing a type from remote execution can make sense if you've created a custom comparison class, or need to carefully manage language encoding with non-Latin SQL collations. In most cases, skipping the filter on the first rowset and processing a second rowset using custom logic is more useful than discarding an entire type. Figure 9.7 shows the effect on a query of removing `DateTime` from the list of remotable types.

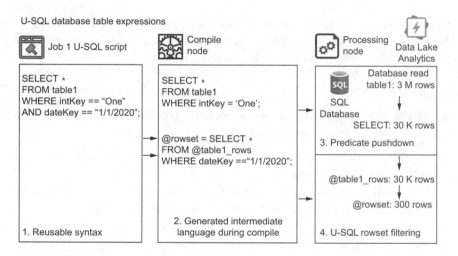

Figure 9.7   Using Data Source remotable types to control row filtering

The primary .NET types for remoting are `bool`, `byte`, `short`, `int`, `long`, `decimal`, `float`, `double`, `string`, and `DateTime`. Run the script in listing 9.32 to create the SQLDB data source.

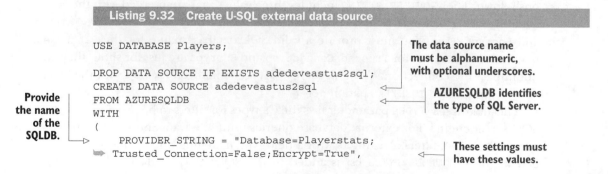

Listing 9.32   Create U-SQL external data source

```
USE DATABASE Players;

DROP DATA SOURCE IF EXISTS adedeveastus2sql;
CREATE DATA SOURCE adedeveastus2sql
FROM AZURESQLDB
WITH
(
    PROVIDER_STRING = "Database=Playerstats;
Trusted_Connection=False;Encrypt=True",
```

Provide the name of the SQLDB.

The data source name must be alphanumeric, with optional underscores.

AZURESQLDB identifies the type of SQL Server.

These settings must have these values.

```
       CREDENTIAL = PlayerStatsAdmin,
       REMOTABLE_TYPES = (bool, byte, short, int, long,
       decimal, float, double, string, DateTime)
  );
```

The credential you created in the previous step

Pass the list of applicable types.

> **TIP** You can find the entire list of .NET-to-T-SQL type mappings at http://mng.bz/K2jg. Some types, such as byte[]/binary, do not lend themselves to use as filters.

With the Data Source created, you can query any tables and views in the external database that your specified credential has access to.

9.3.4 Tables and views

Database tables accessed via the U-SQL data source are read-only. You can read data from the external database using two options with the U-SQL `SELECT` expression.

- The first option adds `EXTERNAL [Data Source Name]` to the expression. The data source will be specific to the U-SQL database context of the script. Be sure to add a `USE DATABASE [Name];` expression to the script.
- The second option adds `LOCATION [Table Name]`, replacing the standard U-SQL table name reference. Use double quotes around the external database table name, which forces the compiler to look outside the current U-SQL database context. You can include the target schema for the table if different from the default `dbo`.

Listing 9.33 SELECT from external Data Source

```
@results =
    SELECT  *
    FROM EXTERNAL [Data Source]
    LOCATION "[schema].[TableName]";
```

The following listing shows a query that reads from the PlayerNames table in the external SQLDB, using the Data Source you set up.

Listing 9.34 Reading data from a U-SQL external data source

```
USE DATABASE Players;

@results =
    SELECT  *
    FROM EXTERNAL adedeveastus2sql LOCATION "dbo.PlayerNames";

OUTPUT @results
TO "/Sandbox/User1/Player/external1.csv"
USING Outputters.Csv(outputHeader: true);
```

Because access is read-only, you can use views instead of base table access to your external database without losing any functionality. Because access is read-only, you can structure your external database access using views instead of base table access without losing any functionality. Using views allows greater control over data access, including by shifting control of the access granted to the database. Using a view works the same as querying a table, only you specify the view name instead. The following listing demonstrates using a view with the external database.

> **Listing 9.35   Reading data from a U-SQL external data source**

```
USE DATABASE Players;

@results =
    SELECT  *
    FROM EXTERNAL adedeveastus2sql LOCATION "dbo.vw_PlayerNames";

OUTPUT @results
TO "/Sandbox/User1/Player/external1.csv"
USING Outputters.Csv(outputHeader: true);
```

Accessing external SQL Server data sources gives you one more method of generating data in ADLA for analysis. When you add additional assemblies, many options for analysis become available with ADLA jobs, all with the built-in parallel processing you get from large batch processing jobs.

9.4   Exercises

The following exercises can help you internalize the new features introduced in this chapter.

9.4.1   Exercise 1

Given a set of user-submitted JPEG images loaded to Data Lake store folder /Staging/Users/User1/images/, create a U-SQL script to analyze the images and return the locations of any identified faces.

SOLUTION

The `EmotionAnalysisEmotionExtractor` can be used to locate faces in photographs, as well as identify the emotion present on the face. Reference the registered assembly, along with the `ImageIO.dll` assembly. Refer to the table of output fields from the `EmotionExtractor` for the EXTRACT statement. Include all the fields.

```
USE DATABASE master;
REFERENCE ASSEMBLY ImageCommon;
REFERENCE ASSEMBLY EmotionAnalysis;
DECLARE @in = "/Staging/Users/User1/images/{FileName}.jpg";
@people = EXTRACT
    Camera string,
    FaceIndex int,
    RectX float,
```

```
RectY float,
Width float,
Height float,
Emotion string,
Confidence float
FROM @in
USING new Cognition.Vision.EmotionExtractor();
```

9.4.2 Exercise 2

Given the following JSON file, create a script to return the `SaleNo`, `LotNo`, `ItemName`, and `LotDescript` fields.

```
{
  "Results":[
    {
      "SaleNo"        ":"A1QSCI20001",
      "LotNo"         ":701,
      "AucStartDt"    ":"2019-11-27",
      "AucEndDt"      ":"2019-12-04",
      "ItemName"      ":"MISC FORENSICS LAB EQUIPMENT",
      "PropertyAddr1" ":"State Of Oregon, Das",
      "PropertyAddr2" ":"Federal Surplus Property",
      "PropertyAddr3" ":"1655 Salem Industrial Dr NE",
      "PropertyCity"  ":"Salem",
      "PropertyState" ":"OR",
      "PropertyZip"   ":"973010375",
      "AuctionStatus" ":"A",
      "BiddersCount"  ":     4,
      "LotInfo":[
          {"LotSequence":"001", "LotDescript":"Misc\u0020Forensics\u0020Lab\u
0020Equipment\u0020\u0028Internal\u003A"},
          {"LotSequence":"002", "LotDescript":"470496\u002D9309\u002D0001\u00
3B\u0020\u00281\u002D17\u0029\u0020TV\u0029\u0020Please\u0020see\u0020at
tached"},
          {"LotSequence":"003", "LotDescript":"list\u0020for\u0020more\u0020d
etails\u002E\u0020Shipping\u0020weight\u0020\u0026"},
          {"LotSequence":"004", "LotDescript":"dimensions\u0020will\u0020be\u
0020determined\u0020after\u0020award\u002C"},
          {"LotSequence":"005", "LotDescript":"depending\u0020on\u0020whether
\u0020it\u0020will\u0020be\u0020picked\u0020up\u0020locally"},
          {"LotSequence":"006", "LotDescript":"or\u0020shipped\u002E\u00201\u
0020Lot"},
          {"LotSequence":"007", "LotDescript":"47049693090001"}
        ],
      "ItemDescURL    ":"https://gsaauctions.gov/gsaauctions/aucdsclnk/?sl=A1
QSCI20001701",
      "ImageURL       ":"https://gsaauctions.gov/lotimages/regnA/A1QSCI200017
01.jpg"
    }
  ]
}
```

NOTE JSON data courtesy of https://open.gsa.gov/api/.

SOLUTION

You can use the `JsonExtractor` or `MultiLevelJsonExtractor` functions to read the rows. Using the `MultiLevelJsonExtractor`, you will use a JSONPath statement to directly retrieve each field. Note the fixed-width fields in the JSONPath expressions.

```
USE DATABASE DB;
REFERENCE ASSEMBLY [Newtonsoft.Json];
REFERENCE ASSEMBLY [Microsoft.Analytics.Samples.Formats];
USING Microsoft.Analytics.Samples.Formats.Json;

DECLARE @in = @"/Staging/open.gsa.gov/v1/auctions/Filename}.json";

@jsonRows = EXTRACT
    Filename string,
    SaleNo string,
    LotNo int,
    ItemName string,
    LotDescript string
FROM @in
USING new MultiLevelJsonExtractor("Results[*]",
true,
"SaleNo       ",
"LotNo        ",
"ItemName     ",
"LotInfo[*].LotDescript");
```

Summary

- ADLA accounts include Cognitive Services .NET assemblies. These assemblies allow U-SQL scripts to extract data from images using ML algorithms.

- You can add your own .NET assemblies to the U-SQL catalog. This allows developers to extend the built-in functions of U-SQL.

- U-SQL scripts can connect to external SQL Server databases using a Data Source and credential. Using external databases lets you add relational data to the rowsets in ADLA jobs.

Service integration
with Azure Data Factory

10

This chapter covers

- Building a single-step processing pipeline
- Using a secret key store
- Scheduling batch data processing

In previous chapters, you've learned how to use Azure services to ingest and transform data. Except for Stream Analytics (SA), which automatically processes incoming data, you have added the data or triggered a process manually. In this chapter, you'll learn how to move data between services on a schedule. You'll learn how to move files between Azure Storage accounts and your Data Lake store (ADLS store). You'll also learn how to run U-SQL scripts on a schedule to transform data. You'll use Azure Data Lake Analytics (ADLA) to read and transform data from multiple sources. You'll learn how to store secrets in Azure Key Vault (AKV). Azure Data Factory (ADF) provides the connections that power this automation.

ADF manages execution of tasks. These can be as simple as calling a web service endpoint, or as complicated as creating a new server cluster to run custom code and removing it once the code completes. Each task is a resource entity consisting of a JSON resource definition. Each resource is related to one or more other resources. Resources and relationships are defined as follows:

- Each task is called an *activity*.
- Connections to external services are called *linkedservices*.
- Files and data tables in linkedservices define a schema interface called a *dataset*.
- Activities connect to external services using a linkedservice. Most activities use a source and target dataset to define a transformation.
- One or more activities chain to form a *pipeline*.
- One or more pipelines form a *data factory*.

Figure 10.1 shows some of the activities an ADF pipeline can perform, including copying files between storage locations, database imports, and executing ADLA U-SQL jobs.

1 Data lands in storage, on-premises, and in Azure.
2 ADF moves raw data from on-premises to a Data Lake.
3 ADF triggers Azure services, like ADLA, to modify or import data.
4 ADF moves processed data to user endpoints in Azure or on-premises.
5 Azure services, like Azure SQL Database (SQLDB), provide end-user access.
6 Failure in ADF processing triggers alert messaging.

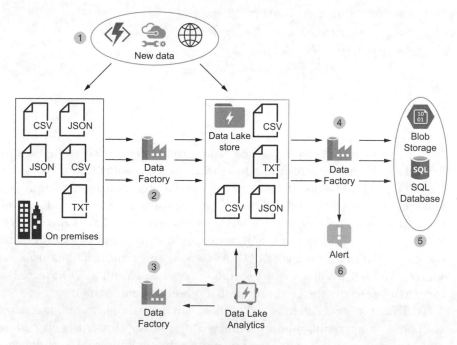

Figure 10.1   Data Factory moves data between services.

ADF moves data and integrates with data processing and serving endpoints. With this in mind, imagine you need to automate data movement and processing tasks. In previous chapters you've learned multiple methods for copying files, including command-line tools and PowerShell scripts. Azure includes several other services that can be developed to copy and transform data, including Azure Functions, ADLA, and SA. Each has strengths and weaknesses, like significant development costs or maintenance costs. ADF was designed around scheduling data movement and transformation, so that's where its strengths lay.

ADF combines a no-code graphical development environment with modern cloud-native principles. The resources are compiled into a set of steps to execute. Each execution creates one or more calls to separate processes, to perform the steps. Each step is monitored and can be retried. Each step can run independently or subsequent to another step. Multiple steps can be run simultaneously, and the service automatically scales to handle multiple executions.

File copies, data imports, and running ADLA jobs are some of the most common tasks in a production analytics system like we've been building. ADF does have a few limitations to be aware of.

- A limit of 800 ADF services per subscription.
- A limit of 5,000 resources in a single ADF service. This includes activities, linked-services, datasets, and pipelines.
- A maximum of 40 activities per pipeline.

This chapter shows you how to set up the basic blocks for building complex automated analytics processing in Azure. You should create these blocks in this order:

1 Azure Data Factory service
2 Azure Key Vault service
3 Azure Key Vault linkedservice
4 Subsequent ADF linkedservices
5 Any ADF datasets for the linkedservices
6 First ADF activity and pipeline
7 Subsequent ADF activities and pipelines

Before we discuss creating activities and pipelines, let's set up the container for these resources—the ADF service itself.

> **TIP** You can find the code listings in the GitHub repository for this book at https://github.com/rnuckolls/azure_storage.

10.1 Creating an Azure Data Factory service

The ADF service functions as an organizing structure for a collection of resources. This includes pipelines and the activities within them. The ADF service doesn't do anything on its own: the pipelines manage the activities that execute. In this way, it's similar to other Azure services, like the Event Hubs namespace, SQL Server, and Storage accounts, which need additional services configured.

Because it's an organizing structure, creating a new ADF service requires a few choices. You can create the new service in the Azure portal by browsing to the New Data Factory blade at https://portal.azure.com/#create/Microsoft.DataFactory. Creating an ADF service in the Azure portal requires the standard selections of name, region, and resource group. You also need to select the ADF version to use. Version 2 (V2) includes a graphical designer for creating pipelines, activities, and other resources. V2 also separates scheduling pipeline runs from the pipeline itself. Version 1 uses the same JSON definitions for ADF resources. You should use V2 to take advantage of newer features.

ADF V2 also supports version control, using Git, a popular open-source version control system. We'll enable version control with Git later in the chapter.

> **NOTE** ADF V2 supports all the functionality of V1, and adds a graphical designer and other new features. Improved pipeline scheduling and Azure resource-to-resource transfers make V2 the better option. This book focuses on ADF V2.

You can also create the new ADF service using Azure PowerShell, which allows automation and repeatability. Use the `New-AzDataFactoryV2` command to create a new ADF service. Supply the standard `ResourceGroupName`, `Name`, and `Location` parameters to create the service. You do not need to select the ADF version, because separate commands are used to create V1 and V2 services. Run the script in the following listing to create the ADF V2 service.

Listing 10.1   Creating a new ADF service with Azure PowerShell

```
New-AzDataFactoryV2 -ResourceGroupName "ade-dev-eastus2"
  -Name "ade-dev-eastus2-adf" -Location "EastUS2"
```

When you first create an ADF service, it has no resources. For data engineers, most of the ADF setup lies in creating and configuring the linkedservices, dataset, pipeline, and trigger resources. ADF builds the pipelines using a no-code approach. All resources are defined using JSON configuration files. You can create the configuration files using the ADF authoring tool, or using a text editor and Azure PowerShell. The JSON elements define each resource's properties, including the relationships to other resources, as follows:

- Linkedservices define the connections to Azure and on-premises services, like Blob Storage, ADLA, and SQL Server databases.
- Datasets define the schema of data available from a connection. This makes it possible to move data between dissimilar services.
- Pipelines define one or more activities to act on linkedservices. Some activities trigger actions, like starting a U-SQL job in ADLA. Some activities move data between two services, using linkedservices and datasets.
- Triggers define scheduled or event-driven execution of pipelines.

- An Integration Runtime (IR) manages the work of executing each activity, either in Azure or on-premises.
- An ADF service collects the resource definitions together, defines the version control connection, and provides an integration point for the ADF GUI.

Figure 10.2 shows the relationships of these resources.

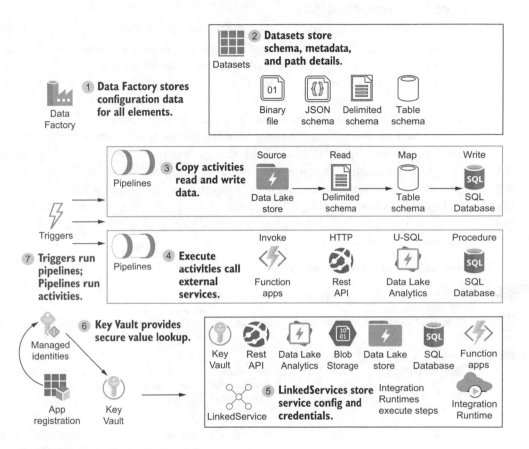

Figure 10.2   Data Factory moves data.

To build a complete pipeline, you need to configure services in order.

1 Start at the lowest level, the *linkedservice*. Arrange required credentials and access to the service.
2 Add a *pipeline* to group the actions to perform.
3 Add an *activity* to perform an action that doesn't read or write data. Activities require a pipeline.

4 Add a *dataset* for files or data tables that provide access to data. Datasets require a linkedservice.

5 Add an *activity* to perform reads and writes on data between two datasets.

With your new ADF service to hold the resources, let's start with a secure foundation for all the linkedservices, AKV.

10.2 *Secure authentication*

ADF holds the authentication configuration for each linkedservice, both external services and Azure services. *Authentication* happens between the requester and the endpoint, and is closely tied to *authorization*. Authentication identifies the requester; authorization defines what the requester can do. The requester must know which authentication method and which credentials to use. AKV provides a secure method for storing the credentials. The linkedservice stores the authentication method.

The ADF IR connects to linkedservice endpoints to perform actions. Some linkedservice endpoints, like public REST APIs, do not require credentials, but most require some form of authentication and authorization. Authorization methods vary between endpoints, even within Azure services, and must be configured at the endpoint.

Linkedservices use multiple methods for authenticating with their target services. These methods fall into three categories: AAD-integrated, key-based, and username/password (see table 10.1).

Table 10.1 Authentication methods

Method	Type	Services	Description
Managed identity	AAD account	Blob Storage, Key Vault, Data Lake store, SQLDB, SynapseDB	An AAD entity with ID tied to the ADF service
Service principal	AAD key	Blob Storage, Data Explorer, Data Lake store, Data Lake Analytics, SQLDB, SynapseDB, ML service	An AAD entity with ID and secret key
Secret key	Key	Blob Storage, Table Storage, Batch, Databricks, Functions, ML Studio, Search	One or more keys to pass with REST API requests
Username/password or connection string	Password	File Storage, HDInsight, CosmosDB, SQLDB, SynapseDB	One or more key/value pairs to pass with HTTP requests or SQL Server connections

AAD-integrated authentication methods are used for Azure services. Some services can use multiple types of authentication, such as key-based methods, and keys can be used with many REST API endpoints. Some websites restrict access with Basic authentication, and you can authenticate to SQL Server with database credentials. Let's look at the AAD integrated methods in more detail.

10.2.1 *Azure Active Directory integration*

AAD integrations use two methods: a key-based method called a *service principal*, and a service-based method called a *managed identity*.

The service principal is an entity you create in AAD, similar to a user account. It provides an identity for authentication and authorization that can be used by services requesting or providing access. The service principal must be given access to Azure services, just like a user account. Using AAD integration with ADF lets you create a single credential, instead of many, for use with multiple Azure services.

To create a new service principal for ADF, we'll use a template called an *App registration*. The App registration defines credentials and authorization methods for an application or applications, and the service principal identifies the application or applications. Instead of a username and password, applications use the application ID and a secret key to get an authentication token from the service principal.

When Azure services are created in AAD, a *managed identity* is created for them. Unlike App registrations, managed identities can be used by only a single Azure service. Managed identities also must be given access to Azure services, just like a user account or service principal.

> **NOTE** App registrations reside in a single AAD directory. The app has one or more unique URIs to identify it. An app can have more than one service principal associated with it, but only one per directory. Additional service principals can be added in other AAD directories. This means you can authenticate your ADF service with a single method and access services in other AAD directory scopes. This is an example of *multi-tenant integration* with AAD.

Before we create any linkedservices, we need to create the App registration and service principal, so we can include the ID and key in the resource configuration file.

CREATING AN APP REGISTRATION

An App registration will be used to identify ADF to other Azure services. Those services can use a common credential for authentication and authorization, reducing the number of credentials to manage in ADF.

Creating an App registration for service-principal authentication consists of two steps: creating the app and adding a key. You can perform both in the Azure portal. Browse to the AAD App Registrations blade in AAD via All Services > Azure Active Directory > App Registrations. The Register an Application blade will open if you don't have any apps; otherwise click New Registration. Type a name for the App registration, distinct from the ADF service name, for example, `ade-dev-eastus2-adf-id`. For this scenario, choose Default Directory Only - Single Tenant. The other account types are for services shared across multiple AAD directories and tenants, which is useful in SaaS applications with multiple customers. Leave the Redirect URI blank, because we won't be interacting with this app through a web request.

> **TIP** You should choose a name for your App registration that is distinct from the application or applications that use it. When you create a service in AAD,

managed identities are also created with the same name as the Azure service they represent. When you add an App registration with the same name as the ADF service and its managed identity, it becomes difficult to select between them when assigning permissions. Managed identities are less flexible than App registrations. We'll discuss managed identities later in the chapter.

After registering the app, browse to the Certificates & Secrets blade of the new App registration. Click New Client Secret to open the Add a Client Secret blade. The *client secret* is the key that applications will use to impersonate the App registration—in this case, the ADLA linkedservice. Add a description and choose an expiration window. The expiration window forces you to rotate your access key, the client secret, on a regular basis. You should select an expiration window that works with your organization's policy on key rotation. The default value is sufficient if you have no policy. Once you click Add, the blade will generate and display a new client secret key. You will have just one opportunity to copy this key before moving away from the blade. Copy the key or leave the blade open while you create the AKV linkedservice in the next section.

You can also use Azure PowerShell to create a new App registration. The steps are the same, but in a slightly different order.

1 Create the App registration.
2 Create the secret key at the same time.
3 Create the service principal, using the new App registration ID.

Creating an App registration for principal impersonation in Azure PowerShell requires three values: a name, a URI, and a password. The parameter `DisplayName` assigns the app name. You should use a name that's distinct from the ADF service name. `IdentifierUris` is required, and is used as part of an authentication chain with this service principal. You do not need to provide a valid endpoint but it must be unique, because ADF uses `IdentifierUris` to identify this app. You need to provide a `SecureString` object for the `Password` parameter. The encrypted value of this object will be stored as the client secret key. In listing 10.2, you provide a value for the `Secure-String` interactively when running the script, using the `Read-Host` command.

Run listing 10.2 to create the new App registration. The output will display the ApplicationId. Copy the ApplicationId value, along with the password you entered, for use in configuring the new ADLS linkedservice in the next section.

Listing 10.2   Creating a new App registration with Azure PowerShell

```
$Secure = Read-Host -AsSecureString          ⟵┤ Read a secret key
                                                 value interactively.

$App = New-AzADApplication -DisplayName "ade-dev-eastus2-adf-id"
    -IdentifierUris "http://none.none"
    -Password $Secure          ⟵┐ Previously submitted
                                  secret key
$App.ApplicationId.Guid     ⟵┐
                              │ The new service principal ID
Throwaway value
```

NOTE The `Read-Host -AsSecureString` command provides a more secure method of providing the password than storing it in a file, but does limit the script's automation potential. PowerShell provides several functions for generating a `SecureString`.

The App registration alone does not give access to Azure services. You need to create a service principal, in the same AAD directory, and authorize it to access the services used by ADF. When creating an App registration using the Azure portal, AAD creates the service principal for you. You must do it yourself when using Azure PowerShell.

`New-AzADServicePrincipal` creates a new service principal. You can create a standalone service principal, but it's more useful when attached to an app. To attach it and use the authentication methods defined in the app, pass the app's GUID using the `ApplicationId` parameter. You can authorize access to a service using AAD RBAC when you use Azure PowerShell to create the service principal. This is not available through the Azure Portal. Pass the target service `resourceId` value using the `Scope` parameter. You can target a whole subscription, a resource group and its children, or a specific Azure service. The default is the current subscriptions. Pass the desired role using the `Role` parameter. The default is `Contributor`, but you can use `Admin`, `Reader`, or other more specific roles.

Listing 10.3 shows an Azure PowerShell script that creates a new service principal and attaches it to an app. The new service principal does not have any permissions. You'll assign permissions as needed when you create linkedservices. Run the script in the following listing to create the service principal.

Listing 10.3 Creating a new service principal with Azure PowerShell

```
$App = Get-AzADApplication -DisplayName "ade-dev-eastus2-adf-id"        ◁──┐
New-AzADServicePrincipal                                           Look up the
  -ApplicationId $App.ApplicationId.Guid          ◁──┐            app by name.
                                                      │
                              Use the app's ID       │
                              for authentication.
```

WARNING When authorizing access during service principal creation, be sure to include both `Role` and `Scope` parameters. If only one is included, the other parameter will be applied with the default value. This can result in the authorization inadvertently being applied to all services in a subscription, or with greater access than necessary.

Azure provides a general service for storing the service principal identity key. ADF can integrate with AKV to securely store passwords, keys, and other secrets.

10.2.2 *Azure Key Vault*

AKV securely stores and gives access to secrets. You can programatically add and access any string less than 25 KB in size, and AKV will encrypt and decrypt the secret value for you.

Applications and Azure services authenticate to AKV using service principals and managed identities. Using a managed identity doesn't require AKV to provide any secrets; the service authenticates as itself. The AKV linkedservice uses the ADF managed identity to connect.

Linkedservices store the authentication method in their definition files. This includes usernames, passwords, and secret keys if provided. AKV forms a critical point in the authentication chain by securely storing these secrets. Because ADF can use Git version control, you could accidentally make the secrets in your definition files available to unauthorized parties. Using an AKV service prevents this by storing the secret, and provides it to the IR when needed. The secret can be a password, an API key, or any other string. Figure 10.3 shows this process in action.

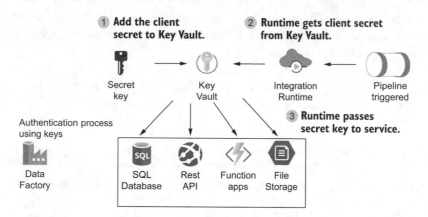

Figure 10.3   Data Factory secret key authentication

Secrets in AKV can also be used with linkedservices using service principals. With the AKV, you can store the secret name in the JSON configuration file and allow the IR to retrieve it directly from AKV. Azure services authorize the service principal to access the service and perform actions. Figure 10.4 shows this process in action.

There are a couple of steps to begin using AKV for authentication in ADF pipelines. First, you need to have an available key vault. Next, you authorize ADF to access it. Last, you add secrets to the vault. Let's start by creating a new key vault.

CREATING A KEY VAULT

You can create the new vault in the Azure portal with just a few options. In the Azure Portal, browse to the New AKV blade at https://portal.azure.com/#create/Microsoft .KeyVault. Choose a subscription and resource group, name, and location for the key

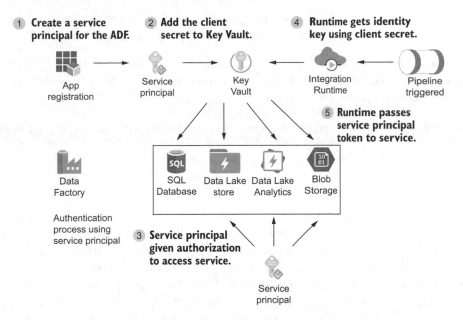

Figure 10.4 Data Factory service principal authentication and authorization

vault. As usual, you should select the same location as the other Azure services that will integrate with AKV. You can choose between Standard and Premium tiers.

- Both tiers use a hardware security module (HSM) to generate and store encryption keys.
- Both levels support RSA 2048-bit and higher keys, and use the same charge per transaction level.
- The Premium tier adds support for HSM encryption processing. At this tier, HSM provides more secure encryption by keeping keys and encrypted values within the device, and running encryption algorithms on the HSM.

In the Azure portal, you can configure options for preserving values in your key vault. *Soft delete* retains the vault for a period of days after deletion. This is enabled by default. Deleted vaults will remain hidden in the Azure portal until the retention period has passed. Disabling soft delete will allow the vault to be removed in one step. You can recover or delete soft-deleted vaults using Azure PowerShell. Enabling purge protection prevents soft-deleted vaults from being removed during the retention period. The retention period is 90 days by default, but you can set it between 7 and 90 days when you create the vault in the Azure portal. Listing 10.4 shows how to recover a deleted vault.

> **NOTE** At the time of writing, operations on secrets cost $0.03 per 10,000 transactions for RSA 2048-bit keys. RSA 3072-bit and higher operations are

$0.15 per 10,000 transactions. HSM keys add $1 per key. There is no monthly charge. See http://mng.bz/4B6j for the latest pricing details.

If you need to recover a soft-deleted vault, use the `Undo-AzKeyVaultRemoval` command in Azure PowerShell. Supply the standard `ResourceGroupName`, `Location`, and `VaultName` for the vault to recover.

Listing 10.4   Recovering a soft-deleted key vault with Azure PowerShell

```
Undo-AzKeyVaultRemoval -VaultName "ade-dev-eastus2-key"
    -ResourceGroupName "ade-dev-eastus2"
    -Location "East US 2"
```

Using Azure PowerShell

You can also create the key vault using Azure PowerShell. Use the `New-AzKeyVault` command to create a new AKV service, supplying the standard `ResourceGroupName`, `Name`, and `Location` parameters. When using this command, you do not need to provide the tier when choosing Standard. Use the parameter `Sku` with value `Premium` for the Premium tier. Use `EnablePurgeProtection` to enable recovery of deleted secrets and AKV services for 90 days. The following listing shows the script for creating the new key vault.

Listing 10.5   Creating a new key vault with Azure PowerShell

```
New-AzKeyVault -Name 'ade-dev-eastus2-key'
    -ResourceGroupName 'ade-dev-eastus2'
    -Location 'East US 2'
    -EnableSoftDelete -EnablePurgeProtection
```

The new key vault can store keys and secrets for use by ADF. You'll add secrets later in the chapter. Now you need to authorize ADF to access the vault.

AUTHORIZING ADF USING MANAGED IDENTITIES

Before ADF can look up secrets in AKV, you need to authorize ADF to do so. AKV linkedservices use managed identities to authenticate to AKV, so this is the type of AAD entity you will need to grant access to. You can add the ADF service to AKV using the Azure portal.

Using Azure portal

Browse to the Access Policies blade under the AKV service. Click Add Access Policy to show the Add Access Policy blade. In the blade, you can grant permission for keys, secrets, and certificate actions like Get, Set, List, and Delete. Choose Get and List from the Secret Permission drop-down. The authoring GUI can test if a secret exists during the creation of a linkedservice. Click the Select Principal option to search for the ADF service. Type the name of the ADF `ade-dev-eastus2-adf` in the Principal search box. Select the entity representing the ADF service, not the App registration. Click Add to add the policy.

Using Azure PowerShell

You can also add the Access policy using Azure PowerShell, using the `Set-AzKey-VaultAccessPolicy` command. Listing 10.6 shows the script to do this. It retrieves the ADF Managed Identity object and passes the ID to `Set-AzKeyVaultAccessPolicy` using the `ObjectId` parameter. The `PermissionsToSecrets` parameter takes a CSV string of the permissions to apply. The values include Get, List, Set, Delete, Backup, Restore, Recover, and Purge.

Listing 10.6 Assign permissions to Data Factory in a key vault with Azure PowerShell

```
$App = Get-AzADServicePrincipal -DisplayName "ade-dev-eastus2-adf"      ⟵  Look up the
Set-AzKeyVaultAccessPolicy -VaultName "ade-dev-eastus2-key"                ADF managed
  -ObjectId $App.Id                    ⟵  Use the Id           identity.
  -PermissionsToSecrets Get,List       ⟵     property.
      Assign read and list access.
```

By assigning access to the ADF managed identity, you can now create an AKV linkedservice in ADF and use it to retrieve secrets for other linkedservice connections. Let's create the linkedservice now.

CREATING AN AKV LINKEDSERVICE

Linkedservices define the connection details to the external service, including endpoint addresses and authentication methods. They store these details in their definition files.

Tight integration with Azure services makes it easy to configure the endpoint details. For Azure services, you choose the subscription, resource group, and service name, and ADF manages the endpoint lookup. For services outside of Azure, you must provide a URL or host address that is accessible by either the Azure or on-premises Integration Runtime (IR). Azure hosts an IR for use by ADF when connecting to Internet-accesible services. An on-premises IR allows access to services behind firewalls, in your datacenter or in private networks in Azure. This chapter discusses services accessible to the Azure IR.

You can create a linkedservice with the Azure portal authoring GUI in a single step, if you have the authentication method set up beforehand. For the AKV linkedservice, authentication happens using the ADF managed identity. You authorized the managed identity in the previous section. Most other Azure services, like ADLS, authorize access by the App registration for the ADF service you created earlier in the chapter. Linkedservices for those services retrieve the App registration key through the linkedservice, then impersonate the App registration to authenticate with the Azure service. Authentication methods for ADLS and ADLA are covered later in the chapter.

Configuring linkedservices for Azure services takes advantage of integrations. For PaaS services hosted in Azure, you rely on Azure infrastructure to provide the connection details for a named instance of the service. You can select the subscription and service from drop-down lists when creating linkedservices in the authoring GUI.

NOTE   Other Azure services, like Azure Functions and Azure Key Vault, use other methods for authentication. Functions uses a secret key, and AKV authenticates with the ADF managed identity. ADF provides methods for authentication depending on what integrations are available. We review these in the chapter discussing the specific service. For services hosted outside Azure, you generally provide a host name and port for communicating over the Internet. You also provide an authentication method, either a key or a username and password. You can find details of authentication and integration for the other linkedservices at http://mng.bz/QxRv.

Using Azure portal

To create the AKV linkedservice in the Azure portal, launch the authoring GUI.

1   Browse to the Overview blade of the ADF service.
2   Click Author & Monitor to launch the Authoring GUI in a new window.
3   Switch to the Authoring tab in the left nav.
4   Show Connections, from the bottom of the Factory Resources navigation.
5   Click New to open the selection blade.
6   Show the Azure tab.
7   Select Azure Key Vault from the list and click Continue.
8   Choose a name for the resource. Only alphanumerics and underscores are allowed.
9   Select the Azure subscription from the drop-down.
10   Select the Azure key vault name (ade-dev-eastus2-key) from the drop-down of available AKV services.
11   Because you have already granted access to the key vault for ADF, you don't need to authorize it at this point.

At this point you can click Create and save the new linkedservice. The authoring GUI provides a helpful feature here: the Test Connection button. This will try to connect to the service with the configuration details you just provided. This can be helpful when troubleshooting a new linkedservice, because connection failures provide error messages.

Using Azure PowerShell

You can also use Azure PowerShell to create a new linkedservice. This allows for a repeatable process and consistent configuration across environments. Access Azure PowerShell by visiting Azure Cloud Shell at https://shell.azure.com/, or clicking the >_ header menu in the Azure portal.

Like creating Stream Analytics services with Azure PowerShell, creating ADF resources requires a JSON configuration file. Using the authoring GUI will generate these files. When configuring ADF with Azure PowerShell, you need to generate them yourself.

The JSON configuration file contains a few common root elements: `name` and `properties`. The `properties` element contains a set of elements common to other linkedservices. The `annotations` element is a CSV string array. The values can be used as additional identifiers for linkedservices, much like the `Tags` attribute of Azure resources. The `type` element identifies the type of linkedservice. For AKV, the type is `AzureKeyVault`. You'll see more types later in this chapter.

The `typeProperties` contains the connection information for the linkedservice. This element varies significantly between linkedservices. There are some elements that multiple Azure services use, because the services are structured similarly or authenticate similarly. For Azure services, these most common elements include:

- `subscriptionId`—The Azure subscription containing the service
- `tenant`—The AAD organization used for authentication
- `servicePrincipalId`—The registered app used to authenticate the ADF service
- `servicePrincipalKey`—The definition for the AKV identity lookup

The only `typeProperties` element for AKV is `baseUrl`. You cannot find this value in the Azure portal or the through Azure PowerShell. It's generated by adding the AKV name to the AKV Azure domain, like the following:

```
https://[AKVName].vault.azure.net
```

Listing 10.7 shows the AKV JSON configuration file. Save this file to an Azure Cloud Shell folder (/adf) or a local drive accessible by your local PowerShell install. Refer to chapter 6 for more details on uploading files to Azure Cloud Shell.

Listing 10.7 Azure Key Vault definition file

```json
{
    "name": "AzureKeyVault1",
    "properties": {
        "annotations": [],
        "type": "AzureKeyVault",
        "typeProperties": {
            "baseUrl": "https://ade-dev-eastus2-key.vault.azure.net/"
        }
    }
}
```

`Set-AzDataFactoryV2LinkedService` is used for creating all linkedservices. The command takes the ADF resource group, ADF name, and the name of the new linkedservice. The parameter `DefinitionFile` takes the JSON configuration file path. Run the script in the following listing to create the new linkedservice.

Listing 10.8 Creating a new AKV linkedservice with Azure PowerShell

```
Set-AzDataFactoryV2LinkedService -ResourceGroupName "ade-dev-eastus2"
➡   -DataFactoryName "ade-dev-eastus2-adf"
➡   -Name "AzureKeyVault1"
➡   -DefinitionFile "~/adf/AzureKeyVault.json"
```

With the AKV linkedservice created, you can now use the key vault to store passwords securely and access them in ADF pipelines. Let's put AKV to use by creating a pipeline to copy files.

10.3   *Copying files with ADF*

The Jonestown Sluggers facilities team has taken an interest in your Data Lake store. They currently store badge tracking data from the stadium in Azure using a File Storage network share and CSV files. They want to copy these files to the Data Lake store so they can do advanced analytics processing. How can you accommodate this request?

Azure Files storage is a storage container type that supports using SMB file sharing. You can map a drive on your local desktop directly to a Files container and use it as a network share. This makes for easy integration with on-premises servers that want to use Azure Storage. You have a few options to copy data from Azure Files:

- Use Azure Storage Explorer to copy from Files > desktop > ADLS.
- Use Azure AzCopy to copy from Files > Blobs, then use ADLCopy to copy from Blobs > ADLS.
- Use Azure portal to copy from a file share attached to Files > ADLS.
- Create an Azure Function to copy from Files > ADLS.
- Use ADF to copy from Files > ADLS.

> **TIP**   You can read more about Azure storage containers in chapter 3.

Some solutions involve manual interactions; others use extra network traffic. Azure Functions requires writing code using the Azure Storage SDK. ADF has a linkedservice available for connecting to Files storage. Let's see what's involved in creating the ADF pipeline for fulfilling this request.

10.3.1   *Creating a Files storage container*

Recall from chapter 3 that creating a Blob Storage service is a two-part process:

1   You first create the Azure storage account
2   Then you create the Blob service under the account

Creating a Files service works the same; the Files service exists under an Azure storage account.

For this scenario, you will need a Files service. You can create one under your existing Azure storage account using the Azure portal or Azure PowerShell.

USING AZURE PORTAL

In the Azure portal, browse to the File Service > File Shares blade under your Azure Storage account. Click the File Share button to show the New File Share dialog. Give your new file share a name (accesscard), using alphanumeric characters and hyphens. You can choose to limit the maximum size of the share, by specifying a value up to 5120 in GB. Click Create to add the new file share.

USING AZURE POWERSHELL

Creating a new file share with Azure PowerShell is just as easy. You need to provide the resource group, storage account, and a name for the new file share. You can also set a maximum storage size using the `QuotaGiB` parameter, in GBs. The following listing shows the script for creating this Files container. Run this script to create the container.

> **Listing 10.9   Create a File Storage service with Azure PowerShell**

```
New-AzRmStorageShare -ResourceGroupName "ade-dev-eastus2"
  -StorageAccountName "adedeveastus2"
  -Name "accesscard" -QuotaGiB 500       ⟵──  Set a reasonable quota according
                                               to expected usage of the file
                                               share, to limit spending.
```

Now that you have the Files container, you need some files. You can download a 100 K-row badge-tracking data file at http://mng.bz/90Bq. Upload this file, and maybe a few copies, to the Files service using the Azure portal, Storage Explorer, or mapping a drive.

ADF authenticates to the Files container using what appear to be a username and password. The values are actually just the storage account name and an account access key. Because ADF will use a key to authenticate, you need to retrieve one with the appropriate access level. ADF integration uses Azure Storage account access keys as the only option. These keys come with more than enough permissions to access the Files container. You then store this key in AKV, thereby not exposing the key in the configuration file.

10.3.2   Adding secrets to AKV

Adding keys to AKV should become a common practice for Azure developers. Authenticating with AAD lets you retrieve secrets from the AKV instead of configuration files. Rotating keys should also become a developer best practice. AKV supports rotation by allowing several active values for a single named secret. Each value has its own start and end date, and can be manually disabled. This lets you stage key updates over time. Linkedservice integration with AKV lets you specify a particular value from a named secret, or use the latest value.

USING AZURE PORTAL

Browse to the AKV > Settings > Secrets blade, or use the search box to find Secrets in the top left of your AKV in the portal. Click Generate/Import to open the Create a Secret blade. Use the Manual upload method, because other options are deprecated. Provide a name for the secret, using alphanumeric values and hyphens. The name of the secret should reference the source or use of the secret. For example, the name adedeveastus2-files-key provides three pieces of information: the name of a Storage account using the standard naming convention, the type of storage service or use for this secret, and the type of secret. You can design your own secret naming format. You can provide both an activation date and an expiration date if you want tighter control over the secret's availability. By default, the new secret value will be enabled. You can choose to create it disabled, and enable at a later time manually.

To configure access for the AKV linkedservice, you will provide one of the two access keys from the Storage account containing the new Files service (adedeveastus2). You can copy the key from the Storage account's Access Keys blade. Create the secret without an activation or expiration date, unless you have an existing key rotation policy. Leave the new secret enabled. This will create a secret that is ready to be used in ADF.

USING AZURE POWERSHELL

Listing 10.10 shows the script for adding the key to AKV. The `Set-AzKeyVaultSecret` command creates a new secret, or adds a new value to an existing secret. This command takes the name of the AKV and the name of the secret. The script retrieves the key from the Storage account, and adds it to the `SecretValue` parameter. It also adds the parameter `ContentType` with a value of `key` to add a description to the secret, when viewing the list of secrets. Run this script to create the secret.

The script uses `Get-AzStorageAccountKey` to retrieve the primary key from the named Storage account. The output of the command is the key value. `Set-AzKeyVaultSecret` takes a `SecureString` object as input to the `SecretValue` parameter, so the script uses `ConvertTo-SecureString` to create a `SecureString`. This command nominally takes an encrypted string as an input, often via the `Read-Host` command. In this script, the key from the Storage account is not encrypted, so `ConvertTo-SecureString` uses the `AsPlainText` and `Force` parameters to read the input key value. You could provide the key value manually using `Read-Host` instead.

> Listing 10.10   Add new AKV key with Azure PowerShell

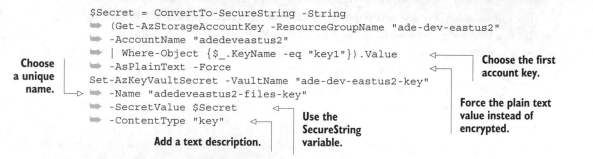

```
$Secret = ConvertTo-SecureString -String
⇨  (Get-AzStorageAccountKey -ResourceGroupName "ade-dev-eastus2"
⇨  -AccountName "adedeveastus2"
⇨  | Where-Object {$_.KeyName -eq "key1"}).Value          ◁        Choose the first
⇨  -AsPlainText -Force                                    ◁        account key.
Set-AzKeyVaultSecret -VaultName "ade-dev-eastus2-key"
⇨  -Name "adedeveastus2-files-key"
⇨  -SecretValue $Secret        ◁
⇨  -ContentType "key"     ◁
```

Choose a unique name.

Add a text description.

Use the SecureString variable.

Force the plain text value instead of encrypted.

After creating the AKV, linkedservice, and a secret, and giving ADF access, you are ready to create a Files linkedservice in ADF. With this, and the ADLS linkedservice you created earlier, you'll create the pipeline and activity to copy the badge-tracking data file.

10.3.3 *Creating a Files storage linkedservice*

Creating a Files linkedservice works like creating an AKV linkedservice, but there are a few extra values to configure.

USING AZURE PORTAL

To create the linkedservice in the Azure portal, launch the authoring GUI.

1. Browse to the Overview blade of the ADF service.
2. Click the Author & Monitor button to launch the authoring GUI in a new window.
3. Switch to the Authoring tab in the left nav.
4. Show Connections, from the bottom of the Factory Resources navigation.
5. Click New to open the Selection blade.
6. Show the Azure tab.
7. Select Azure File Storage from the list of Azure services, and click Continue.
8. Choose a name for the resource. Only alphanumerics and underscores are allowed.
9. Because this is an Azure service, leave the default `AutoResolveIntegration-Runtime` selected. This is the Azure integration runtime.
10. Set the Files Container Host to `\\adedeveastus2.file.core.windows.net\\accesscard`. This is the Azure storage account URL and the Files container name.
11. Set the Files User Name to `AZURE\\adedeveastus2`. This is the string `AZURE\\` followed by the Storage account URL.
12. Switch to using Azure Key Vault. This will change the available values, letting you choose a vault from the same resource group, and add the secret key name.
13. Select the AKV you created earlier (ade-dev-eastus2-key).
14. Set the Secret Name to the secret you created to store the Files access key (`adedeveastus2-files-key`).

The `host` element identifies the Files container to connect to. You cannot find this value in the Azure portal or the through Azure PowerShell. It's generated by adding the Storage account name and the Files container name to the storage domain, like the following:

```
\\\\[StorageName].file.core.windows.net\\[ContainerName]
```

Note that the start of the path is preceded by four backslashes.

USING AZURE POWERSHELL

Save this JSON configuration file to an Azure Cloud Shell folder or a local drive accessible by your local PowerShell install in listing 10.11. You'll use the file to create the Files linkedservice.

> **Listing 10.11 Files linkedservice definition file**

```
{
    "name": "AzureFileStorage1",
    "properties": {
        "annotations": [],
        "type": "AzureFileStorage",
        "typeProperties": {
```

```
            "host": "\\\\adedeveastus2.file.core.windows.net\\accesscard",
            "userId": "AZURE\\adedeveastus2",
            "password": {
                "type": "AzureKeyVaultSecret",
                "store": {
                    "referenceName": "AzureKeyVault1",
                    "type": "LinkedServiceReference"
                },
                "secretName": "abedeveastus2-files-key"
            }
        }
    }
}
```

The `Set-AzDataFactoryV2LinkedService` command is the same one used for the AKV linkedservice. Run the script in the following listing to create the Files linkedservice.

Listing 10.12   Creating a new Files linkedservice with Azure PowerShell

```
Set-AzDataFactoryV2LinkedService -ResourceGroupName "ade-dev-eastus2"
➥   -DataFactoryName "ade-dev-eastus2-adf"
➥   -Name "AzureFileStorage1"
➥   -DefinitionFile "~/adf/AzureFileStorage1.json"
```

Now you have the source linkedservice. You need to add a target linkedservice, using ADLS.

10.3.4 *Creating an ADLS linkedservice*

Creating an ADLS linkedservice works much like creating a Files linkedservice.

USING AZURE PORTAL

The steps for creating the ADLS linkedservice in the portal are the same as for a Files linkedservice, except the authentication options are different. You can choose to use a managed identity or service principal instead of a username and password. Authorization settings for an ADLS linkedservice work much like providing a username and password. You provide a service principal ID and secret key. Azure populates the Tenant ID field from the currently logged in account, much like the subscriptions and services drop-downs are populated. For the ADLS linkedservice, service principal authentication works just as well as using a managed identity. You need to add the service principal secret to AKV before the authentication will work.

ADDING THE SERVICE PRINCIPAL SECRET TO AKV

To authenticate with the ADLS linkedservice using AKV, you need to supply AKV with the service principal (ade-dev-eastus2-adf-id) client secret. That way ADF can look up the secret during pipeline execution. Azure services authorize the service principal to access the service and perform actions. Figure 10.5 shows this in action.

You can use the same process you used to create the AKV secret for the Files storage access key. The new secret can be created using the Azure portal or Azure PowerShell.

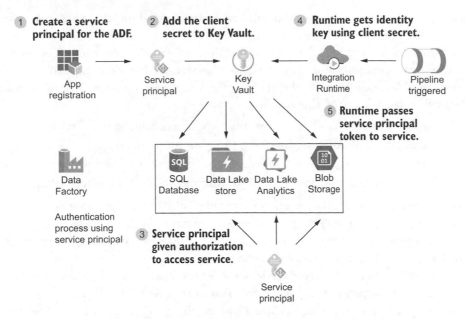

Figure 10.5 Data Factory service principal authentication and authorization

Using Azure PowerShell to add an AKV secret

When you created the App registration earlier in the chapter, you added a client secret. Now you will enter that same value again, so that the encrypted `SecureString` can be entered as a new secret in AKV. Listing 10.13 shows the script for adding the key to AKV using Azure PowerShell. The script uses the same command to add the secret as you used for creating the Files storage key.

Listing 10.13 Add a new service principal key with Azure PowerShell

```
$Secret = Read-Host -AsSecureString
Set-AzKeyVaultSecret -VaultName "ade-dev-eastus2-key"
➥ -Name "ade-dev-eastus2-adf-key"
➥ -SecretValue $Secret
➥ -ContentType "key"
```

Once you have added the service principal key to your AKV, you can complete the creation of the ADLS linkedservice via the Azure portal, just as with the Files storage linkedservice.

Using Azure PowerShell

Creating the ADLS linkedservice with Azure PowerShell uses the same process as the Files linkedservice. The JSON configuration file contains a few common root elements: `name` and `properties`. The `properties` element contains a set of elements common to other linkedservices. For ADLS, the `type` is `AzureDataLakeStore`. The ADLS linkedservice contains a `type` root element with the fixed value `Microsoft.DataFactory/`

`factories/linkedservices`. Many linkedservices, including AWS S3, Azure CosmosDb, and SQLDB, use this same element and value.

`typeProperties` contains the connection information for the linkedservice. This element varies significantly between linkedservices. Some elements are used by multiple Azure services, because the services are structured similarly or authenticate similarly. For Azure services, these include:

- `subscriptionId`—The Azure subscription containing the service
- `tenant`—The AAD organization used for authentication
- `servicePrincipalId`—The registered app used to authenticate the ADF service
- `servicePrincipalKey`—The definition for the AKV identity lookup

The `servicePrincipalKey` element has three children. The value of `type` is always `AzureKeyVaultSecret`. The `secretName` is the name of the secret in AKV. The `store` element points to a previously configured AKV linkedservice, using its `referenceName` and a type of `LinkedServiceReference`.

In addition, ADLS linkedservices require a `resourceGroupName` and `dataLakeStoreUri` to identify the ADLA service. You cannot find the `dataLakeStoreUri` in the Azure portal or the through Azure PowerShell. It's generated by adding the ADLS name to the ADLS domain, like

```
https://[ADLSName].azuredatalakestore.net/webhdfs/v1
```

These elements combine in a JSON document like in the following listing.

Listing 10.14   ADLS linkedservice definition file

```json
{
    "name": "AzureDataLakeStore1",
    "type": "Microsoft.DataFactory/factories/linkedservices",
    "properties": {
        "annotations": [],
        "type": "AzureDataLakeStore",
        "typeProperties": {
            "dataLakeStoreUri": "https://adedeveastus2.azuredatalakestore.net
/webhdfs/v1",
            "servicePrincipalId": "9ebef9cc-904b-4948-abb6-237e60cca836",
            "servicePrincipalKey": {
                "type": "AzureKeyVaultSecret",
                "store": {
                    "referenceName": "AzureKeyVault1",
                    "type": "LinkedServiceReference"
                },
                "secretName": "ade-dev-eastus2-adf-key"
            },
            "tenant": "f41e678f-812a-43cf-b020-7c1f89e52901",
            "subscriptionId": "fdc22d66-7061-4721-abbc-b4c6c93c3d5c",
            "resourceGroupName": "ade-dev-eastus2"
        }
    }
}
```

Listing 10.15 shows a script creating the linkedservice. It uses the same command we used for the AKV linkedservice. Save the JSON configuration file in listing 10.14 to an Azure Cloud Shell folder or a local drive accessible by your local PowerShell install. Run the script from listing 10.15 to create the new linkedservice.

> **Listing 10.15 Creating a new ADLS linkedservice with Azure PowerShell**

```
Set-AzDataFactoryV2LinkedService -ResourceGroupName "ade-dev-eastus2"
➥ -DataFactoryName "ade-dev-eastus2-adf"
➥ -Name "AzureDataLake1"
➥ -DefinitionFile "~/adf/AzureDataLake1.json"
```

With the new linkedservice configured to use AKV, ADF activities will try to connect to ADLS using the ADF registered app's service principal. In order for your service principal to access the ADLS store, you need to authorize the App registration.

AUTHORIZING THE SERVICE PRINCIPAL TO ADLS

As you recall from chapter 4, ADLS access requires two permissions:

1 Access to the Azure service itself
2 Access to the file and folder structure within ADLS

You can assign both using the Azure portal and Azure PowerShell.

Using Azure PowerShell

Listing 10.16 shows how to assign the ADF App access to the ADLS store. Run the script to grant access.

> **Listing 10.16 Assigning a service principal role with Azure PowerShell**

```
$Adla = Get-AzResource -Name "adedeveastus2" -ResourceType
    "Microsoft.DataLakeStore/accounts"
$App = Get-AzADApplication -DisplayName "ade-dev-eastus2-adf-id"
New-AzRoleAssignment -RoleDefinitionName "Contributor" -ApplicationId
    $App.ApplicationId
```

In chapter 4, you saw how to assign access control lists (ACLs) to files and folders in ADLS. ADF needs elevated permissions to the ADLS store to successfully read and write files. You can apply these ACLs through the ADL Data Explorer blade in the Azure portal, or through Azure PowerShell.

The script in listing 10.17 shows how to set Read, Write, and Execute permissions for all existing files and folders. Use the `Set-AzDataLakeStoreItemAclEntry` command to set the ACLs. In this case, the service principal uses the `User` value for `Ace-Type` parameter. If your ADLS store has files and folders, use the `Recurse` parameter to apply the ACLs down the folder tree. By using multiple calls to the command, with different `Path` and `Recurse` values, you can tailor the access given to ADF. ADF does need at least Read and Execute on the root folder in order to read the structure of the folders it can access. Add the `Default` parameter to give ADF default access for new folders and files.

Listing 10.17   Assigning a service principal ACLs in ADLS with Azure PowerShell

Service principal gets User type ACLs.

```
Set-AzDataLakeStoreItemAclEntry -AccountName "adedeveastus2"
-Path / -AceType User
-Id (Get-AzADServicePrincipal -DisplayName "ade-dev-eastus2-adf-
    id").ApplicationId.Guid
-Permissions All -Recurse
Set-AzDataLakeStoreItemAclEntry -AccountName "adedeveastus2"
Path / -AceType User
-Id (Get-AzADServicePrincipal -DisplayName "ade-dev-eastus2-adf-
    id").ApplicationId.Guid
-Permissions All -Recurse -Default        ⊲—  Apply the default ACLs
                                              in the same manner.
```

Give ADF app full rights through the
entire existing folder hierarchy.

With a Files linkedservice and an ADLS linkedservice, you can now create a pipeline
and activity to copy the files.

10.3.5 *Creating a pipeline and activity*

In ADF, pipelines contain *activities*. This structure is expressed in the JSON files defining pipeline. Aside from the ubiquitous `annotations` element, all of the pipeline
resource's `properties` are the activities in the pipeline. The `activities` element holds
an array of activity definitions. Each pipeline can have one or more activities.

ADF PIPELINE WORKFLOW

Executing an ADF pipeline with a copy activity looks like this:

- The pipeline has a single activity, a file copy.
- The pipeline has a single trigger, using a schedule.
- The pipeline uses the *Integration Runtime* (IR) to manage the copy activity
  between the two linkedservices.
- The IR handles the commands for both linkedservices, and monitors the activ-
  ity for progress and errors.
- The Azure IR runs in Azure and connects to Azure resources.
- Each activity and each pipeline execution collects metrics that you can review later.

Figure 10.6 shows the steps for running this ADF pipeline.

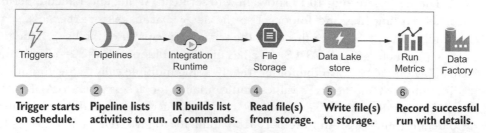

Triggers	Pipelines	Integration Runtime	File Storage	Data Lake store	Run Metrics
① Trigger starts on schedule.	② Pipeline lists activities to run.	③ IR builds list of commands.	④ Read file(s) from storage.	⑤ Write file(s) to storage.	⑥ Record successful run with details.

Data Factory

Figure 10.6   Pipeline processing steps

The process of creating a pipeline is practically the reverse. The steps for creating the ADF pipeline go like this:

1   Create any linkedservices to connect to the services needed.
2   Create any datasets to define any transformations.
3   Create the activities using the linkedservices and datasets.
4   Create the pipeline with the activities.
5   Create the pipeline triggers.

Each activity defines the steps the IR will take, what resources the activity will use, and any other activities that it depends on. Activities fall into three categories:

1   *Flow control activities* provide variable assignment, validation, looping, and decision support to other activities. They don't depend on other services.
2   *Copy activities* move and transform data. They connect two datasets.
3   *Execute activities* call functions on linkedservices. They require at least one linkedservice to interact with.

The IR takes the steps defined by each activity in the pipeline, and their relation to each other, and runs the steps in order. The IR uses the datasets and linkedservices listed in the activities to get connection details and perform transformations. Execute activities list what linkedservices to connect to. Copy activities list what datasets to utilize. The dataset definition then lists what linkedservice to connect to. Figure 10.7 shows this relationship between activities, datasets, and linkedservices.

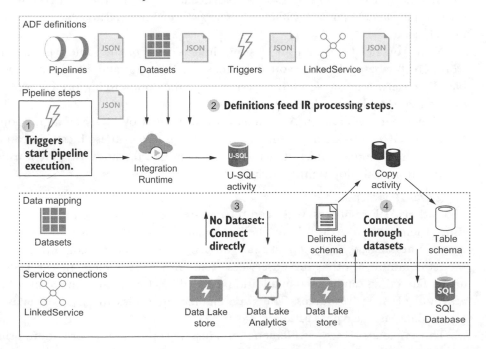

Figure 10.7   Pipeline activities interact with other resources.

Copy activities use one or more dataset definitions to transform one type of data file or schema into another. You will need a dataset for both the source and target linkedservices.

CREATING DATASETS

The dataset resource has three important details: the linkedservice connection to use, the data target of a file path or a table name, and the data's schema definition. The exception is the binary dataset. This format doesn't read the file or define a schema. Copy activities using binary datasets do a direct byte-for-byte copy between two linked-services. Multiple datasets can connect to the same linkedservice.

Using Azure portal

To create the ADF datasets in the Azure portal, launch the authoring GUI.

1 Browse to the Overview blade of the ADF service.
2 Click the Author & Monitor button to launch the authoring GUI in a new window.
3 Switch to the Authoring tab in the left nav.
4 Click Datasets, from the Factory Resources navigation, to reveal a list of existing datasets.

Click the dots to the right of the datasets section to reveal the New Dataset button. When creating a new dataset in the GUI, you first choose a data store. These roughly equate to the available service integrations, aside from the strictly compute services like Batch, Functions, and ADLA. File-based data stores then let you choose the file format: Parquet, Delimited, JSON, AVRO, ORC, or Binary. Table-based stores don't use a format.

Next, you need to select an existing linkedservice of the same type as the data store. For file-based datasets, you also choose the file path and a filename. For table-based datasets, you choose a table. Last, you get the option to import a schema based on the file or table you selected.

Like other resources in ADF, datasets are defined by JSON configuration files. Using the GUI to create a dataset resource outputs one of these files. You can access the file when viewing a dataset, activity, or pipeline in the authoring GUI, using the Code button in the top right corner.

Using Azure PowerShell

Like other ADF resources, you need to prepare the JSON configuration files before using them with an Azure PowerShell command. The file contains a few common root elements: `name` and `properties`. The `properties` element contains a set of elements common to other linkedservices. The `annotations` element is a CSV string array. The values can be used as additional identifiers for datasets, much like the `Tags` attribute of Azure resources. The `type` element identifies the type of dataset. For binary datasets, the type is `Binary`.

The `linkedServiceName` element contains the connection information, using the linkedservice's `referenceName` and a `type` of `LinkedServiceReference`.

The `typeProperties` contains the dataset's path information. For SQL table datasets, the `schema` and `table` elements are directly under `typeProperties`. For file datasets, the path definitions are under a `location` element. The defining elements include `type`, `folderPath`, and `fileName`. The value for `type` will depend on the target, but is usually `[linkedservicetype]Location`. You can omit `folderPath` if the file is in the root directory. Omit `fileName` to select all files in the directory. Listings 10.18 and 10.19 show the JSON configuration files for two binary datasets, one for Files and one for ADLS.

Listing 10.18   Files binary dataset definition file

```
{
    "name": "Binary1",
    "properties": {
        "linkedServiceName": {
            "referenceName": "AzureFileStorage1",
            "type": "LinkedServiceReference"
        },
        "annotations": [],
        "type": "Binary",
        "typeProperties": {
            "location": {
                "type": "AzureFileStorageLocation",
                "fileName": "access_01.csv",
                "folderPath": "2019"
            }
        }
    }
}
```

Listing 10.19   ADLS binary dataset definition file

```
{
    "name": "Binary2",
    "properties": {
        "linkedServiceName": {
            "referenceName": "AzureDataLakeStore1",
            "type": "LinkedServiceReference"
        },
        "annotations": [],
        "type": "Binary",
        "typeProperties": {
            "location": {
                "type": "AzureDataLakeStoreLocation",
                "folderPath": "Staging/Stadium/Doors"
            }
        }
    }
}
```

Save both files to an Azure Cloud Shell folder or a local drive accessible by your local PowerShell install. You'll use the files in the next command to create the binary datasets.

Set-AzDataFactoryV2Dataset is used to create or update ADF datasets. Run the script in the following listing to create the two binary datasets.

Listing 10.20   Creating new binary datasets with Azure PowerShell

```
Set-AzDataFactoryV2Dataset -ResourceGroupName "ade-dev-eastus2"
➥ -DataFactoryName "ade-dev-eastus2-adf"
➥ -Name "FilesBinary1"
➥ -DefinitionFile "~/adf/FilesBinary1.json"
Set-AzDataFactoryV2Dataset -ResourceGroupName "ade-dev-eastus2"
➥ -DataFactoryName "ade-dev-eastus2-adf"
➥ -Name "ADLBinary1"
➥ -DefinitionFile "~/adf/ADLBinary1.json"
```

TIP   Using the authoring GUI lets you create all of the ADF resources quickly. You can then copy the configuration files if you want to reproduce the ADF without the manual work in the GUI. You can get the JSON configuration files for all the ADF resources in this chapter at http://mng.bz/X0qa.

To create a pipeline that can execute a binary copy, you only need one activity: a copy activity. The copy activity reads the file(s) from one linkedservice and writes to another. With the two datasets available, you can create a copy activity to use them. Next you will define the activity.

CREATING ACTIVITIES

The three activity categories each have common and unique configuration elements. Table 10.2 shows some common elements.

Table 10.2   Common activity elements

Element	Value	Description
name	String	Limit to alphanumeric, hyphens, and underscores for JSON compatibility.
type	Unique string identifier for activity	DataLakeAnalyticsU-SQL, Copy, SqlServer-StoredProcedure, Wait, etc.
dependsOn	JSON array element with activity and dependencyConditions properties	The list of activities immediately preceding this activity, with the outcome condition for next step
userProperties	JSON array element with name and value properties	An array of user specified key:value pairs added to the activity
typeProperties	Varies	Define the attributes of the specific type of activity.

You need to look up the correct type value for the activities you are creating. For the Copy job, the value is Copy.

> **TIP** You can get configuration details for each type of activity from the ADF How-to guides at https://docs.microsoft.com/azure/data-factory/.

The `dependsOn` element holds an array of JSON elements, each with an `activity` and `dependencyCondition` element. The `activity` element is the name of another activity in the pipeline. The `dependencyCondition` has one of four values: `Completed`, `Failed`, `Skipped`, `Succeeded`. With these values, you can create pipeline flows that handle multiple scenarios. For example, you may want to call an Azure Function or web hook to be notified of a certain failure. You could add a second copy activity that only copies if the first succeeded. Or you could continue after external website calls regardless of outcome. `Succeeded` is the default in the authoring UI. Here you can see a `dependsOn` snippet for an activity that follows activity `Copy1` when it succeeds.

```
"dependsOn": [
  {
    "activity": "Copy1",
    "dependencyConditions": [
      "Succeeded"
    ]
  }
]
```

The `typeProperties` element has the greatest variety of implementations. For copy activities, it has three elements: `source`, `sink`, and `enableStaging`. The `source` and `sink` align with the datasource and the linkedservice driving the activity. The following snippet copies from the Azure Files service without reading and translating the data. It writes to an ADLS store in the same mode. The `source` element can be configured to select files from the current directory, defined in the dataset, and from child folders using the `recursive` flag.

`enableStaging` lets the IR do a two-part copy using an intermediate storage location. Staging the files is most common for copying between two datacenters, between on-premises storage and cloud databases, and when the database can use technologies like Polybase to improve import throughput. For a copy between two fast Azure storage services, no staging is required.

```
"typeProperties": {
    "source": {
        "type": "BinarySource",
        "storeSettings": {
            "type": "AzureFileStorageReadSettings",
            "recursive": true
        }
    },
    "sink": {
        "type": "BinarySink",
        "storeSettings": {
            "type": "AzureDataLakeStoreWriteSettings"
        }
```

```
    },
    "enableStaging": false
}
```

Binary copy activities don't need to define schema or the `translator` that defines mappings between the two datasets. There is no parsing or translation. You can see a copy with schema in chapter 12.

Last, the copy activity includes `inputs` and `outputs` elements. These use the familiar `referenceName` and `type` structure common to other ADF resource references. For both, the `type` is `DatasetReference`. For `inputs`, `referenceName` is the named dataset used as the source. For `outputs`, `referenceName` refers to the sink dataset. The following listing shows the entire pipeline and activity JSON definition file.

Listing 10.21   Pipeline and activity definition file

```
{
    "name": "pipeline1",
    "properties": {
        "activities": [
            {
                "name": "Copy data1",
                "type": "Copy",
                "dependsOn": [],
                "policy": {
                    "timeout": "0.01:00:00",
                    "retry": 1,
                    "retryIntervalInSeconds": 30,
                    "secureOutput": false,
                    "secureInput": false
                },
                "userProperties": [],
                "typeProperties": {
                    "source": {
                        "type": "BinarySource",
                        "storeSettings": {
                            "type": "AzureFileStorageReadSettings",
                            "recursive": true
                        }
                    },
                    "sink": {
                        "type": "BinarySink",
                        "storeSettings": {
                            "type": "AzureDataLakeStoreWriteSettings"
                        }
                    },
                    "enableStaging": false
                },
                "inputs": [
                    {
                        "referenceName": "Binary1",
                        "type": "DatasetReference"
                    }
```

```
        ],
        "outputs": [
            {
                "referenceName": "Binary2",
                "type": "DatasetReference"
            }
        ]
    }
],
"annotations": []
}
}
```

Using Azure PowerShell

You can upload this JSON configuration file to Azure Cloud Shell just as you did for the AKV and ADLS linkedservices. Then you can run `Set-AzDataFactoryV2Pipeline` to create the pipeline and copy activity. The following listing shows the Azure Power-Shell script.

Listing 10.22 Creating a new pipeline with Azure PowerShell

```
Set-AzDataFactoryV2Pipeline -ResourceGroupName "ade-dev-eastus2"
➥ -Name "pipeline1"
➥ -DataFactoryName "ade-dev-eastus2-adf"
➥ -File "~/adf/pipeline1.json"
```

Using Azure portal to publish the pipeline

Creating pipelines in the authoring GUI removes the need to look up many values and construct a JSON file. The GUI guides you through the choices with drop-down selection of existing linkedservices and datasets. You can create a blank pipeline workspace in the GUI and add an activity to it by dragging the activity into the pipeline workspace. Clicking on the new activity displays the editing panel, where you can make changes. The activities populate the values in the backing JSON configuration files for you, based on the activity you choose, the drop-down values you select, or values you input manually.

The last step in creating a pipeline with the GUI is publishing. The GUI operates in a sandbox, and once you're done constructing the pipeline, click Publish All to publish the backing JSON configuration files to the production ADF environment. Publishing sets up the triggers and configures logging and metrics around pipeline executions. Figure 10.8 shows this workflow in action.

Creating and modifying pipelines with Azure PowerShell publishes to the production environment automatically. Because both authoring methods output JSON configuration files, ADF can be version controlled. We'll discuss version control with ADF in chapter 12.

Now that the pipeline has been created, you can kick it off manually. You can do this in the authoring GUI using the Add Trigger > Trigger Now menu option.

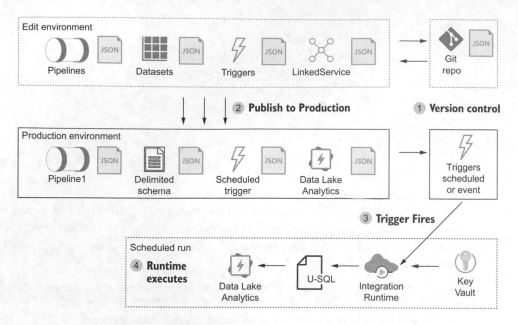

Figure 10.8   Data Factory code promotion

Using Azure PowerShell to start a pipeline execution

You can start the pipeline with Azure PowerShell too. Use the `Invoke-AzDataFactory-V2Pipeline` command, passing resource group, ADF name, and pipeline name. The following listing shows this script in action.

> **Listing 10.23   Starting a pipeline manually with Azure PowerShell**

```
Invoke-AzDataFactoryV2Pipeline -ResourceGroupName "ade-dev-eastus2"
   -DataFactoryName "ade-dev-eastus2-adf"
   -PipelineName "pipeline1"
```

But you didn't come this far to kick off pipelines manually. A major benefit of using ADF is running pipelines on a schedule and recording the success and failure states of each step. You can use third-party schedulers to accomplish these executions, by using the ADF REST or PowerShell interfaces to trigger them. For IT departments with existing automation systems, adding ADF pipeline steps to their workflow can be a good approach. This ADF pipeline supports a new system built in Azure. Let's add a schedule trigger on the new pipeline in Azure too.

10.3.6 *Creating a scheduled trigger*

Creating a trigger resource in ADF works like creating other resources.

USING AZURE POWERSHELL

You provide a JSON configuration file for the trigger, as with other ADF resources. The JSON configuration file contains two common root elements: `name` and `properties`.

The `properties` element contains a set of elements common to other resources. The `annotations` element is a CSV string array, and is used as in other resources. The `type` element identifies the trigger type: `ScheduleTrigger`, `BlobEventsTrigger`, or `Tumbling-WindowTrigger`. Set the activated state with `runtimeState`, either `Started` or `Stopped`.

The `pipelines` element defines the pipeline(s) triggered by the trigger. Triggers can start more than one pipeline, and a pipeline can have more than one trigger. Like other resource references, the `pipelines` element is an array of references, each with a `referenceName` and `type`. For trigger pipelines, the type is `PipelineReference`.

```
"pipelines": [
  {
    "pipelineReference": {
      "referenceName": "pipeline1",
      "type": "PipelineReference"
    }
  }
]
```

Element `typeProperties` varies for the three types of triggers. For the Schedule trigger, all elements are under the `recurrence` element. There are five elements to configure: `frequency`, `interval`, `startTime`, `timeZone`, and `schedule`.

The `frequency` element can be one of the following:

- Minute
- Hour
- Day
- Week
- Month

`interval` takes a number and works together with `frequency`, e.g. 12 hours, 2 days, 1 month. `startTime` takes a date value in UTC. The format is ISO8601, with `T` separator and trailing `Z` for UTC time. The `timeZone` is always `UTC`. The trigger will run at the start time and every interval thereafter, or if the start time was in the past, the next occurring interval in the future when you create the trigger. For example, to start a trigger with an hourly interval one hour from now, set the start time to one hour from now and save the trigger. Or set the start time to now (or one hour ago, or 24 hours ago) and save it. The next available interval will be one hour from now.

To run more complicated schedules, you can add the `schedule` element to `recurrence`. This element can take arrays for `minutes`, `hours`, `weekDays`, and `monthDays`, and will start the trigger on the specified marker(s). The following example runs a pipeline at 5:00 a.m. and 5:00 p.m. every Monday.

```
"recurrence": {
  "frequency": "Day",
  "interval": 1,
  "startTime": "2019-11-01T02:01:00.000Z",
```

```
    "timeZone": "UTC",
    "schedule": {
      "minutes": [
        0
      ],
      "hours": [
        5,
        17
      ],
      "weekDays": [
        "monday"
      ]
    }
  }
}
```

The following listing shows the complete trigger configuration file for a 5:00 a.m. UTC daily run.

Listing 10.24   Scheduled trigger definition file

```
{
  "name": "trigger1",
  "properties": {
    "annotations": [],
    "runtimeState": "Started",
    "pipelines": [
      {
        "pipelineReference": {
          "referenceName": "pipeline1",
          "type": "PipelineReference"
        }
      }
    ],
    "type": "ScheduleTrigger",
    "typeProperties": {
      "recurrence": {
        "frequency": "Day",
        "interval": 1,
        "startTime": "2019-12-31T02:01:00.000Z",
        "timeZone": "UTC",
        "schedule": {
          "minutes": [
            0
          ],
          "hours": [
            5
          ]
        }
      }
    }
  }
}
```

With a completed JSON configuration file available, you can use the script from the following listing to create the trigger and enable it.

> **Listing 10.25   Creating a trigger with Azure PowerShell**

```
Set-AzDataFactoryV2Trigger -ResourceGroupName "ade-dev-eastus2"
➥ -DataFactoryName "ade-dev-eastus2-adf"
➥ -Name "trigger1"
➥ -DefinitionFile "~/adf/trigger1.json"
Start-AzDataFactoryV2Trigger -ResourceGroupName "ade-dev-eastus2"
➥ -DataFactoryName "ade-dev-eastus2-adf"
➥ -Name "trigger1"
```

USING AZURE PORTAL

Adding triggers in the authoring GUI is a two-step process. You create the trigger, then assign it to a pipeline. You can do both at the same time, creating then assigning the trigger from within the pipeline, using the Trigger drop-down in the pipeline workspace, and selecting New/Edit. The Trigger drop down can also start the pipeline manually.

You can also create triggers separately from the pipeline and assign them later. In the GUI, switch to the Triggers window using the button at the bottom of the left navigation. Provide a name and leave the default Schedule type selected. Change the Start Date to when you want the first execution to run. Setting the date in the past does not trigger the execution any earlier than the publish date, but you can set the date in the future to delay execution. Select a recurrence pattern in terms of a number of minutes, hours, days, weeks, or months. You can specify an End Date too, if you want to limit the number of recurring executions.

By default, the trigger is disabled. Switch Activated to Yes to enable it. Save the trigger. Switch to any pipeline you want to use the new trigger. Use the Trigger drop-down in the pipeline workspace, and select New/Edit. Select your new trigger from the drop-down, and click through the dialogs. Once you save the trigger, you need to click the Publish menu option to push the trigger into production.

Once you have created the trigger, your new File Copy pipeline is complete. From this point onward, you can reuse the linkedservices you have created, and create new ones. You can use the datasets as sources or sinks for other activities. You can add more activities to the first pipeline, or create new pipelines. You can even add an activity that starts another pipeline. Let's see what adding another activity is like, now that you've created the primary support resources.

10.4   Running an ADLA job

The trials of the Jonestown Sluggers biometric-uniform sensor suite are running, and the data is being collected in the Data Lake store. The analysts want the data to be updated on a regular basis. You previously loaded data into a U-SQL table manually. How can you accommodate this request?

You have a few options with ADLA jobs.

- Resubmit a job using the Azure portal.
- Submit a new job using Azure PowerShell or other tools.
- Submit a new job with an ADF pipeline.

Resubmitting the previous job is pretty easy to implement. You can even add some C# code to make the script import the previous day. However, you do need to find the job in the Azure portal, click the Reuse Script button, and then submit the job. These are manual steps to be performed by someone.

Submitting a new job is also pretty easy. You have the table import a U-SQL script (see chapter 8), and you can automate executing PowerShell scripts with a number of tools, like Windows Task Scheduler. You will need to have a server to execute the script. The logging and diagnostic information may be lacking, depending on your PowerShell skill level.

Creating a process with ADF works better than these other options. ADF offers both event-driven and scheduled triggers. ADF integrates directly with ADLA to execute jobs. Because it's integrated, monitoring and error handling, including retries, are included. Let's see how creating an ADF pipeline can make scheduling data processing easy. The first step is creating a new linkedservice for the ADLA service.

10.4.1 *Creating an ADLA linkedservice*

Creating an ADLA linkedservice works just like an ADLS linkedservice. You can create one with the Azure portal or Azure PowerShell. The steps are the same as for an ADLS linkedservice, with one exception: ADLA linkedservices use only service principal authentication.

The JSON configuration file contains two common root elements: `name` and `properties`. The `properties` element contains a set of elements common to other linkedservices too. For ADLA, the `type` is `AzureDataLakeAnalytics`. The linkedservice also has a `type` root element, with the fixed value `Microsoft.DataFactory/factories/linkedservices`. Many linkedservices, including AWS S3, Azure CosmosDb, and SQLDB, use this same element and value.

The `typeProperties` contains the linkedservice's connection information. This element varies significantly between linkedservices. There are some elements that multiple Azure services use, because the services are structured similarly or authenticate similarly. For Azure services, these include:

- `subscriptionId`—The Azure subscription containing the service
- `tenant`—The AAD organization used for authentication
- `servicePrincipalId`—The registered app used to authenticate the ADF service
- `servicePrincipalKey`—The definition for the AKV identity lookup

The `servicePrincipalKey` element has three children. The value of `type` is always `AzureKeyVaultSecret`. The `secretName` value is the name of the secret in AKV. The `store` element points to a previously configured AKV linkedservice, using a `referenceName` of the AKV linkedservice and `type` of `LinkedServiceReference`.

In addition to these elements, ADLA linkedservices require an `accountName` and `resourceGroupName`. These elements combine in a JSON document like the following listing.

Listing 10.26   ADLA linkedservice definition file

```json
{
    "name": "AzureDataLakeAnalytics1",
    "type": "Microsoft.DataFactory/factories/linkedservices",
    "properties": {
        "annotations": ["adla","usql"],
        "type": "AzureDataLakeAnalytics",
        "typeProperties": {
            "accountName": "adedeveastus2",
            "servicePrincipalId": "9999999c-904b-4948-abb6-2222222ca836",
            "servicePrincipalKey": {
                "type": "AzureKeyVaultSecret",
                "store": {
                    "referenceName": "AzureKeyVault1",
                    "type": "LinkedServiceReference"
                },
                "secretName": "ade-dev-eastus2-adf"
            },
            "tenant": "ffffffff-812a-43cf-b020-777777752901",
            "subscriptionId": "fdffffff-7061-4721-abbc-bbbbbbbc3d5c",
            "resourceGroupName": "ade-dev-eastus2"
        }
    }
}
```

USING AZURE POWERSHELL

Save this JSON configuration file to an Azure Cloud Shell folder or a local drive accessible by your local PowerShell install. You'll use the file in the Azure PowerShell command to create the ADLA linkedservice.

The `Set-AzDataFactoryV2LinkedService` command is the same one used for the ADLS linkedservice. Run the script in the following listing to create the linkedservice.

Listing 10.27   Creating a new ADLA linkedservice with Azure PowerShell

```
Set-AzDataFactoryV2LinkedService -ResourceGroupName "ade-dev-eastus2"
➥ -DataFactoryName "ade-dev-eastus2-adf"
➥ -Name "AzureDataLakeAnalytics1"
➥ -DefinitionFile "~/adf/AzureDataLakeAnalytics1.json"
```

Now you have a ADLA linkedservice in your ADF service. Before you can create a pipeline and activity, one more step remains. You need a source for the U-SQL script. You have two options: Blob Storage and ADLS stores.

As you recall from chapter 9, you created a top-level folder structure to hold code artifacts. This included folders for .NET assemblies and U-SQL scripts. Because moving data into and out of ADLS is a central part of this analytics system, having a linkedservice in ADF is critical. In fact, you have already seen how to create the ADLS earlier in the chapter. If you haven't created the ADLS linkedservice already, refer to the instructions in section 10.3.4 to create one now.

With these two linkedservices created, you can create a new pipeline and activity to run your U-SQL script. Once you have at least one pipeline, you can decide if new activities should run in the existing pipeline or a new one. You can add the new U-SQL job activity to your existing pipeline, which does a copy activity for Facilities. Because the request comes from a different source, and works with different data, a better choice would be to create a new pipeline for that project, and add the new U-SQL job activity to it. Let's see what that entails.

10.4.2   *Creating a pipeline and activity*

Let's focus on some new settings for the U-SQL job activity. U-SQL activities include three elements that apply to the new job, and one that locates an ADF resource. The `scriptPath` element stores the path to the U-SQL script, from the root folder of the storage resource. `degreeOfParallelism` specifies the number of AUs to use when executing the job. `priority` provides a priority level for queued jobs when the number of available AUs is less than the `degreeOfParallelism` requested. 1000 is the default for ADLA jobs. Smaller numbers are higher priority.

Because ADF does not store files, but accesses files from linked storage services, use `scriptLinkedService` to provide a linkedservice that will host the U-SQL script. The ADLS linkedservice you added earlier can support this element. You specify the linkedservice using a `referenceName` and `type`. Use the name of the ADLS linkedservice you created. The value of `type` is always `LinkedServiceReference`.

```
"typeProperties": {
  "scriptPath": "Code/Usql/Players/readview.usql",
  "degreeOfParallelism": 2,
  "priority": 100,
  "scriptLinkedService": {
    "referenceName": "AzureDataLakeStore1",
    "type": "LinkedServiceReference"
  }
}
```

Copy and execute activities also implement several parameters using the `policy` element. These parameters are listed in table 10.3.

Table 10.3   **Policy elements**

Element	Type	Description
timeout	Timespan	d.hh.mm.ss, e.g. One day, 12 hours, 30 mins, 5 secs would be 1.12.30.05.
retry	Integer	Maximum retry attempts, specify 0 for no retries
retryIntervalInSeconds	Integer	Delay between retries
secureOutput	Boolean	Save output values in logs
secureInput	Boolean	Save input values in logs

Some activities take parameters as input, or generate values from lookups or responses from external services. With the `secureOutput` and `secureInput` elements, you can prevent these values from being entered in the ADF execution logs.

Execute activities have some common elements. Because all activities use a `type` value, you need to look up the one that matches the activity. For the U-SQL job, the value is `DataLakeAnalyticsU-SQL`. Finally, most execute activities use the `linkedServiceName` element to specify what service to connect to for execution. The `referenceName` specifies the name of the linkedservice, and the `type` identifies the element as a linkedservice.

```
"linkedServiceName": {
  "referenceName": "AzureDataLakeAnalytics1",          ← The name of the
  "type": "LinkedServiceReference"                        ADLA linkedservice
}                                                        ← Use LinkedServiceReference.
```

The following listing shows the entire pipeline and activity JSON definition file.

Listing 10.28 Pipeline and activity definition file

```
{
    "name": "pipeline2",
    "properties": {
        "activities": [
            {
                "name": "U-SQL1",
                "type": "DataLakeAnalyticsU-SQL",
                "dependsOn": [],
                "policy": {
                    "timeout": "0.01:00:00",
                    "retry": 1,
                    "retryIntervalInSeconds": 60,
                    "secureOutput": false,
                    "secureInput": false
                },
                "userProperties": [],
                "typeProperties": {
                    "scriptPath": "Code/Usql/Players/readview.usql",
                    "degreeOfParallelism": 2,
                    "priority": 10,
                    "compilationMode": "Semantic",
                    "scriptLinkedService": {
                        "referenceName": "AzureDataLakeStore1",
                        "type": "LinkedServiceReference"
                    }
                },
                "linkedServiceName": {
                    "referenceName": "AzureDataLakeAnalytics1",
                    "type": "LinkedServiceReference"
                }
            }
        ],
        "annotations": []
    }
}
```

USING AZURE POWERSHELL

You can upload this JSON configuration file to Azure Cloud Shell just as you did for the AKV and ADLS linkedservices. Then you can run the `Set-AzDataFactoryV2-Pipeline` command to create the pipeline and U-SQL job activity. The following listing shows the Azure PowerShell script to create the pipeline.

Listing 10.29   Creating a new pipeline with Azure PowerShell

```
Set-AzDataFactoryV2Pipeline -ResourceGroupName "ade-dev-eastus2"
➥ -Name "pipeline2"
➥ -DataFactoryName "ade-dev-eastus2-adf"
➥ -File "~/adf/pipeline2.json"
```

10.5   Exercises

The following exercises can help you internalize the new features introduced in this chapter. You should be able to create and schedule an ADF pipeline.

10.5.1   Exercise 1

In chapter 4, you learned about the zones framework for structuring a Data Lake store. A fundamental part of the framework involves loading data into a "staging" folder first. Any data cleaning and validation occurs on these files, before approved files are loaded to the "raw" folder. In some scenarios, the original data files delivered to staging are ready for use. Given valid CSV files in Data Lake adedeveastus2, design a pipeline with a single activity that copies files from folder /staging/players/v2 to /raw/players/v2.

SOLUTION

The solution resembles the copy pipeline you saw in the chapter. The copy pipeline uses a copy activity, two datasets to define the copy action and file paths, and two linkedservices.

For this scenario, the two datasets would use the same ADLS linkedservice. Create two binary datasets to point to each of the folder locations.

```
{
    "name": "Binary1",
    "properties": {
        "linkedServiceName": {
            "referenceName": "AzureDataLakeStore1",
            "type": "LinkedServiceReference"
        },
        "annotations": [],
        "type": "Binary",
        "typeProperties": {
            "location": {
                "type": "AzureDataLakeStoreLocation",
                "folderPath": "/staging/players/v2"
            }
        }
    }
}
```

Create a pipeline with the copy activity, using the datasets. This pipeline and activity look just like the pipeline for copying from the Files storage service, except the source element refers to an ADLS store.

```
"source": {
  "type": "BinarySource",
  "storeSettings": {
    "type": "AzureDataLakeStoreReadSettings",
    "recursive": true
  }
}
```

10.5.2 *Exercise 2*

The File Copy pipeline for Facilities has entered production, and the new files are available in ADLS daily. You have been asked to schedule a U-SQL job after the copy runs, to detect suspicious activity. Given a U-SQL script in the ADLS store at /Code/Usql/Facilities/dailycheck.usql, add an ADLA U-SQL job activity to the File Copy pipeline. Set the U-SQL job to run on successful completion of the copy activity.

SOLUTION

You've seen both the copy and U-SQL job activities. The `activities` element of the pipeline properties is an array, and can define multiple activities. You can add a new U-SQL job activity to the array.

```
"properties": {
  "activities": []
}
```

The key item to add is the `dependsOn` element.

```
"dependsOn": [
  {
    "activity": "Copy1",
    "dependencyConditions": [
      "Succeeded"
    ]
  }
]
```

Add the `dependsOn` element to the U-SQL job activity, and reference the File Copy activity.

```
{
"name": "U-SQL1",
"type": "DataLakeAnalyticsU-SQL",
"dependsOn": [
  {
    "activity": "Copy1",
    "dependencyConditions": [
      "Succeeded"
    ]
```

```
        }
      ],
      "typeProperties": {
        "scriptPath": "/Code/Usql/Facilities/dailycheck.usql",
        "scriptLinkedService": {
          "referenceName": "AzureDataLakeStore1",
          "type": "LinkedServiceReference"
        }
      }
    }
  }
```

Summary

- ADF uses JSON configuration files to define the steps and connections to move and transform data. These configuration files are both the output of the authoring GUI, and the input for the execution engine. The ADF service can be configured by modifying the JSON files.

- ADF uses AKV to securely store secrets. Using AKV keeps passwords, keys, and other secrets out of the JSON configuration files.

- ADF has separate resources for connections, data definitions, actions, and scheduling. Building a pipeline calls for creating the resources in a specific order.

Managed SQL with Azure SQL Database

This chapter covers

- Creating a highly-available distributed Azure SQL database
- Restoring an Azure SQL Database
- Moving an Azure SQL Database between subscriptions
- Optimizing costs for Azure SQL Database

In the previous chapter, you learned how to create a scheduled pipeline for processing data in Azure. Azure Data Factory lets you automate the common steps in the analytics processing workflow. In chapter 6, you saw another piece of the workflow, with Stream Analytics calculations that flowed into a SQL Server database.

In this chapter, you'll learn more about the Azure SQL Database (SQLDB). You'll learn how SQLDB abstracts the underlying SQL Server to make complex functionality work with only a few clicks. You'll create a highly available database, and learn how to balance cost and performance. You'll work through some of the most common tasks in working with SQLDB. By the end, you'll have a system ready to support end users with analytic queries in SQL.

Relational databases form an important part of the Lambda architecture. Both the Speed layer (powered by Stream Analytics) and the Batch layer (powered by Data Lake Analytics) output data. The processing in these layers is defined by investigating and analyzing data output by these systems, which then feeds new iterations of processing. Resulting data products can themselves can be delivered as text files and as database tables. Text files serve well for machine processing, and end users with SQL knowledge can use data stored in relational databases. Data products, in both text files and database tables, make up the output of the Serving layer (see figure 11.1).

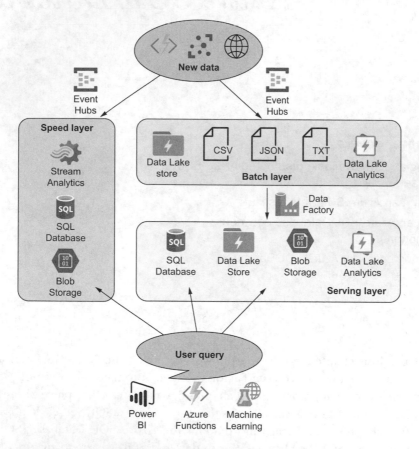

Figure 11.1   Lambda architecture with Azure PaaS services

With the PaaS model of Azure SQL Server, you can add, copy, and remove databases on demand. This makes it easier to support the Serving layer of your analytics system. You can segregate users and data products, run short-lived projects, and respond to increased data usage by end users. Let's see what's involved in spinning up a new SQLDB.

> **TIP** You can find the code listings in the GitHub repository for this book at https://github.com/rnuckolls/azure_storage.

11.1 Creating an Azure SQL Database

The development team wants a SQL Server database that will eventually be hosted in Azure. They want to use it for development work ahead of a production deployment. You've been asked to create the database in Azure. How can you fulfill this request?

> **WARNING** Like most services in Azure, running SQL Server databases comes with a cost. Without controls in place, and consideration of usage and ROI, you can easily spend thousands of dollars a month for little return. Later sections of this chapter cover optimizing costs for SQLDB.

There are several options for running SQL Server databases in Azure: single databases, multiple databases, warehouses, and VMs. For most users, the choice of what type of SQL Server database can be simplified to a few questions, which are shown in figure 11.2.

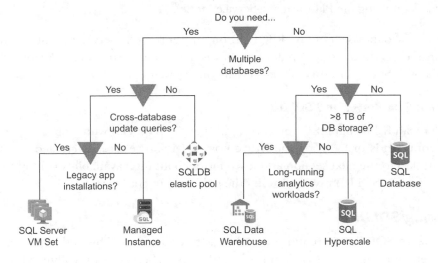

Figure 11.2 Choosing the SQL Server installation in Azure

The underlying type of SQL Server instance is the main determining factor.

- The *SQL Managed Instance* hosts multiple databases on a single instance that supports cross-database update queries and shared SQL Server logins between databases. If you need these functions, choose SQL Managed Instance. This service is limited to 8 TB databases, so if you need larger databases, select the Azure SQL Server VM Set.
- The *SQL Server VM Set* provides redundancy, and you can add drives to increase storage for your databases.

- The Azure SQL Server instance runs the engine behind SQLDB, Synapse (SQLDW), and SQLDB Hyperscale.

  - Azure SQLDB provides the most cost-effective database.
  - Hyperscale moves data storage for SQLDB onto separate storage nodes, backed by Azure Storage infrastructure. This allows SQLDB to grow beyond the normal 4 TB limit.
  - SQLDW similarly separates storage, and adds the option of multiple compute nodes to support long-running and complex queries used in analytics workloads.

NOTE   You can install SQL Server on an *Azure virtual machine* (VM) if you need 100% compatibility with your on-premises installation, or want total control of upgrades and versions. You can also install applications on the same VM as the SQL Server. But you must manage security updates for the VM and SQL Server, and handle administration duties like backups and recovery planning. The SQL Server VM Set falls under the Infrastructure-as-a-Service model; this book focuses on using the Platform-as-a-Service model.

For the new database, choose a SQLDB on an Azure SQL Server instance. This will minimize costs during development as well as management overhead. Every database needs a SQL Server instance, so let's create one now.

11.1.1   Create a SQL Server and SQLDB

As you recall from chapter 6, you can create a SQLDB quickly with a few Azure PowerShell commands or by using the Azure portal. (If you've already created a SQLDB, you can skip to the next section and learn more about high-availability configurations. If not, create a SQLDB now, following the guidance in chapter 6.)

11.2   Securing SQLDB

Every Azure SQL Server requires an administrator account. This is the equivalent of the system administrator (sa) login on standard SQL Servers. Controlling administrative access reduces attack paths on the database. You cannot disable the sa on Azure SQL Servers.

You can, and should, provide a strong password for the Admin account. You can reset the Admin password at any time from the Azure portal by browsing to the Overview blade and clicking Reset Password. You need to have the Owner role to reset the password.

You can use the Set-AzSqlServer command to reset the Admin password using Azure PowerShell. Pass the resource group and server name to identify the server. Then use SqlAdministratorPassword to pass the password. The following listing shows the command, using Read-Host to get a secure password string from the Azure PowerShell console.

Listing 11.1 Set the SQL Server Admin password

```
Set-AzSqlServer -ResourceGroupName "ade-dev-eastus2"
➥ -ServerName "ade-dev-eastus2-sql"
➥ -SqlAdministratorPassword
➥ (Read-Host "Enter Password" -AsSecureString)
```

> **IMPORTANT** Securing access to data should be a top priority when creating Azure resources. Although the Azure SQL Server instance runs at no cost, there is an option for a small cost that brings a big benefit. You can enable Advanced Data Security (ADS) for $15 per server per month, at time of writing. ADS includes threat detection alerts, including attempts at SQL injection, brute force password attacks, and unusual login attempts. Enable it using Azure PowerShell and the `Enable-AzSqlInstanceAdvancedDataSecurity` command. Pass the resource group and the server name.
>
> ```
> Enable-AzSqlInstanceAdvancedDataSecurity
> ➥ -ResourceGroupName "ade-dev-eastus2"
> ➥ -InstanceName "ade-dev-eastus2-sql"
> ```

You can learn more about ADS in the Microsoft documentation at http://mng.bz/jgw8.

In order to reduce use of the Admin account, Azure SQL Servers let you set an AAD user or group as a second administrator. Using AAD authentication brings all the benefits of centrally managed AAD accounts to SQLDB, including using AAD to authenticate applications.

You can set the AAD Admin using the Azure portal or Azure PowerShell. Browse to the Active Directory Admin blade in the Azure SQL Server and click Set Admin to select an account or group. In Azure PowerShell, use the `Set-AzSqlServerActive-DirectoryAdministrator` command, which takes the resource group and server name. You provide the name of the AAD account or group using the `DisplayName` parameter. You can optionally provide a specific AAD principal ID using `ObjectId`, if more than one principal matches the `DisplayName`. The following listing shows this command in use.

Listing 11.2 Set an AAD group as the SQL Server admin

Set the name of the AAD group as a variable for reuse.

Look up the group by name and get ID.

```
$Group = "Technical Operations"              ◄┘
$GroupId = (Get-AzADGroup -DisplayName $Group).Id    ◄┘
Set-AzSqlServerActiveDirectoryAdministrator -ResourceGroupName "ade-dev-eastus2"
➥ -ServerName "ade-dev-eastus2-sql"
➥ -DisplayName $Group              ◄┘ Name of the group
➥ -ObjectId $GroupId          ◄┘
```

Use ID to specifically identify principals with the same DisplayName.

With an AAD admin account, you can connect to your SQLDB with tools like SSMS or the Azure portal Query Editor to create logins and DB users. Performing routine database actions with non-admin accounts reduces risks to the system and lowers the impact of account compromise. Data and system problems can still occur. Let's look at some of the functionality available to mitigate risks and impact of these problems.

11.3 Availability and recovery

Developing and implementing a disaster-recovery plan is an important task for data engineers. At a minimum, you can do the following:

- Ensure backups occur regularly
- Ensure restores from backups result in functioning databases

SQLDB covers the first requirement for you. Databases are backed up with restore points every 5 minutes. The automated backups include full backups each week, differential backups every 12 hours, and log backups every 5 minutes. Backups are kept for 7 days by default. You can test the backups at any point by restoring to a new database.

Every restore of SQLDB is a new database. You pick the point-in-time to restore the database, and a name for the new database. The new database is always created on the same SQL Server as the backed-up database. This means that if you delete a SQL Server in Azure, you won't be able to restore the databases that were on it. But you can move SQLDB between SQL Servers easily. Let's look at this by retrieving a database copy from production for development work.

11.3.1 Restoring and moving SQLDB

The development team has deployed their new application in production, and the production SQLDB is accumulating useful data. They want to refresh the development SQLDB with a copy of the production data. How can you fulfill this request?

Copying databases for development is a common use case. Development teams frequently need to troubleshoot issues in production databases, and prefer to not directly access production servers. This follows a best practice for restricting access to sensitive production data, and minimizes the risk of errors in production. For an on-premises SQL Server database, this works as follows:

1 Back up the production database.
2 Optional: restore the backup to new database, remove sensitive data, and make a new backup.
3 Copy the backup file from production to the development network.
4 Restore the backup over the existing development database of the same name.

This process can include steps for wiping sensitive data and updating data rows with development values after restore. The process for copying a database in Azure offers two options: restore backup, and export.

EXPORTING A DATABASE

Exporting a database is similar to making a manual backup of an on-premises database. You select a file name for the export, choose a storage location, and provide an Admin account. The account must be a server-level admin, because the export removes database encryption that is managed at the server level. The export process uses Blob Storage to store the file in .bacpac format. This format can be used to restore a SQLDB database to an on-premises SQL Server.

Using Azure portal

To export a SQLDB using the Azure Portal, browse to the SQLDB Overview blade and click Export to show the Export Database blade. Provide the file name, and a target subscription for the Blobs service to store the file. Select the Azure Storage and Blobs service to use, and provide the Admin user and password. You can use either AAD Admin or SQL Admin accounts.

Using Azure PowerShell

You can use Azure PowerShell to export the SQLDB too. When using the `New-AzSqlDatabaseExport` command, you provide the resource group, server and database names, and Admin credentials. The `AdministratorLogin` parameter accepts either an AAD account or SQL account. Use a SQL Admin by default, or set `AuthenticationType` to `ADPassword` to use an AAD account. Use `AdministratorLoginPassword` to pass the password. (In listing 11.3, the `Read-Host` command is used to read input for these values.)

You must provide the Blobs service path and access when using the Azure PowerShell command. The command doesn't have drop-down choices to select values like the Portal has. You specify the entire URL to define the location for the bacpac file using the `StorageUri` parameter. The URL looks like the following:

```
https://[STORAGEACCOUNT].blob.core.windows.net/[BLOBSERVICE]/[FILENAME].bacpac
```

You also need to provide the key to provide access to write the bacpac files to Blob Storage. Set the key value using `StorageKey`, and set the key type with `StorageKey-Type`. The type can be `SharedAccessKey` for SAS keys or `StorageAccessKey` for Storage access keys. (See chapter 3 for more information on Azure Storage account access.) The following listing sets a variable for the Storage URL and key, then calls the export command.

Listing 11.3 Export a SQLDB bacpac to Blobs storage

```
$Blob = "https://adedeveastus2sql.blob.core.windows.net
    /backups/playerstats_2020_02_02.bacpac"
$Key = (Get-AzStorageAccountKey -ResourceGroupName "ade-dev-eastus2"
    -Name "adedeveastus2sql").Value[0]
New-AzSqlDatabaseExport -ResourceGroupName "ade-dev-eastus2"
    -ServerName "ade-dev-eastus2-sql"
    -DatabaseName "Playerstats"
```

The Blobs service and file name

The Azure Storage URL

Specify the first key.

Get the Azure Storage access keys.

```
⇒    -StorageKeyType "StorageAccessKey"                    ◁──── Choose the Storage access key.
⇒    -StorageKey $Key -StorageUri $Blob
↦    -AdministratorLogin (Read-Host "Enter Admin")   ⌉ Set the key and file URL.
⇒    -AdministratorLoginPassword (Read-Host "Enter Password" -AsSecureString)
```

**Read the Admin user and password
from the PowerShell console.**

IMPORTING A DATABASE

Importing the bacpac file works the same as exporting, but you need to specify the service level of the new SQLDB. The steps in the Azure portal are the same, using "Import" instead of "Export." The steps are the same for Azure PowerShell as well, but include a few extra parameters to specify the size of the new SQLDB.

Using Azure PowerShell

The import function uses the `New-AzSqlDatabaseImport` command. The same parameters are used for server and database names, access to storage, and the SQL Server. The `Edition` and `ServiceObjectiveName` parameters set the provisioning model of the database—either DTU or vCore-based—and the service level. The `DatabaseMaxSizeBytes` parameter sets a maximum value for the vCore model database storage, in bytes. Use a big number for vCore storage. The following listing sets a variable for the Storage URL and key, then calls the import command.

Listing 11.4   Import a SQLDB bacpac to SQL Server

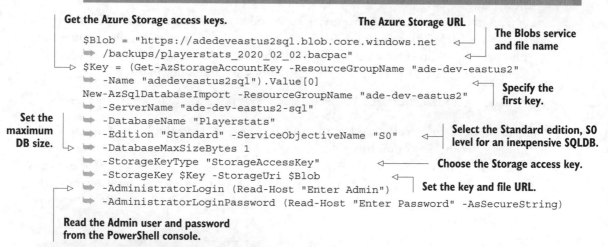

Get the Azure Storage access keys.   **The Azure Storage URL**

```
$Blob = "https://adedeveastus2sql.blob.core.windows.net    ◁──┐ The Blobs service
⇒    /backups/playerstats_2020_02_02.bacpac"          ◁──────  and file name
$Key = (Get-AzStorageAccountKey -ResourceGroupName "ade-dev-eastus2"
⇒    -Name "adedeveastus2sql").Value[0]                      ◁──┐ Specify the
New-AzSqlDatabaseImport -ResourceGroupName "ade-dev-eastus2"      first key.
⇒    -ServerName "ade-dev-eastus2-sql"
⇒    -DatabaseName "Playerstats"
⇒    -Edition "Standard" -ServiceObjectiveName "S0"   ◁──┐ Select the Standard edition, S0
⇒    -DatabaseMaxSizeBytes 1                                level for an inexpensive SQLDB.
⇒    -StorageKeyType "StorageAccessKey"              ◁──── Choose the Storage access key.
⇒    -StorageKey $Key -StorageUri $Blob              ◁──┐
⇒    -AdministratorLogin (Read-Host "Enter Admin")   ⌋ Set the key and file URL.
⇒    -AdministratorLoginPassword (Read-Host "Enter Password" -AsSecureString)
```

**Set the
maximum
DB size.**

**Read the Admin user and password
from the PowerShell console.**

> **NOTE** At the time of writing, the `DatabaseMaxSizeBytes` parameter has no effect on SQLDBs using the DTU model. The maximum DB size is a function of the edition and service level. You can't use Azure PowerShell to import a bacpac file to a Managed Instance. You must use SSMS or another tool.

You can import bacpac files to the same or different SQL Servers, even across subscriptions. When using the Azure portal, the logged-in account should have at least contributor access to the Azure Storage account, to read the access keys. The SQL

Server target has a special blade in the Azure Portal to monitor the import or export processes. The Import/Export History blade shows the status and progress of imports and exports.

You can create security boundaries in Azure using resource groups and subscriptions. These boundaries can define and enforce separation of logical environments. Users can be given access to Azure services at the service level, resource group level, and subscription level. The export and import process lets you copy SQL Databases to different resource groups and different subscriptions, as long as you have access to both.

Azure SQLDB also maintains automatic backups that can be restored directly to the same server. Let's see how the copy process works when using point-in-time backups.

USING A DATABASE RESTORE AND MOVE

In the Azure portal, you restore a SQLDB from the SQLDB's Overview blade, or the host SQL Server's Deleted Databases blade. Deleted SQLDBs can be restored on the SQL Server where they were hosted for seven days after deletion, when the last backup is automatically removed.

Restoring a SQLDB from backup takes only a couple steps. You choose the point-in-time for the backup, the provisioning model and service level of the SQLDB, and a name for the new SQLDB. When restoring from earlier than the 7-day window, you choose a backup by timestamp.

Using Azure portal

In the Azure portal, select the SQLDB Overview blade and click Restore. In the Restore blade, select either Point-in-Time or Long-Term Backup Source. Choose a name for the new database and a timestamp for the restore target. Select the provisioning model and service level for the new database. You can optionally chose to add the new database to an elastic pool.

> **NOTE** An *elastic pool* lets multiple databases share a single service level's resources. We'll talk more about elastic pools later in the chapter.

USING AZURE POWERSHELL

Restoring a database with Azure PowerShell works much the same as with the Azure portal. Because you don't have the GUI to populate drop-down lists for you, you need to look up the database and the available restore times. You also need to find the ID of the database that generated the backups. Listing 11.5 combines all these steps. The following paragraphs explain each PowerShell command.

You can use `Get-AzSqlDatabase` to look up the database properties. Pass the resource group, server name, and database name. Capture the database ID for later use. You can get a list of database restore points, or point-in-time range, using `Get-AzSqlDatabaseRestorePoint`. Pass the resource group, server name, and database name. The command output for a SQLDB is the earliest time when point-in-time restores are available, and looks like the following:

```
ResourceGroupName           : ade-dev-eastus2
ServerName                  : ade-dev-eastus2-sql
DatabaseName                : Playerstats
Location                    : East US 2
RestorePointType            : CONTINUOUS
RestorePointCreationDate    :
EarliestRestoreDate         : 2/8/2020 11:06:06 AM
RestorePointLabel           :
```

Restores are available for any time between the `EarliestRestoreDate` and the current time. The restore will use the latest point-in-time backup earlier than the chosen time.

`Restore-AzSqlDatabase` uses the database ID and the restore time to locate a restore point and create a new database. To use a point-in-time backup, add the `FromPointInTimeBackup` flag, and pass the time with `PointInTime`. As with `New-AzSqlDatabaseImport`, pass the resource group, server name, edition, and service level. The `TargetDatabaseName` parameter, rather than `DatabaseName`, sets the new database name.

Listing 11.5 combines all these commands into a single script for a specific date. First, get the properties of the database to restore and save them in a variable. Second, review the available point-in-time date range. Third, create a `DateTime` variable using the `Get-Date` command, using values in the range. Last, restore the database using the variables.

Listing 11.5   Restore a SQLDB to SQL Server using a point-in-time backup

**Set the type of backup source
and the target time.**   **Get the database properties,
                                                               including the ID.**

```
$Db = Get-AzSqlDatabase -ResourceGroupName "ade-dev-eastus2"
  -ServerName "ade-dev-eastus2-sql" -DatabaseName "Playerstats"
Get-AzSqlDatabaseRestorePoint -ResourceGroupName $Db.ResourceGroupName
  -ServerName $Db.ServerName -DatabaseName $Db.DatabaseName
$Date = Get-Date -Year 2020 -Month 2 -Day 2 -Hour 13 -Minute 0 -Second 0
Restore-AzSqlDatabase
  -FromPointInTimeBackup -PointInTime $Date
  -ResourceGroupName $Db.ResourceGroupName
  -ServerName $Db.ServerName
  -TargetDatabaseName "Playerstats_2020_02_02_13_00"
  -ResourceId $Db.ResourceID
  -Edition "Standard" -ServiceObjectiveName "S0"
```

**Use the Db variable property,
because it's there.**

**Choose a name
different from the
original database.**

The database ID is a ResourceId property.

The restore option creates a copy of the SQLDB up to the last backup. You can use the `copy` command to get a copy of the SQLDB current up to when the action was completed.

CREATE THE DATABASE COPY

The copy command for SQLDB is the easiest method for moving a database between SQL Servers in the same subscription. In the Azure portal, you start with the Overview blade for the database you wish to copy, and click Copy. You need to choose only the new database name, the target SQL Server, and the service level of the new SQLDB. You can choose a target SQL Server in any resource group your account has access to. For vCore-based databases, you chose the vCores; for DTU-based, you chose the service level objective. The SQLDB edition remains the same for the new copy.

The copy command `New-AzSqlDatabaseCopy` is easier to use than the restore command in Azure PowerShell. It takes the resource group, server name, and database name of the source SQLDB. Provide the target SQLDB specifics using `CopyResource-GroupName`, `CopyServerName`, and `CopyDatabaseName`. Listing 11.6 demonstrates copying a SQLDB from a production resource group called `ade-prod-eastus2` to a development resource group called `ade-dev-eastus2`. To run this command, you need a second resource group and SQL Server to represent different environments.

> ### Listing 11.6 Create a SQLDB on another SQL Server using the copy command

```
New-AzSqlDatabaseCopy -ResourceGroupName "ade-prod-eastus2"
    -ServerName "ade-prod-eastus2-sql" -DatabaseName "ade-prod-playerstats"
    -CopyResourceGroupName "ade-dev-eastus2"
    -CopyServerName "ade-dev-eastus2-sql"
    -CopyDatabaseName "ade-dev-playerstats_2020_02_02_13_00"
    -ServiceObjectiveName "S0"
```

Copying databases across resource groups or servers, potentially security boundaries, works fine if no data must be cleansed before leaving the original security zone.

Database copies come from a recent snapshot of the database. Database restores come from the last week of managed full, differential, and log backups. If you need to get database copies from more than seven days in the past, SQLDB makes adding a back-up rotation easy.

LONG-TERM BACKUP RETENTION

SQL Server *long-term retention policies* let you keep backups well beyond the seven-day window. Storage for backups is provisioned in the background. The storage is RA-GRS type for data center redundancy. Storage costs accrue for the backups after seven days.

A basic policy can extend the backup retention up to 35 days, and also allows for a grandfathering rotation of backups. With this rotation, you can keep the first of the week's backups for *N* number of weeks, the first of the month's backups for *N* number of months, and the first of the year's backups for *N* number of years. You can use these in any combination. If you use all three rotations, with 2-year, 12-month, 4-week rotations, after a while you could have the following backups available. Table 11.1 counts the backups available over time.

By the end of week 1, a point-in-time restore is available for every 5-minute period. By the end of week 2, point-in-time restores cover both weeks, and a backup of the previous week is available. By the end of week 5, point-in-time restores cover 4 weeks, 4 new weekly restores are available, and a new monthly restore is available. By the end of 27 weeks, 6 monthly restores are available. By the end of 53 weeks, the most recent 3,360 point-in-time restores, the last 4 weeks' restores, the last 12 months'

Table 11.1   Long-term backup rotation

Weeks	Point-in-time	Weekly	Monthly	Yearly
1	480*7, 3360			
2	480*14, 6720	1		
5	480*28, 13440	4	1	
27	480*28, 13440	4	6	
53	480*28, 13440	4	12	1

restores, and 1 restore from the previous year is available. You can expect the monthly storage cost for this kind of rotation for a database size N in GB to be around the following:

```
(N*4*2(4 full weekly + differential point-in-time) + N*4(full weekly)
     + N*12(full monthly) + N(full yearly) - N*2(included)) * $0.035
```

You can create the retention policy using the Azure portal. You configure the policy using the SQL Server's Manage Backups blade. Select one or more databases on the SQL Server to participate in the policy, and click Configure Retention. You can extend the built-in point-in-time window to 14, 21, 28, or 35 days. This gives you point-in-time restores up to 5 weeks in the past. You can also add long-term retention to weekly backups at the week, month, and year levels. The yearly retention level lets you choose which week of the year to retain, from 1st to 52nd. The first day of the month at the monthly level is retained. Choose the retention at each level in days, weeks, months, or years. Use Apply to save the policy when done.

To add a retention policy with Azure PowerShell, use `Set-AzSqlDatabaseBackup-ShortTermRetentionPolicy` for point-in-time retention, and `Set-AzSqlDatabase-BackupLongTermRetentionPolicy` for long-term retention. The commands really are that long. You provide the resource group, server name, and database name for the policy. To extend the point-in-time retention, specify the days using the `Retention-Days1` parameter, using a value of 14, 21, 28, or 35. For long-term retention, you can set weekly, monthly, and yearly periods separately or all at once. `WeeklyRetention`, `MonthlyRetention`, and `YearlyRetention` are self-evident. When setting the yearly retention period, add a `WeekOfYear` parameter between 1 and 52 to choose what weekly backup to retain. The retention parameters use an ISO 8601 pattern for specifying the duration, as follows, for either (Y)ears, (M)onths, or (W)eeks:

```
P(n)Y(n)M(n)W
```

Use an integer to specify the period in days. The following listing sets both the point-in-time retention period and a long-term retention policy for 8 weekly, 12 monthly, and 2 yearly backups.

Listing 11.7 Configure long-term backup retention for SQLDB

```
$Db = Get-AzSqlDatabase -ResourceGroupName "ade-dev-eastus2"
➡ -ServerName "ade-dev-eastus2-sql" -DatabaseName "ade-dev-playerstats"
Set-AzSqlDatabaseBackupShortTermRetentionPolicy
-ResourceGroupName $Db.ResourceGroupName
-ServerName $Db.ServerName -DatabaseName $Db.DatabaseName
-RetentionDays 28
Set-AzSqlDatabaseBackupLongTermRetentionPolicy
➡ -ResourceGroupName $Db.ResourceGroupName
➡ -ServerName $Db.ServerName -DatabaseName $Db.DatabaseName
➡ -WeeklyRetention 70
➡ -MonthlyRetention P52W
➡ -YearlyRetention P2Y -WeekOfYear 1
```

35 days is the longest point-in-time window.

Set 8 weeks of weekly retention.

Keep 1 backup for 2 years.

Keep 1 year of monthly backups.

Once you have safeguards in place against data loss, you can look at protecting your SQLDB from outages. The top performance tiers come with active replication, and the standard tiers with cloud-based system redundancy. You can also add regional replication as another layer of redundancy, to ensure access to your SQLDB.

11.3.2 Database safeguards

Business continuity plans for data consist of strategies to maintain access to business data assets during an outage. *Disaster recovery* plans define the technical solutions that come out of these strategies. For example, to deal with a lost or deleted database event, a strategy would be to maintain backups of the database. To deal with a data-center outage, another strategy would be to maintain a second data center. The concrete decisions of who, how, where, and how much are covered by the disaster recovery plan.

Azure SQLDB covers many of the typical requirements for disaster recovery by default. These include accidental data loss, hardware failure, and data center outages. Cluster management of the SQL Server process allows for automatic recovery during updates or server failures. Redundant storage for data and log files prevents disk failures. Seven days of backups and 5-minute point-in-time targets help you cover most *restore point objectives* (RPO) for data loss. Geo-replication of backups ensures even entire regional outages won't prevent getting your database back online.

> **NOTE** Each region in Azure is made of multiple data centers. Services in Azure have redundancy within a data center and between data centers. You can choose which region to host your Azure services, but you can't see which data center is running your instances.

Defining an RPO lets you judge if your backup windows meet the requirements of the disaster recovery plan. The RPO represents the most data the business can lose while the database is offline. Ensuring availability of backups is the main step to ensuring continuity of business data. Defining a *recovery time objective* (RTO) lets you judge between options for restoring data access. The RTO for a database is the maximum time allowed for restoring access.

You've seen two methods already for meeting an RTO and RPO for a disaster. You can export a backup and restore the database to the same or a different server at any time. This can be automated but, depending on the RPO, the data could be too old, and the import is slower than a standard restore. You can restore point-in-time backups to the same server. This will let you recover a deleted database or recover deleted data, but it doesn't work if the server is unavailable due to a data-center outage. To recover a database when the host data center is unavailable, Azure replicates SQLDB backups between data centers. You can create a new database from the most recent replicated backup into a new data center. You can also choose a backup stored by a long-term retention policy. Either option can meet your needs, depending on your RTO and RPO. Or neither could meet your needs, if the restore time is greater than the RTO.

Suppose the Technical Operations team wants to test a catastrophic disaster recovery scenario in Azure, including your Azure SQL Database. In this scenario, the primary data center will go offline, and you have an RTO of four hours and an RPO of one hour. Restoring your 1500 GB database takes six hours. How can you configure your database to meet these requirements?

When neither automated imports nor restores from backup are sufficient to meet your disaster recovery targets, SQLDB offers another option: *geo-replication* maintains a second read-only copy of the database in the same region, or a separate region. The geo-replicated database synchronizes all transactions with the secondary database, and can be manually failed over to the secondary at any time. Promoting the secondary to primary takes less than a minute, and the data loss window is less than five seconds. This means you can have a functioning database available again very quickly, and well within your plan's RTO and RPO. Let's see what's involved in configuring a SQLDB for geo-replication.

SET UP GEO-REPLICATION

In order to configure geo-replication, you need an existing database. You also need a SQL Server instance in the target region. Using the Azure portal, you can create this SQL Server while setting up geo-replication. In Azure PowerShell, you need to create the SQL Server as a separate step.

Geo-replication creates a second read-only copy of the database. If your application supports it, you can use the secondary for read operations. This lets you scale out read access to the database. Reading from the secondary reduces traffic on the primary database and table and row contention during data operations. The database runs at the selected service level and accrues costs at the hourly rate for that level. You can set the service level to handle the expected use.

NOTE Geo-replication creates copies of the database across regions. It's available at the basic and higher levels of SQLDB. The Premium and Business Critical provisioning modes include replicating databases to different data centers within the same region. This replication is similar to the Always On Availability Groups for on-premises SQL Server. You'll see more about provisioning modes and service tiers for SQLDB later in the chapter. You can read more about SQLDB's high availability features at http://mng.bz/WPol.

You configure geo-replication for each SQLDB as needed. First, choose a region to target. You can target a region near your users or applications to reduce latency for read access, or a region farther from you primary region to reduce the likelihood of the same outage befalling both regions. Next, create the SQL Server in that region. Last, create the secondary database by selecting the region, SQL Server, and service level. The secondary database will be created, loaded with data from the primary database, and synchronization will begin. Figure 11.3 shows the relationship between SQL Servers and databases using geo-replication.

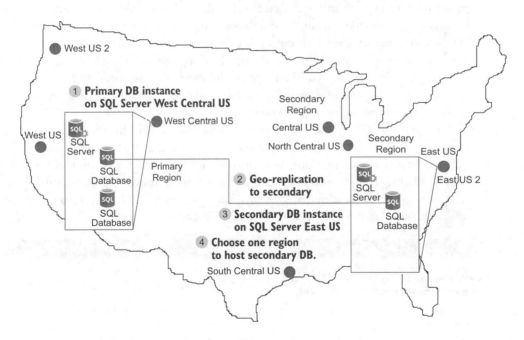

Figure 11.3   Geo-replication of SQLDBs

The time to bring the secondary database online depends on the database size, the service level of the primary and secondary, and the latency between the regions. You can shorten the creation time by increasing the secondary's service level when starting geo-replication setup.

> **IMPORTANT**   Active geo-replication of a database requires an available source database and some time to create the secondary database. Don't wait until

after an outage occurs to configure it! Once the secondary database is created, transactional replication will keep it up to date. You can reduce the service level of the secondary to reduce ongoing costs.

To configure geo-replication in the Azure portal, start from the SQLDB to replicate. Browse to the Geo-replication blade, and select the target region from the list. The Create Secondary blade will open, letting you select or create the SQL Server in the target region, and select the service level. Clicking OK will create the secondary database and begin the synchronization process.

Configuring geo-replication in Azure PowerShell has more steps. First, create a new resource group. Because this SQLDB, and potentially other Azure resources, will be in a separate region, you should group them together. Next, create a new SQL Server in the target region, in the new resource group. Last, configure the replication.

The `New-AzSqlDatabaseSecondary` command configures the replication. The parameter list is very similar to that for `New-AzSqlDatabaseCopy` because they do similar tasks. You provide the source database values and the target server values. The replication command gives the target server values using `PartnerResourceGroupName` and `PartnerServerName`. Set the service level of the new database with `Secondary-ServiceObjectiveName`. You can optionally use a different name for the replicated database, passing the new name with `PartnerDatabaseName`. If you leave it off, the name of the source database will be used.

The primary difference between the commands deals with read access to the replicated database. You can disable read access by passing `No` with `AllowConnections`. Pass `All` to allow read connections. You cannot disable read access when using the Azure portal. Listing 11.8 demonstrates creating the new resource group and server, then configuring geo-replication on the Playerstats database. You can compare to listing 11.6 to see the similarities with `New-AzSqlDatabaseCopy`.

Listing 11.8   Create new Azure SQL Server

Provide a server admin credential. This can match the primary server or be different.

```
New-AzResourceGroup -Name "ade-dev-westus2" -Location "West US 2"
New-AzSqlServer -ResourceGroupName "ade-dev-westus2"
    -Location "West US 2" -ServerName "ade-dev-westus2-sql"
    -ServerVersion "12.0"
    -SqlAdministratorCredentials (Get-Credential)
New-AzSqlDatabaseSecondary -ResourceGroupName "ade-dev-eastus2"
    -ServerName "ade-dev-eastus2-sql"
    -DatabaseName "Playerstats"
    -PartnerResourceGroupName "ade-dev-westus2"
    -PartnerServerName "ade-dev-westus2-sql"
    -AllowConnections "All"
    -AsJob -SecondaryServiceObjectiveName "S0"
```

The partner resource group contains the target SQL Server.

Allow read access to the database.

Use the new SQL Server.

Submit synchronization command as a job.

Replication takes some time to completely initialize. Once the databases are in sync, transactions are replicated automatically. With the databases synchronized, you can use the Azure portal to collect the connection string to each database. Browse to the database and click Connection String in the left nav or on the Overview blade. The connection strings have a common form, as follows:

```
Server=tcp:[SERVERNAME].database.windows.net,1433;
➥ Initial Catalog=[DBNAME];Persist Security Info=False;
➥ User ID=[USER];Password=[PASSWORD];
➥ MultipleActiveResultSets=False;Encrypt=True;
➥ TrustServerCertificate=False;Connection Timeout=30;
```

If you use the same database name, you can vary the server name and use the same connection string. The connection string drops the user and password parameters when using AAD authentication.

```
Data Source=tcp:ade-dev-eastus2-sql.database.windows.net;
➥ Initial Catalog=ade-dev-playerstats;
➥ MultipleActiveResultSets=False;Encrypt=True;
➥ TrustServerCertificate=False;Connection Timeout=30;
➥ Authentication=Active Directory Integrated;
```

If you don't use the server administrator account to connect to the SQLDB—and it's a best practice not to—you need to create contained users in the database that you are replicating. The database replication does not include the "master" database nor the SQL logins contained there. This is similar to creating regular database users, but without linking them to a SQL login.

You can create a SQL user with a local password, or use an AAD linked user. You must connect to the database in order to execute these commands. Use your preferred SQL Server tool, like SQL Server Management Studio, Visual Studio, or the SQLDB Query Editor built into the Azure portal. Use the SQL Server Admin account to connect to the database and create new users. To create an AAD linked user, you must connect to the SQLDB with an AAD account, not the SQL Server Admin account. The following script adds an AAD group as a user in the connected database, then adds the user to the db_owner SQL role. The FROM EXTERNAL PROVIDER option denotes an AAD account:

```
CREATE USER [Technical Operations] FROM EXTERNAL PROVIDER;
EXEC sp_addrolemember [db_owner], [Technical Operations];
```

Now you have an online copy of your database, ready to use in case of an outage. But what happens in an outage? During an outage, the primary database is unavailable. The secondary remains online, and does not become primary automatically. With geo-replicated SQLDBs, the secondary database is read-only. You must choose if and when to fail over to the secondary to let clients read and write to it. Failover promotes the secondary database to the primary, and requires changing your application connection string. To complete our disaster recovery scenario, let's promote the secondary database.

FAILOVER OF REPLICATED DATABASE

With SQLDB geo-replication, the secondary database is online and synchronized automatically. When you fail over to the secondary database, it becomes the primary. The former primary becomes the secondary and begins replication once it's back online.

> **NOTE** SQLDB in a geo-replicated pair can also add a failover policy, called a *failover group*. With a failover group, a geo-replicated database can fail over automatically during an outage. This requires at least one hour of downtime before failover will initiate. See http://mng.bz/8pD5 for more information.

Failover can be initiated in the Azure portal. Browse to the SQLDB, either the primary or secondary, and click Geo-Replication to open the Geo-Replication blade. Click the listed secondary database to open the Failover and Replication blade. Click Forced Failover to begin failover. It should take less than 30 seconds, regardless of database size or location.

Using Azure PowerShell to trigger the failover works a bit differently. The `Set-AzSqlDatabaseSecondary` command specifies the secondary database name, resource group, and server. You identify the primary database resource group using `Partner-ResourceGroupName`. The parameter `Failover` is required to initiate the failover. The following listing shows failover from a SQL Server in the East US 2 region to a secondary database hosted in the West US 2 region.

Listing 11.9   Initiate SQLDB failover to secondary

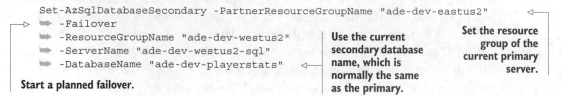

```
Set-AzSqlDatabaseSecondary -PartnerResourceGroupName "ade-dev-eastus2"
    -Failover
    -ResourceGroupName "ade-dev-westus2"
    -ServerName "ade-dev-westus2-sql"
    -DatabaseName "ade-dev-playerstats"
```

Start a planned failover.

Use the current secondary database name, which is normally the same as the primary.

Set the resource group of the current primary server.

You can also add the parameter `AllowDataLoss` to force a failover. When testing a disaster recovery scenario, Azure PowerShell allows a more graceful failover, because you can wait for transactions and synchronization to complete.

Once the secondary database has been promoted, it will be fully active and allow read and write operations. You may need to perform operations against other Azure services, like updating Stream Analytics connections or changing SQL Server linked services in Data Factory. Once service is restored in the region, the formerly primary SQLDB will assume the secondary role. Synchronization will bring the two databases back to a matching state. You can then fail over again.

Geo-replication provides a method for rapid recovery of database function for little additional effort. It's easy to test. But how will you know when to use it? In the next section, you'll see how to create monitors that alert you to problems in your database.

11.3.3 *Creating alerts for SQLDB*

Azure services provide a set of common alert features for monitoring the health of your service. The Azure portal includes a common interface for creating alerts in each service. You can access this from the Monitoring > Alerts blade of the specific service.

Azure alerts consist of two parts:

1 The alert rule
2 The alert action

You define rules based on a metric specific to the service and a threshold for activation. You can choose specific types of notification actions, including the following:

- Email
- SMS
- Phone call
- Azure App push notification
- Webhook
- Automation runbook
- Azure Function
- Azure LogicApp
- IT Service Management endpoint call

One or more actions are bundled into an *action group*. The rule triggers the action group, which executes the actions. The Alerts service comes with an Owner action group by default, which notifies the resource owner.

Each action uses specific configuration options, and most require external services to work. SMS and Phone each take a country code and phone number. SMS notifications allow the recipient to unsubscribe. Email actions include sending email to static targets, and to a configured role on the service, like owner, contributor, or reader. You can send notifications to the Azure mobile app for a specific user. You can POST to a webhook/website endpoint, sending a JSON payload with alert details. The automation runbook, Function, and LogicApp actions let you build complex responses to alerts with PowerShell runbooks, C# functions, or codeless apps, respectively.

> **TIP** The Azure mobile app lets you review and manage your Azure resources from your mobile device. You can download it at http://mng.bz/yrZd.

You can create new alert rules and manage existing alerts from the Alerts blade. Use New Alert Rule to open the Create Rule blade. Here you can select the service or resource to monitor; it defaults to the service you were viewing. Add a condition, which selects a metric called a Signal, with its threshold for activation. Also select an action group to send the alert to.

The condition evaluates the metric over an aggregation window at a particular rate. You can choose an aggregation of average, minimum, or maximum. By default the window is 5 minutes, checked every minute. You can choose a window up to 24 hours and a rate of every 1, 5, 15, 30, or 60 minutes.

Each service includes its own metrics for monitoring. SQLDBs include 32 different signals. These include CPU percentage, DTU percentage, Data space used percentage, Failed connections, Deadlocks, and more. By monitoring these metrics, you can take action when your database needs attention. For each database, you should create alerts to check for CPU/DTU utilization and data space utilization; >80% CPU/DTU utilization over an hour, and data space used >80% over an hour are conservative measurements. These alerts can prompt you to increase storage or service level objectives to keep your database running well.

Now that you have disaster recovery, high-availability, and monitoring configured, your databases will be ready for use. Once your systems are running in Azure, you should review ongoing usage for utilization, performance, and cost. Controlling cost and planning end-of-life becomes more important for cloud resources, where expenditures are easy to generate and don't expire. Let's look at some of the ways you can ensure you get the most out of your SQLDB expenditure.

11.4 *Optimizing costs for SQLDB*

Some services and features in Azure are free: AAD, Azure Functions at low utilization rates, SQL Server, and Azure Shell. Other services are not free, SQLDB being a prime example. The cost generally falls within two categories: hardware sizing and data storage.

These two categories combine into several pricing models for PaaS databases. You can select from them to get the features you require and scale the compute and storage to your needs. The modes and tiers can be changed later as the database usage changes.

Let's look at a scenario that examines the costs and benefits of using SQLDB. The Finance office would like to reduce Azure resource costs. Your environment consists of five Premium tier S400 databases, three Standard S100 databases, and a single 10-vCore Hyperscale database. You need to both justify your current expenditures and provide options for reducing costs.

> **TIP** Microsoft provides a utility to analyze your current on-premises SQL Server load and calculate the appropriate DTU service level when migrating to SQLDB. It's called Azure SQL Database DTU Calculator, and you can download it at https://dtucalculator.azurewebsites.net/.

Budget and expense audits can help control costs when using Azure services. Reviewing expenses can uncover opportunities for consolidation, deletion, and upgrades to reduce costs and improve performance. Audits can also reveal options for improving systems, which can increase costs. The U.S. government requires audits of its largest departments annually, in accordance with the Federal Information Security Management Act (FISMA). Departments provide updates quarterly or semi-annually, depending on size. Quarterly reviews of Azure expenses with annual security reviews would align with these practices. Improve your systems by finding the right balance of cost and features for your business case. To provide a response to the request from Finance, let's look at how SQLDB defines its pricing.

11.4.1 Pricing structure

SQLDBs have three pricing models for computing hardware: stand-alone, elastic pools, and Managed Instances:

- *Stand-alone databases* use a defined set of resources.
- *Elastic pools* group SQLDBs together to share resources, much like an on-premises SQL Server hosting multiple databases.
- *Managed Instances* perform like an on-premises SQL Server, with the underlying OS abstracted away.

Both stand-alone and elastic pools scale hardware resources using a synthetic metric called DTUs, or with the vCore pricing model. The vCore model defines a CPU and memory combination. Manage Instances only use the vCore model.

The hardware provisioning models also have distinct performance tiers. The DTU model has three: Basic, Standard, and Premium.

- Basic include the minimum number of DTUs and up to 2 GB of storage.
- Standard includes a full range of DTU tiers, and up to 250 GB of storage.
- Premium includes options for even more DTUs, and up to 4 TB of solid state drive (SSD) storage. This tier also includes a read-only replica and multiple hot standby replicas for high availability. Because of this, Premium costs about three times as much as Standard.

The vCore model has four variations, with distinct features. For comparison, 100 DTUs are roughly about 1 vCore at the Standard tier.

- *General purpose provisioned* allocates pairs of vCores, up to 80. You pay for the storage allocated, up to 4 TB. This model and tier runs all the time.
- *General purpose serverless* allocates a single vCore or pairs of vCores, up to 16. You pay for the storage allocated, up to 3 TB. This model and tier allow burst usage of vCores up to the maximum set, for a higher per-hour cost. This tier also allows the database to automatically pause when no queries are executing.
- *Hyperscale* allocates vCores up to 24. You pay for storage allocated, but without a maximum amount. You can add up to four read-only replicas, each at two-thirds the cost of the original.
- *Business critical* allocates pairs of vCores, up to 80. You pay for the SSD storage allocated, up to 4 TB. This tier also includes a read-only replica and multiple hot standby replicas for high availability. Because of this, the Business critical tier costs about three times as much as Standard.

Managed Instances use the vCore pricing model. You select the number of CPUs and maximum data storage for the instance. You can create as many databases as you want on the instance, all sharing the compute and storage allocated.

Typically you determine the use case and availability requirements for a database at creation time. Use cases include online transaction processing (OLTP) and online analytical processing (OLAP). OLTP systems improve work best with lower latency and high availability. OLAP systems benefit most from large storage sizes. All database systems benefit from more CPUs and more memory. You need to determine how much to spend on each aspect.

The primary differences between the Premium/Business-critical and lower tiers are faster SSD drives for higher I/O and lower latency, and high-availability configurations. We've already seen how adding a geo-replicated secondary database improves availability for databases at the Standard and General-purpose tiers. So you mix different tiers and models to meet your requirements at the lowest cost.

Start by choosing between Azure SQL Server VMs, Managed Instance, or individual SQLDBs.

- SQL Server VMs have the highest compatibility, but require support.
- Managed Instances offer high compatibility and cross-database queries.
- Individual SQLDBs are the least expensive option.

Determine the performance tier you need.

- Do you need high-availability features? You can build multiple VMs, use the Business-critical or Premium tiers, or add geo-replication.
- Do you need the fast read/write speeds of an SSD? Choose the Business-critical or Premium tier.

Then pick a pricing model, between DTUs and vCores.

- Managed Instances only use the vCore model.
- Hyperscale databases only use the vCore model.
- DTUs have less expensive service levels than the vCore model.

Then determine the service level objective.

- Check CPU utilization. Increase DTUs or vCores when average CPU is more than 80% for multiple minutes, and decrease when less than 20%.
- Compare vCores in SQLDB with on-premises CPU cores, and start with a matching level.
- Find the cost for your last purchase of on-premises SQL Server hardware, storage, networking, and licensing. Divide by a 24- or 36-month hardware refresh cycle.
- Start low. It's easy to increase the service level later.

Then consolidate on a different hardware model if needed.

- Single databases can be scaled separately, for fine-matching of usage and service level.

- SQL Server VMs and Managed Instances share resources between databases.
- Hyperscale databases remain single.
- Combine multiple single SQLDBs onto an elastic pool.

To find the right level of performance for the database, you can do some tests, monitor the performance of the system in production, and make estimates based on installed hardware if migrating. Once you determine the usage patterns and the average usage, you may want to change some configurations to reduce costs. Azure SQLDBs include some useful features to help match your usage scenario. Let's look at some of these.

11.4.2 *Scaling SQLDB*

By default, a new SQLDB is created as a stand-alone database at the lowest-level vCore general purpose tier. This level may be sufficient or you may want to increase it. The SQLDB's Overview blade in Azure portal shows a utilization chart for the past hour, day, or week.

Thresholds for scaling up and down will differ based on database utilization. For databases with steady usage levels, a target service level is easy to find. First, determine your performance targets. If your users are complaining, or your database performance is preventing your application from meeting performance SLAs, consider scaling up. Next, if you are meeting your performance targets, consider scaling down. If your system is running fine, reduce the service level objective until the database becomes a bottleneck. Scaling down the database compute resources will save money. For databases with spikes in usage and sustained idle periods, refer to the next section on SQLDB serverless. You can change the compute mode, performance tier, or service level objective at any time.

> **WARNING**   Once you create or convert a database to Hyperscale, you can't change to DTU mode or to a higher tier.

You can change the database settings using the Azure portal with the SQLDB's Configure blade. Choose DTU compute mode in Basic, Standard, or Premium tiers. Choose a DTU or vCore service level objective, and a maximum data size for the database. 250 GB are included with DTU performance tiers; above this, you pay an additional charge per GB. You pay for the full data size reserved for the database in the vCore tiers.

You can change the database settings using Azure PowerShell. You define the hardware provisioning model, performance tier, and service level objective with the `Set-AzSqlDatabase` command. Specify the resource group, server, and database to change.

Change the tier with the `Edition` parameter. The following values are allowed:

- Basic
- Standard
- Premium
- DataWarehouse

- Hyperscale
- Stretch
- GeneralPurpose
- BusinessCritical

Basic, Standard, and Premium are DTU-based tiers. GeneralPurpose, Hyperscale, and BusinessCritical are vCore-based. Stretch allows automated movement of data from an on-premises database into a linked SQLDB in Azure.

The `RequestedServiceObjectiveName` parameter sets the level for DTUs between 10 and 3000; VCore sets vCores between 2 and 80. VCore also requires you to set the processor generation to `Gen4` or `Gen5` using the `ComputeGeneration` parameter. `Gen5` includes a higher available core count than `Gen4`.

> **TIP**   The lowest Standard S0 10 DTUs pricing is $0.0202/hour at the time of writing. You can find current pricing for SQLDB at http://mng.bz/Mo9B.

The `MaxSizeBytes` parameter lets you increase the database's maximum data size. You can change the data size, compute type, and performance tier in a single command, as shown in listing 11.10. This script sets the SQLDB to the Business-Critical performance tier with 4 vCores. Using the same configuration as current has no effect.

Listing 11.10   Scale SQLDB to 4 vCores Business Critical tier with 1 TB of disk space

```
Set-AzSqlDatabase -ResourceGroupName "ade-dev-eastus2"
⇒ -ServerName "ade-dev-eastus2-sql"
⇒ -DatabaseName "ade-dev-playerstats"
⇒ -ComputeGeneration "Gen5" -VCore 4          ⟵  Specify VCore with a
⇒ -MaxSizeBytes 1099511627776     ⟵               supported tier in Edition
⇒ -Edition "BusinessCritical"    ⟵               to change from DTUs.

            Specify a tier that supports vCores.    One terabyte is a
                                                    large number.
```

The `Set-AzSqlDatabase` command can also be used to convert a SQLDB to the Hyperscale tier. Use the `Edition` value `Hyperscale` to do so. Set the number of vCores with the `VCore` parameter. The Hyperscale tier includes an option for read-only copies, much like the Business-critical tier. You can add from 0 to 4 copies using the `ReadReplicaCount` parameter. The following listing shows this conversion to Hyperscale, with no read-only copies.

Listing 11.11   Initiate SQLDB conversion to Hyperscale

```
Set-AzSqlDatabase -ResourceGroupName "ade-dev-eastus2"
⇒ -DatabaseName "ade-dev-PlayerStats"
⇒ -ServerName "ade-dev-eastus2-sql"
⇒ -Edition "Hyperscale" -VCore 1
⇒ -ReadReplicaCount 0 -AsJob
```

Monitoring a Hyperscale SQLDB works like other SQLDBs. Scale the number of vCores to match the usage levels, up or down. Hyperscale SQLDBs charge for all storage, but you don't need to monitor the upper data storage maximum. You can remove data from the SQLDB and reduce storage costs. You could also reduce the number of read-only copies.

Single database usage for the Hyperscale tier relies on an administrator monitoring usage and calculating appropriate capacity. SQLDBs have an approach to automatically balancing available capacity while minimizing cost for other single databases. It's called *SQLDB serverless*, and it allows scaling of compute based on demand.

11.4.3 Serverless

You could call the SQLDB serverless provisioning model the "usage billing mode" instead. The serverless SQLDB still runs on a SQL Server. It still has backup tied to a server, and uses the SQL Server firewall. SQLDB serverless uses the vCore compute mode, it's just not statically provisioned.

Instead of being billed at a static level, the billed usage increases with demand. When configuring SQLDB serverless, you set the minimum and maximum number of vCores for the database. While the SQLDB has activity, the SQL engine can assign queries to any available CPU core. This allows databases with periods of multiple requests to use multiple cores to handle them in parallel. Each available vCore represents a hyper-thread, and can execute part or all of a query. Usage of each vCore is tracked by the second for billing. The hourly rate is approximately double that for statically provisioned SQLDBs.

During periods of low or no activity, usage is billed at the minimum vCore provisioned per second. But after a period of no activity, a new feature activates, or rather deactivates—by default, after one hour of no activity, the database pauses. The database is taken offline and billing for the vCores ceases while it is paused.

Figure 11.4 compares the cost of a two-vCore provisioned SQLDB and a four-vCore serverless SQLDB with 25 minutes of high usage and 25 minutes of low usage. SQLDB serverless costs about twice as much per vCore-hour as SQLDB provisioned. Over this period, the serverless database costs about a third more than the provisioned one.

After auto-pause, the database remains offline until the next request is received, then it comes online. The first request fails with a retryable error, and the database is online again in less than a minute. Storage reserved for the database accrues charges at the normal rate regardless of the database state. Databases with sporadic activity can see a significant reduction in cost by using auto-pause.

> **IMPORTANT** If you add geo-replication or a long-term backup retention policy to the database, the auto-pause feature will not trigger.

SQLDB serverless is available in the vCore General Purpose tier only. You can set your database to serverless using the Azure portal by browsing to the SQLDB and viewing

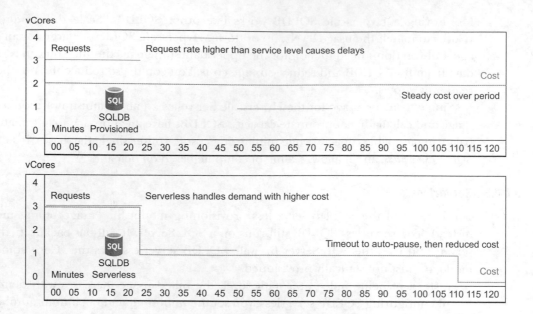

Figure 11.4   Comparing SQLDB provisioned cost versus serverless

the Configure blade. Choose Serverless instead of Provisioned, set the minimum and maximum vCores, and the timeout to auto-pause. The auto-pause delay can run from one hour to seven days. or you can disable it.

You can switch to the serverless via Azure PowerShell too. Use the `Set-AzSqlDatabase` command to change an existing database. The `ComputeModel` parameter sets the option to `Serverless` or `Provisioned`. Use `VCore` to set the available vCores, with `MinimumCapacity` defining the minimum to use. Set the auto-pause delay with the `AutoPauseDelayInMinutes` parameter, or use -1 to disable auto-pause. The following listing sets up SQLDB serverless with six vCores maximum and one vCore minimum, with a two-hour auto-pause delay.

Listing 11.12   Initiate SQLDB conversion to Serverless

```
Set-AzSqlDatabase -ResourceGroupName "ade-dev-eastus2"
    -ServerName "ade-dev-eastus2-sql"
    -DatabaseName "ade-dev-playerstats"
    -Edition "GeneralPurpose"
    -ComputeModel "Serverless"
    -ComputeGeneration "Gen5"
    -VCore 6 -MinimumCapacity 1
    -AutoPauseDelayInMinutes 120
```

SQLDB serverless provisioning works for databases that have long idle periods. What if your databases don't see significant idle periods, or can't tolerate failed initial connections? You can still find savings by sharing provisioned resources, using an elastic pool.

11.4.4 Elastic Pools

A SQLDB elastic pool falls somewhere between a single SQLDB and a Managed Instance. It's used to share billing for multiple databases, but it doesn't enable any cross-database features. The SQLDBs in the pool remain separate. The databases in the pool share available compute resources.

When shared across multiple databases, the elastic pool compute model costs less per database and less overall. Figure 11.5 shows the cost relationships of the various models.

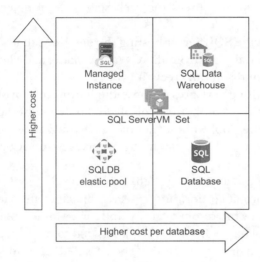

Figure 11.5   Comparing SQLDB costs

The shared nature means that databases in the pool can compete for compute resources. Each database can use the full DTUs of the pool for intensive queries. Other databases in the pool have to wait for DTUs to free up. This is fine for multiple low-utilization databases with spikes of demand. The elastic pool comes with a DTU-bounding feature to limit this behavior so databases don't have to wait to start their queries.

When creating an elastic pool, you set the upper and lower bounds on the databases, based on the DTUs provisioned for the pool. The upper and lower bounds apply to all databases in the pool. For example, three SQLDBs in a S1 100-DTU pool could have a minimum of 10 DTUs and a maximum of 100 DTUs. In practice, any of the three databases could use up to 80 DTUs at any time, while the other two reserved 10 DTUs each to execute any new queries. The following is the DTU-bounding calculation for *N* databases:

```
Available DTUs = (Maximum DTUs) - ((N-1) * Minimum DTUs)
```

The available DTUs are constantly in flux in a busy pool, as queries begin and complete, consuming and releasing DTUs. It's a good practice to provision more DTUs than you'd need for any single database, if your databases are frequently used or you reserve significant DTUs for each database. You can always run the busiest SQLDBs on their own, outside a pool.

Thanks to elastic pool cost savings, it's possible to get a higher maximum service level for any database, for the total cost of the separate databases at a lower service level. Standalone SQLDBs run $1.50 per DTU, while elastic pools run $2.25 per DTU For example, three SQLDBs at S2 50-DTU level cost $225 per month at the time of writing. You can move all three into a S1 100-DTU elastic pool for $225 per month. Each elastic pool service level objective has a break-even point, the minimum number of databases at a minimum service level where it is cheaper to host them in a pool than separately. You can get the current prices for each service level objective at http://mng.bz/awmm.

You create a new elastic pool on the SQL Server hosting the databases that will join the pool. When using the Azure portal, start from the Overview blade, and click New Elastic Pool. Give the pool a name and you can create it.

By default, the new pool runs with two vCores. Choose the hardware provisioning mode and performance tier using the Configure Pool blade. You can also add any databases on the target server to the pool while configuring. If you want to reserve compute for each database, do that now. The vCore model reserves entire vCores; the DTU model reserves DTUs.

You can create elastic pools with Azure PowerShell. You create the pool, define the provisioning mode and performance tier, and reserve capacity with the `New-AzSqlElasticPool` command. Specify the resource group and server for the pool. Use `ElasticPoolName` to define the pool name. Because the pool is tied to the SQL Server, use a variation of the SQL Server name to name the pool. Use `Edition` to set the mode. Use `Basic`, `Standard`, or `Premium` edition for DTUs. Use `GeneralPurpose` or `BusinessCritical` for vCores. The `Dtu` parameter sets the tier for DTUs between 50 and 4000, and `VCores` parameter sets vCores between 2 and 80. VCore also requires you to set the processor generation to `Gen4` or `Gen5` using the `ComputeGeneration` parameter. `Gen5` includes a higher available core count than `Gen4`.

To reserve compute power for the databases in the pool, you include one or two parameters for the lower and upper bounds. `DatabaseDtuMin` reserves a minimum number of DTUs, and `DatabaseDtuMax` defines the maximum DTUs any database can use. The minimum DTUs can be set using the same set of values as the service level objective for a standalone database. `DatabaseVCoreMin` and `DatabaseVCoreMax` do the same for vCores. The minimum vCores can be set using the same scale as the standalone service level objective, and at 0.25, 0.5, and 0.75 fractional vCores.

TIP As of time of writing, table 11.2 lists the service level objectives for elastic pools.

Table 11.2 Service level objectives

Compute mode	objectives
DTU Basic	50, 100, 200, 300, 400, 800, 1200, 1600
DTU Standard	50, 100, 200, 300, 400, 800, 1200, 1600, 2000, 2500, 3000
DTU Premium	125, 250, 500, 1000, 1500, 2000, 2500, 3000, 3500, 4000
vCore General Purpose	2, 4, 6, 8, 10, 12, 14, 16, 18, 20, 24, 32, 40, 80
vCore Business Critical	4, 6, 8, 10, 12, 14, 16, 18, 20, 24, 32, 40, 80

Check http://mng.bz/awmm for the latest values for vCore and DTU service level objectives.

You can move a SQLDB into a pool by specifying the pool name with the `Elastic-PoolName` parameter of the `Set-AzSqlDatabase` command. The following listing shows the command to create a new pool and move a database into it.

Listing 11.13 Add SQLDB to new elastic pool

```
New-AzSqlElasticPool -ResourceGroupName "ade-dev-eastus2"          Use a pool name that
    -ServerName "ade-dev-eastus2-sql"                              references the host server and
    -ElasticPoolName "ade-dev-eastus2-sql-pool1"          ◁        distinguishes between pools.
    -Edition "Standard" -Dtu 400                          ◁        Use DTU or VCore
    -DatabaseDtuMin 10 -DatabaseDtuMax 400                ◁        parameter to match
Set-AzSqlDatabase -ResourceGroupName "ade-dev-eastus2"             the Edition selected.
    -ServerName "ade-dev-eastus2-sql"
    -DatabaseName "ade-dev-playerstats"                            Use both minimum and
    -ElasticPoolName "ade-dev-eastus2-sql-pool1"                   maximum parameters.
```

Elastic pools limit the amount of storage available to all databases in the pool. The storage limit scales with the DTUs or vCores, up to 4 TB. Because of this, you should monitor storage growth of your databases in pools, and plan for increasing service level objectives as overall usage and storage grows. Splitting pools, moving databases between pools, and moving databases to single compute models can balance compute and storage usage. All these changes are done on demand with minimal interruption.

Elastic pools provide a method for sharing capacity between multiple databases automatically. They rely on an administrator monitoring usage and calculating appropriate capacity for multiple SQLDBs.

You now have all the background to provide recommendations and justifications to the Finance department. With data sizes less than 100 GB and moderate utilization, two or more of the five Premium-tier S400 databases could be moved into an equivalent elastic pool, which would reduce costs. If any do not require rapid failover or maximum IOPS, they can be converted to the Standard tier. With significant periods of inactivity, the three Standard S100 databases may be good candidates for SQLDB serverless. A review of usage for the Hyperscale database might lead you to increase or decrease vCores, or add a read-only copy. Now create some databases, give them some load, and create some alerts!

11.5   Exercises

The following exercises can help you internalize the new features introduced in this chapter. You should be able to create, restore, and optimize cost for SQLDBs.

11.5.1   Exercise 1

Given these three databases and this usage graph, make a recommendation for optimizing the database configuration.

- DB1: Standard 400 DTU, 80% usage 3 hours per day
- DB2: Standard 100 DTU, 100% usage 4 hours per day
- DB3: Standard 800 DTU, 50% usage 4 hours per day

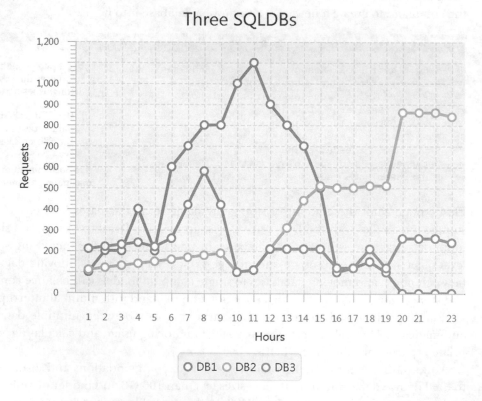

Figure 11.6   Usage chart of three SQLDBs over 24 hours

SOLUTION

The current cost ratio for the 3 SQLDBs is $4X + 1X + 8X = 13X$, where X is the cost of 100 DTUs on a single SQLDB. DB1 looks likes it's set in the sweet spot, DB2 may be under-provisioned, and DB3 may be over-provisioned. If you increase DB2 to 200 DTUs and decrease DB3 to 400 DTUs, the cost ratio yields $4X + 2X + 4X = 10X$. This level of provisioning could reduce the monthly spend by 3 times the cost of 100 DTUs.

Alternately, you could place all 3 SQLDBs in an 800 DTU elastic pool for $8Y$, where Y is the cost of 100 DTUs on an elastic pool. If $8Y < 13X$, then you would save the difference each month. The usage patterns of the three databases are such that usage peaks vary throughout the day, so there would less likelihood of competition between the databases in the pool. Using an 800 DTU pool would benefit DB1 and DB2.

11.5.2 Exercise 2

Given these three databases and this usage graph, make a recommendation for optimizing the database configuration.

- DB1: General Purpose 6 vCore, 100% usage 4 hours per day
- DB2: General Purpose 1 vCore, 50% usage 19 hours per day
- DB3: Business Critical 8 vCore, 20% usage 11 hours per day

Figure 11.7   Usage chart of three SQLDBs over 24 hours

SOLUTION

DB1 presents a classic pattern for the SQLDB serverless provisioning model. The current usage yields $6X * 24 = 144X$, where X is the cost of a vCore-hour. DB1 could be set for 10 vCore serverless with 0.25 vCore minimum. The usage would then yield $(2X * 10 * 4) + (2X * 1 * 0.25) = 80.5X$, where X is the cost of a vCore-hour. DB2 appears to have appropriate usage. DB3 appears to be over-provisioned, and could be reduced to 4 or 6 vCores.

11.5.3 *Exercise 3*

Given these three scenarios, give the closest target restore window.

1. Restore target 14 days previous, default SQLDB settings
2. Restore target 14 days previous, default SQLDB settings with 4 weeks of weekly long-term backup retention
3. Restore target 14 days previous, 28 days point-in-time retention with 12 months of long-term backup retention

SOLUTION

1. The database can be restored to 7 days previous.
2. If more than 3 weeks have passed since the retention policy was applied, the database can be restored to midnight on the first or second Monday that is more than 7 days in the past. If more than 2 but less than 3 weeks have passed, only the first Monday more than 7 days in the past is available.
3. The database can be restored to 14 days previous.

11.5.4 *Exercise 4*

A group of users requires access to data in a production database for reporting. The database contains private data that must not be shared. How can you provide access?

SOLUTION

You will need to create a copy of the SQLDB that can be sanitized. You can then export the sanitized SQLDB for later import, or move the copied SQLDB to be accessible to the group of users. This scenario is covered in the sections on exporting and copying databases.

1. Create a SQL Server in the production environment.
2. Create a copy of the SQLDB onto the new SQL Server.
3. Sanitize the copied SQLDB data using SQL statements.
4. Provide access to the SQLDB by moving the SQL Server into a different security network for the user group, and/or providing IP access through the SQL Server firewall.
5. Provide SQL credentials to the user group, either with SQL authentication or AAD authentication.

Summary

- You can make your SQLDB highly available using the Premium and Business Critical performance tiers, and by adding a geo-replicated secondary database. Both options include read-only access to a database replica, and allow you to meet short recovery time objectives.
- SQLDB provides point-in-time backups for up to 35 days, and long-term retention for weeks, months, and years. You can tailor your retention policy to suit your requirements.
- SQLDB has multiple approaches to optimizing cost for database usage. You can pay for just the performance needed by a single database, or collect multiple databases together to share resources and split costs.

Integrating Data Factory with SQL Database

This chapter covers

- Importing data into Azure SQL Database with external data sources
- Configuring cross-database queries in Azure SQL Database
- Importing file data into Azure SQL Database with Azure Data Factory

In the last chapter, you learned about creating and configuring Azure SQL Database (SQLDB). Relational databases like SQLDB provide an accessible endpoint for queries into both the Serving layer and Speed layer of a Lambda architecture analytics system. In chapter 6, you saw the real-time part of the workflow, with Stream Analytics calculations that flowed into SQLDB. Chapter 10 demonstrated using Azure Data Factory (ADF) to automate the batch-processing part using Azure Data Lake Analytics (ADLA). SQLDB sits at the center of this web of data flows and forms the primary service of the Serving layer. You can see the entire design in figure 12.1.

In this chapter, you'll learn how to move data in Azure services into SQLDB. This includes the outputs of ADLA batch processing, data in Blob Storage, and data in other SQLDBs. Providing data via an RDBMS gives more users access, with a wider range of tools, than data files only.

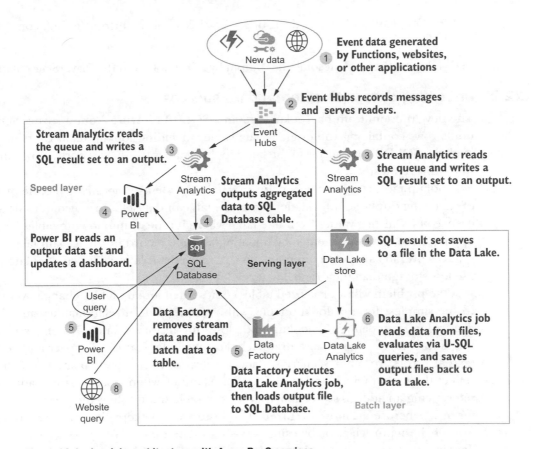

Figure 12.1 Lambda architecture with Azure PaaS services

This chapter explores two methods of importing data into SQLDB: external tables and ADF. External tables read data from data stores other than the one storing the SQLDB's native tables. These data stores can be external files or separate databases. ADF connects to both file services and databases, and copies data between services. Along the way you'll enhance your use of both SQLDB and ADF. You'll learn how to share data between otherwise isolated SQLDB instances, which works the same as accessing data from file stores. You'll also attach Git repositories to your ADF services, providing change management for your configuration files.

12.1 Before you begin

The scenarios in the next section deal with querying data from sources outside the database, using external tables. To see how external tables work, you'll need a couple of databases and a file in Blob Storage. You can use the scripts in appendix A to create the databases and Storage account required in this chapter.

> TIP   You can find the code listings for this book at https://github.com/ rnuckolls/azure_storage.

Let's take another look at some files output by ADLA jobs and the PlayerStats database.

12.2   *Importing data with external data sources*

The development team has lookup data in a SQLDB in Azure. Your analytics SQLDB holds rows containing the original data values including lookup data. Users of your analytics SQLDB want access to the latest lookup values for their reports. How can you fulfill this request?

Lookup tables have many benefits in database systems. *Normalization* is the process of removing duplicate information from one table or dataset into a second using a reference key. Shifting values from one table where it repeats into lookup tables lets you update these values efficiently, by updating a single record in the lookup table. This reduces overall storage requirements too, because the relational key and lookup table use less storage than the original data.

One problem with normalized tables comes when lookup tables change over time. In the simplest form of lookup table, with a single-column relational key and single data column, updating the lookup value loses the historical value. In some scenarios this is a feature rather than a drawback. For example, you can discover and correct textual errors. In other scenarios, data sets drawn from a particular period should reflect the extant values of that period. For example, when a user changes addresses, referencing an address stored in a user lookup table should show the previous address for orders before the move occurred. This history can be kept either in a separate version of the main table, or by using a from/to date range. We're not going to delve deeply into data warehouse designs, but we'll use remote data sources to look up data. Dealing with slowly changing values in analytics systems is a topic for another book.

In this scenario, your users want a report that shows a single value for a column that changed over the period of time the report covers. Or, the data in the lookup table in your analytics database has become out of sync with the data in the development team's database. In either case, you need to let your users query the latest data. You can do this by loading the updated data into your database or by querying the data remotely.

SQLDB is inherently insular. Unlike its cousins, the Managed Instance and full SQL Server install, SQLDB can't connect to multiple databases in a single query. Server-level logins aren't supported for connecting between SQLDBs, so these cross-database queries don't connect. There's no method for linking servers together either, as with a full SQL Server install. SQLDB does support connections from outside applications that can insert data into and read data from the database. The SQLDB is an island with no bridges.

You can build bridges from SQLDB to other databases using *external data sources*. An external data source uses a saved credential, a connection definition, and a table definition to let queries read from outside databases. This saved credential is called a *database scoped credential*. The external data source defines the location of the external database and the credential to use. An external table provides a schema definition to use when reading data from the external connection. Together, these three objects allow *read* access to data in separate databases.

An external data source can use either another SQLDB or a Blob file. Different schema, read, and authentication steps are used for each source. Figure 12.2 shows the process of reading data from external data sources using a SQL query.

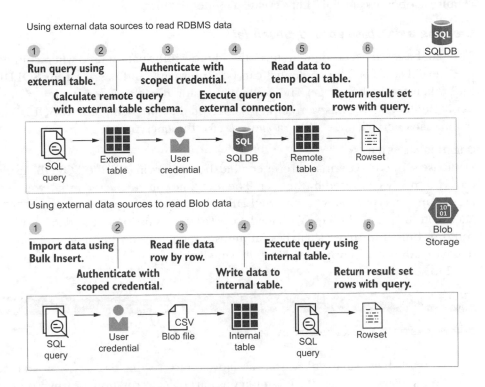

Figure 12.2   Connecting SQLDB to an external data source

SQL queries using external tables retrieve rows from the external data source and perform processing like JOINs and column calculations afterward. The retrieved rows are stored in an intermediate temp table during processing. To use data from Blob files in SQL queries, you must first import the data into a database table. Then you can use the table in your query.

While preparing query execution, filters in the query are evaluated for predicate pushdown, which executes some filters remotely to optimize performance. This works for SQLDB external data sources, but not for Blob sources.

> **TIP**   When using external tables with large row counts, consider loading data into local tables. Queries with Blob data sources load all data rows into a table

before filtering. Some queries for remote SQLDB tables will read all data to a local temp table too. Queries without filters read all data locally, as do external tables in a correlated sub-query. Querying the data source returns the latest values; any performance trade-offs against local tables may be worth it in your use case.

To read data from external sources, you must create the credentials, external data sources, and external tables. External tables require external data sources, which require scoped credentials. Let's create a credential first.

12.2.1 *Creating a database scoped credential*

The database scoped credential stores the identity information used when connecting to external sources. The credential can be a username and password for SQLDB, or SAS token for Blob Storage. The credential is stored in the system tables of the containing database. The password or key is encrypted before being stored. SQLDB uses a symmetric encryption key called a *master key* for this encryption.

CREATING A MASTER KEY

Database-scoped credentials are encrypted before storing in the SQLDB, using an encryption key generated by the user. The first time you add a credential, you need to create an encryption key in the SQLDB. The SQL command CREATE MASTER KEY ENCRYPTION creates the key. You need *CONTROL* permission at the database level to run the command, so use a database administrator account. You can learn more about database admins in chapter 11. The following listing shows the command using a password to secure the key.

Listing 12.1   Create a master encryption key with password

```
CREATE MASTER KEY ENCRYPTION BY PASSWORD='{YOURPASSWORD}';
```

If you already have a master key, you can move on to creating database-scoped credentials. You may want to reset the master key as part of a key rotation, or when personnel changes. You can use ALTER MASTER KEY to do so. The REGENERATE WITH parameter decrypts and encrypts any secrets encrypted with it. You can check for the existence of a master key using the sys.symmetric_keys catalog view. The following listing shows its usage by checking for the ##MS_DatabaseMasterKey## record.

Listing 12.2   Alter an existing master encryption key with password

```
IF EXISTS (SELECT * FROM sys.symmetric_keys WHERE [name] =
    '##MS_DatabaseMasterKey##')
ALTER MASTER KEY REGENERATE WITH ENCRYPTION BY PASSWORD = '{YOURPASSWORD}';
```

> **NOTE**   Most of the listings in this section show T-SQL commands, rather than PowerShell commands. You'll want to use a SQL editor to connect to the databases and execute the commands. Both SQL Server Management Studio

and Visual Studio are available for free download from Microsoft, at http:// mng.bz/EdMX and https://visualstudio.microsoft.com/downloads/. You can also use the SQL Query Editor in the Azure portal by browsing to the SQLDB overview blade and clicking Query Editor from the left nav.

With a master key in place, you can create a database-scoped credential. Do you have a plan for accessing the remote database securely, and a user available with the right permissions? If not, check section A.5.10 in appendix A for scripts to create a login and user. Let's move on to creating a scoped credential.

CREATING A CREDENTIAL

Creating a database-scoped credential saves the credential in the database. It is used when connecting to external sources, using a configured external connection. The credential can match an AAD user, a SQLDB user, or a Blob Storage key. The same format is used to store all types.

> **NOTE** Authentication using Azure Active Directory (AAD) users for external tables is not supported at time of writing. This means different credentials must be used for different external source types. You'll need to use a SQL user in the remote database that has access to the data tables, views, or stored procedures you want to call remotely.

To save the credential, you use the SQL command CREATE DATABASE SCOPED CREDENTIAL. The command takes a unique name for the credential within the database, and two parameters.

- Identity stores the username for SQLDB sources, using the value SHARED ACCESS SIGNATURE for Blob sources.
- SECRET stores the password for SQLDB sources, or a SAS token for Blob sources.

In this example, you'll connect later to database ade-dev-sql2-gamestats on server ade-dev-eastus2-sql2. Create a scoped credential in the ade-dev-sql-playerstats database using the command in the following listing.

Listing 12.3 Saving an external username and password as scoped credential

```
CREATE DATABASE SCOPED CREDENTIAL [ade-dev-sql2-gamestats-user]
⇨ WITH IDENTITY = '{USERNAME}',
⇨ SECRET = '{USERPASSWORD}';
```
◁— Use remoteuser login if using the DB creation scripts from appendix A.

> **TIP** You can use your own SQLDB, create a new one yourself, or use the scripts in appendix A to create a second SQL Server and SQLDB for creating a remote connection.

To connect to a Blob Storage file, the credential uses a default identity value, SHARED ACCESS SIGNATURE, and a SAS token. You can use a SAS token for the Blob container, or a specific Blob file.

TIP   You can read more about Storage accounts, Blob files, and working with SAS tokens in chapter 3.

In chapter 7, you uploaded the PlayerDetails.txt file to Blob Storage, at https://adede-veastus2.blob.core.windows.net/biometricstats/Staging/Players/PlayerDetails.txt. You can use this file as the target for your external data source too.

TIP   You can retrieve a file for use in this scenario at http://mng.bz/NKlv.

You'll need to generate the SAS token for the particular file that you will read. Use the Azure portal to browse to the file in the Storage account container and generate an SAS token. You can generate a token at the Storage account level for containers, too. For container-level tokens, remove the leading ? from the token. You can also generate an SAS token for any containers or on the Blob file itself using Azure PowerShell. (See section 3.4 in chapter 3 for more details.) Once you have the signature part of the SAS token, you can use it with the SQL statement in the following listing to create a credential.

Listing 12.4   Saving an external SAS token as a scoped credential

```
CREATE DATABASE SCOPED CREDENTIAL [ade-dev-eastus2-blob-playerdata]
⇒ WITH IDENTITY = 'SHARED ACCESS SIGNATURE',
⇒ SECRET = '{SASTOKEN}';
```

Now that you have a scoped credential for authentication, you can create the external data source.

12.2.2   *Creating an external data source*

SQLDB supports connections to other Azure SQL databases and Storage account Blob files. The data source defines the target location for the data and the authentication scheme to use when connecting.

Creating an external data source requires a couple of pieces of information: a name for the data source and the connection details. Use the SQL command CREATE EXTERNAL DATA SOURCE {NAME}, providing the details using the WITH () attribute. You provide four parameters to the CREATE command:

1 TYPE
2 LOCATION
3 DATABASE_NAME
4 CREDENTIAL

TYPE can have three values:

1 RDBMS for SQLDB
2 SHARD_MAP_MANAGER for querying sharded databases with elastic queries
3 BLOB_STORAGE for Blob Storage

The location parameter uses the fully-qualified server name, under the database.windows.net domain. Specify the database using DATABASE_NAME, and the database scoped credential using CREDENTIAL.

> **NOTE** External data sources and tables are part of the SQL Database elastic query framework. *Vertical* partitioning in SQLDB separates tables across multiple databases and uses external tables for queries. *Horizontal* partitioning duplicates tables across multiple databases and splits rows between the databases. This is called *sharding*. Horizontal partitioning uses a metadata database to manage queries across the sharded tables. When linking an external data source to a sharded source, you connect to this managing database, specifying the SHARD_MAP_MANAGER source type.

Listing 12.5 shows a script for creating the external data source, on the ade-dev-sql2-gamestats SQLDB, using the scoped credential you created in the previous section.

Listing 12.5   Creating an external data connection to SQLDB

```
CREATE EXTERNAL DATA SOURCE [ade-dev-eastus2-sql2-gamestats]
  WITH (TYPE = RDBMS,
  LOCATION = 'ade-dev-eastus2-sql2.database.windows.net',
  DATABASE_NAME = 'ade-dev-sql2-gamestats',
  CREDENTIAL = [ade-dev-sql2-gamestats-user]);
```

Creating an external data source on a Blob file uses the same SQL command. Pass the type, location, and credential parameters. The location is the fully-qualified URL to the Blob file. Because you're connecting to a file, you don't use the database name parameter. Connecting to a Blob external data source uses a Blob Storage key or AAD user scoped credential, instead of a SQLDB user. The following listing shows a script for creating the blob file external data source.

Listing 12.6   Creating an external data connection to a Blob file

```
CREATE EXTERNAL DATA SOURCE [ade-dev-eastus2-blob-playerdata]
  WITH (TYPE = BLOB_STORAGE,
  LOCATION = 'https://adedeveastus2.blob.core.windows.net      ◀── Leave the trailing /
  /biometricstats/Staging/Players',                                off of the location
  CREDENTIAL = [ade-dev-eastus2-blob-playerdata]);                 path.
```

With a data source created, you can now add the table schema using the data source for the SQLDB connection, or import the Blob file. This is the last step to enable querying of external data.

12.2.3 Creating an external table

External tables form the entry point to retrieving data from remote SQLDBs. Use external tables like internal tables in queries, views, and stored procedures, with a few caveats.

- External tables allow only read access. You can use remote execution of stored procedures to update the remote table, or you can copy the data into a local table for use.
- External tables don't get local indexes. Queries using external tables will scan tables as necessary, but remote processing can include indexes on the remote table to improve query speed.

Creating an external table requires a few pieces of information: a name for the table, and the name of the data source. You also define the schema for the table, just as when creating a local table.

> **WARNING** The schema for the external table *should* match the schema of the remote table. While the external schema can vary from the remote table, you will get errors if you use fields that don't match in queries.

Use the SQL command CREATE EXTERNAL TABLE {NAME} to create the external table. The name of the external table must match the name of the remote table. Provide the data source using WITH (DATA_SOURCE = {NAME}). Listing 12.7 shows a script to create a table that matches the PlayerDetails.txt file from chapter 7. A script for creating this table in the remote database can be found in appendix A.

Listing 12.7 Creating an external table

```
CREATE EXTERNAL TABLE [dbo].[playerdetails]          Table name matches
    (PlayerId nvarchar(8),PlayerName nvarchar(100),  remote table name.
    TeamName nvarchar(100),TeamPosition nvarchar(100),
    PositionStart DateTime,PositionEnd DateTime)               Using external
    WITH (DATA_SOURCE = [ade-dev-eastus2-sql2-gamestats]);     RDBMS data
                                                               source
```

External table queries work like local table queries. Keep predicate pushdown in mind when structuring queries. SQL Server will pass filter clause values to the remote database to reduce the number of rows returned. Increasing the performance tier of the remote database can improve query speed.

With a configured credential and data source, you can read external data without defining an external table. Reading from a Blob file is an import instead of a remote query.

12.2.4 *Importing Blob files*

Using external data sources with Blob files works differently than with remote SQLDBs. External tables can read directly from remote databases and can be used in queries directly. Blob file data sources must import the data first, before using it in queries. The import target can be temp tables, table variables, or local tables.

To import data from Blob files, use the BULK INSERT SQL command. The FROM parameter provides the file to import, and WITH specifies other options. Pass the external data source using DATA_SOURCE. Use FORMAT = 'CSV' to specify a comma-separated file with carriage return and line feed row endings. The target table already has a header defined for the columns; you can skip the header row in the Blob file by passing FIRSTROW = 2. The following listing shows an example script for importing PlayerDetails.txt.

Listing 12.8 Importing data from a Blob file with Bulk Insert

```
BULK INSERT [#blob_playerdetails]                                          Using a
⇒   FROM 'PlayerDetails.txt'                                               temp table
⇒   WITH (DATA_SOURCE = 'ade-dev-eastus2-blob-playerdata',
⇒   FORMAT = 'CSV',                                                        Filename
⇒   FIRSTROW = 2);                          Data source name               to import
                                            uses single quotes.
```

> **TIP** BULK INSERT offers many parameters to customize usage for your particular use case. You can see the options at http://mng.bz/D2XA.

Now you've seen two methods for accessing data stored in external locations through SQLDB queries. Depending on your use case and data size, importing Blob files inline with your queries may be sufficient. Reading from external databases minimizes data duplication and is fast for small files. If you need to import more substantial data or files from your data lake, or perform imports on a schedule, you can move file import processing to Azure Data Factory (ADF). Let's see what loading data into SQLDB with ADF looks like.

12.3 Importing file data with ADF

As data moves through the Batch layer, it is captured in ADLS files. These files are available for reading directly. For ease of use, your analytics system will also provide access to the data via an RDBMS. You've seen how SQLDB can directly access data in remote databases and remote files in Blob Storage. Azure Synapse Analytics (formerly SQL Data Warehouse) can access files in ADLS. To provide the same access for SQLDB, you can use ADF.

Now that you have automated some ADLA batch processing jobs using ADF, your users have begun downloading the output files. They want the output data to be available in their business application database without having to load it manually. How can you fulfill their request?

You've seen already that SQLDB can import Blob files. An option for loading the data involves modifying the U-SQL job to output to Blob Storage instead of ADLS. Updating database data can be done as a pull. This approach relies on restructuring the application query to perform the import, or some other means of automating the import.

You can instead use ADF to load the output of the U-SQL job into the database. Recall from chapter 10 that ADF can both read from ADLS and trigger ADLA executions. ADF also supports linkedservices connecting to databases, including SQL Server. You can use the same pipeline that triggers the ADLA job to push the output into the database. This business application database would become part of the Serving layer of your analytics system. Figure 12.3 shows ADF handling this data movement.

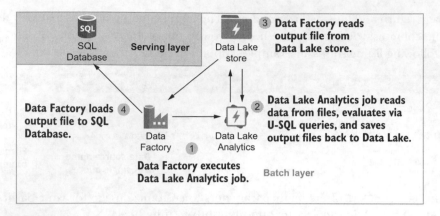

Figure 12.3   Moving data from the Batch layer into the Serving layer

Using ADF to push data into SQLDB requires a few configuration tasks, beyond using existing factory, database, and table entities. You must create an authorized credential, create an ADF linkedservice, and create an ADF dataset.

The new ADF pipeline workflow will look like figure 12.4. The U-SQL activity connects to an ADLS linkedservice and an ADLA linkedservice, to execute a U-SQL activity that generates a new data file in the ADL. You will add a new copy activity to the pipeline, to import the data file into SQLDB. This activity will use the existing ADLS

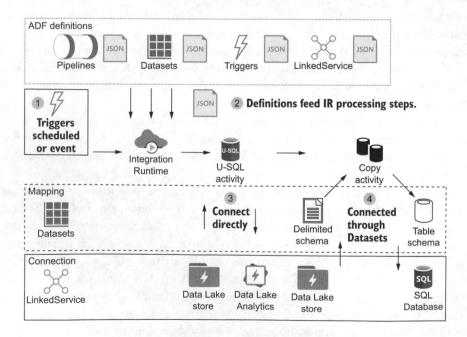

Figure 12.4   Data Factory batch processing and SQLDB import

linkedservice, and require a new SQLDB linkedservice, the copy activity, and two schema datasets.

Let's look at adding each of these ADF resources. We'll start by preparing access to the SQLDB before creating the linkedservice.

12.3.1 *Authenticating between ADF and SQLDB*

When connecting to data sources, it's important to provide access with minimal privileges and protect credentials. You may need to work within an existing framework of security controls or ad-hoc user accounts. Using ADF will let you configure access securely.

Connecting to SQLDB follows a flexible authentication model. Both SQL Server users and AAD principals are supported. Recall from chapter 10 that ADF supports retrieving secrets from Azure Key Vault (AKV). When using a SQL username and password, store the password in AKV securely. The same goes for AAD service principal authentication. You store the service principal key in ADF, and authorize the AAD principal to access the data. SQLDB linkedservices also allow authentication via the ADF managed identity itself, the same way ADF authenticates to AKV. Managed identities allow secure authentication without the need for secret key storage.

> **TIP** You can learn more about ADF authentication methods in chapter 10, which covers integrating with AKV, using managed identities, and creating service principals.

To set up authentication to a SQLDB, choose which type you want to use. SQL Server users work for SQLDBs that don't have AAD authentication configured. Managed identity and service principals both use the same command to create a new SQLDB user. If you have already used a service principal to access other Azure services, and have the secret key stored in AKV, using the service principal again for SQLDB will make the linkedservice creation easy.

First start by creating the user account in SQLDB. If you are using a standard SQL Server login and user, you can use the scripts included in appendix A or create them yourself. Creating a user for managed instance or service principal authentication doesn't use a SQL Server login; instead, the CREATE USER command uses FROM EXTERNAL PROVIDER to indicate this is an AAD login. Listing 12.9 shows a script to add the ADF App registration principal to the SQLDB, with write permissions. To add a service principal as a user, you must be connected to the SQLDB as an AAD-authenticated user with sufficient permissions to add users. You can use the SQL Server Active Directory Admin account for this purpose.

Listing 12.9 Authorize ADF to access SQLDB

```
CREATE USER [ade-dev-eastus2-adf-id] FROM EXTERNAL PROVIDER;
ALTER ROLE [db_datareader] ADD MEMBER [ade-dev-eastus2-adf-id];
ALTER ROLE [db_datawriter] ADD MEMBER [ade-dev-eastus2-adf-id];
```

If you prefer to use a managed identity, you can use the same SQL command to add the ADF principal, by using the ADF name instead of the App registration.

> **TIP** See chapter 11 for more detail on adding an Active Directory Admin to Azure SQL Server. See chapter 10 for directions on creating App registrations.

With a user created and given access to the SQLDB, you can add a linkedservice to connect ADF to the SQLDB.

12.3.2 *Creating SQL Database linkedservice*

The steps for creating a SQLDB linkedservice in Azure portal are the same as an ADLS linkedservice, except the authentication options are more expansive. You can choose to use a managed identity, service principal, or SQL username and password for authentication. Authorization settings for service principal authentication work much like providing a username and password. You provide a service principal ID and secret key.

USING AZURE PORTAL

To create the SQLDB linkedservice in the Azure portal, launch the authoring GUI and use the following steps:

1 Browse to the Overview blade of the ADF.
2 Click the Author & Monitor button to launch the authoring GUI in a new window.
3 Switch to the Authoring tab in the left nav.
4 Show Connections, from the bottom of the Factory Resources navigation.
5 Click New to open the Selection blade. Figure 12.5 shows the Selection blade.
6 Show the Azure tab.
7 Select Azure SQL Database from the list and click Continue.
8 Choose a name for the resource. Only alphanumerics and underscores are allowed.
9 Select the Azure subscription from the drop-down.
10 Select the Server Name (ade-dev-eastus2-sql2) from the drop-down of available SQL servers.
11 Select the Database Name (ade-dev-sql2-gamestats) from the drop-down of available databases.
12 Select Service Principal, Managed Identity, or SQL Authentication as the authentication type.
13 For Service Principal or SQL authentication, switch to using Azure Key Vault. This will change the available values to let you use a key vault from the same resource group, and add the secret key name.
14 Select the vault you created earlier (ade-dev-eastus2-key).
15 Set Secret Name to the secret you created to store the ADF App registration (ade-dev-eastus2-adf-id-key).

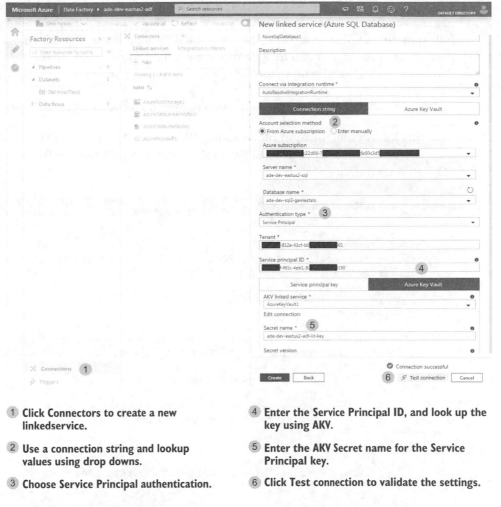

1. **Click Connectors to create a new linkedservice.**

2. **Use a connection string and lookup values using drop downs.**

3. **Choose Service Principal authentication.**

4. **Enter the Service Principal ID, and look up the key using AKV.**

5. **Enter the AKV Secret name for the Service Principal key.**

6. **Click Test connection to validate the settings.**

Figure 12.5   Creating a new SQLDB linkedservice using the ADF authoring GUI

Figure 12.5 shows the creation of a SQLDB linkedservice using the ADF authoring GUI. At this point you can click Create and save the new linkedservice.

USING AZURE POWERSHELL

As with others, a SQLDB linkedservice uses a JSON file to define its properties. Azure PowerShell uses the same process to create a SQLDB linkedservice as for an ADLS linkedservice. The JSON configuration file contains two common root elements: `name` and `properties`. `properties` contains a set of elements common to other linkedservices. For SQLDB, the `type` is `AzureSqlDatabase`.

`typeProperties` contains the connection information for the linkedservice. In addition to the common `servicePrincipalId`, `servicePrincipalKey`, and `tenant` elements, a SQLDB linkedservice requires a `connectionString`. The connection-String requires a `Data Source` and `Initial Catalog` values. The Data Source is the fully-qualified SQL Server name, and the Initial Catalog is the SQLDB name. For the `connectionString`, you can include or leave off the protocol `tcp:` that is required for connecting with other remote tools. `Server` cannot be substituted for `Data Source`.

TIP   See chapter 10 for more detail on creating linkedservices in ADF.

Save this JSON configuration file in listing 12.10 to an Azure Cloud Shell folder or a local drive accessible by your local PowerShell install. You'll use the file to create the SQLDB linkedservice.

> **Listing 12.10   SQLDB linkedservice definition file**

```
{
    "name": "AzureSqlDatabase1",
    "type": "Microsoft.DataFactory/factories/linkedservices",
    "properties": {
        "annotations": [],
        "type": "AzureSqlDatabase",
        "typeProperties": {
            "connectionString": "Data Source=ade-dev-eastus2-
    sql2.database.windows.net;Initial Catalog=ade-dev-sql2-gamestats;",
            "servicePrincipalId": "d915e8ef-f61c-4eb1-82b5-b4b20f0a6190",
            "servicePrincipalKey": {
                "type": "AzureKeyVaultSecret",
                "store": {
                    "referenceName": "AzureKeyVault1",
                    "type": "LinkedServiceReference"
                },
                "secretName": "ade-dev-eastus2-adf-id"
            },
            "tenant": "f41e678f-812a-43cf-b020-7c1f89e52901"
        }
    }
}
```

`Set-AzDataFactoryV2LinkedService` is the same command used for other linkedservices. Run the script in the following listing to create the SQLDB linkedservice.

> **Listing 12.11   Creating a new SQLDB linkedservice with Azure PowerShell**

```
Set-AzDataFactoryV2LinkedService -ResourceGroupName "ade-dev-eastus2"
➥ -DataFactoryName "ade-dev-eastus2-adf"
➥ -Name "AzureSqlDatabase1"
➥ -DefinitionFile "~/adf/AzureSqlDatabase1.json"
```

With the SQLDB linkedservice and the existing ADLS linkedservice, you can move on to creating datasets for the source file and target database table.

12.3.3 *Creating datasets*

Datasets in ADF define the location and schema of the data to read and write via linkedservices. ADF includes many dataset types, including various flavors of RDBMS and document databases, flat and semi-structured file types, and even web services like Google AdWords. Datasets connect activities to linkedservices and provide the interface for translating data between two endpoints.

You'll be using a copy activity to copy data from a CSV file into a SQLDB table. To create the activity, you'll need to have defined both the source and target dataset. The source dataset will use a file in your ADLS store, and the target dataset will use a table in your SQLDB.

Earlier in the chapter, you uploaded PlayerDetails.txt to Blob Storage. For this scenario, the source file is stored in your ADLS store. Upload the PlayerDetails.txt file to folder /Raw/Players/v1 in the ADLS store. In chapter 10, you created a linkedservice to the ADLS; you can reuse that linkedservice as part of the SQLDB import pipeline.

> **TIP** You can retrieve a file for use in this scenario at http://mng.bz/lG6d.

Like other ADF resources, datasets use a JSON file to define their properties. The dataset resource defines three important details: the linkedservice connection to use, the data target of a file path or a table name, and the data schema definition.

> **TIP** See chapter 10 for more detail on creating datasets in ADF.

Let's go over creating a file-based dataset in the Azure portal, and a table-based dataset using Azure PowerShell.

USING AZURE PORTAL

To create the ADF datasets in the Azure portal, launch the authoring GUI.

1. Browse to the Overview blade of the ADF.
2. Click the Author & Monitor button to launch the authoring GUI in a new window.
3. Switch to the Authoring tab in the left nav.
4. Click Datasets, from the Factory Resources navigation, to reveal a list of existing datasets.
5. Click the dots to the right of the datasets section to reveal the New Dataset button.
6. Choose Azure Data Lake Storage Gen1 from the list of data stores.
7. Choose DelimitedText from the list of formats.
8. Select a name for the dataset, and choose the linkedservice that accesses the file.
9. Browse to the file you uploaded earlier (/Raw/Players/v1/PlayerDetails.txt) to select it, or enter the folder and filename path manually.
10. Because this file has a header, select the First Row as Header option. This will provide a human-readable name for the fields, and skip the first row during import.
11. Choose Import Schema from Connection/Store. This will read the selected file directly, and generate a schema for you. You can choose to skip this step and

generate the schema manually, or upload a sample file here using the From Sample File option.

Clicking OK at this point will read the schema from the file and save the new data source. You can review the result of the file read. In the GUI, the data source provides two tabs, Connection and Schema, to review and edit the file details and review the schema. The Connection tab shows the specific row characteristics used to read the file. This includes:

- Field delimiters
- Row delimiters
- Escape and quoting characters
- File encoding
- Compression

You can modify the row import using a drop-down for each characteristic. The Schema tab lets you clear the schema and rescan the file to update the schema. You can leave the file portion of the File Path value empty, and the Preview and Import Schema functions will read from the first file in the folder. The Import Schema function will prompt you to select a file extension, sample file, or a wildcard. You can specify a single file or wildcard when creating the copy activity later. Keeping files of different schemas in separate folders, and having a defined folder structure, makes this easier.

Creating the dataset resource with the authoring GUI generates a JSON definition file. You can access the file via the Code button to the far right of the canvas. You can edit the JSON directly in the GUI, and the changes will be reflected in the GUI tabs. You can generate a template for the dataset this way, to be used with Azure PowerShell for programmatic creation of datasets. Let's see how the JSON configuration is constructed for a SQLDB dataset.

USING AZURE POWERSHELL

Like other ADF resources, you need to prepare the JSON configuration files before using them. The JSON configuration file contains two common root elements: `name` and `properties`. The `properties` element contains a set of elements common to other datasets too. The `type` element identifies the type of dataset. For a SQLDB dataset, the type is `AzureSqlTable`.

The `typeProperties` contains the data path information for the dataset. For SQL table datasets, the `schema` and `table` elements are directly under `typeProperties`. These elements contain the database schema and table name that identify the target table.

The most complicated part of the dataset definition lies in defining the schema. The `schema` array element lists each table field with a `name` and SQL `type` elements. Some types require `precision` and `scale` elements to match the target table types. Table 12.1 shows a list of supported SQL field types, their ADF types, and whether precision or scale elements are needed. Except for the numeric and rowversion types, SQL type names match ADF type names. Matching types are excluded from the table.

Table 12.1 SQL schema types

SQL Type	ADF type	Default precision	Default scale
bigint	bigint	19	
datetime	datetime	23	3
decimal	decimal	18	0
float	float	15	
int	int	10	
money	money	19	4
numeric	decimal	18	0
real	real	7	
smalldatetime	smalldatetime	16	0
smallint	smallint	5	
smallmoney	smallmoney	10	4
time	time	7	
tinyint	tinyint	3	

Binary, bit, char, date, image, nchar, ntext, nvarchar, text, timestamp, uniqueidentifier, varbinary, varchar, and xml use matching type names, and don't require a precision value. Listing 12.12 shows an excerpt of the SQLDB dataset schema element. Note that the nvarchar ADF type doesn't use the SQL format nvarchar(NNNN) and doesn't specify a length. This is typical of the rest of the types.

Listing 12.12 SQLDB dataset schema detail

```
"schema": [
        {
            "name": "PlayerId",
            "type": "nvarchar"
        },
        {
            "name": "PositionEnd",
            "type": "datetime",
            "precision": 23,
            "scale": 3
        }
    ],
```

Save the JSON configuration file in listing 12.13 to an Azure Cloud Shell folder or a local drive accessible by your local PowerShell install. You'll use the file to create the SQLDB dataset.

Listing 12.13   SQLDB table dataset definition file

```json
{
    "name": "AzureSqlTable1",
    "properties": {
        "linkedServiceName": {
            "referenceName": "AzureSqlDatabase1",
            "type": "LinkedServiceReference"
        },
        "annotations": [],
        "type": "AzureSqlTable",
        "schema": [
            {
                "name": "PlayerId",
                "type": "nvarchar"
            },
            {
                "name": "PlayerName",
                "type": "nvarchar"
            },
            {
                "name": "TeamName",
                "type": "nvarchar"
            },
            {
                "name": "TeamPosition",
                "type": "nvarchar"
            },
            {
                "name": "PositionStart",
                "type": "datetime",
                "precision": 23,
                "scale": 3
            },
            {
                "name": "PositionEnd",
                "type": "datetime",
                "precision": 23,
                "scale": 3
            }
        ],
        "typeProperties": {
            "schema": "dbo",
            "table": "PlayerDetails"
        }
    }
}
```

The `Set-AzDataFactoryV2Dataset` command is used to create or update ADF datasets. Run the script in the following listing to create the SQLDB dataset.

Listing 12.14   Creating new SQLDB dataset with Azure PowerShell

```
Set-AzDataFactoryV2Dataset -ResourceGroupName "ade-dev-eastus2"
➥ -DataFactoryName "ade-dev-eastus2-adf"
➥ -Name "AzureSqlTable1"
➥ -DefinitionFile "~/adf/AzureSqlTable1.json"
```

This covers both the ADLS file dataset and the SQLDB dataset creation. With these datasets you can create a copy activity in a pipeline. Both datasets are bi-directional. Although this scenario calls for reading the file data into SQLDB, the copy activity can use the SQLDB dataset as a source and the ADLS dataset as a file target. Let's create a copy activity to import the ADLS file into the SQLDB now.

12.3.4 Creating a copy activity and pipeline

In ADF, pipelines contain activities. This structure is expressed in the JSON files that define the pipeline. Aside from the ubiquitous `annotations` element, all the `properties` of the pipeline resource are activities in the pipeline. The `activities` element holds an array of activity definitions. There isn't a separate activity definition outside of a pipeline. Each pipeline can have one or more activities.

Recall from chapter 10 that an ADF pipeline with a copy activity looks like this:

- The pipeline has a single activity, a file to DB copy.
- The pipeline has a single trigger, using a schedule.
- The pipeline uses the *Integration Runtime* (IR) to manage the copy activity between the ADLS linkedservice and the SQLDB linkedservice.
- The IR handles commands for both linkedservices and monitors the activity for progress and errors.
- The Azure IR runs in Azure and connects to Azure resources.
- Each activity and pipeline execution collects metrics which can be reviewed later.

Figure 12.6 describes the steps for running this ADF pipeline.

Importing data with a copy activity works like the copy activity for binary files you saw in chapter 10. Two linkedservices are used for the source and destination, and two

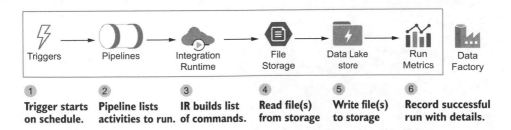

Figure 12.6   Pipeline processing steps

datasets define the read target and write target. For non-binary copies, the copy activity includes a schema translation.

The two datasets define their respective target schemas. To create a copy activity with a translation, you define the mapping between the schemas. For your user request, the target SQLDB data table uses a matching field structure as the CSV file target. Let's see how this schema mapping plays out.

SCHEMA MAPPING IN ACTIVITIES

ADF copy activities use many common elements, including name, type, dependency, and inputs and outputs. Recall from chapter 10 that the `dependsOn` array lists any pipeline activities that must execute before the copy activity. The inputs and outputs arrays define the source and destination datasets used in the copy.

Pipeline definitions with copy activities tend to be long documents. Listing 12.17 shows the JSON definition file for copying an ADLS data file into SQLDB with a single schema mapping. Before we get to the whole document, let's break out the new sections for the copy activity: source, sink, and translator. The source section is shown in listing 12.15, and the sink section in listing 12.16.

Under `typeProperties`, each ADF copy activity includes `source` and `sink` elements that describe the operations available. For a `source` targeting a row-based text file, like a CSV, we use `DelimitedTextReadSettings` under `formatSettings`.

Listing 12.15 Delimited source dataset in copy activity

```
"source": {
    "type": "DelimitedTextSource",
    "storeSettings": {
        "type": "AzureDataLakeStoreReadSettings",
        "recursive": true
    },
    "formatSettings": {
        "type": "DelimitedTextReadSettings"
    }
}
```

For a `sink` targeting a row-based text file, like a CSV, we use `DelimitedTextReadSettings` under `formatSettings`.

Listing 12.16 Delimited sink dataset in copy activity

```
"sink": {
    "type": "DelimitedTextSink",
    "storeSettings": {
        "type": "AzureDataLakeStoreWriteSettings"
    },
    "formatSettings": {
        "type": "DelimitedTextWriteSettings",
        "quoteAllText": true,
        "fileExtension": ".csv"
    }
}
```

Because the copy activity inserts data into the SQLDB, you should consider the impact of duplicates on the table. For instance, you may read the same data file into the table multiple times, each time appending the same data rows. To handle this duplication, you could do the following:

- Structure the table with an import date field that is set automatically, and adjust your queries to use the latest rows.
- Add an activity to execute a stored procedure that will clean up the duplicates or clear the table.
- First import the data into a staging table, and then add an activity that executes a stored procedure to merge the staging table.

For a `sink` targeting SQLDB, you have the option of running a SQL script before the data begins copying. This lets you prep the table where the data will land. With the `sinkpreCopyScript` element, you can execute a SQL script that clears the table before import.

```
"sink": {
    "type": "AzureSqlSink",
    "preCopyScript": "DELETE FROM [dbo].[PlayerDetails];",
    "disableMetricsCollection": false
}
```

> **TIP** ADF collects information about the database endpoint during execution, especially the scale unit like DWU, DTU, or RU for SQLDW, SQLDB, and Cosmos. You can set `disableMetricsCollection` to `true` to disable this. You can read more about creating activities in chapter 10.

When adding a copy activity, you also need to define the translation between the source and sink schemas in the `translator` element of `typeProperties`. Here we use a type of `TabularTranslator` and a `mappings` array to join a strongly typed field from the `source` to a strongly typed field in the `sink`. Each translation in the array is a pair of `name` and `type` elements, for the `source` and `sink`. The types are the same as listed earlier in the section.

```
"translator": {
    "type": "TabularTranslator",
    "mappings": [
        {
            "source": {
                "name": "PlayerId",
                "type": "String"
            },
            "sink": {
                "name": "PlayerId",
                "type": "String"
            }
        }
    ]
}
```

You can add any or all of the fields from the source as translations to the sink. The ADF authoring GUI in the Azure portal offers a wizard for adding copy activities to a pipeline. The wizard steps through configuring the details for the activity, source, and sink, and includes an automatic schema mapping feature. The completed activity and pipeline are backed by a JSON definition file that you can edit and download too.

> **TIP** There are many targets for copy activities in Data Factory. You can get an up-to-date list of them and the formats of their JSON definition files at http://mng.bz/QxRv.

Let's look at publishing the complete JSON file to ADF using Azure PowerShell.

USING AZURE POWERSHELL

Listing 12.17 shows the JSON definition file for copying an ADLS data file into SQLDB with a single schema mapping.

> **TIP** You can get the full version of listing 12.17 in the GitHub repository for this book at http://mng.bz/B2nw.

Listing 12.17   SQLDB copy activity and pipeline definition file

```json
{
    "name": "pipeline1",
    "properties": {
        "activities": [
            {
                "name": "Copy1",
                "type": "Copy",
                "dependsOn": [],
                "policy": {
                    "timeout": "0.01:00:00",
                    "retry": 0,
                    "retryIntervalInSeconds": 30,
                    "secureOutput": false,
                    "secureInput": false
                },
                "userProperties": [],
                "typeProperties": {
                    "source": {
                        "type": "DelimitedTextSource",
                        "storeSettings": {
                            "type": "AzureDataLakeStoreReadSettings",
                            "recursive": true
                        },
                        "formatSettings": {
                            "type": "DelimitedTextReadSettings"
                        }
                    },
                    "sink": {
                        "type": "AzureSqlSink",
                        "preCopyScript": "DELETE FROM [dbo].[PlayerDetails];",
                        "disableMetricsCollection": false
```

```
            },
            "enableStaging": false,
            "translator": {
                "type": "TabularTranslator",
                "mappings": [
                    {
                        "source": {
                            "name": "PlayerId",
                            "type": "String"
                        },
                        "sink": {
                            "name": "PlayerId",
                            "type": "String"
                        }
                    }
                ]              //Array
            }                  truncated
        },
        "inputs": [
            {
                "referenceName": "DelimitedText1",
                "type": "DatasetReference"
            }
        ],
        "outputs": [
            {
                "referenceName": "AzureSqlTable1",
                "type": "DatasetReference"
            }
        ]
    }
    ],
    "annotations": []
},
"type": "Microsoft.DataFactory/factories/pipelines"
}
```

You can upload this file to Azure Cloud Shell just as you did for the SQLDB linkedservice. Then you can run the Azure PowerShell command `Set-AzDataFactoryV2-Pipeline` to create the pipeline and copy activity. The following listing shows the script to create the pipeline.

> **Listing 12.18 Creating a new pipeline with Azure PowerShell**

```
Set-AzDataFactoryV2Pipeline  -ResourceGroupName "ade-dev-eastus2"
    -Name "pipeline2" -DataFactoryName "ade-dev-eastus2-adf" -File
    "~/adf/pipeline2.json"
```

This pipeline now contains the SQLDB copy activity. You can add the ADLA U-SQL activity and the daily schedule trigger from chapter 10 to complete this request. Copy activities form the core function of ADF, and significantly extend SQLDB's data ingestion capabilities.

With multiple methods for loading data into your SQLDB, your users can access analytic data in multiple ways. The Serving layer for your analytics system is ready to provide answers.

12.4   Exercises

The following exercises can help you internalize the new features introduced in this chapter. You should be able to create an ADF pipeline and connect two SQLDBs to support cross-database queries.

12.4.1 Exercise 1

Given an Azure Storage Blob file 2020-02-21.txt in container stats in account data, create the SQL scripts necessary to import the data into your SQLDB. The file has a header row, and two columns: an integer ID, and a decimal Level. Assume you have a master encryption key.

SOLUTION

The solution requires three steps:

1 Create a scoped credential with access to the Storage account.
2 Create an external data source pointing to the Storage container.
3 Use a BULK INSERT SQL command to import the file data.

> Listing 12.19   Saving an external username and password as scoped credential

```
CREATE DATABASE SCOPED CREDENTIAL [creds]
➥ WITH IDENTITY = 'SHARED ACCESS SIGNATURE',
➥ SECRET = '==key==';
```

> Listing 12.20   Creating an external data connection to a Blob file

```
CREATE EXTERNAL DATA SOURCE [blob1]
➥ WITH (TYPE = BLOB_STORAGE,
➥ LOCATION = 'https://data.blob.core.windows.net/stats',
➥ CREDENTIAL = [creds]);
```

> Listing 12.21   Importing data from Blob file with Bulk Insert

```
CREATE TABLE #Stats (ID int, Level decimal(18,5));
BULK INSERT [#blob_playerdetails]
➥ FROM 'PlayerDetails.txt'
➥ WITH (DATA_SOURCE = 'ade-dev-eastus2-blob-playerdata',
➥ FORMAT = 'CSV',
➥ FIRSTROW = 2);
```

12.4.2 Exercise 2

You have two SQLDBs, both running standalone—not in a Managed Instance or Hyperscale mode. Which of the following are required to read a database table from the other database?

1 Both SQLDBs must be on the same SQL Server.
2 Both SQLDBs must have matching user accounts.
3 Each SQLDB must have the table defined in the database.
4 Each SQLDB must define a database scoped credential.
5 The source SQLDB must list the source table as an external data source.

SOLUTION

Number 3 is required for reading from external tables. The source database stores a regular table. The target database stores an external table with the same schema.

The SQLDBs can be on different servers. The target database creates a scoped credential with a user from the source database, but a matching user doesn't need to be present in the target database. The source database doesn't need to add a scoped credential to allow outside connections. The target database defines the connection parameters for the source database in an external data source. The source database doesn't require any external data sources, external tables, or scoped credentials.

12.4.3 Exercise 3

Complete the following schema element from a copy activity definition.

Listing 12.22 Sample source file

```
"Id", "Level", "SampleTime"
1,20.3,"05:12:34:123"
2,1.0,"05:12:34:225"
3,180.33,"05:12:34:320"
```

Listing 12.23 Sample target table

```
CREATE TABLE Stats (ID int, Level decimal(18,5), SampleTime Time);
```

Listing 12.24 Sample mappings element

```
"mappings": [
  {
    "source": {
        "name": "Id",
        "type": _____
    },
    "sink": {
        "name": _____,
        "type": "Int"
    }
  },
```

```
    {
      "source": {
          "name": _____,
          "type": _____
      },
      "sink": {
          "name": "Level",
          "type": "Decimal"
      }
    },
    {
      "source": {
          "name": _____,
          "type": "Time"
      },
      "sink": {
          "name": _____,
          "type": _____
      }
    }
  }
]
```

SOLUTION

The mappings element defines the schema mapping from one data source to another. Using the file header and table definition, you can determine the source and sink name values. From the table definition, you can determine the sink type values. Most type values match between ADF and SQL types. You can refer to table 12.1 for more details.

Listing 12.25 Sample mappings element

```
"mappings": [
  {
    "source": {
        "name": "Id",
        "type": "Int"
    },
    "sink": {
        "name": "Id",
        "type": "Int"
    }
  },
  {
    "source": {
        "name": "Level",
        "type": "Decimal"
    },
    "sink": {
        "name": "Level",
        "type": "Decimal"
    }
  },
```

```
    {
      "source": {
          "name": "SampleTime",
          "type": "Time"
      },
      "sink": {
          "name": "SampleTime",
          "type": "Time"
      }
    }
]
```

You now have the knowledge to move data into and out of SQLDBs in multiple ways. The Serving layer of your Lambda analytics system is now complete.

Summary

- External data sources define connections to files and databases. Data sources allow importing data from Blob files and reading data from remote databases.
- External tables in SQLDB allow queries between isolated databases. Standalone SQLDB do not support cross-database queries using a server login.
- External tables can connect across security boundaries. They remain intact in databases restored from backups.
- The copy activity in Data Factory copies data between two data sources. The sources can be files, databases, and other endpoints.
- Schema mapping allows translation between the source formats. Using Data Factory allows loading data from sources not supported by SQL Database.

Where to go next

13

This chapter covers

- Making your data assets user friendly
- Keeping your data assets safe
- Keeping your development assets safe
- Proving your skills with Microsoft exams

You've reached the end of this book on building an analytics system in Azure using the Lambda architecture. Each chapter demonstrates part of the overall system. You can see flow of data through the system in figure 13.1.

The knowledge you've learned in this book can be applied more broadly too. Consider the following:

- Storage account services support backups of other Azure services, disks for Azure Virtual Machines, and durable, scalable storage for web applications.
- Queues and Event Hubs decouple components of applications. Use them in other systems for scalability and asynchronous processing.
- Relational databases are used in many multi-tiered software applications. The many flavors of SQLDB allow drop-in substitution for on-premises SQL Server databases.

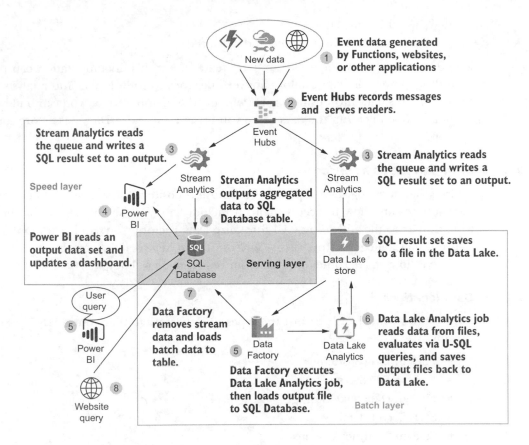

Figure 13.1 Lambda architecture with Azure PaaS services

- Azure Data Factory can connect to external cloud services like AWS S3 and Google Cloud Storage. It can trigger web hooks, and retrieve data from websites, FTP servers, and services like Salesforce.

As you begin gathering data and supporting analysis work, consider how you can encourage adoption and protection of the analytics system you've built. You can start by making a descriptive list of your data.

13.1 Data catalog

A data catalog is a source describing who, what, where, when, and how for the data you provide. Your data catalog is made up of metadata describing your data sources, including:

- Who are your data subject matter experts
- What application or entity generates the data
- Where the data resides

- When the data is updated
- How the data is transformed and delivered

The data catalog may seem like an extra feature, but this documentation can prove incredibly powerful. Data catalogs answer questions for developers and analysts who need to access data and business users who need to trust the data. You can build your catalog by documenting the data when you bring it into your Data Lake store for the first time.

13.1.1 Data Catalog as a service

Azure's Data Catalog service provides a central repository for storing metadata about data sources and how to access them. It includes a search facility and an authoring tool, similar to the authoring GUI for Azure Data Factory. You can learn more about Azure Data Catalog at https://azure.microsoft.com/services/data-catalog/.

The following are some questions your data catalog will help answer.

13.1.2 Data locations

Where does your data live? List the types of data storage that your analytics system supports:

- Files in Blog Storage
- Files in File Storage
- Files in Data Lake Storage
- SQL Server databases
- Stream Analytics streams
- Other Azure database services

Data in Queue Storage, Event Hubs, and Service Bus topics count as data generators rather than data stores. You may want to track the upstream source of these data streams.

How is your data generated? Your analytics system uses data that has been saved to persistent storage. This can take the form of database tables, data files, and unstructured sources like video and audio. You can record the generating application and the type of storage used for discrete output—delimited file, data table, structured data files, images, audio, and video. You can also record which department or team is responsible for the application.

13.1.3 Data definitions

What is the shape of the data at rest? Record the schema used for the data. This could be delimited file columns, table columns, or a data structure like JSON. Include any row and column delimiters, and data gaps and errors that must be controlled. Include versions of the schema as data drift occurs over time. This will allow users to work with the data easily, without inspecting it and choosing the schema themselves.

How is the data transformed? New data often undergoes several processing steps before it is ready for consumption. This can include validation, error identification and remediation, and aggregation. If these steps are available as separate data sources, record the step as a data source and reference the preceding and following steps in the process. Reports and data aggregations lie at the end of the chain, and the chain lets you review the data sources. This chain of data transformations will give users greater confidence in the data they use.

13.1.4 Data frequency

What is the schedule for data generation? Some data is available in real-time or near real-time. For example, you may collect data from IoT devices, or web and mobile applications. Some data is collected offline and delivered when network access is available. Some data is exported on hourly, daily, or monthly schedules. This schedule will limit the use cases available. For example, dashboards use real-time data, but aren't suitable for weekly and monthly data sets.

When is the data updated? Some data sets are written to durable storage once and never updated. Some are overwritten with each new export. Some are corrected after the initial generation. Each approach to data updates can be described in your data catalog.

If you have designed your analytics system with a Lambda architecture, you will maintain an original version of the data. Subsequently updated data is stored separately from the original. This allows updates and corrections to be made as many times as needed to derive the best data.

Storage data sets using dates in the folder paths also helps determine the state of data updates over time. For data updated each month, as opposed to data added each month, separating the updates into monthly folders or files lets you analyze data at a point in time. Updated or appended data should be noted in the data catalog.

13.1.5 Business drivers

Creating and maintaining a data catalog for your analytics system provides business value. The data catalog should make it easier for your end users to extract value from the data you manage. This can come in the form of reports, machine learning algorithms, or questions answered by data scientists. If you don't have those types of business drivers, you may not need a data catalog. You should implement backup and recovery processes in all cases.

13.2 Version control and backups

This book describes Azure services that function as Platform-as-a-Service (PaaS) or Software-as-a-Service resources (SaaS). PaaS services require some configuration to get running, then some amount of development work to use. Azure Stream Analytics, Data Lake Analytics, and Data Factory fall into this category. For PaaS services, you want to protect the configuration and the development output from loss. For SaaS services, the configuration and data are most important for recovery. No development work per se is required, but the act of using the software generates valuable assets. You can and should include backups for these assets. Let's explore the options available for your Azure resources.

13.2.1 *Blob Storage*

If you are using Azure PowerShell to provision your Storage accounts, it's a trivial exercise to version control the configuration assets, the PowerShell scripts. You can save the scripts as text files, and include them in a source control repository of your choice. Data backups are more problematic.

Storage accounts are built on redundant storage. At the Local Redundant Storage (LRS) level, at least three copies are kept in the local data center. Other levels include replication to other data centers. This prevents file loss but doesn't prevent data loss within the file.

Blob Storage has a facility for versioning a file, called *snapshots*. A snapshot is a version of a file saved at a specific time. Each snapshot is set individually on each individual file. Deleting the file deletes the snapshots. There is no feature to turn on automatic snapshots for Blob Storage.

You can use Azure Data Factory (ADF) to back up Blob Storage. Using a binary copy activity in a pipeline, you can schedule file copies from one Storage account to another. You can configure the activity to only copy new and modified files. The ADF authoring GUI includes templates to set up pipelines like this easily. See the documentation at http://mng.bz/dyBg for more information.

13.2.2 *Data Lake Storage*

Much like Blob Storage, Azure Data Lake Storage (ADLS) replicates files locally. ADLS doesn't include a backup service for versioning files. ADF copy activities also work for backing up files to guard against data loss.

Using multiple copy activities in ADF pipelines lets you control which data sets are copied. Some questions to consider include the following:

- Are some data sets exports from external systems with their own backups?
- Are some projects obsolete and don't require recovery in the event of data loss?
- Are there requirements for data retention?
- For aggregate or batch processing outputs, how much time is required to re-create the data sets?
- Do data sets lose business value over time, and if so, should they be excluded from backup?

Structuring your ADLS store using the zones framework gives you options for selective backup. For example:

- Staging data sets don't require backups.
- Curated data sets can usually be re-created via batch processing.
- Raw data sets can be selected by most recent version or excluded by project.

Complexity and maintenance of backup activities must be balanced against storage cost and business value.

13.2.3 Stream Analytics

Beyond the basics of Stream Analytics (SA) service creation, you have the streaming calculations themselves. When using Azure PowerShell to create SA jobs, you save the job queries in JSON definition files. These can be kept in a source control repository.

When using Visual Studio for Azure development, you can build SA jobs and transformations in an SA project. Install the Azure Stream Analytics tools for Visual Studio to create this type of project. The tools let you create jobs and publish to your SA services. Get them at http://mng.bz/rrpx.

13.2.4 Data Lake Analytics

Beyond the basics of Data Lake Analytics (ADLA) service creation, you have the U-SQL scripts themselves. When using Azure PowerShell to create U-SQL jobs, you save the U-SQL scripts in text files. These files can be kept in a source control repository.

When using Visual Studio for Azure development, you can build and debug U-SQL scripts in an ADLA project. Install the Data Lake Tools for Visual Studio to create this type of project. The tools let you submit jobs to your ADLA services. Get them at http://mng.bz/Vg5N.

13.2.5 Data Factory configuration files

Now that you can create pipelines for multiple types of functionality, you might wonder how you can provide safeguards for your ADF processes. Although the ADF system runs on distributed, redundant Azure systems, by default it provides limited backup functionality. But thanks to the JSON configuration files backing the ADF resources, you can make copies of the files and resources as you wish. ADF also comes with a more sophisticated version of file copies.

The Azure portal provides a web-based GUI for creating pipelines, linkedservices, data sets, and triggers. This GUI generates JSON files that define the resources. The GUI helps you look up Azure services to use in linkedservices, read schemas from files to configure datasets, and create triggers for pipelines. It also validates the resulting JSON definition files before deploying for execution. You can access the GUI in the Azure portal by browsing to your ADF service > Overview > Author & Monitor button.

Each ADF service has two environments: one to edit resources (development) and one to execute pipelines (production). Using the authoring GUI, you can make changes in development without impacting existing pipeline runs. Once you have created your linkedservices, data sets, pipelines and activities, and triggers, you must promote the definition files to production. Once in production, enabled triggers will invoke IRs to process the pipeline activities.

1 ADF uses the definition files to configure the production environment. This environment is completely managed for you.

2   Once you have completed configuring the resources for your ADF, you must publish the definition files to production.

3   The pipelines are then operational and can be started by the configured triggers.

4   The activities within a running pipeline are executed by an IR, either in Azure or on-premises.

Figure 13.2 shows this workflow in action.

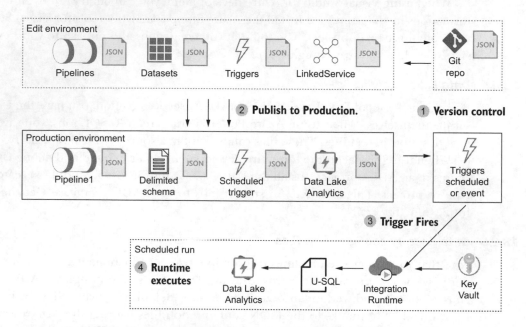

Figure 13.2   Data Factory code promotion

Because ADF uses JSON files to define all its resources, the ADF store can be version controlled too. You have two approaches to version control with ADF: external or integrated. You can use any form of external version control you like. With external version control, save the files in your repository as you would other files. For integrated version control, ADF services can be configured using Git. You can run your edit environment with or without integrated version control. Let's see how to configure an ADF with Git.

GIT VERSION CONTROL

ADF services can be configured using Git version control. Git is used to keep track of changes to source code, the JSON definition files. You can keep your ADF resource definitions under version control to make it easier to revert to previous configured states and provide recovery options if the service is deleted.

Saving and publishing are tightly integrated with Git when using version control. Saving changes to ADF resources automatically commits to Git. You can create new branches from the ADF authoring GUI or directly to the Git repository. You can publish to production from any branch. Even without using a branching strategy, enabling version control lets you review change history and revert changes in the ADF service.

ADF provides integrations for two version control systems: Azure DevOps Git and GitHub. Azure DevOps (AZDO) is a collection of services for planning, controlling, compiling, and deploying application code. AZDO uses Git for source code version control. GitHub is a hosting platform for Git. Both integrations require an account name, repository name, branch name, and root folder to support reading a Git repository for configuration.

TIP You can learn more about Azure DevOps in "What is Azure DevOps?" at http://mng.bz/xWN7.

Using Azure portal
In the Azure portal, you provide the Git URL, repository name, branch name, and root folder when creating a new ADF service with version control. You can also enable version control on an existing service in the authoring GUI.

1 Browse to the Overview blade of the ADF service.
2 Click the Author & Monitor button to launch the authoring GUI in a new window.
3 Switch to the Authoring tab in the left nav.
4 Click the Data Factory drop-down in the top left corner, and select Setup Code Repository.
5 Choose a Repository type, either AZDO Git or GitHub.
6 Choose an AZDO account, or enter the GitHub account to use.
7 Choose an AZDO project if using AZDO.
8 Choose an existing repository for GitHub.
   a When choosing a GitHub account, ADF will attempt to authenticate to GitHub and retrieve a list of repositories.
   b ADF will open a pop-up login window to GitHub to authenticate and authorize the service.
9 Choose an existing repository for AZDO, or create a new one.
   a When creating a new repository, choose a collaboration branch to use. Master is the default.
10 Choose a collaboration branch to use. This is the base branch for new branches, typically Master or Default.
11 If you have created resources, choose to import existing ADF resources into version control, or not; it's up to you. I mean, I'd do it. Why not save that work? Branches are practically free.
   a You can import the existing JSON definition files into a new or existing branch.
12 Click Apply to set the version control configuration.

The Git URL can point to a user with access to the repository, or the URL of an AZDO organization and project hosting the repository. Examples include https://github.com/rnuckolls for GitHub, and https://dev.azure.com/azure99999/ade-dev-eastus2-adf for AZDO. In the latter case, azure99999 is the organization, and ade-dev-eastus2-adf is the project. Use the name of the ADF service /ade-dev-eastus2-adf in the root folder value for the repository root. ADF will make commits here.

NOTE Access must be granted to the repository for ADF to make updates when version control is enabled. Access is controlled via OAuth in GitHub, and granted to the AzureDataFactory account. Figure 13.3 shows the GitHub access control screen.

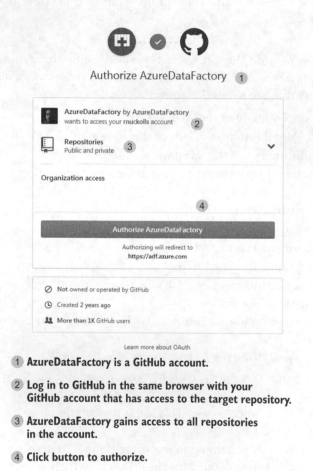

1. **AzureDataFactory is a GitHub account.**

2. **Log in to GitHub in the same browser with your GitHub account that has access to the target repository.**

3. **AzureDataFactory gains access to all repositories in the account.**

4. **Click button to authorize.**

Figure 13.3   Granting GitHub access to ADF via OAuth

Access is controlled via AAD for AZDO, and granted to the active AAD user with the built-in AZDO repository controls.

Using Azure PowerShell

Creating an ADF service under version control with Azure PowerShell works the same as without version control. You can create a new ADF service using the `New-AzDataFactoryV2` command, and add the repository values with parameters. Table 13.1 shows the list of parameters. You can create the service first, then configure version control later using `Set-AzDataFactoryV2` too.

Table 13.1 Version control parameters

Parameter	Service	Value description
AccountName	Both	The organization hosting the DevOps repository, or the GitHub user account
RepositoryName	Both	Limited to alphanumeric plus hyphens and underscores
CollaborationBranch	Both	Typically Master, but can follow your version control branching strategy
RootFolder	Both	Use / for the root, or a path to the definition files
HostName	GitHub	Use https://github.com
ProjectName	Azure DevOps	The specific DevOps project hosting the repository

You can run the script in the following listing to update or create the ADF V2 service under version control with GitHub.

Listing 13.1 Updating a GitHub version controlled ADF service with Azure PowerShell

```
Set-AzDataFactoryV2 -ResourceGroupName "ade-dev-eastus2"
    -Name "ade-dev-eastus2-adf" -Location "EastUS2"
    -HostName 'https://github.com'
    -AccountName "github-account"
    -RepositoryName "ade-dev-eastus2-adf"
    -CollaborationBranch "master" -RootFolder "/"
```

HostName is always https://github.com.

https://github.com/rnuckolls is my GitHub account.

To use GitHub repositories, you need to authorize the AzureDataFactory application. To do this, you must use the ADF GUI. In the ADF GUI, open the Home page and click the Git Repo Settings button in the top right corner. If ADF is not authorized to access the configured account and repository, the GUI will open a pop-up, and prompt you to log in and/or authorize the AzureDataFactory to access the account repositories.

> **WARNING** When using a GitHub account, you will need to authorize the AzureDataFactory user to access the repository via OAuth. The user will have full permissions to all repositories in the GitHub account. You should carefully weigh access controls when using version control with ADF on GitHub. One approach to limiting access is to host your ADF definitions in a separate account. That way, ADF only has access to repositories under that account. You can read more about it at http://mng.bz/AA6e.

To use AZDO, use the `Set-AzDataFactoryV2` command, with the `ProjectName` parameter instead of `HostName`. You can find the `AccountName` and `ProjectName` values using the URL of your AZDO instance, like the following:

```
https://{AccountName}.visualstudio.com/{ProjectName} https://dev.azure.com/{
AccountName}/{ProjectName}
```

You can run the script in the following listing to update or create the ADF V2 service under version control with AZDO.

Listing 13.2   Updating an AZDO version controlled ADF service with Azure PowerShell

```
Set-AzDataFactoryV2 -ResourceGroupName "ade-dev-eastus2"
    -Name "ade-dev-eastus2-adf" -Location "EastUS2"
    -AccountName "azure99999"
    -ProjectName "YourProject"
    -RepositoryName "ade-dev-eastus2-adf"
    -CollaborationBranch "master" -RootFolder "/"
```

Also known as
organization in AZDO

An account can have
multiple projects.

> **IMPORTANT**   Before using an AZDO repository in ADF, you must initialize the repository. This means creating the first branch. AZDO defaults to Master as the main branch. Create the branch, using the DevOps portal or a Git tool, then configure ADF to use the repository.

Enabling version control is typically the last step you'll take when using PowerShell to interact with a specific ADF service, because version control complicates the ADF authoring and deployment workflow. From this point forward, you'll use the authoring GUI or a text editor and Git. Let's look at the reason behind this workflow change.

USING ADF WITH GIT VERSION CONTROL

Version control functions differently between the authoring GUI and Azure Power-Shell. The authoring GUI commits changes to linkedservices, datasets, and triggers upon edit completion. Pipeline and activity changes aren't committed until you click Save All. Overall updates to the service are only pushed to production when you click Publish. Publishing commits to a special repository branch called adf_publish, which contains Azure Resource Manager (ARM) templates for creating the service. These templates create the production environment.

Azure PowerShell writes directly to the non-version controlled development and production environments. When version control is enabled, the authoring GUI uses a Git editing environment, separate from the development environment. This means changes made using Azure PowerShell are not committed to Git, and are not present in the authoring GUI under version control. Publishing in the authoring GUI from the non-version-controlled ADF edit environment and branches other than the collaboration branch is also disabled. Publishing in the authoring GUI is only allowed from the collaboration branch.

So if you use Azure PowerShell to update the ADF after enabling version control, your edit and production environments can fall out of sync. Changes to the version-controlled edit environment are checked against the adf_publish branch during publish. If no differences are detected, the change is not published. In short, once you enable version control on the ADF, stop using Azure PowerShell to update it. Use the authoring GUI or commit directly to your Git repository.

> **WARNING** If your version-controlled authoring GUI editing environment gets out of sync, and you can't publish, disconnect version control and then reconnect. Use the Azure PowerShell `Set-AzDataFactoryV2` command, without the version control parameters, to disconnect. When using the authoring GUI to reconnect, choose to not import existing ADF resources, if the resources would be incorrect.

It's especially important when using version-controlled ADF that you use Azure Key Vault or Managed Identities for linkedservice connections. The configuration files are added to Git repositories, which may have different security restrictions than the ADF and the linkedservice endpoints. Best practice is to not save passwords, keys, and other access tokens in version control repositories.

Using Git prevents creating new resources in ADF from within the New Resource Creation blade. Chain resource creation can be handy when creating new pipelines. But resource creation commits the new resource to Git on save, and validates required resources. This happens against the production environment. The resources with dependencies must be created after the dependency has been published to production. This is done from the collaboration branch. If you use a branching strategy, with code reviews and pull requests, you will need to plan a staggered release of ADF resources.

Even with all these constraints, using version control with ADF is recommended. You get the benefits of version control processes, like code reviews and backups, with an integrated system. Using AZDO also lets you automate the production deployment or multiple environment deployments using AZDO pipelines. You can read more about AZDO at http://mng.bz/Z2yN.

13.2.6 *SQL Database*

SQLDB has backups covered. Recall from chapter 11 that backups are taken at regular intervals and that you can manage long-term retention. But what about version control?

Version control for database schemas or data changes requires a time commitment to a specific solution. Several commercial and open-source options are available, like Redgate SQL Source Control and Liquibase by Datical. These let you track changes to the database objects. Microsoft developers can use Entity Framework (EF) Code First design to build your database based on class code. You classes are tracked with version control. You can read more about EF Code First design at http://mng.bz/RARR.

Backup and recovery plans are part of any production-ready system. You should plan your response to an outage or a disaster. You can present your plan to the system business owner, and implement the processes that the business deems worth the cost. Bolster the case for your plans by demonstrating your expertise with Microsoft certifications.

13.3 *Microsoft certifications*

Microsoft certifications have long been a method for demonstrating competency, when looking for new positions or promotions. Certifications can be part of Microsoft partner programs supporting businesses. Books have traditionally been part of preparing for an exam.

At the time of writing, there are two exams for the Azure Data Engineer Associate certification:

1 DP-200: Implementing an Azure Data Solution
2 DP-201: Designing an Azure Data Solution

Many of the topics for these exams are covered in this book. Learn Blob Storage provisioning in chapter 3, and usage with various services throughout. Configure SQLDB for high availability and security in chapter 11. Integrate SQLDB with other services and choose the right database technology. Build Data Factory pipelines in chapters 10 and 12. Process data with Stream Analytics in chapter 6. Choosing the right authentication method and securing assets is covered in multiple chapters. This includes AAD authentication using Managed Identities and SAS with Storage accounts.

Use this book as part of your overall course of study for Azure exam topics. Get a free Azure account for testing out the services discussed in this book and more. If you have an MSDN subscription, you get credits every month to use for development and testing using Azure services. Most of the services have a free tier or usage level that lets you study and test your knowledge at a low cost. Reading and working hands-on examples is a strong method for learning new skills. Exposure to a broad swath of options is one of the best benefits you can get from studying for Microsoft exams.

13.4 *Signing off*

Good luck in your pursuit of data engineering. I hope you have learned as much from reading this book as I have from writing it. Azure cloud technologies continue to improve and new services come online. This book represents an island in this flow of change, showcasing software with a limited scope. As Azure grows and changes, you'll be able to learn and grow with it. May your data lake be deep and clear, and your cloud processing always come with a silver lining.

Summary

- You build an analytics system for the benefit of data consumers. You can help them use your system by documenting the data assets available.
- Azure handles the work of keeping your services online. To a greater or lesser degree, you must do the work of keeping your configuration effort safe.

- Azure Data Factory integrates with Git repositories. You can add version control processes for ADF and gain the benefits of code review and backups for your JSON definition files.
- Microsoft certifications demonstrate your knowledge. The act of preparing yields a personal benefit beyond just earning the certification.

appendix A
Setting up Azure services through PowerShell

This appendix covers setting up Azure resources for the examples in the book. These PowerShell scripts can help you quickly get your Azure environment setup for use with chapter scripts. The scripts in this book have been developed using Azure PowerShell version 3.8.0 and earlier. See http://mng.bz/X01a for a full command reference. You should already be familiar with the Azure portal. This book uses the portal to set up services, as the GUI makes discovering the many options available easy.

Some features in Azure cannot be configured through the portal, and some can be configured only through the portal. PowerShell is a powerful tool, and the examples in this book only scratch the surface of what's possible. Read *Learn Windows PowerShell in a Month of Lunches, 3rd ed.* (Manning, 2016) by Don Jones and Jeffrey Hicks for a much deeper view.

TIP If you don't have the latest Azure PowerShell module installed, Azure offers Cloud Shell. You can access Cloud Shell from the Azure portal, or by connecting to https://shell.azure.com. First-time Cloud Shell setup requires a Resource group and Storage account. You will also choose PowerShell instead of Bash for your shell environment. You can create a new group and Storage account right from Cloud Shell, specifically for Cloud Shell use. Azure Cloud Shell is tied to a user account, so you will have access to all your subscriptions, but you will need to select a subscription to store the settings and local scripts used in the command window.

A.1 *Setting up Azure PowerShell*

If you already have a working Azure PowerShell setup, or want to use Cloud Shell, you can skip to the next section.

Getting Azure PowerShell installed on your machine may be complicated. Different versions of Windows come with different versions of PowerShell. Azure PowerShell requires PowerShell 5.x and .NET 4.7.2 on Windows. Here are a few steps that can help.

- Run cmd.exe as Administrator.
- Run the following cmdlets to install the Azure PowerShell package.

```
powershell.exe -ExecutionPolicy Unrestricted
```

This command will start PowerShell, and the ExecutionPolicy setting allows the installation of packages.

Install-Module installs PowerShell modules. If you install modules from public repos, even from Microsoft's own PSGallery, the modules are treated as untrusted. PowerShell will ask you to confirm the installation before proceeding. You can override this behavior on a per-install basis using the Force parameter. This following script will install the Azure PowerShell module, updating earlier cmdlets if present using the AllowClobber parameter. You can set the target repository with the Repository parameter.

```
Install-Module -Name Az -Repository PSGallery -Force -AllowClobber
```

This loads Azure PowerShell into memory for use.

```
Import-Module Az
```

This generates a token for connecting the session to Azure. Follow the instructions on-screen, going to https://microsoft.com/devicelogin to enter your token.

```
Connect-AzAccount
```

Connect-AzAccount connects subsequent Az PowerShell commands to the default subscription for the account. You can set a different subscription to use with Set-AzContext. Look up the subscription you want to use and pass the ID to the command.

```
$Sub = Get-AzSubscription -SubscriptionName "{SubNameHere}"
Set-AzContext -SubscriptionId $Sub.Id
```

You can modify a Windows shortcut for PowerShell by passing -ExecutionPolicy Unrestricted, and run these PowerShell script in a PowerShell window. See http://mng.bz/2Woo for more information.

Now that you have a working PowerShell environment, you can use PowerShell and the Azure PowerShell cmdlets to create and modify services in Azure. In the next section, you'll set up the basic resources needed for working with Azure services and completing the examples and exercises in this book. Set up these basic resources before moving on to creating any other Azure services.

A.2   Create a subscription

In order to follow along with the examples, you'll need an Azure subscription. Signing up for a personal account and subscription takes an email address, a phone number, and a credit card. Visit https://azure.microsoft.com/free/ to start your free trial. All of the Azure services described in this book are available during the trial period.

A.3   Azure naming conventions

Every Azure service, also called a *resource*, must have a name. Consistently applying a naming convention helps users find services, and identify ownership and usage of services. Since some resource names require lowercase characters, and most resources are addressable via URL, make your names lowercase from the start. A working naming convention incorporates several aspects of managing cloud resources:

- Project, system, or owning organization
- Environment or deployment stage, such as Development, Staging, or Production
- Region, or lack thereof
- Supported function, such as web, tools, api, batch, daily or other description
- Multiple instances, using a numeric suffix

This book uses a naming convention with these elements where necessary.

> **Listing A.1   Naming convention**

```
[REGION]-[PROJECT]-[ENVIRO]-[FUNCTION]-[SUBFUNCTION]-[NN]
```

Suppose we need two SQL Databases for development, in the East US 2 region, for Azure Data Engineering (ADE), supporting baseball statistics. This gives us a name like ade-dev-eastus2-sql-baseball. You can read about Microsoft's recommendations for resource naming at http://mng.bz/1g6Q.

A.4   Setting up common Azure resources using PowerShell

In this section, you'll learn how to set up some common Azure resources using PowerShell. You'll need access to an instance of PowerShell with the Azure PowerShell module loaded to run these scripts. This can be a local PowerShell install, or you can use Azure Cloud Shell: https://shell.azure.com. You'll create a resource group which you can use for all the examples and exercises. You'll create an AAD user and security group, which you can use to test security on Azure resources with accounts different than your primary owner account. These basic resource types are useful throughout your Azure service use.

A.4.1 Creating a new resource group

Resource groups in Azure are organizing containers. Every Azure service has one. Every resource group has a region. The resource group anchors a service to a region, with the primary configuration data for the service stored in that region. This is especially true for some global services, like Cosmos DB and Traffic Manager, which have infrastructure in every region. Deleting a resource group deletes all the services attached to it. This book uses ade-dev-eastus2 as the resource group for any scripts which require it. You should choose a naming convention which make sense for your situation. This book uses the East US 2 region for any scripts which require it, since all resources in the book are available in that region. The following listing shows how to create a new resource group and retrieve a list of all resource groups.

Listing A.2 New resource group

```
New-AzResourceGroup -Name "ade-dev-eastus2" -Location "East US 2"
Get-AzResourceGroup
```

Execute this line in PowerShell with the Azure Modules loaded. This script will return an error if a group by that name exists. Otherwise it will create a new resource group, then list the resource groups in the current subscription. There are many regions, or locations, for hosting Azure resources across the globe, including the Americas, Europe, Asia Pacific, and the Middle East and Africa. You can see the current list of services by region at http://mng.bz/OvGR.

A.4.2 Creating a new Azure Active Directory user

Azure uses Azure Active Directory (AAD) extensively for user and service authentication. Setup, examples, and exercises in this book make use of AAD users and groups. You should already be familiar with the Azure portal, and using Active Directory for authentication and authorization to Azure services. The following listing creates two new AAD users.

Listing A.3 New AAD user

```
$SecureStringPassword = ConvertTo-SecureString -String "Password1!"
    -AsPlainText -Force
$User = New-AzADUser -DisplayName "Tech User"
➡   -UserPrincipalName "techuser@domain.onmicrosoft.com"
➡   -Password $SecureStringPassword -MailNickname "techuser"
$SecureStringPassword = ConvertTo-SecureString -String "Password1!"
    -AsPlainText -Force
$User2 = New-AzADUser -DisplayName "Finance User"
➡   -UserPrincipalName "financeuser@domain.onmicrosoft.com"
➡   -Password $SecureStringPassword -MailNickname "financeuser"
```

Execute these lines in PowerShell with the Azure PowerShell module loaded. This script will return an error if a group by that name exists. The first line creates a Password object. Don't use Password1! The second will create a new user `techuser`. You need to construct a `UserPrincipalName` using one of the AAD registered domains. You'll repeat these steps for a new user `finance`.

> **NOTE** If you are using an Azure subscription without a corporate Active Directory, then your domain will be some variation of the email you used to sign up with Azure. You can find this value by going to the AAD service's Overview blade. The domain is listed above the header Default Directory, as well as in the Custom Domain Names blade.

A.4.3   *Creating a new Azure Active Directory group*

Now create a new security group for Technical Operations, and add `techuser` to this group. Execute listing A.4 in PowerShell with the Azure PowerShell module loaded. You'll repeat these steps for the `finance` user. This script will return an error if a group by that name exists.

Listing A.4   New AAD group

```
$Group = New-AzADGroup -DisplayName "Technical Operations" -MailNickname
    "TechOps"
Add-AzADGroupMember -MemberObjectId $User.Id -TargetGroupObjectId $Group.Id
$Group2 = New-AzADGroup -DisplayName "Finance" -MailNickname "Finance"
Add-AzADGroupMember -MemberObjectId $User2.Id -TargetGroupObjectId $Group2.Id
```

Now you've set up the basic resources in Azure using PowerShell. You've learned why you need a resource group in Azure, and how to create one. You've created a user and a security group for Technical Operations and Finance in AAD. Now you can use them when securing other resources in Azure. In the next section you'll create a Storage account.

A.5   *Setting up Azure services using PowerShell*

In this section, you'll provision the required Azure services for your analytics system. These include:

- Storage account
- Data Lake Storage
- Event Hubs
- Stream Analytics
- Data Lake Analytics
- SQL Server and SQL Database
- Data Factory
- Key Vault

A.5.1 Creating a new Storage account

Now you'll create a Storage account using Azure PowerShell. The Storage account cmdlet needs four pieces of information.

1 The resource group created in listing A.2.
2 A name, referencing the same values from the resource group.
3 A replication SKU, for the default Read Access Geo-redundant Storage.
4 A location, the same region as the resource group.

Execute listing A.5 in Azure PowerShell. This script will return an error if a Storage account by that name exists.

Listing A.5 Create a new Storage account

Account name must be alphanumeric.

```
New-AzStorageAccount -ResourceGroupName "ade-dev-eastus2" -AccountName
    "adedeveastus2" `
-SkuName Standard_RAGRS -Location "East US 2" `
-EnableHttpsTrafficOnly 1 -Kind "StorageV2"
```

Allowing only HTTPS traffic increases security.

Choose RAGRS for maximum redundancy, LRS for minimal redundancy.

There are multiple values for the Replication SKU, which we cover in chapter 3. The default value includes the most redundancy. Other values are less expensive, but have less redundancy.

There are multiple values for the Kind command.

- Storage, which includes Blobs, Tables, Queues, Files and Disks services
- StorageV2, the default, which includes Blobs, Tables, Queues, Files and Disks services and adds Hot/Cold/Archive tiered storage
- BlobStorage, which only supports Blob Storage

Now you've learned how to create a Storage account using Azure PowerShell.

A.5.2 Creating a new Data Lake store

Creating a Data Lake store works the same as most Azure resources. Use the New-AzDataLakeStoreAccount command and provide the basic properties of name, resource group, and location. The cmdlet takes three pieces of information.

1 The resource group created in listing A.2.
2 A name, referencing the same values from the resource group, alphanumeric only.
3 A location, the same region as the resource group.

Execute the following listing in Azure PowerShell to create a new Data Lake store.

Listing A.6   Create new Data Lake store

```
New-AzDataLakeStoreAccount -ResourceGroupName "ade-dev-eastus2"
    -Name "adedeveastus2" -Location "East US 2"
```

This script will return an error if a Data Lake store by that name exists, or if the service is not available in the selected region. Keep resources within the same region. Data Lake Storage has the fewest available regions. It's a good idea to select one of these regions before creating the rest of your resource in Azure, to keep all resources in the same region. This lowers the latency of network communication between resources.

You can also specify some other options during setup. You can add key/value pairs, called *tags*, to Azure resources to help locate them later. If you know your storage size, you can pre-purchase storage at a discounted rate using the `-Tier` parameter.

Listing A.7   Create new Data Lake store with options

```
New-AzDataLakeStoreAccount -ResourceGroupName "ade-dev-eastus2"
-Name "adedeveastus2" -Location "East US 2" -Tag @{User="ADE";} -Tier
Commitment1TB -DefaultGroup (Get-AzADGroup -DisplayName "Technical
    Operations").Id
```

`-DefaultGroup` will set the owning group for your root folder and other folders in the Data Lake store. Add a tag for management of resources. This is especially nice when browsing the All Resources blade in the portal, because you can select from a list of all the tags you have provided. Use a consumption plan, until you calculate your monthly storage needs. After you find your usage, sign up for recurring billing of the committed storage.

A.5.3   *Create new Event Hub*

Creating and configuring an Event Hub is covered in chapter 5. Creating an Event Hub using PowerShell requires two steps: creating an Event Hubs namespace and creating the Event Hub. Both AMQP and Kafka protocols require a fully-qualified domain name (FQDN) endpoint to submit messages to. In Event Hubs, this is called the *Event Hubs namespace*. The namespace can be thought of as the gateway or load balancer for one or more Event Hubs. You need to create the namespace before creating an Event Hub. The following listing shows how to create the namespace with Azure PowerShell.

Listing A.8   Create a new Azure Event Hub namespace using PowerShell

Standard tier, 1 throughput unit

```
New-AzEventHubNamespace -ResourceGroupName "ade-dev-eastus2"
    -NamespaceName "ade-dev-eastus2-hubs" -Location "East US 2"
    -SkuName "Standard" -SkuCapacity 1
    -Tag @{User="ADE";}                    ◁─── Tag this resource with
                                                ADE, to aid in searching.
```

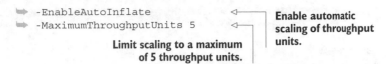

```
-EnableAutoInflate
-MaximumThroughputUnits 5
```
Limit scaling to a maximum of 5 throughput units.

Enable automatic scaling of throughput units.

Once you have the namespace created, you can create the Event Hub. Run the following script to create the Event Hub with two partitions and message retention of one day.

Listing A.9 Create an Event Hub

```
New-AzEventHub -ResourceGroupName "ade-dev-eastus2"
-NamespaceName "ade-dev-eastus2-hubs" -Name "biometricstats"
-MessageRetentionInDays 1
-PartitionCount 2
```
Up to 32 partitions included in the Throughput Unit rate

One day of message retention (storage) included in the Throughput Unit rate

The script in listing A.10 creates a new Staging folder for collecting statistics, and sets the necessary permissions for Event Hubs. The script will prompt to overwrite the folder if present. The final step applies the permissions over any existing folders and files.

Listing A.10 Set access permissions for Event Hubs service

```
$pri = Get-AzADServicePrincipal
-DisplayName Microsoft.EventHubs
$store = "adedeveastus2"
New-AzDataLakeStoreItem -AccountName $store
-Path "/Staging/playerstats" -Folder

Set-AzDataLakeStoreItemAclEntry -AccountName $store -Path /
-AceType User -Id $pri.Id -Permissions Execute
Set-AzDataLakeStoreItemAclEntry -AccountName $store -Path /Staging
-AceType User -Id $pri.Id -Permissions Execute
Set-AzDataLakeStoreItemAclEntry -AccountName $store
-Path /Staging/playerstats -AceType User -Id $pri.Id
-Permissions All -Default
Set-AzDataLakeStoreItemAclEntry -AccountName $store
-Path /Staging/playerstats -AceType User -Id $pri.Id
-Permissions All -Recurse -Concurrency 128
```

Get the account for the Event Hub service.

Create a folder in the Data Lake store.

Set list access for the service at the root and Staging folders.

Set full access for the service at the Staging/playerstats folder, for new items.

Set full access for the service at the Staging/playerstats folder, for existing items.

A.5.4 Create new Stream Analytics job

Creating and configuring a Stream Analytics job is covered in chapter 6. Creating an ASA job using PowerShell requires two steps: creating a JSON configuration file and executing a Azure PowerShell command referencing the file. The following listing contains the creation configuration file.

Listing A.11   ASA job configuration file

```
{
    "location":"EastUS2",
    "properties":{
        "sku":{
            "name":"Standard"
        },
        "eventsOutOfOrderPolicy":"Adjust",
        "outputErrorPolicy": "Stop",
        "eventsOutOfOrderMaxDelayInSeconds":10,
        "eventsLateArrivalMaxDelayInSeconds":5,
        "compatibilityLevel": 1.1
    }
}
```

Follow these steps to create the file.

1 Open and log in to Cloud Shell in a web browser at https://shell.azure.com/.
2 Choose the PowerShell environment instead of Bash. If necessary, switch to PowerShell using the environment selector in the top left corner of the page.
3 Type `mkdir asa` in the window to create a folder "asa" to store the ASA job files.
4 Type `cd asa` to switch to the new folder.
5 Type `code streamingjob.json` to create a new file in the Cloud Shell editor in the folder.
6 Copy the JSON from listing A.11 into the editor.
7 Enter Ctrl+s/Cmd+S to save the file.
8 Enter Ctrl+Q/Cmd+Q to quit the editor.

Now that you have a valid ASA job configuration file available, you can run the Azure PowerShell command to create the job. Execute the command in listing A.12 using Azure Cloud Shell.

Listing A.12   Create new Azure Stream Analytics job using PowerShell

```
New-AzStreamAnalyticsJob -ResourceGroupName "ade-dev-eastus2"
➥  -Name "ade-dev-eastus2-biometricstats"        ◁——  The name for the
➥  -File ~/asa/streamingjob.json      ◁              ADLA service
                Select the Data Lake store for
                management and job storage.
```

A.5.5   *Create new Data Lake Analytics account*

Listing A.13 shows a PowerShell script for creating an ADLA service. Creating an ADLA service with Azure PowerShell requires the standard selections of name, region, and resource group. You also need to select the default Data Lake store and a pricing package. With the Azure PowerShell command, you can also adjust policy limits and storage growth.

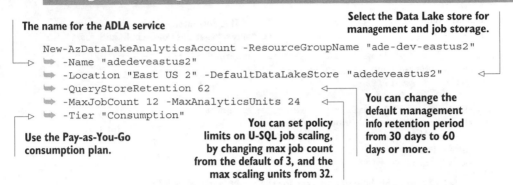

Listing A.13 Creating a new ADLA service with Azure PowerShell

The name for the ADLA service

Select the Data Lake store for management and job storage.

```
New-AzDataLakeAnalyticsAccount -ResourceGroupName "ade-dev-eastus2"
    -Name "adedeveastus2"
    -Location "East US 2" -DefaultDataLakeStore "adedeveastus2"
    -QueryStoreRetention 62
    -MaxJobCount 12 -MaxAnalyticsUnits 24
    -Tier "Consumption"
```

Use the Pay-as-You-Go consumption plan.

You can set policy limits on U-SQL job scaling, by changing max job count from the default of 3, and the max scaling units from 32.

You can change the default management info retention period from 30 days to 60 days or more.

A.5.6 Create new SQL Server and Database

Every SQLDB requires an Azure SQL Server as a host. To create an Azure SQL Server, you'll need to choose a resource group, a name, and a region. You also must choose between version 11 (SQL Server 2012) and 12 (SQL Server 2014). Finally, you'll need to provide an admin username and password. You can use Azure PowerShell to create the SQL Server. Run the following listing in Azure Cloud Shell.

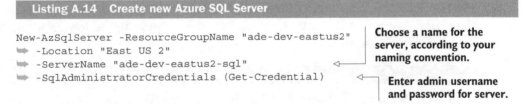

Listing A.14 Create new Azure SQL Server

```
New-AzSqlServer -ResourceGroupName "ade-dev-eastus2"
    -Location "East US 2"
    -ServerName "ade-dev-eastus2-sql"
    -SqlAdministratorCredentials (Get-Credential)
```

Choose a name for the server, according to your naming convention.

Enter admin username and password for server.

You can create a new SQLDB using the Azure portal, and using Azure PowerShell. Run the following listing in Azure Cloud Shell to create a new SQLDB.

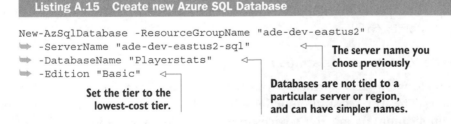

Listing A.15 Create new Azure SQL Database

```
New-AzSqlDatabase -ResourceGroupName "ade-dev-eastus2"
    -ServerName "ade-dev-eastus2-sql"
    -DatabaseName "Playerstats"
    -Edition "Basic"
```

The server name you chose previously

Set the tier to the lowest-cost tier.

Databases are not tied to a particular server or region, and can have simpler names.

The new SQL Server does not allow outside connections to the engine by default. Outside connections are blocked by a firewall. There are two types of firewall rules you can apply: one for Azure resources, and one for specific IP addresses. The script in listing A.16 will set the Allow Azure Endpoints rule and create another rule for your on-premises network. Run the script in Azure Cloud Shell to create the firewall rules.

Listing A.16   Create a firewall rule to allow access by Azure resources

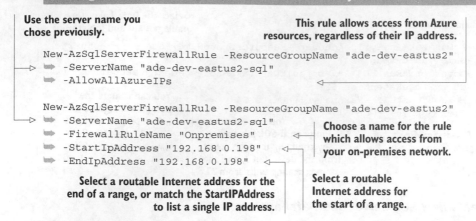

Use the server name you
chose previously.

This rule allows access from Azure
resources, regardless of their IP address.

```
New-AzSqlServerFirewallRule -ResourceGroupName "ade-dev-eastus2"
    -ServerName "ade-dev-eastus2-sql"
    -AllowAllAzureIPs

New-AzSqlServerFirewallRule -ResourceGroupName "ade-dev-eastus2"
    -ServerName "ade-dev-eastus2-sql"
    -FirewallRuleName "Onpremises"
    -StartIpAddress "192.168.0.198"
    -EndIpAddress "192.168.0.198"
```

Choose a name for the rule
which allows access from
your on-premises network.

Select a routable Internet address for the
end of a range, or match the StartIPAddress
to list a single IP address.

Select a routable
Internet address for
the start of a range.

A.5.7   Create a new Data Factory service

ADF functions as an organizing structure for a collection of resources. Because it's an organizing structure, creating a new ADF service requires a few choices. Use the `New-AzDataFactoryV2` command to create a new ADF service. Supply the standard `ResourceGroupName`, `Name`, and `Location` parameters. When using the Azure Power-Shell command, you do not need to select the ADF version. Separate commands are used to create V1 and V2 services. Run the script in the following listing to create the ADF V2 service.

Listing A.17   Creating a new ADF service with Azure PowerShell

```
New-AzDataFactoryV2 -ResourceGroupName "ade-dev-eastus2"
    -Name "ade-dev-eastus2-adf" -Location "EastUS2"
```

When you first create an ADF, it has no resources. The bulk of ADF work lies in creating and configuring the linkedservices, data set, pipeline, and trigger resources. You can get the JSON configuration files for all the ADF resources in this chapter at http://mng.bz/yr8d.

A.5.8   Creating a new App registration

To create a new service principal for ADF to use, we'll use a template called an *App registration*. The App registration defines the credentials and authorization methods for the application(s), and the service principal identifies the application(s). The App registration links to a custom service principal, separate from the service's own service principal. Instead of a username and password to access the service principal, applications use the application ID and a secret key to get an instance of the custom service principal. Using the custom service principal provides a common authentication mechanism for the ADF linkedservices.

Run listing A.18 to create the new App registration. The output will display the `ApplicationId`. Copy the `ApplicationId` value, along with the password you entered, for use in configuring the new ADLS linkedservice in the next section.

Listing A.18 Creating a new App registration with Azure PowerShell

```
$Secure = Read-Host -AsSecureString        ◁─┤ Read a secret key
                                               value interactively.

$App = New-AzADApplication -DisplayName "ade-dev-eastus2-adf-id"
➥ -IdentifierUris "http://none.none"       ◁──── Throwaway value
➥ -Password $Secure                ◁─┐
                                      │ Previously
                                        submitted
$App.ApplicationId.Guid    ◁──┐        secret key
                               │
     The new service principal ID
```

The App registration alone does not give access to services in Azure. You need to create a service principal, in the same AAD directory, and authorize it to access the services used by ADF.

Listing A.19 shows an Azure PowerShell script that creates a new service principal and attaches it to an app. The new service principal does not have any permissions. You'll assign permissions as needed when you create linkedservices. Run the script to create the service principal.

Listing A.19 Creating a new service principal with Azure PowerShell

```
$App = Get-AzADApplication -DisplayName "ade-dev-eastus2-adf-id"    ◁─┐
New-AzADServicePrincipal                              Look up the
➥ -ApplicationId $App.ApplicationId.Guid    ◁─┐      app by name.
          Use the ID of the app for authentication.
```

A.5.9 Creating a new key vault

You can also create the key vault using Azure PowerShell. Use the `New-AzKeyVault` command to create a new AKV service. Supply the standard `ResourceGroupName`, `Name`, and `Location` parameters. When using the Azure PowerShell command, you do not need to provide the tier when choosing Standard. Use the parameter `Sku` with value "Premium" for the Premium tier. Use `EnablePurgeProtection` to enable recovery of deleted secrets and AKV services for 90 days. The following listing shows the script for creating the new vault.

Listing A.20 Creating a new key vault with Azure PowerShell

```
New-AzKeyVault -Name 'ade-dev-eastus2-key'
➥ -ResourceGroupName 'ade-dev-eastus2'
➥ -Location 'East US 2'
➥ -EnableSoftDelete -EnablePurgeProtection
```

Before ADF can look up secrets in AKV, you need to authorize ADF to access secrets. Use the `Set-AzKeyVaultAccessPolicy` command to set the policy. Listing A.21 shows the script to do this. The script retrieves the ADF Managed Identity object, and passes the ID to the `Set-AzKeyVaultAccessPolicy` command using the `ObjectId` parameter. The `PermissionsToSecrets` parameter takes a CSV string of the permissions to apply. The values include Get, List, Set, Delete, Backup, Restore, Recover, and Purge.

Listing A.21   Assign permissions to Data Factory in key vault with Azure PowerShell

```
$App = Get-AzADServicePrincipal -DisplayName "ade-dev-eastus2-adf"      ⟵  Lookup the
Set-AzKeyVaultAccessPolicy -VaultName "ade-dev-eastus2-key"                 ADF Managed
 ➥ -ObjectId $App.Id                 ⟵  Use the ID                          Instance.
 ➥ -PermissionsToSecrets Get,List    ⟵      property.

                        Assign read and list access.
```

A.5.10 *Create new SQL Server and Database with lookup data*

Chapter 12 includes a section on configuring SQLDB to query external data from other SQLDBs. To follow along, you need a second database. Use the following code samples to create the second SQLDB and add a data table to it.

To create an Azure SQL Server, you'll need to choose a resource group, a name, and a region. The SQL Server also requires you to choose between version 11 (SQL Server 2012) and 12 (SQL Server 2014). Finally, you'll need to provide an admin username and password. Run the following listing in Azure Cloud Shell.

Listing A.22   Create a new Azure SQL Server

```
New-AzSqlServer -ResourceGroupName "ade-dev-eastus2"
 ➥ -Location "East US 2"
 ➥ -ServerName "ade-dev-eastus2-sql2"
 ➥ -SqlAdministratorCredentials (Get-Credential)
```

Run the following listing in Azure Cloud Shell to create a new SQLDB.

Listing A.23   Create a new Azure SQL Database

```
New-AzSqlDatabase -ResourceGroupName "ade-dev-eastus2"
 ➥ -ServerName "ade-dev-eastus2-sql2"
 ➥ -DatabaseName "ade-dev-sql2-gamestats"
 ➥ -Edition "Basic"
```

The new SQL Server does not allow outside connections to the engine by default. Outside connections are blocked by a firewall. There are two types of firewall rules you can apply: one for Azure resources and one for specific IP addresses. The script in listing A.24 will set the Allow Azure Endpoints rule, and create another rule for your on-premises network. Run listing A.24 in Azure Cloud Shell to create the firewall rules. Remember to update the `StartIpAddress` and `EndIpAddress` with your network IP address.

Listing A.24   Create a firewall rule to allow access by Azure resources

```
New-AzSqlServerFirewallRule -ResourceGroupName "ade-dev-eastus2"
➥ -ServerName "ade-dev-eastus2-sql2"
➥ -AllowAllAzureIPs

New-AzSqlServerFirewallRule -ResourceGroupName "ade-dev-eastus2"
➥ -ServerName "ade-dev-eastus2-sql2"
➥ -FirewallRuleName "Onpremises"
➥ -StartIpAddress "192.168.0.198"
➥ -EndIpAddress "192.168.0.198"
```

To authenticate to the SQLDB, you can use the server admin credential you created with the new SQL Server. Or you can create a login and user for querying the SQLDB. Run the script in listing A.25 to create the SQL Server login. This script connects to the Master database on the SQL Server.

Listing A.25   Create a SQL Server login

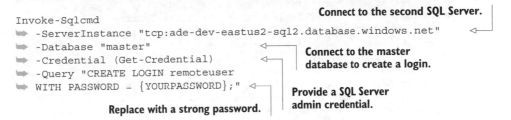

```
Invoke-Sqlcmd
➥ -ServerInstance "tcp:ade-dev-eastus2-sql2.database.windows.net"    ◁──  Connect to the second SQL Server.
➥ -Database "master"    ◁──  
➥ -Credential (Get-Credential)    ◁──  Connect to the master database to create a login.
➥ -Query "CREATE LOGIN remoteuser
➥ WITH PASSWORD - {YOURPASSWORD};"    ◁──  
```

Replace with a strong password.

Provide a SQL Server admin credential.

Run the script in listing A.26 to create the new user in the SQLDB. This script connects to the GameStats database on the SQL Server.

Listing A.26   Create a SQLDB user

```
$Cred = Credential (Get-Credential)
Invoke-Sqlcmd
➥ -ServerInstance "tcp:ade-dev-eastus2-sql2.database.windows.net"    ◁──  Connect to the second SQL Server.
➥ -Database "ade-dev-sql2-gamestats"    ◁──  
➥ -$Cred    ◁──  Connect to the master database to create a login.
➥ -Query "CREATE USER remoteuser
➥ FOR LOGIN remoteuser;"    Provide a SQL Server admin credential.
Invoke-Sqlcmd
➥ -ServerInstance "tcp:ade-dev-eastus2-sql2.database.windows.net"
➥ -Database "ade-dev-sql2-gamestats"
➥ -$Cred
➥ -Query "ALTER ROLE db_datareader    Allow remoteuser to read data.
➥ ADD MEMBER remoteuser;"    ◁──
```

Specify the login created at the server level.

To query external data from this new SQLDB, you need a table with data. The following PowerShell script creates a table and adds some rows of data for use in an external table query. Run the script in the following listing to create the table and populate the data.

Listing A.27   Create a table and populate game data

```
$Cred = Get-Credential
Invoke-Sqlcmd
    -ServerInstance "tcp:ade-dev-eastus2-sql2.database.windows.net"
    -Database "ade-dev-sql2-gamestats" -Credential $Cred
    -Query "CREATE TABLE PlayerDetails (PlayerId nvarchar(8),
    PlayerName nvarchar(100),TeamName nvarchar(100),TeamPosition
    nvarchar(100),PositionStart DateTime,PositionEnd DateTime);"    ◁──┐ Create the
                                                                         data table.
Invoke-Sqlcmd
    -ServerInstance "tcp:ade-dev-eastus2-sql2.database.windows.net"
    -Database "ade-dev-sql2-gamestats" -Credential $Cred
    -Query "INSERT INTO PlayerDetails values ('abera101',
    'Arnold Berathal','Jonestown Sluggers','Pitcher',
    '2010-07-11','2020-07-11');"                         ◁──┐ Insert a row.
Invoke-Sqlcmd
    -ServerInstance "tcp:ade-dev-eastus2-sql2.database.windows.net"
    -Database "ade-dev-sql2-gamestats" -Credential $Cred
    -Query "INSERT INTO PlayerDetails values ('jstro101',
    'John Strong','Poplar Bats','First Base',
    '2010-07-11','2020-07-11');"
Invoke-Sqlcmd
    -ServerInstance "tcp:ade-dev-eastus2-sql2.database.windows.net"
    -Database "ade-dev-sql2-gamestats" -Credential $Cred
    -Query "INSERT INTO PlayerDetails values ('mjone101',
    'Michael Jones','Harrisburg Drivers','First Base',
    '2018-07-11',NULL);"
```

appendix B
Configuring the Jonestown Sluggers analytics system

This appendix covers setting up Azure resources to form the Jonestown Sluggers analytics system featured in the book. It uses Azure PowerShell to create and configure the services. PowerShell is a powerful tool, and the examples in this book only scratch the surface of what's possible. This appendix provides some enhancement to similar scripts found elsewhere in the book, but these enhancements are to support script reuse by multiple readers. *Learn Windows PowerShell in a Month of Lunches, 3rd ed.* (Manning, 2016) by Don Jones and Jeffrey Hicks provides a much deeper view of the technology.

> **TIP** You can find the code listings at https://github.com/rnuckolls/azure_storage.

B.1 Solution design

The Lambda architecture for analytics systems forms the basis of this design. The Lambda architecture defines a Speed layer, Batch layer, Serving layer, and master data set. Data flows through both a hot path and a cold path, allowing both low-latency calculations and large batch processing to occur.

The end-to-end solution presented in this appendix provides one possible design for implementing a Lambda architecture in Azure. The solution uses the same Azure services discussed in the book. Instead of presenting all the options for feature implementation, this solution focuses on producing output from a single data source along the hot and cold paths. The output is a set of average values within two different windows of time: 5 minutes and 24 hours. Figure B.1 shows the services used to implement the various layers of the Lambda architecture in this solution.

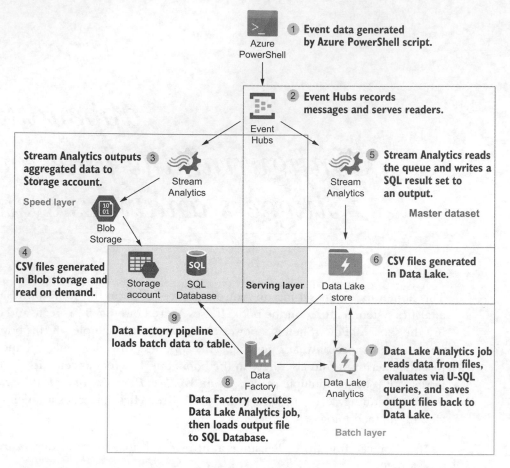

Figure B.1   Azure service analytics system, showing Lambda architecture layers over hot path and cold path data processing steps

1   A PowerShell script generates event messages and submits them to an Event Hubs endpoint.

2   Event Hubs serves as a distribution point for the Speed layer and the master data set.

3   An Azure Stream Analytics (ASA) job prepares a real-time view and outputs the average calculations to a CSV file in Blob Storage.

4   A Storage account provides access to the real-time view data.

5   The same ASA job saves the raw event messages to Data Lake store (ADLS store) for long term storage.

6   The event messages are stored in CSV files each hour in the /Staging folder in ADLS.

7 On a daily schedule, a Data Factory (ADF) pipeline calls Data Lake Analytics (ADLA) to execute a batch job.

8 ADLA runs a U-SQL job to calculate the daily average and generate a CSV file in the /Curated folder.

9 The same ADF pipeline then copies the data from the daily average CSV file into a SQL Database (SQLDB) table.

10 The SQLDB provides access to the batch view data.

B.1.1 Hot path

Event data flows through the Speed layer for real-time views in the Lambda architecture. This design uses only a single query to generate a single real-time view in the Speed layer. This view uses a 5-minute window to average the values in a specific field for events that match the query criteria. While all data is analyzed, not all data follows the hot path to the end. Only data that matches the query filter for this view are included. For this reason, the PowerShell script generates many thousands of event messages so that some qualify for inclusion in the calculation. Figure B.2 shows the steps this data follows as it is processed on the hot path.

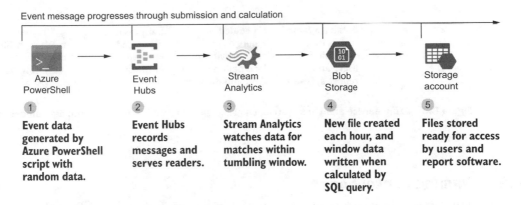

Figure B.2 Azure service analytics system, showing Lambda architecture hot path data processing steps

B.1.2 Cold path

Event data flows into the Batch layer for storing in the master data set. From the master data set, data is drawn for calculations to generate the batch views. This design uses only a single query to generate a single batch view in the Batch layer. This view uses a 24-hour window to average the values in a specific field for all events in the window. All data is analyzed, and all data follows the cold path to the end. This daily average U-SQL job query includes only the previous day's data. The ADF service schedules the query execution to calculate the averages. ADF also copies the resultant data into a

SQLDB table. This table represents the batch view in the Batch layer. Figure B.3 shows the steps this data follows as it is processed on the cold path.

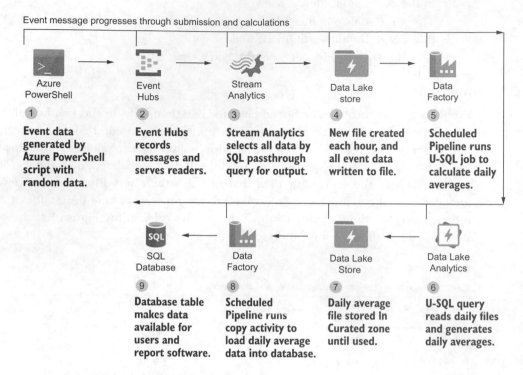

Figure B.3   Azure service analytics system, showing Lambda architecture cold path data processing steps

B.2   *Naming convention*

This appendix contains multiple code listings, including Azure PowerShell scripts, JSON configuration files, and U-SQL query files. These are intended to create an entire analytics processing system based on the solution provided in this appendix. Most of this can be accomplished with Azure PowerShell commands, but some tasks cannot. The code listings are interspersed with instructions to complete before moving on. These include configuring specific service features in the Azure portal, and copying configuration files to folders for use by the subsequent Azure PowerShell scripts. Please follow the steps in order to ensure each piece is configured correctly.

Listing B.1 sets up the naming convention for your system. Modify these variables to match a system name you prefer. These variables are used in later scripts. The listing provides a single place to set the names to make set up easier.

Listing B.1 Azure naming convention

```
# Define the named parts for your system
# Choose the region
$region = "eastus2"
$regionName = "East US 2"
# Choose unique client name
$client = "jones"
$env = "dev"
$project = "biometricstats"
$rgName = $region + "-" + $client + "-" + $env
# Make sure RG name is less than 21 characters
("RG name length " + $rgName.length)
$storeName = $region + $client + $env
# Make sure Storage name is less than 25 characters
("Storage name length " + $storeName.length)
$hubsName = $rgName + "-" + "hubs"
$streamName = $rgName + "-" + "asa" + "-" + $project
$sqlName = $rgName + "-" + "sql"
$dbName = $sqlName + "-" + "stats"
$vaultName = $rgName + "-" + "key"
# Make sure AKV name is less than 25 characters
("AKV name length " + $vaultName.length)
$adfName = $rgName + "-" + "adf"
$adfAppName = $adfName + "-" + "id"
# Lookup your workstation public IP Address
$ipAddress = "192.168.0.1"
```

B.3 Creation script

Listing B.2 takes approximately 10 minutes to run. You must provide values for a SQL Server admin and password interactively. You will receive a prompt halfway through the script to allow you to enter these values.

Listing B.2 Create Azure services

```
# Create services
Get-AzResourceGroup -Name $rgName -ErrorVariable notPresent -ErrorAction
    SilentlyContinue
if ($notPresent)
{
New-AzResourceGroup $rgName -Location $regionName
}

# Storage Account
Get-AzStorageAccount -Name ($storeName) -ResourceGroupName $rgName `
-ErrorVariable notPresent -ErrorAction SilentlyContinue
if ($notPresent)
{
New-AzStorageAccount -ResourceGroupName $rgName `
-AccountName $storeName -SkuName Standard_LRS -Location $regionName `
-EnableHttpsTrafficOnly 1 -Kind "StorageV2"
```

```
$accountObject = Get-AzStorageAccount -ResourceGroupName $rgName `
-AccountName $storeName
New-AzRmStorageContainer -StorageAccount $accountObject `
-ContainerName $project -PublicAccess None
}


# Data Lake store
if (!(Test-AzDataLakeStoreAccount -Name $storeName))
{
New-AzDataLakeStoreAccount -Name $storeName -Location $regionName `
-ResourceGroup $rgName -Encryption ServiceManaged
}


# Event Hubs
if ((Test-AzEventHubName -Namespace $hubsName).NameAvailable)
{
New-AzEventHubNamespace -ResourceGroupName $rgName `
-NamespaceName $hubsName -Location $regionName `
-SkuName "Standard" -SkuCapacity 1
New-AzEventHub -ResourceGroupName $rgName `
-NamespaceName $hubsName -Name $project `
-MessageRetentionInDays 1 -PartitionCount 2
New-AzEventHubAuthorizationRule -ResourceGroupName $rgName `
-NamespaceName $hubsName -AuthorizationRuleName "hubsreader" `
-Rights @("Listen")
New-AzEventHubAuthorizationRule -ResourceGroupName $rgName `
-NamespaceName $hubsName -AuthorizationRuleName "hubswriter" `
-Rights @("Send")
}


# Stream Analytics
Get-AzStreamAnalyticsFunction -JobName $streamName -ResourceGroupName $rgName `
-ErrorVariable notPresent -ErrorAction SilentlyContinue
if ($notPresent)
{
mkdir asa
cd asa
$jobConfig = @{}
$jobProp = @{}
$jobSku = @{name="standard"}
$jobProp.Add("sku",$jobSku)
$jobProp.Add("eventsOutOfOrderPolicy","adjust")
$jobProp.Add("eventsOutOfOrderMaxDelayInSeconds",11)
$jobProp.Add("compatibilityLevel",1.1)
$jobProp.Add("outputErrorPolicy","Stop")
$jobProp.Add("eventsLateArrivalMaxDelayInSeconds",6)
$jobConfig.Add("properties",$jobProp)
$jobConfig.Add("location","EastUS2")
$jobConfig | ConvertTo-Json -Depth 10 | Out-File -FilePath ./streamingjob.json
New-AzStreamAnalyticsJob -ResourceGroupName $rgName `
-Name $streamName -File ./streamingjob.json
cd ..
}
```

```
# Data Lake Analytics
if (!(Test-AzDataLakeAnalyticsAccount -Name $storeName))
{
New-AzDataLakeAnalyticsAccount -ResourceGroupName $rgName -Name $storeName `
-Location $regionName -DefaultDataLakeStore $storeName -Tier "Consumption"
}

# SQL Database
Get-AzSqlServer -Name $sqlName -ResourceGroupName $rgName `
-ErrorVariable notPresent -ErrorAction SilentlyContinue
if ($notPresent)
{
# Enter new SQL Admin credentials
New-AzSqlServer -ResourceGroupName $rgName -Location $regionName `
-ServerName $sqlName -SqlAdministratorCredentials (Get-Credential -
    Message "Enter new SQL Admin credentials")
}

Get-AzSqlDatabase -Name $dbName -ResourceGroupName `
$rgName -ServerName $sqlName -ErrorVariable notPresent -
    ErrorAction SilentlyContinue
if ($notPresent)
{
New-AzSqlDatabase -ResourceGroupName $rgName -ServerName $sqlName `
-DatabaseName $dbName -Edition "Basic"
}

# Key Vault
if (-not (Get-AzKeyVault -Name $vaultName -ResourceGroupName $rgName))
{
New-AzKeyVault -Name $vaultName -ResourceGroupName $rgName `
-Location $regionName -EnablePurgeProtection -ErrorVariable deleted
}
if ($deleted)
{
Undo-AzKeyVaultRemoval -VaultName $vaultName -ResourceGroupName $rgName `
-Location $region
}

Get-AzDataFactoryV2 -Name $adfName -ResourceGroupName `
$rgName -ErrorVariable notPresent -ErrorAction SilentlyContinue
if ($notPresent)
{
New-AzDataFactoryV2 -Name $adfName -Location $regionName `
-ResourceGroupName $rgName
}

# Verify creation of Resource Group, Storage account,
# Data Lake store, Event Hubs, Stream Analytics,
# Data Lake Analytics, SQL Database, Key Vault,
# and Data Factory resources.
```

When complete, the required services will be created. Each of them requires further configuration.

B.4   Configure Azure services using PowerShell

Once your Azure services have been created, run the following scripts to configure the services.

B.4.1   Stream Analytics Managed Identity

Enable Managed Identity using the Azure portal. This cannot be done via Azure PowerShell at the time of writing.

1. In the Azure portal, use the All Services menu and filter on ASA jobs to show the ASA Jobs blade.
2. Select your ASA job by clicking its name.
3. Click Configure > Managed Identity in the left navigation to open the Managed Identity blade.
4. Click Use System-assigned Managed Identity. Click Save to confirm the setting and generate the Managed Identity.

B.4.2   Data Lake store

Run listing B.3 to configure your ADLS store for use by ASA, ADLA, and ADF. The code creates folders and assigns permissions to the various service principals for these services.

Listing B.3   Configure ADLS

```
# Data Lake store
# Add Data Factory permissions
$principal = Get-AzADServicePrincipal -DisplayName $adfName

Set-AzDataLakeStoreItemAclEntry -AccountName $storeName -Path / `
-AceType User -Id $principal.Id -Permissions Execute

New-AzDataLakeStoreItem -AccountName $storeName -Path "/Staging" -Folder
New-AzDataLakeStoreItem -AccountName $storeName -Path "/Raw" -Folder
New-AzDataLakeStoreItem -AccountName $storeName -Path "/Curated" -Folder
New-AzDataLakeStoreItem -AccountName $storeName -Path "/Sandbox" -Folder
New-AzDataLakeStoreItem -AccountName $storeName -Path "/Code" -Folder

Set-AzDataLakeStoreItemAclEntry -AccountName $storeName `
-Path /Staging -AceType User -Id $principal.Id -Permissions All -Default
Set-AzDataLakeStoreItemAclEntry -AccountName $storeName `
-Path /Raw -AceType User -Id $principal.Id -Permissions All -Default
Set-AzDataLakeStoreItemAclEntry -AccountName $storeName `
-Path /Curated -AceType User -Id $principal.Id -Permissions All -Default
Set-AzDataLakeStoreItemAclEntry -AccountName $storeName `
-Path /Code -AceType User -Id $principal.Id -Permissions All -Default

# Add Stream Analytics permissions
$principal = Get-AzADServicePrincipal -DisplayName $streamName
```

```
Set-AzDataLakeStoreItemAclEntry -AccountName $storeName -Path / `
-AceType User -Id $principal.Id -Permissions Execute

Set-AzDataLakeStoreItemAclEntry -AccountName $storeName `
-Path /Staging -AceType User -Id $principal.Id -Permissions All
Set-AzDataLakeStoreItemAclEntry -AccountName $storeName `
-Path /Staging -AceType User -Id $principal.Id -Permissions All -Default

New-AzDataLakeStoreItem -AccountName $storeName -Path ("/Staging/
    " + $project) -Folder
New-AzDataLakeStoreItem -AccountName $storeName -Path "/Code/Assemblies"
    -Folder
New-AzDataLakeStoreItem -AccountName $storeName -Path "/Code/Usql" -Folder
```

Copy the U-SQL file in listing B.4 to ADLS folder /Code/Usql/DailyAggregate.usql. This file will be used for the ADLA daily average batch job.

Listing B.4 U-SQL script for daily aggregation

```
DECLARE EXTERNAL @year string = DateTime.Today.AddDays(-
    1).Year.ToString("#0000");
DECLARE EXTERNAL @month string = DateTime.Today.AddDays(-
    1).Month.ToString("#00");
DECLARE EXTERNAL @day string = DateTime.Today.AddDays(-1).Day.ToString("#00");
DECLARE EXTERNAL @in string = string.Format("/Staging/biometricstats/{0}-{1}-
    {2}{3}.csv", @year, @month, @day, "{*}");

@Players =
    EXTRACT
        Id Guid,
        NodeValue decimal,
        Player string,
        Node int,
        EventTime DateTime,
        PartitionId int,
        EventEnqueuedUtcTime DateTime,
        EventProcessedUtcTime DateTime
    FROM @in
    USING Extractors.Csv(
    skipFirstNRows: 1
    );

@DailyAgg =
    SELECT
        Player,
        Node,
        EventTime.ToString("d") AS AvgDate,
        AVG(NodeValue) AS Average
    FROM @Players
    GROUP BY Player, Node, EventTime.ToString("d");

DECLARE EXTERNAL @out string = "/Curated/biometricstats/v1/
    daily_value_avg.csv";
```

```
OUTPUT @DailyAgg
    TO @out
    USING Outputters.Csv(outputHeader: true);
```

See chapter 4 for detailed descriptions of the ADL service.

B.4.3   *Stream Analytics job configuration*

ASA uses JSON files for configuring the inputs, outputs, and transforms via Azure
PowerShell. You must save these files in a folder location accessible by your Power-
Shell instance.

> **TIP**   The files can be downloaded from the GitHub repository for this book at
> http://mng.bz/MoZB.

Create an Event Hubs input file using the JSON in listing B.5. Save this file into a new
folder named /asa, and name the file HubsInputBiometrics.json. Retrieve the Event
Hubs access key using the following Azure PowerShell command, and update the
sharedAccessPolicyKey value in the file.

Listing B.5   Get Event Hubs key

```
$key = (Get-AzEventHubKey -ResourceGroupName $rgName `
-Namespace ($rgName + "-" + "hubs") `
-AuthorizationRuleName "hubsreader").PrimaryKey
```

Update the value for serviceBusNamespace and sharedAccessPolicyKey in the following listing.

Listing B.6   Configure Event Hubs input

```
{
    "properties": {
        "type": "Stream",
        "datasource": {
            "type": "Microsoft.ServiceBus/EventHub",
            "properties": {
                "eventHubName": "biometricstats",
                "serviceBusNamespace": "eastus2-jones-dev-hubs",
                "sharedAccessPolicyName": "hubsreader",
                "sharedAccessPolicyKey": "==KEY==",
                "consumerGroupName": "$Default"
                }
        },
        "compression": {
            "type": "None"
        },
        "serialization": {
            "type": "Json",
            "properties": {
                "encoding": "UTF8"
            }
```

```
        }
    },
    "name": "HubsInputBiometrics",
    "type": "Microsoft.StreamAnalytics/streamingjobs/inputs"
}
```

Create a Blob output file using the JSON in listing B.8. Save this file into the folder named /asa, and name the file BlobOutputPitcher.json. Retrieve the Storage account access key using the following Azure PowerShell command, and update the `accountKey` value in the file. Update the `accountName` value to match your naming convention.

Listing B.7 Get Storage account key

```
$key = (Get-AzStorageAccountKey -ResourceGroupName $rgName `
-Name $storeName).Value | Select-Object -First 1
```

Update the value for `accountName` and `accountKey` in the following JSON file in the following listing.

Listing B.8 Configure Storage Blobs output

```
{
    "properties":{
        "datasource":{
            "type":"Microsoft.Storage/Blob",
            "properties":{
                "container":"biometricstats",
                "pathPattern":"{date}/{time}",
                "dateFormat":"yyyy/MM/dd",
                "timeFormat":"HH",
                "storageAccounts":[
                    {
                        "accountName":"eastus2jonestowndev",
                        "accountKey": "==key=="
                    }
                ]
            }
        },
        "serialization":{
            "type":"CSV",
            "properties": {
                "encoding": "UTF8",
                "fieldDelimiter":","
            }
        }
    }
}
```

Create the ADLS output for your Stream Analytics job in the Azure portal. Creating an ADLS output via Azure PowerShell is not supported at time of writing. Use the following settings:

- Name—`DataLakeOutputRaw`
- Account name—your chosen ADLS name
- Path prefix pattern—/Staging/biometricstats/{date}-{time}
- Date format—YYYY-MM-DD
- Time format—HH
- Event serialization format—CSV
- Delimiter—comma
- Encoding—UTF-8
- Authentication mode—Managed Identity

See "Create an ADLS output using the Azure Portal" in chapter 6 for a detailed description of creating the ADLS output.

Create a query transforms file using the JSON in listing B.9. Save this file into the folder named /asa, and name the file Transforms.json.

Listing B.9   Configure ASA job transforms

```
{
    "properties":{
        "streamingUnits":1,
        "query":"WITH PitchAverage AS (
SELECT Player, Node, AVG(NodeValue) AS AvgValue
FROM HubsInputBiometrics TIMESTAMP BY EventTime
WHERE Player = 'abera101' AND Node = 12 AND NodeValue > 80
GROUP BY Player, Node, TumblingWindow(second, 150)
)
SELECT a.Player, a.NodeValue, b.AvgValue
INTO BlobOutputPitcher
FROM HubsInputBiometrics a TIMESTAMP BY EventTime
INNER JOIN PitchAverage b
ON a.Player = b.Player
AND a.Node = b.Node
AND DATEDIFF(second, a, b) BETWEEN 0 AND 150
WHERE a.NodeValue > 80;

SELECT
Id,
NodeValue,
Player,
Node,
EventTime,
PartitionId,
EventProcessedUtcTime,
EventEnqueuedUtcTime
INTO DataLakeOutputRaw
FROM HubsInputBiometrics TIMESTAMP BY EventTime;"
    }
}
```

Run the following listing to configure the ASA job with these configuration files, and start the job running.

Listing B.10 Configure ASA

```
# Stream Analytics
cd asa
# Create Input
New-AzStreamAnalyticsInput -ResourceGroupName $rgName `
-JobName $streamName -Name "HubsInputBiometrics" `
-File "./HubsInputBiometrics.json"

# Create output
New-AzStreamAnalyticsOutput -ResourceGroupName $rgName `
-JobName $streamName -Name "BlobOutputPitcher" `
-File "./BlobOutputPitcher.json"

# Create query
New-AzStreamAnalyticsTransformation -ResourceGroupName $rgName `
-JobName $streamName -Name "Transformation" `
-File "./Transforms.json" -Force

Start-AzStreamAnalyticsJob -ResourceGroupName $rgName `
-Name $streamName -OutputStartMode "JobStartTime"
```

See chapter 6 for detailed descriptions of the ASA service.

B.4.4 SQL Database

Run listing B.11 to configure the SQLDB for your analytics system. The code adds firewall rules, a SQL credential for access, and creates the daily averages table.

Listing B.11 Configure SQLDB

```
# SQL Server
New-AzSqlServerFirewallRule -ResourceGroupName $rgName `
-ServerName $sqlName -AllowAllAzureIPs
New-AzSqlServerFirewallRule -ResourceGroupName $rgName `
-ServerName $sqlName -FirewallRuleName "Onpremises" `
-StartIpAddress $ipAddress -EndIpAddress $ipAddress

# Add user and login
$sqlAddress = ("tcp:" + $sqlName + ".database.windows.net" )
# Provide SQL Server admin and password
$sqlCred = Credential (Get-Credential -Message "Enter SQL Admin credentials")
$YOURPASSWORD = "MMMMMMMMMm.1"
Invoke-Sqlcmd `
-ServerInstance $sqlAddress -Database "master" -Credential $sqlCred `
-Query ("IF NOT EXISTS(SELECT sid FROM sys.sql_logins WHERE name =
        'remoteuser') `
BEGIN CREATE LOGIN remoteuser WITH PASSWORD = '" + $YOURPASSWORD + "'; END")

Invoke-Sqlcmd -ServerInstance $sqlAddress `
-Database $dbName -Credential $sqlCred `
```

```
-Query "IF NOT EXISTS(SELECT uid FROM sys.sysusers WHERE name = 'remoteuser') `
BEGIN CREATE USER remoteuser FOR LOGIN remoteuser; END"
Invoke-Sqlcmd -ServerInstance $sqlAddress `
-Database $dbName -Credential $sqlCred `
-Query "ALTER ROLE db_datareader ADD MEMBER remoteuser;"
Invoke-Sqlcmd -ServerInstance $sqlAddress `
-Database $dbName -Credential $sqlCred `
-Query "ALTER ROLE db_datawriter ADD MEMBER remoteuser;"

# Add data table
Invoke-Sqlcmd -ServerInstance $sqlAddress `
-Database $dbName -Credential $sqlCred `
-Query "DROP TABLE IF EXISTS DailyAverages; `
CREATE TABLE DailyAverages (Player nvarchar(50), Node int, `
AverageDate DateTime, AverageValue decimal(18,9));"
```

See chapter 11 for detailed descriptions of the SQLDB service.

B.4.5   *Data Factory*

Run listing B.12 to configure security for ADF. This code registers a new app for the
ADF service, then gives access to the ADLS store and Azure Key Vault (AKV) to the app.
For a new AKV service, a user account must be given permission via a policy before
adding additional policies. Update the $user value with your AAD user. A format is
provided for users without a corporate AAD account. It also adds two secrets to the
AKV service, one for impersonating the ADF service, and one to hold the SQLDB
remoteuser password. You'll want to provide the remoteuser password from the previous section when prompted.

Listing B.12   Configure Active Directory service principal for ADF

```
# Data Factory
# App registration
$App = Get-AzADApplication -DisplayName $adfAppName
if ([string]::IsNullOrWhiteSpace($App))
{
# Enter new app password
$Secure = Read-Host -AsSecureString -Prompt "Enter new app password"
$App = New-AzADApplication -DisplayName $adfAppName `
-IdentifierUris ("https://" + $adfName + ".none") -Password $Secure
}
$adfGuid = $App.ApplicationId.Guid

$notPresent = Get-AzADServicePrincipal -DisplayName $adfAppName
if ([string]::IsNullOrWhiteSpace($notPresent))
{
New-AzADServicePrincipal -ApplicationId $adfGuid
}
# Give Data Factory access to Data Lake store
$principal = Get-AzADServicePrincipal -DisplayName $adfAppName
Set-AzDataLakeStoreItemAclEntry -AccountName $storeName -Path / `
-AceType User -Id $principal.Id -Permissions All -Recurse
```

```
Set-AzDataLakeStoreItemAclEntry -AccountName $storeName -Path / `
-AceType User -Id $principal.Id -Permissions All -Recurse -Default


# Key Vault
# Find your AAD user and add access policy, so that following steps succeed
$user = "[USER]_[DOMAIN].com#EXT#@[USER][DOMAIN].onmicrosoft.com"
$userId = (Get-AzADUser -UserPrincipalName $user).Id
Set-AzKeyVaultAccessPolicy -VaultName $vaultName `
-ObjectId $userId -PermissionsToSecrets Get,List,Set,Delete

$principal = (Get-AzDataFactoryV2 -ResourceGroupName $rgName -Name
    $adfName).Identity.PrincipalId.Guid
Set-AzKeyVaultAccessPolicy -VaultName $vaultName -ObjectId $principal
    -PermissionsToSecrets Get,List

# Add Data Factory key
$Secret = Read-Host -AsSecureString -Prompt "Enter registered app password"
Set-AzKeyVaultSecret -VaultName $vaultName `
-Name ($adfName + "-" + "key2") -SecretValue $Secret `
-ContentType "key"

# Add SQL Database user
# Enter remoteuser password from SQL Database configuration
$Secret = Read-Host -AsSecureString -Prompt "Enter remoteuser password from
    SQL Database"
Set-AzKeyVaultSecret -VaultName $vaultName `
-Name ($dbName + "-" + "2") -SecretValue $Secret `
-ContentType "key"
```

> **IMPORTANT** Assign permissions to Data Lake services and folders using the ID of the ADF registered app's service principal, not the registered app itself.

Run listing B.13 to create an AKV linkedservice in the ADF service. This can be accomplished in a single step, without having to save a configuration file first, using the code in the listing.

Listing B.13 Configure AKV linkedservice

```
# Key Vault
Get-AzDataFactoryV2LinkedService -ResourceGroupName $rgName `
-DataFactoryName $adfName -Name "AzureKeyVault1" `
-ErrorVariable notPresent -ErrorAction SilentlyContinue

if ($notPresent)
{
mkdir adf
cd adf
$akvConfig = @{}
$akvProp = @{}
$akvType = @{baseUrl=("https://" + $vaultName + ".vault.azure.net")}
$akvProp.Add("typeProperties",$akvType)
$akvProp.Add("type","AzureKeyVault")
```

```
$akvConfig.Add("properties",$akvProp)
$akvConfig.Add("name","AzureKeyVault1")
$akvConfig | ConvertTo-Json -Depth 10 | `
Out-File -FilePath ./AzureKeyVault.json
Set-AzDataFactoryV2LinkedService -ResourceGroupName $rgName `
-DataFactoryName $adfName -Name "AzureKeyVault" `
-DefinitionFile "./AzureKeyVault.json"
cd ..
}
```

Look up `subscriptionId`, `tenantId`, and ADLS `servicePrincipalID` using the Azure PowerShell commands in listing B.14. Update the JSON configuration files for linkedservices with these values.

Listing B.14 Lookup service and environment identifiers

```
# Subscription and Account
Get-AzSubscription
# Data Factory Service Principal
Get-AzADServicePrincipal -DisplayName ($adfName + "-" + "id")
```

TIP The files can be downloaded from the GitHub repository for this book at http://mng.bz/MoZB.

Create a config file using the JSON in listing B.15. Save this file into the folder named /adf, and name the file AzureDataLake.json. Make the following changes to the file:

- Update `dataLakeStoreUri`, replacing subdomain with the name of the ADLS store.
- Update `servicePrincipalId` using the ADF app service principal `ApplicationId`.
- Update `secretName` with the AKV secret name.
- Update `tenant` with the Active Directory ID.
- Update `subscriptionId` with your resource group subscription ID.
- Update `resourceGroupName` with your resource group name.

Listing B.15 ADLS linkedservice configuration file

```
{
    "name": "AzureDataLakeStore1",
    "type": "Microsoft.DataFactory/factories/linkedservices",
    "properties": {
        "annotations": [],
        "type": "AzureDataLakeStore",
        "typeProperties": {
            "dataLakeStoreUri": "https://
eastus2jonesdev.azuredatalakestore.net/webhdfs/v1",
            "servicePrincipalId": "12345678-904b-4948-abb6-123456789012",
            "servicePrincipalKey": {
                "type": "AzureKeyVaultSecret",
                "store": {
                    "referenceName": "AzureKeyVault1",
```

```
                            "type": "LinkedServiceReference"
                        },
                        "secretName": "eastus2-jones-dev-adf-key"
                    },
                    "tenant": "12345678-812a-43cf-b020-123456789012",
                    "subscriptionId": "12345678-7061-4721-abbc-123456789012",
                    "resourceGroupName": "eastus2-jones-dev"
                }
            }
        }
```

Create a config file using the JSON in listing B.16. Save this file into the folder named /adf, and name the file AzureDataLakeAnalytics.json. Make the following changes to the file:

- Update servicePrincipalId using the ADF app service principal ApplicationId.
- Update secretName with the AKV secret name.
- Update tenant with the Active Directory ID.
- Update subscriptionId with your resource group subscription ID.
- Update resourceGroupName with your resource group name.

Listing B.16 ADLA linkedservice configuration file

```
{
    "name": "AzureDataLakeAnalytics",
    "type": "Microsoft.DataFactory/factories/linkedservices",
    "properties": {
        "annotations": ["adla","usql"],
        "type": "AzureDataLakeAnalytics",
        "typeProperties": {
            "accountName": "eastus2jonesdev",
            "servicePrincipalId": "9999999c-904b-4948-abb6-2222222ca836",
            "servicePrincipalKey": {
                "type": "AzureKeyVaultSecret",
                "store": {
                    "referenceName": "AzureKeyVault",
                    "type": "LinkedServiceReference"
                },
                "secretName": "eastus2-jones-dev-adf-key"
            },
            "tenant": "ffffffff-812a-43cf-b020-777777752901",
            "subscriptionId": "fdffffff-7061-4721-abbc-bbbbbbbc3d5c",
            "resourceGroupName": "eastus2-jones-dev"
        }
    }
}
```

Create a config file using the JSON in listing B.17. Save this file into the folder named /adf, and name the file AzureSQLDatabase.json. Make the following changes to the file:

- Update connectionString, replacing the server name and database name.
- Update secretName with the AKV secret name for the remoteuser password.

Listing B.17   SQLDB linkedservice configuration file

```
{
    "name": "AzureSqlDatabase",
    "type": "Microsoft.DataFactory/factories/linkedservices",
    "properties": {
        "annotations": [],
        "type": "AzureSqlDatabase",
        "typeProperties": {
            "connectionString": "Data Source=eastus2-jones-dev-
    sql.database.windows.net;Initial Catalog=eastus2-jones-dev-sql-stats;User
    ID=remoteuser",
            "password": {
                "type": "AzureKeyVaultSecret",
                "store": {
                    "referenceName": "AzureKeyVault",
                    "type": "LinkedServiceReference"
                },
                "secretName": "eastus2-jones-dev-sql-stats"
            }
        }
    }
}
```

Create a config file using the JSON in listing B.18. Save this file into the folder named /adf, and name the file PlayerAverageFile.json.

Listing B.18   Player average file datasource configuration file

```
{
    "name": "PlayerAverageFile",
    "properties": {
        "linkedServiceName": {
            "referenceName": "AzureDataLake",
            "type": "LinkedServiceReference"
        },
        "annotations": [],
        "type": "DelimitedText",
        "typeProperties": {
            "location": {
                "type": "AzureDataLakeStoreLocation",
                "fileName": "daily_value_avg.csv",
                "folderPath": "Curated/biometricstats/v1"
            },
            "columnDelimiter": ",",
            "escapeChar": "\\",
            "firstRowAsHeader": true,
            "quoteChar": "\""
        },
        "schema": [
            {
                "name": "Player",
                "type": "String"
            },
```

```
        {
            "name": "Node",
            "type": "String"
        },
        {
            "name": "AvgDate",
            "type": "String"
        },
        {
            "name": "Average",
            "type": "String"
        }
    ]
  }
}
```

Create a config file using the JSON in listing B.19. Save this file into the folder named /adf, and name the file PlayerAverageTable.json.

Listing B.19   Player average table datasource configuration file

```
{
    "name": "PlayerAverageTable",
    "properties": {
        "linkedServiceName": {
            "referenceName": "AzureSQLDatabase",
            "type": "LinkedServiceReference"
        },
        "annotations": [],
        "type": "AzureSqlTable",
        "schema": [
            {
                "name": "Player",
                "type": "nvarchar"
            },
            {
                "name": "Node",
                "type": "int",
                "precision": 10
            },
            {
                "name": "AverageDate",
                "type": "datetime",
                "precision": 23,
                "scale": 3
            },
            {
                "name": "AverageValue",
                "type": "decimal",
                "precision": 18,
                "scale": 9
            }
        ],
        "typeProperties": {
```

```
                     "schema": "dbo",
                     "table": "DailyAverages"
                }
            }
        }
    }
```

Create a config file using the JSON in listing B.20. Save this file into the folder named /adf, and name the file Pipeline.json.

Listing B.20   ADF pipeline configuration file

```
{
    "name": "Pipeline",
    "properties": {
        "activities": [
            {
                "name": "DailyAggregate",
                "type": "DataLakeAnalyticsU-SQL",
                "dependsOn": [],
                "policy": {
                    "timeout": "0.01:00:00",
                    "retry": 1,
                    "retryIntervalInSeconds": 30,
                    "secureOutput": false,
                    "secureInput": false
                },
                "userProperties": [],
                "typeProperties": {
                    "scriptPath": "Code/Usql/DailyAggregate.usql",
                    "scriptLinkedService": {
                        "referenceName": "AzureDataLake",
                        "type": "LinkedServiceReference"
                    }
                },
                "linkedServiceName": {
                    "referenceName": "AzureDataLakeAnalytics",
                    "type": "LinkedServiceReference"
                }
            },
            {
                "name": "Import",
                "type": "Copy",
                "dependsOn": [
                    {
                        "activity": "DailyAggregate",
                        "dependencyConditions": [
                            "Succeeded"
                        ]
                    }
                ],
                "policy": {
                    "timeout": "0.01:00:00",
                    "retry": 0,
                    "retryIntervalInSeconds": 30,
```

```
            "secureOutput": false,
            "secureInput": false
      },
      "userProperties": [],
      "typeProperties": {
            "source": {
                  "type": "DelimitedTextSource",
                  "storeSettings": {
                        "type": "AzureDataLakeStoreReadSettings",
                        "recursive": true
                  },
                  "formatSettings": {
                        "type": "DelimitedTextReadSettings"
                  }
            },
            "sink": {
                  "type": "AzureSqlSink"
            },
            "enableStaging": false,
            "enableSkipIncompatibleRow": false,
            "translator": {
                  "type": "TabularTranslator",
                  "mappings": [
                        {
                              "source": {
                                    "name": "Player",
                                    "type": "String",
                                    "physicalType": "String"
                              },
                              "sink": {
                                    "name": "Player",
                                    "type": "String",
                                    "physicalType": "nvarchar"
                              }
                        },
                        {
                              "source": {
                                    "name": "Node",
                                    "type": "String",
                                    "physicalType": "String"
                              },
                              "sink": {
                                    "name": "Node",
                                    "type": "Int32",
                                    "physicalType": "int"
                              }
                        },
                        {
                              "source": {
                                    "name": "AvgDate",
                                    "type": "DateTime",
                                    "physicalType": "String"
                              },
                              "sink": {
                                    "name": "AverageDate",
```

```
                                        "type": "DateTime",
                                        "physicalType": "datetime"
                                    }
                                },
                                {
                                    "source": {
                                        "name": "Average",
                                        "type": "Decimal",
                                        "physicalType": "String"
                                    },
                                    "sink": {
                                        "name": "AverageValue",
                                        "type": "Decimal",
                                        "physicalType": "decimal"
                                    }
                                }
                            ],
                            "typeConversion": true,
                            "typeConversionSettings": {
                                "allowDataTruncation": true,
                                "treatBooleanAsNumber": false
                            }
                        }
                    },
                    "inputs": [
                        {
                            "referenceName": "PlayerAverageFile",
                            "type": "DatasetReference"
                        }
                    ],
                    "outputs": [
                        {
                            "referenceName": "PlayerAverageTable",
                            "type": "DatasetReference"
                        }
                    ]
                }
            ],
            "annotations": []
        }
}
```

Create a config file using the JSON in listing B.21. Save this file into the folder named /adf, and name the file Trigger.json.

Listing B.21   ADF pipeline trigger configuration file

```
{
    "name": "DailyTrigger",
    "properties": {
        "annotations": [],
        "runtimeState": "Started",
        "pipelines": [
            {
```

```
                    "pipelineReference": {
                        "referenceName": "Pipeline",
                        "type": "PipelineReference"
                    }
                }
            ],
            "type": "ScheduleTrigger",
            "typeProperties": {
                "recurrence": {
                    "frequency": "Day",
                    "interval": 1,
                    "startTime": "2020-06-25T01:00:00.000Z",
                    "timeZone": "UTC"
                }
            }
        }
    }
}
```

Run listing B.22 to configure the ADF pipeline with these configuration files, and start the trigger. The pipeline trigger will run the pipeline activities at the scheduled time.

Listing B.22   Configure ADF

```
# Add Key Vault Linkedservice
cd adf -ErrorAction SilentlyContinue
# Add Data lake Linkedservice
Set-AzDataFactoryV2LinkedService -ResourceGroupName $rgName -DataFactoryName
    $adfName -Name "AzureDataLake" -DefinitionFile "./AzureDataLake.json"
# Add Data Lake Analytics Linkedservice
Set-AzDataFactoryV2LinkedService -ResourceGroupName $rgName -DataFactoryName
    $adfName -Name "AzureDataLakeAnalytics" -DefinitionFile "./
    AzureDataLakeAnalytics.json"
# Add SQL Database Linkedservice
Set-AzDataFactoryV2LinkedService -ResourceGroupName $rgName -DataFactoryName
    $adfName -Name "AzureSQLDatabase" -DefinitionFile "./AzureSQLDatabase.json"

# Add Player average file dataset
Set-AzDataFactoryV2Dataset -ResourceGroupName $rgName -DataFactoryName $adfName
    -Name "PlayerAverageFile" -DefinitionFile "./PlayerAverageFile.json"
# Add Player average table dataset
Set-AzDataFactoryV2Dataset -ResourceGroupName $rgName -DataFactoryName $adfName
    -Name "PlayerAverageTable" -DefinitionFile "./PlayerAverageTable.json"

# Add pipeline
Set-AzDataFactoryV2Pipeline -ResourceGroupName $rgName -DataFactoryName
    $adfName -Name "Pipeline" -File "./Pipeline.json"

# Add trigger
Set-AzDataFactoryV2Trigger -ResourceGroupName $rgName -DataFactoryName $adfName
    -Name "Trigger" -File "./Trigger.json"
Start-AzDataFactoryV2Trigger -ResourceGroupName $rgName -DataFactoryName
    $adfName -Name "Trigger"
```

See chapter 10 for more information about ADF.

B.5   Load event data

The PowerShell script in listing B.23 loads data into the Event Hubs endpoint. The code creates a SAS key and generates random values in the Player Biometricstats format. These events are created in a loop and sent to Event Hubs.

Listing B.23   Submit events to Event Hubs

```
# Write data to Event Hubs
[Reflection.Assembly]::LoadWithPartialName("System.Web") | out-null

$key = Get-AzEventHubKey -ResourceGroupName $rgName -NamespaceName $hubsName
    -AuthorizationRuleName "hubswriter"
$URI= $hubsName + ".servicebus.windows.net/" + $project

$Expires=([DateTimeOffset]::Now.ToUnixTimeSeconds())+3600
$SignatureString=[System.Web.HttpUtility]::UrlEncode($URI)+ "`n" +
    [string]$Expires
$HMAC = New-Object System.Security.Cryptography.HMACSHA256
$HMAC.key = [Text.Encoding]::ASCII.GetBytes($key.PrimaryKey)
$Signature = $HMAC.ComputeHash([Text.Encoding]::ASCII.GetBytes($SignatureString))
$Signature = [Convert]::ToBase64String($Signature)
$SASToken = "SharedAccessSignature sr=" +
    [System.Web.HttpUtility]::UrlEncode($URI) + "&sig=" +
    [System.Web.HttpUtility]::UrlEncode($Signature) + "&se=" + $Expires
    + "&skn=" + $key.KeyName

$endpoint = "https://" + $hubsName + ".servicebus.windows.net/" + $project + "/
    messages" + "?timeout=60&api-version=2014-01"

$headers = New-Object "System.Collections.Generic.Dictionary[[String],[String]]"
$headers.Add("Authorization", $SASToken)
$headers.Add("Content-Type", "application/atom+xml;type=entry;charset=utf-8")
$headers.Add("Host", ($hubsName + ".servicebus.windows.net"))

for($i = 0; $i -lt 14400; $i++)
{
$player = switch (Get-Random -Minimum 1 -Maximum 4) {
  1 {"abera101"; break}
  2 {"jjone101"; break}
  3 {"ksmit102"; break}
}
$node = GET-Random -Minimum 1 -Maximum 40
$val = Get-Random -Minimum 0 -Maximum 254
$eventDate = (Get-Date).ToUniversalTime().ToString("o")

#Construct body using Hashtable
$htbody = @{
    Id=(New-Guid).Guid
    Player= $player
    Node= $node
    NodeValue= $val
```

```
    EventTime= $eventDate
  }
$body = ConvertTo-Json $htbody

Invoke-WebRequest -Uri $endpoint -Method POST -Body $body -Headers $headers
}
```

B.6 *Output of batch and stream processing*

Once the analytics system has been created, the ASA job is running, data has been submitted to the Event Hubs endpoint, and the ADF pipeline has executed, you will have multiple files to verify. Check for data files in ADLS, including in the /Staging and /Curated folders, to verify that the cold path is working. Check for data files in the Blob Storage container to verify that the hot path is working. Check the data table in the SQLDB to ensure that the pipeline import is working. With all these outputs verified, you have successfully created the end-to-end solution.

B.7 *Removing services*

To remove all of the Azure resources, four steps are required.

1 Delete the resource group. This will delete all of the Azure resources that were created, except two. The registered app for the Data Factory remains, and the AKV service becomes hidden.

2 Delete the registered app. This can be found in Azure Active Directory blade, under Enterprise Applications. Show all application types, and filter by the registered app name.

3 Delete the /asa and /adf folders from your Azure PowerShell directory. Include the configuration files.

4 Wait 90 days for the AKV service to be removed. After this soft-delete retention period, the Azure Resource Manager will remove the AKV service. The name will be available once the old AKV service is removed.

WARNING Don't delete secrets you have added to the AKV service. You can't add a new secret with the same name, unless you have deleted and purged the old secret. They can be difficult to restore. Instead add a new version of the secret, or add a secret with a new name.

index